Walter Benjamin

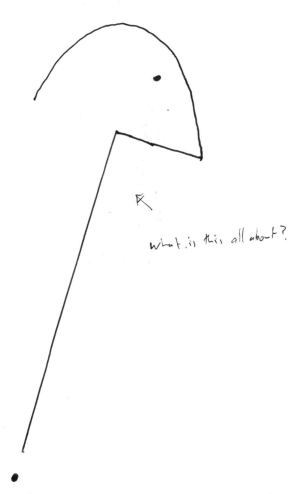

what is this all about?

Modern European Thinkers

Series Editor: Professor Keith Reader,
University of Newcastle upon Tyne

The Modern European Thinkers series offers low-priced introductions for students and other readers to the ideas and work of key cultural and political thinkers of the postwar era.

Jean Baudrillard
Mike Gane

Edgar Morin
Myron Kofman

Pierre Bourdieu
Jeremy F. Lane

André Gorz
Conrad Lodziak and Jeremy Tatman

Gilles Deleuze
John Marks

Guy Hocquenghem
Bill Marshall

Georges Bataille
Benjamin Noys

Régis Debray
Keith Reader

Julia Kristeva
Anne-Marie Smith

Walter Benjamin
Overpowering Conformism

Esther Leslie

Pluto **АP** Press

LONDON • STERLING, VIRGINIA

First published 2000 by Pluto Press
345 Archway Road, London N6 5AA
and 22883 Quicksilver Drive,
Sterling, VA 20166–2012, USA

British Library Cataloguing in Publication Data
A catalogue record for this book is available from the British Library

ISBN 0 7453 1573 9 hbk

Library of Congress Cataloging in Publication Data
Leslie, Esther.
    Walter Benjamin : overpowering conformism / Esther Leslie.
        p. cm. — (Modern European thinkers)
    Includes bibliographical references.
    ISBN 0–7453–1573–9
        1. Benjamin, Walter, 1892–1940—Political and social views.
    I. Title. II. Series.

    PT2603.E455 Z726 2000
    838'.91209—dc21
                                                            00–020282

Designed and produced for Pluto Press by
Chase Production Services, Chadlington, OX7 3LN
Typeset from disk by Stanford DTP Services, Northampton
Printed in the European Union by T.J. International, Padstow

Contents

Acknowledgements

The *Collected Writings*, *Gesammelte Schriften*, of Walter Benjamin appeared in 1991 as a 14-part box set. It contained not only juvenilia alongside multiple versions of the famous pieces and notes and drafts, but also an extensive 'editorial apparatus', with datings, excerpts of relevant correspondence, indication of first places of publication, types of paper and ink used and all the other things that an obsessive scholar needs and wants to know. (In this, it is unlike the English-language *Walter Benjamin: Selected Writings* from The Belknap Press of Harvard University Press.) The robust box set has served me well, and I thank the editors for all their scholarly effort. The *Gesammelte Schriften* was my main source of information, and this meant that I often translated quotations from Benjamin myself as I made notes for this book. I sometimes stick with those translations here, but I also provide page references to the relevant place in published English translations where those are available.

This book took on its shape over the 1990s. That decade opened with the calendrical opportunities for reflection offered by the 50th anniversary of Benjamin's death. Then came the centenary celebrations, which were followed by the flurry around the opening of Dani Karavan's monument at Portbou. All these events produced more and more words about Walter Benjamin. My contribution found first form as a doctorate, whose successful completion was much aided by my supervisor, Dr Margarete Kohlenbach, and my examiners, Professor Edward Timms and Dr Steven Giles. Since that completion, this contribution to the ever-growing pile of Benjaminiana has been recomposed time and again. Sometimes sentences or paragraphs found their way out of my study into articles or reviews or conference papers, only then to be altered and imported back again. Some might recognize certain turns of phrase. For opportunities to unravel further my thoughts on Benjamin I thank the editors of *Things*, *Mute*, the *Journal of Design History*, *Art Criticism Theory*, *De-*, *Dis-*, *Ex-*, *Revolutionary History*, *New Formations* and the organizers of the digital 'Artwork project' at London's Camerawork and all the others who published my words or gave me a stage for an hour.

Above all, I thank my parents, George and Sheila, and Ben Watson.

Preface: An Accumulation of Technological Themes

On 'overpowering conformism'

The phrase 'overpowering conformism' is a half-quote whose connotations mark out some parameters for a study of Walter Benjamin's work. The phrase alludes to Benjamin's caution in one of his final compositions, '*Über den Begriff der Geschichte*', written at the end of the 1930s:

> In every epoch the attempt must be made anew to wrest tradition away from a conformism that is about to overpower it.[1]

Conformism here refers to the energies of conventional interpretation. These ensnare tradition and the receivers of tradition in tales devised, or at least approved, by the ruling class and its ideology-mongers. The accumulated experience of the oppressed is overwritten in histories that re-transmit the existing balance of power: business as usual. Long dead, Benjamin is himself now part of transmissible tradition. Using here the phrase 'overpowering conformism' flags a desire to wrest Benjamin from a conformism inherent in those appropriations that excise him from a culture of engaged political critique. 'Overpowering conformism' suggests a confrontation with domesticating readings of Benjamin's work.

Wresting Benjamin's writings from the conformism that threatens to overpower their reception is the task. Such an assignment is aided by taking cognizance of Benjamin's onslaught on a second conformism mentioned in 'Über den Begriff der Geschichte' – the conformity of reformist theory and practice.[2] Reformism is still the conformity that overpowers the supposedly critically-minded. Nowadays it is frequently reformist-minded theorists who see reflected in Benjamin their own defeatist melancholy and desperate half-hope that, ameliorated by their wishful thinking, things might just work out for the best in the end, somehow. No major shake-ups intended. This is quite contrary to Benjamin's intent. In his final notes on the concept of history, Benjamin attacks reformist political tactics and economic delusions for their bypassing of the insurgent, self-organized moment of proletarian revolution. For Benjamin, without revolution there can be no redemption from 'this life here', since revolution and redemption are fused.[3] In the wretched late 1930s, while some of his contemporaries looked to Moscow and others vacillated (and numerous others hailed Hitlerite Munich), Benjamin attacked the 'innate' conformism of the left parties.[4] Conformism of one sort manifests itself for him in 1939, in the chimera of an ever-onwards-and-upwards progress of history, a salvation that can take place without the intervention of revolutionary subjects. This desperate and blind faith flies in the face of an *actual* devastation – plain for all to see – of the working class and the labour movement. Benjamin recalls that such devastation set in after the failure of the Spartakus rebellion in Germany, and it was exacerbated by the regimes of Hitler and Stalin. He sees a downhill tumble of the prospects for workers' self-activity. Not that he loses hope. But the reformist-meets-Stalinist trust in the progress of history, and the more or less wilful ignorance of Marx's insistence on proletarian self-emancipation, mean that proclaimedly progressive ideologues overlook the catastrophic impact of the defeat of revolution in Germany in the Weimar years and after, and in the Soviet Union under Stalin. They put their faith in history, economy and theory, and do not put their energies into the re-animation of class struggle. Conformism incubates business as usual; that is to say, nothing changes, because to the conformists it seems that nothing very much needs to change. Benjamin thought that the so-called critics were mistaken. Business as usual is a state of emergency. In a defence of the absolutely revolutionary fracture, in thought and in practice, he concludes: 'That it continues "like this" *is* the catastrophe.'[5]

From the mid-1920s, Benjamin investigates Marxism. He explores Marxist theory, enters into dialogue with Marxists and visits the Soviet Union. Benjamin is a nonconformist, often sceptical about trends engendered by the Communist Party of his day. His misgivings multiply as Stalinism solidifies its rule, and what passes for Marxist analysis extinguishes its revolutionary spark. He deploys the tools of historical materialism quirkily, and yet no more idiosyncratically than does the 'official' Marxism of the party. Benjamin's nonconformism is conspicuous in his critical interrogations of the ways in which party communists make use of Marxist maxims.

It may be tedious to participate in prolonging the game of selecting quotations, reinserting ellipses, arguing over the political affiliations of a dead man. But asserting the revolutionary under-pinning of somebody's thought is, if nothing else, a poke in the eye of those perpetrators of scholarship who endlessly defuse, debarb and domesticate that which has slipped into the intellectual bequest. However, recovering theory is not a matter of archival accuracy alone. Benjamin's political work is still of interest if its strategies and insights can be of use for analysis and action today, if it can be used as a resource and research tool for overpowering present political and cultural conformism, if it can be found to possess continuing relevance or, maybe, *Aktualität*.

Aktualität is a word that recurs in Benjamin's writing. For example, it appears in 1921, when he announces the formation of a journal, *Angelus Novus*. The *Aktualität* of *Angelus Novus* is said to mean the capturing of the underlying, decisive 'spirit of the epoch'.[6] *Aktualität* is mentioned again in 1925 when, having resigned himself to a career in upmarket *feuilleton* journalism, Benjamin defends the topicality of popular illustrated magazines – that they speak to the moment.[7] In a letter to Hugo von Hofmannsthal introducing *Einbahnstraße* in 1928, he insists that *Aktualität* is the obverse of the eternal in history, and is endlessly more significant for historical, political and cultural research.[8] The concoction of the theoretical concept *Aktualität* was evidence of Benjamin's attempt to avoid high-minded abstraction. He wants to engage in the world as he finds it. Refusing to focus purely on the formal aesthetics of the painterly canvas surface or extrapolating for purposes of bloodless philosophizing and eternity beckoning the subtleties of Hegelian thought, Benjamin, the 'anthropological materialist', enters drawing rooms and attics, spaces and scenes of historical, material human traces. Materialism – in Benjamin's sense – assumes an interaction between people and world. Humans work upon physical things and materialism questions the ways in which they do this and the relationships into which they enter in order to do this, and how this alters their thoroughly historical human nature. In order to study such matters, Benjamin is enticed into lodgings crammed full with baubles and valuables and vibrating with scratchy phonographs. He proposes taking seriously the clutter of material existence, and wants expressly to analyse the commodity trash of mass production, scrutinizing what his friend Siegfried Kracauer called 'inconspicuous surface-level expressions' which, 'by virtue of their unconscious nature, provide unmediated access to the fundamental substance of the state of things'.[9] An attitude informed by *Aktualität* grabs quotidian objects whose very insignificance and 'unconscious nature' warrant their indexical relationship to social truth and social lies. Whether on the track of theorists' more or less secret politics, or on the trail of the embedded social and historical meanings of things, to negotiate *Aktualität* is to enmesh critique in precise social observations and to be responsive to the urgencies and apprehensions of the moment, to be topical. An attitude informed by *Aktualität* understands Benjamin in context, underscoring his reactive engagement with contemporary controversies and phenomena.

But how can Benjamin's stress on *Aktualität* be interpreted today? The meaning of *Aktualität* is fractured, for it has to acknowledge a constellation between the past and present. *Aktualität* entails responsiveness to the specific historical and political conditions of the scrutinized object's emergence into the world and into theory. The questions must be posed: what conditions impinged on Benjamin's thought, how was his theory inflected by its sorties into historical and political actuality? But also to be faced in this idea of *Aktualität* is the relationship between the object of study, Benjamin, and this present, this urgent moment, now (for all moments are urgent). Benjamin details this linearity-defying perspective: 'Telescoping of the past through the present.'[10] Even the past is topical, for it has significance in the present. The past reverberates in the present; the present filters the image of the past. Critique, sensitive to the conditions that shape the past, cannot evade the concerns of the present.

A perspective convinced of past Benjamin's continuing relevance for the present draws on the *Aktualität* of his offensive against a technology fetishism that is ignorant of the stipulations accorded by the private mode of appropriation. Such ignorance may be newly prevalent in the hyper-cyberbabble of the new millennialism. The notion of the technoid subject might give a neon-green light to cybermaterialism and its visions of machinic subjects, enhanced with prosthetics, wired up and plugged into inflowmation (a version of Marinetti's futurist rhapsody for a postindustrial age). What happens in this cyber-conception of material is that the distinction between machine–technology–worker – a technician producing within technical relations of production – is collapsed into a single, mythic, postnatural subject. This subject embodies, quite literally, technology, technical relations of production and producer, and so can only with difficulty be envisaged as involved in a process of exploitation. But a communion with high-tech that evades relations of exploitation is a rare privilege. Cybermaterialism sets up a frozen concept of technology, a blindly determining force, shooting us back to Second International Marxism, and it is no wonder that Charles Darwin and friends enjoy a new popularity: the talk, for all its rhetoric of revolution, is of evolution. The cybers seek through technology a new determination of the species. Benjamin might sometimes be wheeled on to articulate the early birth of this machine-man, but he would be shocked at the cybermonster's class-blindness.

Under investigation here is the *Aktualität* of Walter Benjamin, then in his time, and now in mine. Nowadays, constantly, the attempt has to be made to wrest his work away from a conformism about to overpower it – bred of an historical and political amnesia about the past and the present, affecting those quite able to forget.

'Overpowering' possesses another sense. It means exertion of an unavoidable effect, suggesting another layer of significance embedded in the phrase 'overpowering conformism'. In Benjamin's analyses, adaptation to new technological forms by all elements of the social ensemble results from an irresistible conformism. This second sense of overpowering conformism points out a certain formal and technical determinism in Benjamin's work, at moments redolent of the determinism of thinkers on the left, whose automatic, evolutionary presumptions Benjamin is often keen to counter. Such determinism is especially manifest in his thoughts on aesthetics. Numerous essays set out from the presupposition that technology generates new forms, and that adoption of the formal characteristics of new technological forms – in art and in all social practices – becomes unavoidable over time. Technological form precipitates social form. In practice, however, Benjamin asserts, this falling into conformity with new technological forms and consummation of the reorganization of production and reception that they suggest is retarded by capitalist relations of production. The central contradiction of capital's new order consists in the fact that the socializing of production and its col- lectivizing of culture are countervailed by a retrograde movement, instituted to safeguard the social templates of class society. Benjamin concentrates his inquiries in the space opened up by this misalignment between the technological dynamic and the mode of social ordering. He identifies this misalignment as the two-way pull of forces and relations of production. For Benjamin, *Technik* (technique, technics, technology) is implicated in the mismatch of forces and relations of production. His assumption that the orga- nization of the technological forces of production discharges a determining effect on all sections of the social totality is coupled with the insistence on analysis of the relations of production. Such analysis forms part of Benjamin's political strategy to nurture proletarian activism. Forces of production and what are seen by Benjamin to be their 'appropriate', 'conforming' relations of production can be played out pre-emptively in the realm of art. Cultural production and cultural reception are forms of training. The rehearsal in culture of new modes of social relations becomes the precondition for the general overpowering of conformism in its cultural and political guises.

Focusing on technology does not render an analysis a contri- bution to Marxist theory. Marxist theory demonstrates sensitivity to the relationship posited between technology and non-technology – that is, the relationships between technology, nature and world. For a theory to be called Marxist it needs to flaunt an interest not just in the hardware of production but also in relations of production.[11] It is in order to insinuate this dual concern that the term *Technik* is more often than not left untranslated in this study. The German word *Technik* transmits a more open sense than the English word technology concedes. In order to demonstrate that the word *Technik* has caused other translators conceptual grief, a citation from one of Habermas's translators should suffice:

> Although German has adopted to some extent the corrupt usage of technology (*Technologie*) to mean technics rather than its study, the adjective *technisch* means technical and technological. That is, it emphasizes the form of making and controlling as well as the machines used in these processes. It has been translated in both ways. Similarly, *Technik* means technique, technics and technology.[12]

Technik intimates a sense of both technology *and* technique. Benjamin seems to squeeze full meaning from this compact word. In signifying simultaneously technology and technique, *Technik* alludes to the material hardware, the means of production *and* the technical relations of production. To accent technical relations of production is to acknowledge that there exist social and political relationships between producers and means of production. Technique also refers to the accumulated skill and knowledge, the scientific data necessary for the manipulation of machinery. The point to be made here is simply that Benjamin uses the term *Technik* rather than the word *Technologie*, and this might be because *Technik* covers social and political relations, as well as the empirical fact of machinery. *Technik* includes reference to social relations and, as such, is a category of experience. Whenever Benjamin uses the term *Technik*, he is mindful of a complex of human relations of ownership and control.[13] Benjamin's dynamic of social actuality, informed at its core by human labour and the interactions between technology and technique, insists on an awareness of both the factuality of the objective world and its contents and the actuality of subjective human interaction with that objective world. A dual concern with technology and technique is manifest not only in Benjamin's strictly social and political assessments, but also exerts direct bearing on his aesthetic formulations. These formulate a specific interest in technological art-forms and ask questions about the relations of production and reception that those forms intimate. Of course, the word *Technik* has aesthetic resonances too. To highlight this point, here is a citation from a book by two people both connected to Benjamin, who represent two poles of influence on him. His friend and critical theorist, Theodor Wiesengrund Adorno, and Bertolt Brecht's musical collaborator, Hanns Eisler, published, in English first, a study of film scores titled *Composing for the Films* (1947), while living near Hollywood. The limits and confusions of the terminology of technism, and the contradictions that this opens up for their cultural analyses of modern mass culture, are indicated in a footnote:

In the realm of motion pictures the term 'technique' has a double meaning that can easily lead to confusion. On the one hand, technique is the equivalent of an industrial process for producing goods: e.g. the discovery that picture and sound can be recorded on the same strip is comparable to the invention of the air brake. The other meaning of 'technique' is aesthetic. It designates the methods by which an artistic intention can be adequately realized. While the technical treatment of music in sound pictures was essentially determined by the industrial factor, there was a need for music from the very beginning, because of certain aesthetic requirements. Thus far no clear-cut relation between the factors has been established, neither in theory nor in practice.[14]

Adorno was harking back to a dispute with Benjamin from a decade before, where the difference between them concerned the content of the word *Technik* – and whether dependent or autonomous art was more technical and what that means anyway.[15] Such complications surrounding the term *Technik* explain indeed why questions concerning technology and technique are so important. So much hangs off *Technik*. Accessing Benjamin's thinking on *Technik*, a task made easy, if endless, by Benjamin's persistent spotlighting of the technical, in one context or another – his frequent analyses of experience as dependent on the interplay between technology and procedures of its implementation, his intricate detailing of the dialectical relationship between technology and technique, between forces and relations of production – leads right into the dialectical and materialist tenor of Benjamin's output.

It might be objected that *Technik* is both too narrow and too broad a category to use to investigate the writings of Walter Benjamin. Too narrow because it seems to ostracize other influential factors, notably Judaism and mysticism; too broad because this interpretation of *Technik* understands it as technology and technique, technological means of production, relations of production, technological artefacts and literary technique. I counter the charge of tunnel-vision perception by contending that, drawing on an historical perspective, Benjamin apparently finds no contradiction between scientific and magical approaches and this contributes to his anthropological materialism and his perspective on technology and technique. I counter the charge of too broad an understanding of the technical by countering weakly that Benjamin too understood the term in all its variety and devoted theoretical energies to both expanding it analytically and specifying it critically. It was for him a lodestar.

Particular writings by Benjamin are related here to their historical and political contexts. In an article on the collector Eduard Fuchs, Benjamin cites Engels' criticism of any history of ideas which represents new dogmas as a development of an earlier stage or which sees poetic schools as reactions to the schools that precede them.[16] Benjamin intimates that each philosophy, ideology or programme needs to be located within the living relations in which it is forged. While this study adheres strictly to a traditional chronological structure, such temporal ordering exists not to suggest that sort of interpretation made popular by Gerhard-Gershom Scholem. Scholem maintains that the very last writings are a recantation of the work of the previous decade and a half, and as such a revealing abandonment of Marxist method.[17] This study is chronologically ordered for it wishes to demonstrate that Benjamin's work is situated in the context of debates and events that develop historically. Benjamin's ideas react to form constellations with political events around him. He rebuffs and interacts with contemporary political theory and philosophy. This politics and this philosophy, perhaps like many philosophies and politics, are involved in inquiries concerning technology and technique, the regulation of the exchange between humanity and nature, the matter of reciprocity between technology and operators, the mimetic drive and the question of realism in art. That list sets out the rudimentary concerns of Benjamin's writings from the mid-1920s until 1940, as he searches for an appropriately modern cultural understanding, relevant political practice and a singleton understanding of human activity as the superseding of such distinctions.

CHAPTER 1

Explosion of a Landscape

Analogy between a person and a switchboard, on which are thousands of bulbs; suddenly one set extinguishes, then the other, and then they are relit.

'Pariser Passagen' 1 (1927–29)[1]

'Zum Planetarium': on a betrayed elective affinity

Highly technologized, imperialist war reverberates in Benjamin's writings.[2] A number of his essays and reviews refer to the large-scale destruction delivered by war. These writings clatter in the unnerving silence of a ceasefire, soon to be interrupted by even more catastrophic bloodfests. Benjamin warns that the 1914–18 war cast just the shadow of a brutality soon to be superbly outbid. The armies of the future will deploy technologies of far greater destructiveness;[3] troops will be immeasurably more sadistic and bloodthirsty;[4] war will be total, and inescapable – it will be fought by new technological means. Chemical warfare turns soldiers and civilians alike into targets.[5] A short piece from 1925 named the gaseous killing tools manufactured in I.G. Farben's Hoechst, Agfa and Leverkusen plants and at other 'respectable' laboratories and institutes. 'Die Waffen von morgen: Schlachten mit Chloraze-tophenol, Diphenylamchlorasin und Dichloräthylsulfid' speculates on the consequences of chemical warfare.[6] Gas warfare is described as a military attack by a barely visible but choking penetrant which permeates everything, diffusing from the warfront, slithering into cities and under the skin of civilians. Military atrocity is intensified by technological means. Shell-shock jolts a mass psychosis for civilian populations, who in previous wars remained remote from events in the combat zone.[7] I.G. Farben were not alone in developing poison gases so deadly no gas masks could give protection.[8] Though the Hague Convention before the Great War had outlawed gas deployment, Ypres in 1915 was the testing ground for chemical weaponry which broke the stalemate of trench warfare. The modern, states Benjamin in an early note in the *Passagenwerk*, is a time of hell.[9] The most modern technological inventions, products of capitalist research and development, encompass the latest military gadgets that mete out battlefield punishments. For Benjamin, war features as the destructive life-consuming aspect of technological development. The vast

1

accumulated resources clotted by the factory system in the second half of the nineteenth century increase productive potential, but also boost massively the potential for destruction. Benjamin's commentary on military technology provides a starting-point for his critical analysis of technology in general. The 1914–18 war marks the historical breakdown of the promissory ideology of technological benefit. The Great War provides a clanging riposte to the credo of perpetual historical progress guaranteed through technological innovation.

Einbahnstraße (One Way Street), Benjamin's brochure on modern existence, which draws on the language of commercial slogans and city signs, was begun early in 1923, completed in 1926 and published by Rowohlt in 1928. Benjamin describes it in letters to Scholem as a work that signals a new orientation in his thought.[10] His habilitation project, an academic dissertation entitled *Ursprung des deutschen Trauerspiels* (Origin of the German Mourning Play) (1923–25) had not been passed, and so an academic path was barred. He had to identify himself anew as a cultural critic, a freelance journalist, writing weekly reviews, articles and lectures for the more or less mass media of the Weimar Republic. He describes this period, which begins with the aphoristic spoutings of *Einbahnstraße*, as the start of a new 'production cycle'. It is to end only with the completion of a study of the Parisian arcades.[11] The previous 'production cycle' had been a Germanist one, concluded by his unsuccessful academic submission. The new 'production cycle', however, never does reach a close, despite Benjamin's claims that it will last only a few more weeks. The study of the arcades and their world, now known as the *Passagenwerk* (Arcades Project), is never completed – Benjamin had stated in a letter to Scholem that he had never written with such a risk of failure.[12] Until the end of his life Benjamin explores the 'profane motifs' first exhibited in *Einbahnstraße*. In his *Passagenwerk*, he reveals, these motifs parade past in 'hellish intensification'. Perhaps some sort of systematic orientation in Benjamin's thought can be uncovered around the 'profane motifs' of *Einbahnstraße* and the *Passagenwerk*.[13] What Benjamin meant by 'profane motifs' was not revealed to Scholem, for he was himself unclear. Many themes in these two works, and others, cluster around questions concerning technology and techniques. Benjamin's absorption in the effects of technology and technological change duplicates the fascination of nineteenth-century commentators charting industrial progress, commentaries that are reproduced and explored in the various files of themed notes in the *Passagenwerk*. For Benjamin, technology opens up access to new realms of experience, perception and consciousness. Always relating technological developments to human experience,

Benjamin's study of technology turns into a type of anthropology, as well as political critique. But profanity also intimates Benjamin's turn to the world, the common, the impious. This move meshed with his encounter with Marxism.

Georg Lukács' *Geschichte und Klassenbewußtsein* (History and Class Consciousness) (1923), read in Capri, was an important influence. Benjamin brands communism as that which is rooted in practical experience. This rooting, as Benjamin had alleged in a letter to Gerhard-Gershom Scholem, written on 29 May 1926, makes it the corrective for its political assertions and avowed goals.[14] The stance was adopted from Lukács. Another letter to Scholem in 1924 relates how the key insight in Lukács' book is its philosophical underpinning for the assertion that theory is understood through practice.[15] The activism of the Latvian Bolshevik Asja Lacis (Benjamin met her in Capri in 1924) provided a model of political practice. Lacis was part of a politically active avant-garde dedicated to developing the cultural practice of the Soviet Communist Party. Lacis worked in Germany too, with Brecht's theatre in the 1920s and on Erwin Piscator's agitprop spectaculars. She wanted to generate a revolutionary pedagogy, specifically through theatre work with proletarian children. Benjamin considered her an active builder of the post-revolutionary society: using the fashionable political language of the time, he called her an 'engineer' in the dedication in *Einbahnstraße*. He fell in love with her. He made himself resemble her by adopting Marxism as a framework. And yet, he had to make it his own too. He had to be critical. His commentary on his new political environment was voiced in *Einbahnstraße*.

'Tankstelle' (Petrol Station) is the opening blast in this slim volume which edits philosophy into scenes, freezeframing it into stills hung under captions or titles. 'Tankstelle' tenders a constructivist-inspired analogy between literary technique and machine maintenance.[16] Here Benjamin specifies a type of literary production closer to journalism or political polemic effected by commentators who specialize in knowing the social world and its relations. The order is to avoid vague and grand gestures.

> Opinions are to the huge apparatus of social existence what oil is to machines; one does not go up to a turbine and pour machine oil all over it. One applies a little to concealed spindles and joints that one has to know.[17]

In order to propagate opinions and critique, 'Tankstelle' recommends the fabrication of leaflets, posters, pamphlets and newspaper articles, all apt and valid forms of artistic production. 'Tankstelle' suggests that technology has enabled new literary forms, mass-reproducible and able to respond rapidly to events and situations. Benjamin advocates 'prompt language' and the spurning of the 'pretentious universal gesture of the book'.[18] Such a stance is reiterated in the book's format. Ernst Rowohlt published *Einbahnstraße* as a booklet, and its typography was designed to emulate the shock-effects and chaotic experimentalism of 1920s' advertising and newsprint. Technology facilitates new modes of presentation, and it suggests new matter for representation. The dust jacket, by the montagist Sascha Stone, was a scrambled photomontage of road signs and shop signs; street furniture and urban bric-à-brac demanding, confrontationally, the right to be exposed to philosophical inquiry. Benjamin was devising modes of address appropriate for modern propagandizing.

He also addresses questions of class struggle. A few pages into the book, 'Feuermelder' (Fire Alarm) couples technology and the technological potential for destruction with the balance of class forces.[19] In 'Feuermelder', Benjamin forecasts comprehensive economic and technical catastrophe. 'Feuermelder' does not present a romantic vignette of class warfare as an even fight to the death carried out in a style reminiscent of old-style army officers. Benjamin rebuffs such geometry of transformation with its interminable line of endless movement, and its presentation of history as an open book. Such history alleges that one fine day the struggle of the two opposing classes will result in victory for one side, and defeat for the other. Benjamin counters this by insisting that the bourgeoisie is necessarily condemned to expiration through its internal contradictions, irrespective of whether it succeeds in suppressing the proletariat at any specific moment in time. Capitalist decline is inevitable. The communistic reorganization of social relations is, however, not inevitable. And, because the stakes of the struggle are lopsided, if the proletariat does not win, not just the bourgeois class but the whole of humanity is condemned to extinction. In a scenario of 'socialism or barbarism',[20] Benjamin poses a momentous question: will the bourgeoisie be destroyed by itself or by the proletariat?[21] Capitalist decline without communist revolution, he insists, means absolute annihilation in war and economic collapse. Benjamin does not suppose the triumph of the proletariat to be a question of historical inevitability, but rather a matter of social necessity whose realization is uncertain. He defies the oblivious optimism of the vulgar-Marxist interpretation of social change. Such Marxian optimism typically reveals itself to be inevitabilistic, evolutionist and technologically determinist, that is, innocently reliant on the blossoming of technologies of production. Benjamin claims that technology is not the guarantor of beneficial social evolution – or revolution – as is falsely asserted by the social democrats. As long as technology exists within capitalist production relations, it is bound to turn out to be a vehicle of disaster. Technological development is not in itself a prelude to a reorganization of production relations that automatically redistributes power to the proletariat. Making political activity a matter of deadlines, tactics and class-conscious organization, Benjamin asserts that 'the burning ignition fuse must be severed before the spark reaches the dynamite'.[22] The abolition of the bourgeoisie must be accomplished before an 'almost calculable' moment of economic and technical development, signalled by inflation and gas warfare. Proletarian power is not a mechanical, natural or inevitable result of technological change, but a possible, though not guaranteed, interruption of calamitous technological developments. The fizzling ignition-fuse, emblem of the devastating, explosive power of the bourgeoisie, must be severed before the spark makes contact with the dynamite. Dynamite suggests the contradictions of bourgeois order; its affinity to destruction is matched by its accumulation of a marvellously powerful technical and economic potential. 'Feuermelder' pictures the damage caused by technological expansion, and concludes that only the proletariat can engage in humanitarian damage-limitation.

Though Benjamin refuses the determinism of evolutionary historical advancement through technological change, his re-framing of the concept of *Technik* and its role in class struggle and historical change draws on another determinism, apparent in the assertion of an 'elective affinity'.[23] The final entry in *Einbahnstraße*, 'Zum Planetarium' (To the Planetarium), proposes a marriage between humankind and modern technology. In the ruinous nights of total war, states Benjamin, an ecstatic feeling shook the 'limb structure' of a humanity manoeuvred into connection with powerful technologies.[24] Benjamin conceives the world war as an attempted communion, through technology, between national collectives, but the encounter was warped. The world war was internationalism twisted into gross distortion. Through the media of new technologies, mass populations related to external nature and to each other as if intoxicated, evoking an ancient pre-scientific encounter between humanity and cosmos, which had been displaced since the post-Renaissance promotion of a predominantly optical comprehension of the world. The ecstatic encounter of the masses and technology is described as copulation, an index of both sexual delight and the birth of the new.[25] Technological forces penetrated the earth in their wooing of the cosmos. Human masses, gases and high-frequency electrical currents cut through landscapes, claims Benjamin, exhibiting a distinct fascination in war's potency. New constellations emerged in the sky, while air space and sea-depths hummed with propellers, and shafts were dug deep into the earth.[26] The transmutation of the landscape by industrial warfare means that nature is reinvented through technology. Technological organization infuses human relations, realigning the relationship between self and environment. Bodies are infused and enthused by technology. New technologies are born. From the collusive collision between proletariat and technology, an organic-technological techno-body is generated. Technology and humanity scheme together to form a collective, social body. The mass revolts that follow the world war are, for Benjamin, the first failed attempts by the developing collective historical subject, the proletarian mass, to bring its new-born techno-body under control.[27] This failure is blamed on the inhibition of reciprocity, on the fact that fair exchange is scuppered. Benjamin outlines again and again the existence of a reciprocal or electively affinitive relationship between the forces of production, technology and science, and the collective subject who operates those forces of production within specific relations of production. The concept of reciprocity can be traced through the discipline of *Naturphilosophie*, such as, for example, Goethe's notion of *Wechselwirkung*, or the subjective idealism of Fichte's *Wissenschaftslehre* (1794). Were the novel bond between new powerful technologies and mass populations permitted to develop socially and in full reciprocity, the vortex of annihilation would spew forth a higher stage of development. Instead, Benjamin's parable of recent past history continues, the ruling class's lust for profit leads it to make *Technik* pay out dividends. *Technik*, whose evolution suggests proper ways of negotiating between nature and humanity, asserts its autonomy and double-crosses all humanity, turning the bridal bed of nature into a sea of blood. In 'Zum Planetarium', Benjamin switches the agency of historical change back and forth between technology and the proletariat. Technology calls the shots, regulating the relationship between humanity and nature. But the proletariat battles to prove its masterful robustness, by bringing technology under its control and fighting to consummate, through technological means, a harmonious arrangement with nature. The two-way relation between humanity and technology betrays Benjamin's interest in *Naturphilosophie* and is reminiscent of Novalis's magic idealism or magic observation, a reciprocally productive process of interaction between subject and object, converted by Benjamin into an interaction between nature, humanity and technology. Such a reciprocal process was originally fashioned by the Romantics to counter instrumental Enlightenment concepts of nature.[28] Benjamin sets this relationship in the context of class politics of the early twentieth century. The overriding political factor of structures of ownership, relations of production, promotes a subversion of the 'natural' elective alliance between proletariat and technology, to which technology responds by revolting.[29] Benjamin's analysis works by establishing a formal contractual relationship that binds technology and the proletariat. Imperialism forces the proletariat to break the contract, demanding their role as executors of the deployment of *Technik* for the destructive domination of nature. At this point, when the proletariat, under capital's command, wields technology in order to abuse nature, technology turns with unmatched ferocity on the cosmos. The proletariat, once seemingly thrilled by new technological possibilities for a utopian reformulation of nature, has become a bloody collective object and victim-sacrifice of technology's machinations in war. Viewing the catastrophic hellfire world of one total war and hurtling towards the holocaust of another, the collective appears a sacrificial wreck of a powerless body that had once hoped. In its devastated ruination the beaten collective surfaces as prefiguration of Benjamin's distressed *Angelus Novus*, the angel of history, staring in half-disbelief at the ruins, devastated by the failure to co-operate, made manifest in the sheer destructive capacity of technological progress.[30]

This is a myth of technology. Benjamin nurtures the 'shudder of true cosmic experience'.[31] The elective affinity between the collective and technology draws on an ahistorical structure of communion, first promoted, as Benjamin notes, by the ancient Greeks. But Benjamin's analyses of technological changes and new technological agendas indicate that 'Zum Planetarium' is also concerned with making experience historical, that is aligning experience with technological change. This results in an identifiable tension between the mapping out of a mystical-philosophical theory of experience and the formation of a materialist approach to the historicity of experience. The notion of a collective relationship of the masses to technology, the making of nature subject to historical and technological development, and the notion of the significance of relations of ownership, fix Benjamin's essay in a Marxist-derived framework. The increasing historical likelihood of the eruption of another horrific 'sea of blood' is consequent on a number of misalignments. Realization of these affiliations would constitute a harmonic relation of parts. They are alignments between forces and relations of production, between technology and nature, between the new collective and the new technology, between humanity and nature. Benjamin ventures to stage the specifics of military horror not simply as a mystical-religious moment, but as an historically situated event, consequent upon the subordination of the relationship between nature and humanity to the needs of profit-making. Though he is aware of the disastrous stakes of modern warfare and the exigencies that capitalist relations of ownership compel, technology is no simple bad object for Benjamin, but one element, reactive upon a number of other elements to which it is related. At stake is the regulation of the relationship between producers, nature and *Technik*. As Benjamin puts it:

> Mastery of nature, so the imperialists teach us, is the purpose of all *Technik*. But who would trust a martinet who declared that the control of children by adults is the purpose of education? Is not education above all the indispensable regulation of the relationship between generations and therefore mastery, if we are to use this term, of that relationship and not of children? And likewise *Technik* is not the mastery of nature but of the relation between nature and humanity.[32]

Such an issue finds at least a faint premonition in volume III of Marx's *Das Kapital*, where Marx conceives the meaning of freedom to be associated producers rationally regulating their interchange (*Stoffwechsel*) with nature collectively, rather than being at nature's mercy. (Marx uses a biological term, *Stoffwechsel*, the word for metabolism.) Rather than positing the control of nature itself, it is the interchange between humans and non-human nature that is in need of control.[33]

'Zum Planetarium' hints at deep shifts in the human mode of relating to the object world, made necessary by social change, and made both necessary and possible by developments in *Technik*. Experience in the industrial world is experience mediated through technology. Objects and forms of experience alike are liquidated and reforged in the process of technological metamorphosis. Benjamin's first contribution to a theory of surrealism 'Traumkitsch' (1926) suggests succinctly that *Technik* transfigures the look of things in the world:

> *Technik* cashes in the external images of things, which, just like banknotes about to lose their currency, are never to be seen again.[34]

Technik, like *Notgeld* (emergency money), participates in history by casting things into obsolescence. Or at least the external image of things transforms, even if things remain in essence the same, as fashion compels superficial differences to supply the push-me-pull-me logic of capitalist economic turnaround. *Technik* is the midwife of fashion. Its permanent churning out and its adjustments of styles and types endlessly remainders products. *Technik* ceaselessly dispenses novel ways of presentation, new looks, new images and new purposes. Benjamin's metaphor was grabbed from the German inflation of the early 1920s. Hyperinflation exacerbated the centrality of money – and thus the terrible sovereignty of the commodity – and as the numbers of zeros on banknotes multiplied, human life and rhythm was more and more drastically pegged to the fluctuations of exchange. One of the sections in *Einbahnstraße* was a reflection on that period and was titled 'A Tour of German Inflation'. It was a protest against the way in which money had taken over and had become the only theme – a situation that was probably far worse than anything the money-critic Georg Simmel, who died just before the war ended, might have imagined possible.

The inflation coincided with the publication of a book that powered up Marxist theory for the next period. Lukács' *Geschichte und Klassenbewußtsein* (1923) outlines the phenomenon of reification, a strange illusioning that naturalizes and objectifies social relations.[35] The concept of reification furnished Benjamin's first Marxist theoretical tool. It enabled him to confront, politically, the frozen, reified landscapes he inhabits and that inhabit him. Lukács' theorizing of the modern world's alien but glamorous bleakness and his vision of a thing-bound inorganicism nestle in Benjamin's surveys. Benjamin manipulates the Lukácsian rendition of the socio-political, switching between depiction of the cold landscape of commodity society to reflection on the forms of culture and interaction produced within this society. Through delineation of the effects of the accelerating rate of change, mandated by fashion, and study of the demands of the commodity economy, Benjamin reveals a world in which things rapidly petrify, turn alien and obsolete. In this fetishized thing-world, phantasmagoric and frozen commodity-forms belligerently beset people, only to be tossed, through technical change and economic stimulus, on the rubbish heap of the outmoded. The things have (shelf) lives, albeit short ones. Such a vision is critically recorded in Benjamin's studies of rubbish, urban debris, cultural trash and collectors. According to the logic of reification, it is not just that things become fetishized, but that people become things. Reification specifies how the self turns into a thing amongst the mounting piles of commodity junk. The term relies on Marx's concept of commodity fetishism. In capitalism all workers sell their labour-power as commodity. All submit to commodity fetishism, whereby each person is transformed into a thing, and each relates to others as things. For Benjamin, industrial modernity, ruled by commodities and dead labour and the exertion of machine power over people, elicits alienated human relations. Reification is a name for a social actuality, in which the body has become a thing, specifically a machine for work, the machine-pendant described by Marx. The body annihilated, petrified, subjected to attack, deformed by war weaponry, the body as alien, the skin of the self hardening, inorganic matter, a thing: such images litter Benjamin's work. This person under onslaught is a person subjected to commodification. What has later become known as Western Marxism accentuated Marx's idea of commodity fetishism and the Western Marxists established, as the pivotal part of Marx's analysis, the mechanism of exchange and its effects. But Benjamin differed. While Marx's analysis of commodity fetishism was indispensable to his conceptualization of social relations, Benjamin is also keen to stress exploitation and the conditions in which labouring occurs. The fashion industry provides, for Benjamin, a 'dialectical image' of the deadly social relations of production, illustrating both the reifying effects of the exchange mechanism and the brutal physical conditions that attend work. In Marx's account, the textile industry is central to the formation of the factory system of exploitation. It was in the cotton mills that women and children were employed en masse, cheaply, and mechanically spinning materials harvested by growing numbers of slaves, born to work and worked to death, in the US slave states.[36] *Das Kapital* supplies a materialist core for Benjamin's idea of the fashionable body as, symbolically and concretely, intimate with death. Marx details how 'the murderous, meaningless caprices of fashion' are linked to the anarchy of production, where demand cannot be predicted and where gluts lead to starvation.[37] The connections between products and death alert Benjamin to the fact that everything consumed has been produced under conditions that occasioned suffering. Capital's rule – exercised through its technologies and techniques – fractures and fragments bodies, and these are bodies that have been remade as prostituted, dehumanized commodities. Through the reifying operation of commodity fetishism, capital's organization murderously consumes life.

As a counter-attack, Benjamin plots a redemptive and interpretative history of technological development in which the act of interpretation aspires to draft the possibility of change in the present. It hopes to do this by posing the potential for transformation as latent, pending different social relations. This redemptive, constructive role for theory can be cross-referenced to a comment in the *Passagenwerk* that asserts that 'a historical object is whatever is rescued by knowledge'.[38] When Benjamin noted in the 'Collector' file of his *Passagenwerk* 'Failed material: that is the lifting of the commodity into the state of allegory', he was insisting that theoretical investigation of industrial material culture is the sole starting point for the longed-for release from its reifying grip.[39] In the same file, Benjamin quotes from Adorno's 1931 lecture on Dickens' wondrously sentimental Victorian novel, *The Old Curiosity Shop*. For Adorno, the novel's miscellaneous scenes, the old curiosity shop, the waxworks museum, the puppet theatre, the graveyard, are allegories of the bourgeois industrial world.[40] All these places are occupied by piles of commodity junk or populated by the disturbingly dead. In this industrial world the most commanding social forces are production, commerce, reification and commodification. At the end of the lecture, Adorno decodes Little Nell's death:

> On fleeing, Nell parted unreconciled from her things – she was not able to take anything with her from the bourgeois realm: to speak in modern terms, she failed to manage the dialectical transition, and achieved only the flight, which exerts no power over the world from which she escapes, and so she succumbs to the world.[41]

Adorno concludes that, because Little Nell did not succeed in grasping the thing-world of the bourgeois space, the thing-world grasps her, and her sacrifice is effected. Little Nell accomplished only the flight, first away from the cluttered interior of the junk shop and the chimney-filled metropolis, and then into death – and so having no power over the world, she was snatched by the world. Objects are enslaving, not least because their technical conditions of production are monstrous. Authentic redemption, for Adorno and for Benjamin, is lodged in the thing-world. It means realizing the utopian promises of objects or tokens as yet unredeemed in the frozen commodity-scape. Such realization entails, of course, a revolution in property and labour relations, a revolution of *Technik*, in all senses – in order to re-establish that elective affinity. Critique necessitates serious consideration of conditions of production, and unbinding the potentials muzzled in actuality. The type of redemption undertaken by Benjamin, in his studies of modern culture, necessitates an *Aufhebung*, in that it preserves, annuls and raises to a higher level the current notion of *Technik*. Redemption is first a work of theory, but it advocates a new practice. For example, homeopathically, Benjamin demands an incorporation of the forms of current technologies and techniques into his prescriptions for modern aesthetic arrangements – hence the sloganeering of *Einbahnstraße* or the attraction to Brecht's jerky drama of alienation. Only in this way – through testing and analysis – can potentiality spill over into actuality.

But *Technik* also participates in a bridging of distances – technologies are media and so they set up new lines of communication and intercourse. Developed are new techniques of using this industrialized material – entertainment devices, cheap prints, ornaments and the rest. Novel objects, mass-produced kitsch commodities, force themselves on 'the new person', jostling for attention in cluttered environments. Kitsch and clutter, abortions of industrial technological development, demand the right to existence and love. The objects' kitschiness, their economical availability, their being at hand, obliges a re-evaluation of ideas of closeness and distance between objects and people.[42] In 'Traumkitsch' Benjamin notes that what counted as art – a privileged thing-world – in former days began at 2 metres distance from the body, but through mass-production the thing-world creeps up on the person. It is seen to jut out, just as the mass-reproduced image does or the montaged fragments that explode the frames of art. These kitsch things meet audiences halfway. Kitsch lays bare emotional whims common to all, divulging social fantasies. Benjamin parades the peculiar power of the soon-to-be-outmoded, not just in terms of how much sentiment people invest in the cheap objects in their environment, but also in terms of the relationship between all that stuff and art, in truth the most arresting avant-garde art. Benjamin's list of surrealist muses in 'Pariser Passagen' includes stars of stage, screen, billboard advertisements, illustrated magazines and producers of kitschy culture, who have now largely faded from memory: Luna, the Countess Geschwitz, Kate Greenaway, Mors, Cléo de Mérode, Dulcinea, Hedda Gabler, Libido, Friederike Kempner, Baby Cadum, Angelika Kauffmann.[43] Greenaway was an illustrator of pretty children's books and a name associated with a Victorian style of children's clothes. Baby Cadum was a figure advertising Cadum's soap. Kauffmann was a South German baroque painter, reproductions of whose rather sickly-sweet portraits became popular in the late nineteenth century. Kempner was a late nineteenth-century writer whose work was relished by those who found its ill-phrasings and gushing romanticism unintentionally comic. De Mérode, a celebrated beauty of the 1890s, was aristo-cratic by birth, a lover of the King of Belgium, Leopold II, and a ballerina. Countess Geschwitz is a character in Wedekind's play *Lulu*, and so also appears in Berg's opera and in the film *Pandora's Box*. Dulchinea was Don Quixote's desirable mistress. Hedda Gabler, Luna and Libido have persisted and can be imagined in some form. Mors may refer to the Latin name for death. So much junk and ephemera, a world of kitsch industrial debris, no cultural deep-freeze conserves it, and yet, Benjamin insists, it was, in its day, the most absorbent, the place of fantastic projections, and therefore a snare for social and political meaning. And not just meaning, but catalyst for an urban poetry, a lyricism of the refurbished everyday. Kitsch, because of its industrialized, formulaic mass production or its pretensions or its drooling with cod-emotionality, stages an inquest into social desire, as utopian corrective to the reification of people. Propagated by congealed labour and mechanical effort, kitsch makes possible a psycho-analysis of things, for it encrypts the contents of a social collective consciousness. For Benjamin, modern culture issues from this kitsch, picked up off the streets and snipped out of the screens. This modern stuff is not animated by the eternal values of art or the high-minded quest for purity of form and abstracted truth. The Cubists too had accredited the arcana of labels, brandmarks, posters and newspapers. Café life and cabaret provide the stimuli for Cubist collages which tear out strips of newspaper, bottle labels, cigarette papers, handbills from department stores, bargain wallpaper, all carefully juxtaposed to allow puns and interplay between the parts. Avant-garde and mass smash up against each other, and technologized culture is the mesh. Benjamin's modernism feeds itself on the mass-consumable, industrialized detritus born of and condemned to short life by capitalism and its technological resources. Surrealists too are interested in the world of obsolete things, remaindered by technological change. There are few things more socially poignant than these two: a beauty from another epoch who now appears embarrassingly unfashion-able; a broken gramophone, propelled into uselessness. Like the surrealists, Benjamin's interest in technical culture is directed not just at the new productive possibilities of hi-tech, but also at the revealing psychic reverberations and historically resonant energies of the *passé*, the broken, the inefficient.

One characteristic of surrealism is its drafting of innovative strategies for the imaging and imagining of experience. Such re-imagining takes place in an era captivated by technologized commodity production, with its production of dashed utopian pos-sibilities, urban trash and fashion, elements central to surrealism's worldview. After writing 'Traumkitsch' Benjamin continued his investigations into the surrealist movement.[44]

Surreal Experiences in Moscow and Paris

'Der Sürrealismus' (1929) is Benjamin's first ambitious study of the convolution of revolutionary politics and art. He recognizes the extremism of surrealism.[45] He ratifies its materialism. The surrealists develop a poetry of matter and of chance, tangible and essentially objective, yet interpretable. Theirs was a materialism that appealed to Benjamin, in contrast to others, such as the 'meta-physical' mechanical materialism of Vogt and Bukharin – disembodied, objectified, founded on science and cosmos and yet abstracting from any human measure. For example, Vogt's naturo-materialism assumed that thought was secreted by the brain, just as gall was discharged by the liver and urine by the kidneys. And valuing matter over the concrete, acting human being, Vogt ascribed to atoms a sense of pain. Benjamin contrasts this to the 'anthropological materialism' of the surrealists and before them the proto-Brechtian pedagogue Hebel, activist-poet Georg Büchner, Nietzsche and Rimbaud.[46] Mechanistic materialism is not properly rooted in anthropological materialism's double bind: a double bind that intermeshes physical nature and political materialism (that is consciousness, activity, history). These two forces share the assaults on the abstract spectre of spirit, tearing it limb from limb with anti-bourgeois acumen.

In order to appraise the revolutionary commitment of surrealism, Benjamin adopts Trotskyist, surrealist Pierre Naville's ultimatum: do these artists assume the idealist necessity of altering mental dispositions or the materialist precondition of first altering life-conditions?[47] He endorses the surrealists' commitment to institutionalizing a new communion with technology. But Benjamin suggests annexation of a more politically focused aspect – one that commits to the proletariat as agent of revolution. The proletariat provides the organized and constructive discipline that will save the body of industrialized humanity from the chaos of destruction.[48] Having dealt the surrealists a blow, he turns his weapons on organized communism and well-meaning left-wing intellectuals in France and the Soviet Union, such as Duhamel, who speak of soul. Benjamin mocks the devotion of bourgeois left-wing intellectuals, not to the revolution, but to traditional culture.[49]

Benjamin's cynicism about organized communism and its adherents derived from experience. He travelled to Moscow at the end of 1926. He stayed from 9 December 1926 to 1 February 1927. 1927 was the year in which Trotsky and the left opposition were estranged from the Politburo. It was the time of Stalin's final consolidation of the doctrine of 'Socialism in One Country', first formulated in November 1924, and antipodal to Trotsky's concept of world revolution. The programme of 'Socialism in One Country', announced one year and four months after Lenin's death, was a pithy expression of the political horizons of the Soviet bureaucracy. The Bolshevik revolutionaries of 1917 had insisted on the necessity of internationalism. A revolution, especially one that had broken out in an economically backward country, could be no more than a time-limited holding operation, banking on the stimulation of revolutions in other countries.[50] At the Third Congress of the Comintern in 1921, Lenin restated this position in his phrase 'World Revolution or Perish'. The programme of 'Socialism in One Country' disregarded Lenin's verdict. According to Trotsky's analysis from the late 1920s, 1927 was the beginning of Thermidor. Trotsky defines Thermidor as the first stage of the counter-revolution. It represents bourgeois restoration, 'the direct transfer of power from the hands of one class into the hands of another'.[51] 1926 and 1927 were years in which Benjamin first considered in earnest whether or not to join the Communist Party.[52] The visit to Moscow was an investigation of communism in power, as well as an opportunity to visit Asja Lacis, the woman he loved. He travelled there with a curious yet suspicious attitude, and kept a diary, *Moskauer Tagebuch*, recording street life, cultural events, heartache and meetings with intellectuals and the left literary oppositionists who still remained in Moscow.[53] Fierce battles were under way. The left opposition was drawing its final yet vigorous breaths. The united left opposition of 1926–27 had tried to promote workers' resistance to the government's 'New Economic Policy'.[54] The NEP was supposed to be a temporary measure until the capitalist crisis was reasserted and class struggle was on the rise again internationally. But the NEP turned away from this perspective and, from the mid-1920s, began to reconsolidate the Soviet economy along capitalist lines. By the time of the onset of the capitalist crisis in the late 1920s, the central plan of Bolshevik policy was to build up an independent industrial state, initially within the scope of the mixed, unplanned economy of NEP, later within the rigidly planned economy of the 'Third Period'. Hopes were raised in some quarters for a change in party leadership at the 15th Party Congress in 1927.[55] At the end of 1927, the Stalinists clamped down. Thousands of militants were jailed. Trotsky was arrested, charged with counter-revolutionary activity and exiled to Alma-Ata, on 17 January 1928.

In his writings on the Soviet Union Benjamin notes that developments in the Soviet Union are working to the detriment of the left, but there is still vibrancy present in Soviet society.[56] Everything is still in flux ten years after the revolution, from laws and regulations to the positioning of bus stops. On a cultural level, the proletariat has begun genuinely to take possession of bourgeois culture. Benjamin is struck by how confidently they move through museums and galleries. In contrast, in Germany, if workers at leisure are found in galleries, their demeanour and the reactions of others make it look as if they are there only to steal something.[57] In his diary Benjamin records sudden shifts in policy – the flux affects party politics too. Early on in his visit, for example, someone reports that Trotsky is to address the Comintern to defend Zinoviev, whom Stalin had defeated in 1925 and had removed from the presidency of the Comintern in October 1926.[58] Perhaps, says the man, the party is about to make a U-turn. However the fragility of the opposition in the face of Stalinism suffuses the diary more noticeably. Reinvigorated activity on the opposition's part appears to be a brief resuscitation before expiry. Benjamin registers the pessimism of his friend Bernd Reich who lives in Moscow and gets by making a living as a writer. As soon as Benjamin arrives, he discusses with Reich the idea of joining the Communist Party. Reich's main quibble with party policy stemmed from his involvement with the theatre. He is critical of its stance on cultural matters and laments the reactionary turn. Reich, reports Benjamin, fears that the left movements in art, state approved and used at the time of 'war communism', will be ostracized. The proletarian writers, notes Benjamin, have become, against Trotsky's wishes, state-recognized, although this does not translate into practical state support.[59] This new 'proletarian culture' is a constricted pragmatic vision of a culture based on the perceived characteristics of the working class and its revolution. It is not a utopian-idealist rejection of bourgeois culture, along the lines of futuristic *proletkult*, but rather a bureaucratic artistic policy. It determines the value of culture according to the class origins of cultural producers. Soon it would become an instrument of policy for Stalin. The promotion of 'proletarian culture', primarily through the Association of Artists of the Revolution, went hand in hand with a disregard for the absence of the cultural and productive conditions of communism. Instead of a new culture materializing, the bureaucratic concept required a culture that could be summoned by order of state. This was needed to confirm the lie that communism as total way of life could be forced through from above. Trotsky argued that such bureaucratism leads to artistic aridity and spoliation.[60] But more dangerous, as Benjamin notes, is the restoration of proletarian disempowerment. He writes:

> Externally the government seeks peace, in order to set up trade agreements with imperialist states; but, above all, internally it attempts to suspend militant communism. It strives to institute a harmony between classes, to depoliticise bourgeois life in as far as that is possible. On the other hand, in the pioneer groups, in Komsomol, youth are being educated as revolutionaries. That means that the idea of revolution comes to them not as an experience, but as a slogan. The attempt is made to disconnect the dynamic of revolutionary processes in state life – whether one likes it or not, the restoration has begun – but in spite of that, the attempt is made to store up revolutionary energy in youth like electric power in a battery. That just is not possible.[61]

Benjamin continues his analysis of the decrepit culture of the Soviet Union with reflection on Soviet youth's ignorance of bourgeois culture – a point made by Trotsky too. But he also reasserts that bourgeois cultural values are being officially popularized by the Party, as part of the restitution.[62]

After his visit to the Soviet Union, Benjamin writes a series of cultural-political articles on the situation in post-revolutionary Soviet Union. The essay, 'Neue Dichtung in Rußland', contains a concise depiction of Trotsky's pronouncements on culture.[63] Trotsky promoted complete formal freedom for artists who are on the side of the revolution. The revolution in the Soviet Union was a transitional phase; hence the impossibility of proletarian culture. In a number of articles on art and literature, written between 1923 and 1926, Trotsky waged a struggle against what he terms the 'theoretical corrosion' of the Bolshevik Party. His study, *Literature and Revolution*, insists that the proletariat is not creating a culture that conforms to its needs as proletariat, but is engaged in a struggle to abolish itself. It is the character of the artwork itself that is of decisive importance and not the birthrights of the author. In *Literature and Revolution* Trotsky ties culture to its material roots, insisting at the same time that, while the 'class criteria' are vital in art, art must be 'judged according to its own laws'. The proletariat must master the old culture as well as forging the new. In the course of this they will generate new forms and also revitalize old forms.[64] Importantly, for Trotsky, art analysis must be embedded in a historical and social context: even art that claims to be pure has historical, social roots, and this is a matter worthy of study. Artists are of interest, perhaps, when they forge groups, act as movements. Speaking of the Party in a manner soon to become wishful thinking, Trotsky writes:

> The Party understands the episodic character of the literary groups of a transition period and estimates them, not from the point of view of the class passports of the individual gentlemen literati, but from the point of view of the place these groups occupy and can occupy in preparing a socialist culture.[65]

Benjamin had experienced at first hand the problems of a literary analysis that bases itself solely, contrary to Trotsky's advice, on the class origins of writers. While in Moscow, Benjamin submits an entry on Goethe for the *Great Soviet Encyclopaedia*, but it is rejected.[66] The authorities required a sociological treatment of Goethe's life, concentrating on his class origins. Benjamin had written a materialist analysis of the after-life of Goethe's works, arguing that it is only the history of a poet's influence that can be portrayed in terms of materialism, and not his life. Benjamin wanted to bring political matters to bear on literature as matter that exists after the fleshly personality of the author has died – literature itself and the institutions that cradle it are the object of analysis. Comrade Radek reasoned that the submission was dropped because it overused the phrase 'class struggle'.[67] Benjamin concluded that his approach was too radical for the authorities. His attempt at materialist analysis had fallen victim to the contradictory aims of the editorial board:

> They are shaken by good old Aristotelian fear and pity when it comes to the European intelligentsia; they want a standard work of Marxist science, at the same time, however, they want to create something that will awaken vain admiration in Europe.[68]

Insisting on the centrality of the class origins of cultural producers, the authorities inherit a bourgeois-derived obsession with personalities rather than a materialist interest in the work and its after-life. At the same time, the desire to secure recognition for scholarship in Europe pressurizes them to defuse the political resonance of their analyses. This conundrum is just one of many contradictions that strike Benjamin in Moscow.

The Soviet Union had broken with some of the ways of the West. This was obvious, for example, in the misalignment between money and power, two forces that are aligned in the West.[69] In the West money buys influence; in the Soviet Union social status is determined by the relationship between an individual and the Party. The Party or the bureaucracy retains the power and the NEP men have the money. It is a class state still – and alongside that, castes have emerged. Caste status is determined by relationship to the Party. The NEP man is an outcast because he has money, because he is distrusted and because he has no power and no status. He is a pariah. Benjamin comments:

> If the European correlation of money and power were to emerge here, the country would not be lost, not even perhaps the Party, but communism in Russia would be.[70]

For the Soviet people wealth is human, territorial and connected to the ability to make decisions. This makes life in post-revolutionary Russia so heavy with content, so full of events and prospects. From early till late people dig for power, notes Benjamin. Self-activity, engagement, is the watchword. Power is returned to the people, with all the contradictions and corruption that this involves in a revolution confined to one country.

The revolutionary experiment was faltering or sliding into reverse. On his return from Moscow, Benjamin distils images and annotations from his Moscow diary into an essay for the journal *Kreatur*.[71] He describes the Lenin Cult, noting how little babies are called October or Wolf from the moment they can point to Lenin's picture and how Lenin's picture is sold on icon stalls, with pictures of saints flanking it like a police guard – a contradiction plain to see on the streets.[72] In the Red Army Club there is a map of Europe. The handle can be revolved and all the places where Lenin went in his lifetime light up one after another. Other cities are not marked at all, as if they had no significance without Lenin's visitation. Benjamin comments wryly: 'On it Lenin's life appears like a colonialist conquering all of Europe.'[73] Benjamin also accentuates how life has been increasingly collectivized. Any deviation from the bureaucratic norm smashes into an enormous apparatus and immeasurable costs. The Soviet Union is a country of 24-hour mobilization, where specialists are fetishized. At the Red Military Academy there is a general, relates Benjamin, who had been given a teaching post. He had become notorious in the civil war. Every Bolshevik imprisoned by him had been hanged.[74]

Benjamin asserts that ideology is overlooked in favour of objective skills. Intellectual specialists are also returning to the posts that they sabotaged during the civil war. The opposition or any independent intelligentsia who oppose the Bolsheviks does not exist in any particularly meaningful sense any more.[75] Either it has been destroyed or it has called a truce, writes Benjamin. A new bourgeoisie has risen, reports Benjamin. These economic realignments are the results of political struggle, and the new political turns brought their own cultural accompaniment. On a visit to the theatre in December 1926, Benjamin noted in his diary:

> The smell of perfume hit me immediately upon entering the auditorium. I could not see a single communist in a blue tunic, but there were a few types who would not have been out of place in any of George Grosz's albums. The performance had absolutely the style of a completely dusty royal theatre.[76]

The ideals of the revolutionary avant-garde were definitely on the retreat, and this went, to a certain extent, hand in hand with the forced retreat of the left opposition. The revolutionary avant-garde had opposed the social stratification that the NEP brought in its wake and the reactionary turn in cultural policy to which it also seemed to give succour. Dziga Vertov and Osip Brik, both, of course, partisan on the side of the avant-garde and therefore not disinterested, noted that the proletariat had responded positively to new cultural techniques in art, and they insisted that it was the NEP men who were antipathetic to experimentation, preferring conventional notions of art as a luxury good, emotive and separate from life. NEP culture contravened thus the central core of the avant-garde project of production art. It appeared undeniable that a new class with its cultural shibboleths was in the ascendancy. This re-emergence of the bourgeoisie was further promoted by Stalinist entrenchment. There was little to choose between the aesthetic preferences of NEP culture and Stalinist-approved 'proletarian culture'. Both discouraged experimentation. The new ground-rules of Soviet art encouraged figurative easel-painting and monumental sculpture in order to depict a 'heroic realism'. Trotsky had warned about the fetishism of the style of Great Realism in *Literature and Revolution* (1924). In his city portrait of Moscow, Benjamin discloses the cultural perspectives of the Soviet bureaucracy in 1927, detailing the official demand for 'banal clarity':[77]

> Political affiliations and content are deemed most important. Formal controversies had played a not inconsiderable role during the civil war. Now they have been silenced. And today, the position is official: content and not form is decisive for the revolutionary or counterrevolutionary attitude of a work.[78]

The sad consequences, for art and for artists, of this policy, and the fact of its successful enforcement, can be assessed by its effect on the old revolutionary avant-garde. Trotsky, in an article on the suicide of the Futurist revolutionary poet Mayakovsky in 1930, speaks poignantly of the effects of bureaucratization on art. He writes of a system of bureaucratic command over art. Like Benjamin, he asks where revolutionary theory and practice might be found – and what role might the new cultural forms play.

'Der Sürrealismus', written in February 1929, brings together Trotsky's analysis from *Literature and Revolution* and Benjamin's assessment of the role of the revolutionary intelligentsia:

> If it is the dual task of the revolutionary intelligentsia to topple the intellectual predominance of the bourgeoisie and to gain contact with the proletarian masses, it has virtually failed in the second half of this task, because the masses are no longer to be won over contemplatively. But that has not stopped them from acting as if they could be and calling for proletarian poets, thinkers and artists. Trotsky had to point out, in opposition to this, in *Literature and Revolution*, that they would only emerge in a successful revolution.[79]

Benjamin continues by outlining a new role for cultural producers – a role that is concerned with artistic effectivity and not class origin. The deployment of intellectuals is modified in the modern age, argues Benjamin, casting a side-swipe at the old guardians of cultural heritage, as well as the proletarian novel-writers. By way of his contention that the artist is a producer of functions, but not a proletarian, Benjamin formulates the Marxist debate on art in terms of an active category of agency and not a passive sociologistic observation of class. He notes how official communist art criticism is unable to go beyond a torpid paradigm of reflection of class interests in artworks, inquiring only whether artworks are reactionary or revolutionary in their subject matter.

Benjamin regards the surrealist venture as a contribution to an expanded theory of experience, rather than as simply another aesthetic movement.[80] Just as *l'art pour l'art* is seen not solely as an aestheticist flight from the political and from the world, but rather as a gazetteer to an enhanced concept of experience,[81] so too the social service of surrealism is to gauge the crisis of the arts as an indicator of a general crisis of experience. Surrealism breaches conceptual and institutional borders between art and other practices. It does this, contends Benjamin, by pushing poetic life to the outer limits. Surrealism aestheticizes existence to the maximum degree, and, through such absolutism, hopes to obliterate the aesthetic, having dislodged any antithetical principle against which it could flaunt its autonomy.[82] Everyday life is made aesthetic, though this is not the same transmutation as the dandyish attitude effects through aestheticism. In an essay on Marcel Proust from the same year, Benjamin first edges towards a condemnation of aestheticism, the stance of the consumer *extraordinaire*. In 'Zum Bilde Prousts' aestheticism is evaluated as a specific class-ideology.[83] But aestheticism can become fully critical, and so not aestheticist, if it is coupled with what Benjamin calls the 'materialist-political' or 'politico-materialist'.[84] This coupling appears in surrealism's clash of extreme aestheticism and its various appeals to left campaigns, as much as in its psychic materialism, a charting of the reality of desires, using materials that are available to all – dreams, litter, kitsch.

Surrealists ransack the unconscious and the world of dreams. Benjamin does too, recording his own dreams. For Benjamin, the dream is primarily important because it offers material for analysis. It is a cognitive resource for expanded research into the entangle-ments of the real. To provide a consummate concept of experience (*Erfahrung*) that does not overlook the outlandish or obscure (even as it exists in the most ordinary), the unconscious or the dreamt, entails a refiguration of what reality is. Benjamin takes very seriously the realism in surrealism. Surrealists envisage deep and complex realities and, in envisaging them, imagine they have made them material. In his study of surrealism, Benjamin mentions André Breton's essay 'Introduction au discours sur le peu de réalité' (1924).[85] Breton explains a practical strategy for making dreams real: arguing that it is the poet's duty to fabricate strange objects glimpsed in dreams, in order to expand the contents of the real, whilst fulfilling the desire for perpetual verification.[86] This is an extravagant suggestion, upon which even Breton does not really act, preferring instead to transmute reality by poetic production. Benjamin's supplement to surrealism's envisaging and summoning of deep and complex realities in poetry hopes to evade its glints of idealism by insisting rather more systematically on tapping the individual unconscious and methodically exposing the mytholog-ical forces still latent in modern society. This coincides with Benjamin's methodology in his studies of the Parisian arcades, whereby he demonstrates that mythic drives continue to endure in the supposedly disenchanted modern world, even in those places where instrumental rationality is supposed to have taken hold. Sur-realism's germination of a new form of historical consciousness and the use of associative techniques urge an extension of the zones of analysable, politically significant experience.

Important to an expanded concept of experience is the relevance of secularized ecstasy and intoxication (*Rausch*). Benjamin writes that 'an intoxicated component lives in every revolutionary act' and emphasizes 'winning the powers of intoxication for the revolution'.[87] An extreme intoxication is supposed to lead beyond a 'charmed circle' of mythic prostration to an intensified sense of the realities of this world in a 'profane illumination'.[88] Such illumination is assumed to bestow intelligible structure on exhilarated experience. The significance of intoxicated experience consists in its uprooting of the individual subject and opening experience up as a mass affair.

A couple of years after the study of surrealism, Benjamin writes a tract called 'Der destruktive Charakter' (1931). It continues the breakdown of 'the self', exalting a reforged, post-bourgeois, post-individual type. The destructive character is an enemy of the comfort-seeking 'etui-person', coddled by sheaths and casings. The destructive character is an augmented version of the *flâneur*. This is a type opposed to repression in its political and psychic guises, who – provoking havoc by gashing ways through – prises loose the bonds that shackle people, via sentiment, to the status quo. The destructive character does this in order to facilitate the drafting of experience according to amended, more fitting tenets. The destructive character calls for a futurist vacuum cleaner to suck up the dust of eons in a streamlined, spatially diminishing, massified, techno-modernist age. 'Der destruktive Charakter' presents a persona who destroys normality at the same time as the traditional idea of character.[89]

Dada likewise was, according to Hans Arp, spawned of a 'negation of man's egotism'.[90] Tristan Tzara's 'Dada Manifesto 1918' interjected post-expressionist echoes of the Great War into the avant-garde's nihilism: 'After the carnage we are left with the hope of a purified humanity.'[91] Like Benjamin in 'Der destruktive Charakter', Tzara uses the language of housework. The task of Dada, he writes, is: 'To sweep, to clean'.[92] Dada embarks upon a 'a great destructive, negative work', aiming to undermine all institutions – aesthetic, religious, moral, political – that rely upon the repressed stability of the individual ego.[93] In his notes for the surrealism essay, Benjamin mentions the active, collective overcoming of the rational individual through states of intoxication.[94] The dissolution of the individual ego into the collectivity becomes, further, the precondition for a break with the egoistic seductions of intoxication, about whose dangers, insists Benjamin, the surrealists were not sufficiently clear.[95] The destruction of the bourgeois psyche enables the constitution of a '*Physis*', a term that draws on *phusis*, the ancient Greek word for nature. Psyche, the name of the interiority of the individual, becomes '*Physis*', a new collective, physical humanity, through a process, described in corporeal imagery, as a dismemberment and reconstitution.[96] Surrealism, in contributing to the formation of '*Physis*', through its transformation of receivers into a creaturely, collective body, makes art a question of physiology and politics. The historical birth of this creaturely, collective body provides Benjamin's justification of materialism as the only appropriate framework of analysis. (Benjamin's materialism is stunningly literal, rejecting an interest in 'abstract matter', insistent instead on the fleshy materials.[97]) This collective, creaturely '*Physis*' is organized 'within technology'.[98] Tools and instruments are not external to people but organs of communal life in the collectivity. Benjamin had just completed his first fragmented but extensive study of the Paris arcades, in which he suggests that architectural forms, products of the latest technologies, are part of a reconstruction of the social body. Dismissing Gideon's idea of glass and iron substructures as an unconscious, Benjamin suggests that these scaffoldings are analogous to 'bodily processes'. New architectural spaces become a physiological extension of the bodily collective.[99] Benjamin understands the proletariat as a collective organ, organizable precisely because of its nature as collective. The conception of the joined, interpenetrative collective body of humanity and *Technik* moderates any charges of technocratic anti-humanism.[100] In 'Karl Kraus' (1930–31), Benjamin tries to shift the ground of humanism in the modern era. He uses the descriptive label 'real humanism'. 'Real humanism' is based on materialism and formulated in conscious opposition to dominant, lip-servicing forms of Weimar humanism.[101] 'Der Sürrealismus' instigates a collectivized humanism that is in affinitive dialogue with the technological. This collectivized body is then proposed as the site of a 'bodily collective innervation', which acts as a charge for revolutionary activity.[102] Revolution is a matter of sensuous demand. An entry in the *Passagenwerk*, written contemporaneously, indicates Benjamin's sense of a dialectic of rational organization and a mystical fixation with corporeality. Provided that his caution against religiosity is taken seriously, Benjamin's political outlook does not judge corporeal mysticism anathema to an organized, rationalist communist perspective:

> It is absolutely necessary to understand the apotheosis of orga-nization and rationalism, which the Communist Party must untiringly effect in the face of feudal and hierarchical forces in terms of a polemical reaction. And also to be clear that the movement has its own mystical elements, even if they are of a quite different type. Of course, it is even more important not to confuse these mystical elements, which belong to corporeality, with religious ones.[103]

'Der Sürrealismus' attempts to imagine politics, aesthetics, political activity and aesthetic activity in one glance. Gershom Scholem's insistence that the essay is 'still largely dominated by

an absolutely pre-Marxist line' fails to convince.[104] 'Der Sürrealismus' traces Benjamin's formulation of a partisan proletarian
politics, at least as much influenced by Marxism as was surrealism
itself. It foregrounds a pessimistic attitude – only to emphasize the
immensity of the danger and the injunction to act:

> Surrealism has come ever closer to the communist answer. And
> that means pessimism all along the line. Absolutely. Mistrust in
> the fate of literature, mistrust in the fate of freedom, mistrust in
> the fate of European humanity, but three times mistrust in all
> reconciliation: between classes, between nations, between
> individuals. And unlimited trust only in I.G. Farben and the
> peaceful perfection of the air force.[105]

And once this sober but panicked recognition of industrial
dynamics is acknowledged, then comes the innovating of strategies
of expression. Drawing on Aragon's *Traité du style*, Benjamin
opposes the image to the simile and identifies the image as
predominant in surrealist creations.[106] Similes are the 'as if', future-
oriented effects of optimistic social democracy and moralism which
have no place in Pierre Naville's hard-nosed political directive –
'pessimism all along the line'. The political assignment is 'organization of pessimism'.[107] Similes are the stock-in-trade of pious,
optimistic socialist visions of the future when our children and
grandchildren will act 'as if they were angels', and everyone has as
much 'as if he were rich', and everyone lives 'as if he were free'.
This is nothing more than a bad poem about springtime, stuffed
to bursting with metaphors, sneers Benjamin. It betrays a politics
of unprincipled dilettantist optimism that preaches moralism and
idle fantasy. The 'organization of pessimism' demands something
else: primarily the expulsion of moral metaphor from politics in
the interests of envisaging political action. For this purpose,
Benjamin devises a realm called the 'image-space' (*Bildraum*), his
name for repetitions of the world, the body and technology in
optical form. Metaphor is a technique attuned to the moral and
spiritual realm, and, in some sense, part of the world of the stand
in, the 'as if' realm. Marxist materialism and correct conduct with
images both propagate, instead, a doctrine in which 'an action puts
forth its own image and exists, absorbing and consuming it'. It is
closeness looking with its own eyes.[108] It is the system that
motivates its own overcoming from within its own terms, and as
such, then, according to Benjamin, can be understood as the
production of an equivalent, an image, without spillage, without
substitution of one thing for another – without morality, or spirit
brought in to grease the wheels of transcendence – with no 'as ifs'.
Image, in contrast, has something tangible, graspable. It is a
material force. Image, Benjamin notes, is a 'world of many-sided

and integral actuality', and it resides at the heart of political action. (How much more concrete this becomes if we think contextually of the importance of reproduced images in those years, in the new media forms, and concurrently with that, in art and in popular culture, unprecedented and endless experiments in depicting visual space and shapes across time.) The sphere of images is a realm in which creative contact can be made with proletarian masses: 'a one hundred percent image-space'.[109] Art and politics are fused in the theory of the 'image-space'. The 'image-space' avers that political activity is synonymous with the circulation of images that can be creatively and actively appropriated by the proletariat. Benjamin also denotes 'image-space' as 'more concretely: body-space' ('*Leibraum*').[110] The materialist change in life-conditions, identified by Benjamin, equals an historically effected and inescapable anthropic change. Contemporary reality has become the image of reality, an assertion that indicates Benjamin's emphasis on visuality and the visualized. The struggle for revolution is a fight for 'image-space'. Within the 'image-space' the role of the artist-producer changes, Benjamin having deleted the centrality of artists' class origin and any allure discharged by the prospects of careerism:

> In reality it is far less a matter of turning the artist of bourgeois origin into a master of 'Proletarian Art' than of placing him, even at the expense of his artistic activity, at important points in the image-space. Indeed might not perhaps the interruption of his 'artistic career' be an essential part of this new function?[111]

Imagery becomes a sort of tool, the 'image-body-space' a machinery. Placing the artist 'at important points in the image-space' recalls the constructivist-inspired juxtaposition of literary technique and machine maintenance in 'Tankstelle', the opening gambit of *Einbahnstraße*: writers artfully apply a little oil to the machine's concealed spindles and joints.[112]

Fascist Warriors

In 'Der Sürrealismus' Benjamin establishes tenets of a new post-bourgeois reality, prefigured in the day-by-day decline of bourgeois society. These tenets are intoxication, aestheticized experience retransmitted through technology, destruction of the individual in the enthused mass and the mutual innervation of collective and individual bodies in a simultaneously sacred and profane world. It could perhaps be argued that such ingredients found fulfilment in the actuality of fascism. The political victory of fascism appears as a translation of certain surrealist demands of reality. The cult of ecstatic experience finds its reflection and extension in a vitalistic mythology derived from *Lebensphilosophie*. The aestheticism of the proto-fascists had its roots in the *Lebensphilosophie* of the early twentieth century, touted by Stefan George and his circle. Fascism, in a sense, can be diagnosed as a surrender to those dangers of surrealism against which Benjamin had cautioned in 'Der Sürrealismus'. Benjamin sought to negate those hazards in the demand for connection to the sobering rigours of Bolshevism. However, the general thrust of Benjamin's thinking in 'Zum Planetarium' and 'Der Sürrealismus' is echoed in Ernst Jünger's proto-fascistic photo-text manuals of aesthetic, catastrophic battlefield consciousness. Jünger's authored, edited and co-written books and photo-essays include *In Stahlgewittern* (In Storms of Steel) (1920), *Das Antlitz des Weltkrieges: Fronterlebnisse deutscher Soldaten* (The Face of World War: Front Experiences of German Soldiers) (1930), *Krieg und Krieger* (War and Warriors) (1930), *Hier spricht der Feind: Kriegserlebnisse unserer Gegner* (Here Speaks the Enemy: War Experiences of our Opponents) (1931), *Der gefährliche Augenblick* (The Dangerous Moment) (1931), *Der Arbeiter* (The Worker) (1932), *Die veränderte Welt* (The Transformed World) (1933). The titles alone divulge the fascination with risk, the sense of war as a natural eruption, the shared mentality with the warring enemy and the marking of the landscape by technology and power. Benjamin partakes in Ernst Jünger's thesis of an atrophying of the ability to experience, caused by socio-cultural upheavals in a world dominated by technical rationality and media projections. In the face of an actual atrophying of experience, Benjamin seeks to institute an expanded experience. This expanded experience is precisely the one denied by capitalism and yet made potentially possible by new technologies. In actual technological production, however, experience is further depreciated. For example, in journalism, mass-produced words are cheap and devalued, mediating just snippets of a marketable paper reality. For Jünger, the social world of modernity is a disenchanted realm of mechanical actions. The empty mechanisms of these routine actions crush magical experience. Benjamin had once encountered and appropriated kindred conceptions in the work of Georges Sorel. Sorel bewailed the contemporary loss of the sublime and sought its retrieval in the propagation of a myth of war or the myth of the general strike.[113] Only moments of crisis can obliterate the emptiness. Such moments, for Jünger, include childlike helplessness, narcotic intoxications that involve a loss of self, or life-risking soldiering. Jünger laments the way that, through the development of military technologies, modern warfare is stripped of experiential vividness. 'Inner experience' is lost. He recommends to the elite a revival of magical experience through limit-experiences. But he also discerns that technological developments reintroduce elements of danger and risk to life. Technologies that intensify the danger-stakes cut against the tendency towards banalization.[114] In the face of monstrous, crushing technology on the battlefield, Jünger's soldier submits to depersonalization, by effecting a mystical surrender to the spirit of technologized war. Benjamin and Jünger alike draw off aestheticized chthonian forces for social renewal, released in annihilation on the battlefield. But their dissimilarities become increasingly apparent in the subsequent divergent political paths of the two writers.

Jünger cultivates an aesthetic consciousness of the catastrophe, attuned to a battlefield intensification of experience. Armed with aesthetic consciousness, the soldier-critic is *voyeur-flâneur* on the mesmerizing battlegrounds, adopting an indifferent viewpoint, a '*désinvolture*'. Aesthetic consciousness furnishes for him the fantasy of a metallic body – it is an armour. Nothing can touch him. He is anaesthetized, as he aestheticizes. Fear-negating indifference towards a distanciated reality is hitched for the aesthete-soldier to an acute thrill at the likely perilousness of the event that explodes intensely into the banality of uneventfulness. Jünger's memoirs of the killing fields are prismed through images of lenses, as if they were the narratives of a cameraman or photographer (as indeed Jünger sometimes was), separated, affected, but simultaneously strangely unaffected. Benjamin counters such aestheticization of the battlefield, stressing the material bodily reality of the soldier in action.[115] In his essay on Karl Kraus, Benjamin quotes the Viennese satirist's complaint that in wartime the warrior and the journalist merge to become a journalist-warrior, who is in a prime position to rewrite the actual experience of war.[116] In the 1880s, Baudelaire, whose writings thread their way through many of Benjamin's and who explores the violence on which social relations are founded, connected journalism and war-reportage with the flâneuristic modern eye in his essay 'Le peintre de la vie moderne'. Baudelaire finds war's repertoire of images, battlefields strewn with corpses, ruined structures and munitions, a valuable archive and writes about the terrible poetry of the battlefield. Aestheticization of the battlefield is peculiarly spliced to technological modernity. But Benjamin has no sympathy with the way in which Jünger's aesthetic model of war is checked, from the start, by class myopia. For the broad masses, Jünger tends to affirm the technologization of the workaday world and its concomitant banalizing of experience. The growing dominance of war zone values in everyday life creates a new form of mass humanity, a type of functionalized, de-individualized human being. The officer elite's relation to danger and risk offers them a different quality of technologized experience.

Benjamin manoeuvres against the glorification of war espoused by army officers such as Jünger and Von Salomon in a 1926 review, entitled 'Friedensware'.[117] He told Rilke and Hofmannsthal that he hoped that the review would stir up a fuss.[118] It was an analysis of Fritz von Unruh's seemingly pacifist reportage 'Flügeln der Nike'. Benjamin shows the former militarist von Unruh to be the exporter of an idea of 'eternal peace', derived from a reading of Kant, which has its roots in mysticism and whose major intent is to launch a polemic against communism. War was the issue, and Benjamin's new Marxian arsenal would enable its analysis. He views his work in this period as a contribution to the crisis of new historical thinking in an intellectual civil war. Benjamin extends metaphors of war into the literary realm. One example is a literary-political critique, 'Dreizehn Thesen wider Snobisten' (1925); 'The critic is a strategist in the literature battle.'[119] Such military language evokes Benjamin's general standpoint that the only war worth fighting is the civil war he wages against his fellow critics on paper.[120] By the late 1920s, as the state lurches rightwards in the context of devastating economic and social crises, he writes a number of review essays evaluating the indicators of a new militarism.[121] Profound connections between the event of war and artistic movements are stressed in Benjamin's notes on the practice of criticism, written between 1929 and 1931.[122] He suspects the deeper ideological motives of the authors of the new war literature. Writing specifically about the new objectivist vogue for war novels, he states:

> On the question of the war novel. ... Which (or whose) interests are served by this vogue of war novels? The more the objectivity, the documentary nature of this literature is stressed, the harder one should search for the deeply buried tendencies that they serve.[123]

In 1930 a novel entitled *Gas gegen Gas* written by Benjamin's wife Dora was printed in instalments in a radio station magazine, the *Südwestdeutsche Rundfunk Zeitung*. *Gas gegen Gas* contemplated the possibility and danger of a future gas war. In the same year, an anthology of German proto-fascists and nationalists, edited by Ernst Jünger, appeared.[124] Benjamin felt compelled to attack it, largely for its attitude towards technology. He delineates the fascist daydreams manifest in the literary-philosophical battlefield of the 'post-war', seeping onto the literary scene a decade after the war. Benjamin uses the word '*Nachkrieg*', conferring a definite substantive sense to the figure of the war in that period. The theoretical re-encounter with the war in the post-war period, especially the onslaught of war memoirs from the intellectual right, is interpreted as an attempt to recapture the field of interpretation.

These proto-fascists glorify the fray in their repeated returns to battlefield ruins. There is a fascist-rightist rehabilitation of the Great War, and war in general. Benjamin read Ernst Bloch's critique of the Great War in *Geist der Utopie* (1918).[125] Bloch reproaches those responsible for the 'lies' that covered up the true face of the 'naked war of entrepreneurs', and insists that bombs had shattered the spiritual speculations of academic ideologists, while 'artillery had killed off mysticism'.[126] Benjamin's analyses of German fascism hoped to counter the claim that mysticism had been murdered once and for all.[127] Its re-emergence is identified in the post-war memory of events on the battlefield. The right is reassembling, Benjamin argues in 'Theorien des deutschen Faschismus', by regaining mysticism and mythicization as explanations of historical process, thus turning the war on mythical battlefields into the fantasy of 'the eternal War'.[128] Motivated by the hope that the war could be re-run and re-won in book-form, the fascists clung on to the fact of loss.[129] As they re-ran it, the crushing defeat in the war zone is remoulded as a new victory, experienced in the mystically encountered delirium of catastrophe.[130] For Jünger, a type of success had already occurred in a battle zone spectacle in which soldiers delight in the triumph of form and beauty, represented by the naturalized sublimity of 'storms of steel'. The fascist notion of 'eternal' war presents the battle as a cultic event. Advocacy of an abstract, soldierly posture ('*Haltung*') acts as compensation for losing the war.[131] Quoting Florens Christian Rang, Benjamin describes how, for those who recall it, the world war becomes the scene of a mystical heroism of the pure stance, the place of a deathly intoxication ('*Rausch*') which illuminates its sacrifices in a halo.[132] The retransmission of war, asserts Benjamin, is 'an uninhibited translation to the battlefield of the principles of *l'art pour l'art*' by a mature bourgeoisie in crisis.[133] Benjamin releases 'decadent' *l'art pour l'art* from his more affirmative interpretation in 'Der Sürrealismus', which had analysed the movement as part of the project of expanding experience by aestheticizing life. The aestheticization of experience on the battlefield, the 'intoxication' of the fight, is not redeemable as an expansion of experience or an energetic, ecstatic but misaligned intercourse between humanity, cosmos and machine, akin to that suggested by Benjamin in 'Zum Planetarium'. The analysis of the philosophy and ideology of extreme-right intellectuals in 'Theorien des deutschen Faschismus' marks the beginning of Benjamin's critical attitude towards an 'aestheticization of politics', or, more specifically, an aestheticization of experience, blatant in the proto-fascist celebration of an empty cult of war without specified enemies.[134] The proto-fascistic 'new war theory' transforms the actuality of the war event into the experience-denying mythology of a glorification of war which disavows experience and hammers out a 'war ideology'.[135] War is made into an intensely subjectivized experience in the post-war recollection of a reality rechristened the '*Welthaft-Wirkliches*' ('worldly-real'). This Benjamin theorizes as incommensurate with the experience of actual battlefields of the past or future. Total war for the fascists recollecting afterwards in the post-war is not a conceivable experience, Benjamin notes, but a symbol of the expression of an '*Urerlebnis*' ('primeval experience').[136] Remembered experience becomes an ideological reworking of experience, a site of ideological intention. In the process of retransmitting war, the fascists make the event unreal.

The mystification of war experience undertaken by the warrior-writers is best displayed in their relationship to technological developments. Technological developments on the battlefield are mythologized by members of the rightist intellectual scene who write about war, but treat it as a cultic metaphysical abstraction.[137] The fuzzy haze of yellow gas grenade warfare and high-intensity fire is drawn by the fascists as mysterious, mythological effects that envelop the slaughter in a haze of beauty.[138] The landscape of the front, redrawn in new fiery terms, announces a new aesthetics. Benjamin notes how Jünger calls for a sublime vision of the battlefield ruins. Jünger's 'totally mobilized' reality denotes the destructive self-prostration of natural resources, calling nihilistically for the sacrifice of humans and the rape of nature.[139] Technology becomes part of the spectacle of nature, and war becomes a natural-technical catastrophe. In the face of techno-destruction, there is a strange fascist return to nature, represented by the new 'landscape of the front' drawn in the post-war theory, and described by Benjamin as the true '*Heimat*' of the nationalistic 'soldier type', defended still in his post-war.[140] The rightist landscape of the European killing zone seems to Benjamin an idealist travesty of nature. In all actuality, this ravaged Europe is a garden where deadly metal bullets are planted in flesh, but, for the fascists, it becomes the graveyard of an immortal glory.[141] Representations of this landscape draw the event of war as an inexplicable phenomenon of nature. Benjamin's review of a play by Carl Zuckmayer claims similarly that, in the standard bourgeois fantasy of war, the militaristic apparatus is displayed released from business and capitalist industry, and so it appears as if war were an 'event of nature, with all its horror and bliss'.[142] Indeed, argues Benjamin, the noxious fascist 'parallelogram of forces', nature and nation, is spanned by the 'diagonal' of war.[143] The fascists present the nation as a new economic mystery of a sublime nature, as impenetrable as the secrets of first nature. New nationalism publicizes a shortcircuited, unmediated fusion of nature and technology, instead of passing the two categories through social determination.[144] Grounding the war ideology of the proto-fascists in an economic substructure, Benjamin asserts that the idea of the nation, promoted by the proto-fascists, has hidden behind it the very specific agenda of a 'ruling class' in economic crisis. The old officers become class warriors. Proto-fascists and a ruling class in crisis push to actualize an agenda that guarantees further sources of profit.[145]

For Benjamin, the actual landscape of world war is a wasteland, ravaged by technology. One single aeroplane, loaded with gas bombs, carries all the necessary power to cut off civilian amenities and life. The development of military technology enables the tremendous empowerment of a bureaucracy. This development nourishes fascist fantasies of control. The fascist nation depends on a centralized and devastating violence, necessitating a techno-cratic military machine which, together with the ranks of fascist civil servants, carries out the will of a crisis-stricken state. Lone bombers on a mission for the state, disposing over an ever-more destructive warfare technology, can permanently savage nature.[146] The mush of the battlefield is not an Arcadian landscape, such as encourages the contemplation of aura – a fuzz on the horizon, a strange weave of space and time that encompasses the viewer at peace within nature, gently.[147] And yet, for the fascists, the gases from the battlefield are retranslated as the fire and brimstone of mythology, creating an ersatz, man-made aura.[148] At the end of auratic experience – in modernity's new denaturing – is aura's readmission in the mysticism of the reactionary war chroniclers. The fascist experience marks the landscape with a vicious intel-lectual mystical idealism. Benjamin, in contrast, insists on a sober experience of the new technologies, a correct and rational under-standing of the technological stakes – the proletariat might achieve such understanding. The fascist landscape of the front has become a symbolic landscape within which technology and its effects have become metaphors for idealist categories. Benjamin draws a connection between the formulae of idealism and the waging of war. Both idealism and militarism inhabit the same terrain and it is a terrain of battle:

> It must be bitterly stated: in the face of the totally mobilized landscape the German feeling for nature has experienced an unsuspected upswing. The genii of peace that sensually inhabit it have been evacuated. For as far as one could see over the edges of the trenches, the surroundings had become the very terrain of German idealism. Each shell-crater was a problem, each wire entanglement an antinomy, each barb a definition, each explosion a thesis. And the sky overhead, by day was the cosmic inside of a steel helmet, at night, the moral code above you.[149]

Kant, the theoretician of absolute ethical conduct, had called for just such a man who declares: the immensity of the heavens above me, the imperative of my conscience within me. Alluding perhaps to the ethical basis of the dominant justificatory discourse of the Great War, Benjamin insinuates that a pure ethical stance can be used to justify an idealist withdrawal into the unethical conduct of war. In 'Nochmals: Die vielen Soldaten' (1929), Benjamin states that the issue is never abstract war, but always concrete war, specifically imperialist war, and that is a 'phenomenon of economic life'. If it is not seen thus, the discussion is forced away from the terrain of the political, into the bottomless pit of the ethical.[150] In denying the actuality of past experience, the fascists attempt to negate the real presence of the massed ranks in the world war, emphasizing instead the individualist heroic soldierly ethos that bows before fate. Where the writers do grasp the actuality of the battlefield, for example, in their recognition of the presence of massed ranks, not just heroic officers, or in their acknowledgement of the mechanization of war, they tend to use this admission to account for the war's loss, the degradation of the former aristocratic soldierly ethos and the impurity of this military principle compared to that of earlier battles. One example is the attack, quoted by Benjamin, on the 'senselessly mechanized matériel war'.[151] The warrior of the 1930s, draped in an officer's uniform, a supposed symbol of talent, strategy and genius and emblem of heroism, attempts to ignore the reality of technology, manifested as a matériel battle of battalions, dependent on the superiority of their technology and fighting over long distances. Such factors invalidate in actuality individual heroism.[152] Warrior-writers endeavour to ignore the real stakes of technical development, promoting instead a bad infinity of eternally sparring soldier-heroes.

For Benjamin, any claim to legitimacy of the inherited idealist and nationalistic ideologies of justification is practically obliterated in the experience of material annihilation by the destructive technologies of the 1914–18 world war. War is shown to have absolutely changed because of new technical inventions that occasion sportily proficient mass armies, chemical weaponry, protracted trench warfare and long-distance butchery. Benjamin insists on the reality of the terrain and war as the violent technological mastering of land and people. Any mediation of actual past experience in the war zone would have to take into account the *Technik* of '*Materialschlacht* (material battle). The truth of materialism is found in a '*Materialschlacht*' that produces victims' bodies ripped open. Benjamin assumes that '*Materialschlacht*' signals the death of any justification of idealism: to recognize the brute reality of war is to be a materialist.[153] Benjamin employs the idea of materialism in quite a literal sense – '*matérielles*', '*leibliches*', the collective body politic. The physical materiality of the collective is in crisis in war. Idealist theorizing ignores the annihilating threat to the collectivity. Benjamin pinpoints an aporia in the relationship of matter and mind, objective conditions and human consciousness in the reactionaries' work. Matter, he insists, should have primacy over idealist conceptualizations of mind. This is akin to the orthodox Marxist assertion of materialism as the primacy of matter over mind, or the crucial facticity of determinant brute economic reality. Benjamin seems to be suggesting that if an intellectual caste ignores the nature of objective conditions, a space is then opened up for idealist theorizing. When matter is not prioritized, false consciousness is bound to result. At the close of the essay on fascism Benjamin asserts that it is the economic nature of bourgeois society that forces a split between the mental and the technical, mind and matter.

Benjamin explains his theory of false consciousness in a 1930 review of Siegfried Kracauer's *Die Angestellten*, an examination of the mentalities, dreams and fantasies of urban white-collar workers in Weimar Berlin:

> Marx said that social being determines consciousness, but also, however, that only in the classless society will consciousness be adequate to being. It follows that social being in a class state is inhuman in as much as the consciousness of different classes is inadequate to being, corresponding to it rather in highly mediated, improper and distorted form. Since such a false consciousness in the lower classes has its roots in the interests of the upper classes, and the upper classes' consciousness has its roots in the contradictions of their economic situation, the eliciting of correct consciousness – initially in the lower classes, which have the most to expect from it – is the first priority of Marxism.[154]

Materialist insight is not easily gained. It is blocked by the discrepancies between matter and mind or being and consciousness in the class state. But the Marxist has a framework for interpretation. The materialist critic has an educative role that involves the propagandistic task of 'eliciting correct consciousness'. However, this is not just a matter of thinking inside other people's heads. In his essay on Karl Kraus, Benjamin argues that there is no idealist liberation from myth, but only a materialist emancipation.[155]

The critique of other intellectuals' understanding of *Technik* and an exposure of the political assumptions of those who write about the last and next war is framed by Benjamin's contributions to a theory of *Technik*. Theoretical assertions on technological dynamics in the opening and closing parts of the essay provide the context for Benjamin's critique of the fascist aestheticization and ideological representation of experience. The opening and closing parts of 'Theorien des deutschen Faschismus' trace the dialectical forcefield around *Technik*.[156] The annihilating coincidence of *Technik* and war is articulated inside a theory of the interplay between technological forces and socio-political forces. This is most clearly expounded on the opening page of 'Theorien des deutschen Faschismus'.[157] His 'sober' analysis of technological dynamic encourages continued insistence on an imminent worldwide conflagration, due to (mis)alignments in the relationship between forces and relations of production, that are part of a social inability to administer *Technik*.[158] Technical resources, sources of energy, have been so intensified and yet are not 'adequately' directed into the conduct of private or social lives, because of structures of ownership that affect the particular articulation of the political-moral and the technological.[159] There is a gaping discrepancy between the vast potential uses of *Technik* to the benefit of the proletariat and a lack of 'moral elucidation', which is a consequence of the bourgeois organization of production and politics. This sense of a divergence between the productive and political realm is stressed by Lukács in a discussion of Rosa Luxemburg's *Soziale Reform oder Revolution?*, read by Benjamin in 1924 while he was in Capri. Lukács affirms Luxemburg's comment that:

> The relations of production of capitalist society become increasingly socialist, but its political and legal arrangements erect an even loftier wall between capitalist and socialist society.[160]

For Benjamin, this discrepancy between productive and political realms compels technological forces to find an outlet in war, or, as he expresses it, to 'still push to justify themselves'.[161] Technology erupts into war, finding no other place to expend its energies. Benjamin's *Technik* possesses a certain natural disposability or normativity. *Technik* is endowed with a peculiar subjective autonomy. The term '*adäquat*' implies a notion of essential predetermination of the technical resources: technology's dynamic is an unfolding of energy that will out. Technology's energetic overspill is a by-product of capitalist economic competition and the overproduction of surplus value. The surplus value produced in capitalism cannot be profitably realized within the system and must erupt violently as weaponry deployed by the imperialists. This situation allows capital and the state to become sole and guaranteed consumers of their own military productions, as well as to conquer new markets.[162]

Benjamin's report on *Technik* suggests a necessary realization of technological essence, and provides therefore evidence of a tendency towards a technologism that assigns historical determinacy to technology. The purpose proper to *Technik* is only realized when *Technik* is taken up into political discussion, in a most literal sense. For *Technik* to be taken up into the political or moral realm and to be effective there it must be a subject and it must have a voice. Likewise, in an instance of reciprocity, Benjamin maintains that technology, which has forged the apocalyptic visage of nature and silenced it, was the force that could have given nature a voice.[163] The economic nature of bourgeois society impels the cleavage between the mental and the technical, signifying the exclusion of 'the technical thought from the right to participation in social ordering'.[164] War has become vicious against populations because technology has not been consulted. In a schema that draws on the re-creation out of annihilation proposed in 'Zum Planetarium', Benjamin suggests that war is a terrible opportunity for technology to make known *its* demands. It does this in order to correct 'the incapability of peoples to order relations amongst each other corresponding to the relation to nature that they already possess through their technology'.[165] Benjamin asserts, in a gesture reminiscent of some of the utopian socialist Charles Fourier's axioms, that once *Technik* has become a 'key to happiness' and not a 'fetish of doom', nature will offer up unimaginable experiences to humanity.[166] Benjamin insists on reciprocity, a reciprocation between nature/humanity and technology, in contrast to a certain Marxist model that implies only the one-way recognition of nature as a force to be dominated. By the same token, Benjamin asserts that instead of illuminating itself through its technology, nature as a dynamic force in a non-socially determined fusion with technology flaunts only its most threatening features. The contractual elective affinity, identified as violated in 'Zum Planetarium', is enlisted to make sense of the assertion that 'each coming war is the slave revolt of *Technik*'.[167] Such a view, though fervently mystical in some sense, was not too far removed from Trotsky's political argument in *The War and the International*. Alfred Seidel quotes from this book by Trotsky in a dissertation read by Benjamin in the very early 1920s.[168] Trotsky insists that forces of production have outgrown the limits of nation and state and partake in a dynamic that occasions war:

> The core of the present war is the revolt of forces of production which generated capitalism. They revolt against their exploited form in the nation-state.[169]

Technik and its accommodation within the social world become markers of social maturity. If society can accommodate *Technik* sufficiently, *Technik* and humanity will coexist in 'harmonious playing'.[170] *Technik* will not revolt destructively in war, with the energetic relations in society culminating in violent imperialism.

An autonomous sense of technology's power is partly overridden when Benjamin notes of the social and political constellations, inside which *Technik* operates, that they themselves have a determining effect on technological development and production. Benjamin refers to the decisive effect of the failure of the revolution in Germany in 1919, whose success would have signalled or would have been dependent upon, social maturity.[171] Technology becomes a subject with determining force, in a position to make promises, once it has been so enabled by social-political relations. Those political conditions are dependent on a seizure of control via revolution. By the end of 'Theorien des deutschen Faschismus', the moral illumination of technology is translated into the need for political activity.[172] Benjamin identifies a blocked 'natural' coalition between proletariat and technology. Consultation between proletariat and its ally *Technik* is the precondition for a harmonious coexistence, based on the beneficial and egalitarian usage of *Technik*.

Benjamin notes how the fascists wish to abolish any notion of the rational from war. They are antagonistic towards the 'civil-rational', opposite of the military.[173] But for Benjamin a closer investigation of the definition of the term 'rational' reveals another contradiction. In 'Nochmals: Die vielen Soldaten' (1929) he unmasks the core of bourgeois ratio as domination administered through force. Such domination provides an efficient way of getting things done.[174] The military is at its core. This contrasts with the notion of rational organization, expounded in 'James Ensor wird 70 Jahre' (1930), with its dialectic of the mass. This dialectical view of the mass claims that varying political consequences are to be drawn, depending on whether the mass forms itself or is discovered.[175] War moulds people into a seething mass of worms, in contrast to the communist self-formation of the masses in organization. Organization is a consciously undertaken act. For Benjamin, the idea of the properly rational is allied to a normative usage of *Technik* as part of the organization of the collective. Organization carries within it the word organ, hinting at Benjamin's programme of organizing technology as an organ of the collective body. As stated in 'Zum Planetarium' and 'Der Sürrealismus', the task of a *Technik*, liberated from the strictures of capitalist organization, is to organize this body. Social maturity denotes the ability to make *Technik* an organ of the collective social body. Technology as 'organ' injects new meaning into the notion organic. The word organ cannot be detached from its natural biological connotation, but it also transmits connotations of technical implements. It rests perfectly on that ambiguous nexus of technical-natural that so interests Benjamin. Benjamin's conceptual language of elemental forces and maturity suggests a conflation of the social and the natural.

His metaphors verify traces of a teleology of blocked technological development.

At the close of the essay on German fascism, Benjamin speaks of 'sober children', defined in opposition to the mystic proto-fascists with their hocus-pocus of war. This rational epistemological subject is only newly born.[176] The language echoes *The Communist Manifesto* of Marx and Engels: 'Alles Ständische und Stehende verdampft, alles Heilige wird entweiht, und die Menschen sind endlich gezwungen, ihre Lebensstellung, ihre gegenseitigen Beziehungen mit nüchternen Augen anzusehen' [all that is solid melts into air, all that is holy is profaned and finally people are compelled to face with sober eyes their conditions of life and their mutual relations]. The sober proletariat will not see the next war as magical, but as the everyday, normal emergency state of capital's rule, and will convert that war into civil war.[177] The language, then, is that of sobriety, and shifts the ground away from 'Zum Planetarium' and its positing of a pre-rational ecstatic relationship between humanity and technology. Diverging slightly from the analysis in 'Der Sürrealismus', which had acknowledged the importance of intoxication, Benjamin stresses rather the caveat voiced there about the need for the abstemious rigours of bolshevism and an 'illumination' that is most definitely 'profane'. But Benjamin is unable to relinquish completely the language of sorcery, though there may be a certain ironic or rhetorical intent in his continued usage. He describes the civil war as 'the Marxist trick' that alone is a match for 'runic magic'.[178] In Benjamin's writings, from now on, the proletariat is discussed as the only force that is in the process of sobering up, quite unlike other sections of society. The sobriety of the proletariat comes from its special, elective affinity to the technology with which it is in daily contact – machinery's shocks and demands keep it alert. And the other classes are condemned to dream the nightmare that they sustain: in the *Passagenwerk* it is the petits bourgeois (regarded by Benjamin as the electoral base of Nazism) and grands bourgeois (seen as the economic executors of Nazism) who are intoxicated with commodity capitalism and its promising seductions.[179]

Fascist critics are unwilling to recognize the true meaning of technology. They fetishize its destructive side, without considering under what conditions the possibility of destruction becomes actual. Fascists do not historicize destructivity. No intellectual critic is in a position to realize the essence of technology, but, in Benjamin's view, critics critical of the status quo must recognize and assert technology's latent essence, its possibilities. And if they recognize that essence, they will be forced to concede that the dynamic of *Technik* and its specific relationship to the proletariat means that only through proletarian revolution can the cycle of violence be broken and a post-revolutionary harmony of technology, humanity and nature inaugurated.

Reality/Experience

Benjamin alleges that the rightist intellectual warriors, despite their talk of eternity and the primeval, are, in fact, bound up in the concerns of the moment and ignore history in 'a journalistic rush to capitalize from the actual present, without having grasped the past'.[180] They cannot comment on history because they are blinded by the directives of their present. For Benjamin, to grasp the past would necessitate the transmission in their writings of a complex understanding of political and economic machinations on the battlefield and the new role of technology. After this point, Benjamin summons a critical approach to a reality in which he sets a dual notion of experience, 'Erfahrung' and 'Erlebnis', a recurrent couplet in his writings. In 1933 he reaches the conclusion that conditions on the battlefield have made the continued existence of experience as 'Erfahrung' – practised, well-established and continuous tradition – virtually impossible in this moment.[181] The technological traumas of war confirm and kick home experience as 'Erlebnis' – shock, adventure, disruption. The mistake made by the proto-fascists is to universalize and dehistoricize 'Erlebnis', rewriting the historically specific as 'Urerlebnis' and relinquishing the opportunity to step back and critically assess its qualities.[182]

Post-war experience is shaped by the continued mismanagement of *Technik*. It is also the experience of the end of the bourgeois humanist subject and the beginning of a possible new collective humanity. The loss of experience (as it was previously known) might be the inauguration of a new form of experience that may be deeper, more complex or simply different. In notes on a discussion with the bank official Gustav Glück and composer Kurt Weill in 1931, he observes how an awareness of alterations in conceptions of experience is mediated in the latest popular cartoon films. Mickey Mouse films disavow, more radically than ever before, all experience, implying that a public that recognizes in Mickey Mouse the fact that 'the creature remains, even after all human likeness has been cast off', realizes it may not be worth having experiences in a world like this.[183] Mickey Mouse, the discussants claim, is a figure who shows for the first time on screen that even our own body parts can be repossessed by those with power over us. The cartoons' massive success proves that the public recognizes its own lives in them.[184] Such a statement blooms out of Benjamin's acknowledgment of the historicity of experience and marks his prioritizing of the search for forms of reproduction that retransmit an adequate representation of what it is to experience today.

Discussions of *Technik* or technology and technique are prevalent in 1920s' and 1930s' social, political and cultural theory. While there are those – often Nazi-tinged or mystically inclined – who reject technology outright, seeking the realization of a pre-modern, anti-rational bucolic fantasy, technology also has its assorted fanatics. The fanatics' fantasies are manifested across the political panorama in various forms of techno-enthusiasm, engineer-romanticism, heady pro-Taylorism and Fordism. Halfway through the 1920s a process of virtually uninhibited capitalist rationalization takes place in Germany. Its ideological promoters – Americanists, new objectivists and the like – assume that known structures of representation and political domination are crumbling before technological rationality. It is 1924 and the dollar sun is rising in Germany, while a bourgeoisie bent on rationalizing production charge themselves up on a translation of Henry Ford's bestseller *My Life and Work* (1923). This book recommends, slo-ganistically: 'don't discuss, produce'. It seems as if, in 1924, US capital exports something extra along with the boost to productive capacities delivered by the Dawes Plan for managing German reparations. The US also markets abroad an ideological substance capable of narcoticizing segments of the intelligentsia. Ford's book fanfares a supersession of class conflict and the provision of a system confident in assuring an accord of interests. Ford tackles economic matters as questions of organization and technological efficiency. Industry-cultists disseminate a belief in the purity of the productive power of tonic-*Technik*. Technology is posited as an antidote to class society's sickening irritations. Technology is viewed by leftist and rightist machine-obsessed modernists as a magical apparatus of social refurbishment whose scientific properties can remedy all predicaments through technical rationality. Politics turns technocratic. Biology also turns technical – as Fordism is seen to intrude into human physique and reorganize the labouring body.[185] Nature is denatured. Some see this as material for a modern calamity of lost nature and lost humanity.

Not all commentators critical of Americanism, however, insist that such a technological invasion of physical nature leads to the absolute mechanization of the labour force and the advent of the malleable post-human. Duplicating Benjamin's hope, some anti-capitalist critics see deliverance from the negativity of technologization occurring through technology. Gramsci, pondering the way in which Fordist factory labour relies on a physical, reactive gesture that allows the worker's mind to wander, states:

> American industrialists have understood all too well this dialectic inherent in the new industrial methods. They have understood that trained gorilla is just a phrase, that unfortunately the worker remains a man and even that during his work he thinks more, or

at least has greater opportunities for thinking, once he has overcome the crisis of adaptation without being eliminated: and not only does the worker think, but the fact that he gets no immediate satisfaction from his work and realises that they are trying to reduce him to a trained gorilla, can lead him into a train of thought that is far from conformist.[186]

For Gramsci, Fordism, eventually, potentially, replaces bourgeois individualism with socialized relations. And the space for a new consciousness of exploitation is not closed down by the extreme presence of forceful technological methods, but is rather opened up. Gramsci's is, of course, just one version of how technology might be a prelude to, rather than occlusion of, revolutionary transformation.

The file on Marx in the *Passagenwerk* is in large part a collation of excerpts from Marx's recently released early writings and *Das Kapital*. But it also provides a record of Benjamin's reliance on Karl Korsch in his efforts to comprehend Marx's theory. Another critic to whom Benjamin turned for orientation was Hugo Fischer, a Munich professor who published a book in 1932 entitled *Karl Marx und sein Verhältnis zu Staat und Wirtschaft*.[187] Benjamin paraphrases Fischer's assertion that, in the desolation of the nineteenth century, Marx perceives *Technik* as the only sphere of life in which the person stands 'at the centre of things'.[188] Fischer's study appears to have influenced Benjamin's reading of Marx – or to have met with the sense that he had already made of Marx. Fischer claims that Marx endows *Technik* with a particular facility: the power to combine workers, and indeed the ability to fuse the two classes, in the act of cooperative industrial reproduction. Marx is seen to credit technology with the potency, through its continual enforcement of social combination, to smash through the individual existences of post-medieval citizens, and in the process destroy all distinction between inwardness and externality, appearance and essence.[189] Persuaded by Fischer's characterization of Marx's idea of *Technik*, Benjamin likewise identifies a specific quality of technology that places the person in the middle of things, eliminating distance between persons and objects, bringing things closer to people and people closer to things. Just before the sentence referred to by Benjamin in his file of quotations on and by Marx, Fischer discusses how, in Marx's view, technics works anthropologically – an idea central to Benjamin's understanding of the dialectical interplay between technology and humans.

An anecdote illustrates how far Benjamin's recognition of technical necessity invades his own social relationships. His writing mode excludes intimacy and embraces mechanical mediation. In February 1931, he sends a letter to Scholem. He had used a typewriter, dictating its contents to another and so making it a public affair – instead of his usual and unique, minuscule fountain pen scratchings. Two weeks later Scholem responds, deeply hurt and disturbed by the publicity of the gesture and mechanical intervention in their relationship. On the back of the typed letter he writes:

> Certainly it may be true, as you insist, that its technical production adds what is undoubtedly an extremely modern, revolutionary touch and tenor to our written correspondence, but as someone competent in this area, I may say with equal assurance that this indirect form of communication appears simply and bluntly as a double silence, and, if I am not being too impudent, I would like to state that never was such a letter, one crying out to be written by fountain pen, less suited to dictation to a typist.[190]

Scholem had missed the point. He insists on a romantic idea of the individual, sealed off from technological change. Benjamin understands the risks involved in utilizing the new technology, but he also believes in gambling. After all, in the 1880s Nietzsche had tried his hand at producing typewritten manuscripts, and from that time onwards script, in various contexts, had been more and more mechanized. The immediacy and individualistic expressiveness that might be lost would be well compensated by the candid and punctual adherence to the epoch, in all its mediocrity. Later, Benjamin reflected on the process of letter writing. His book *Deutsche Menschen*, published in 1936 under the pseudonym Detlef Holz, was a study of the art of letter-writing in the progressive bourgeois epoch. Adorno remarked in a letter to him, in November 1936, that he had illuminated how the decline of the bourgeoisie is enacted in the decline of letter-writing. In critical broadsides such as 'Tankstelle' and in his own social practice, Benjamin places technology pivotally in a lurking post-bourgeois epoch of social interaction.

CHAPTER 2

Benjamin's Objectives

> To be past, not to exist any longer works passionately in things.
> The historian entrusts his business to this. He holds on to this
> force and recognizes things as they appear in a moment of no-
> longer-existing.
>
> 'Pariser Passagen' 1 (1927–29)[1]

Technology and Forms

Technology and techniques restructure the human sensory
apparatus: this is Benjamin's conclusion. Technologies organize
perception in particular. Benjamin examines technologies of reproduction emergent in the modern, industrial epoch. A note from
the early stages of the *Passagenwerk* mentions how the optical
devices prevalent in an epoch might reconfigure the world:

> Careful examination of the relationship of the optics of the
> myrioramas to the time of the modern, the newest. They must
> surely be registered as the base coordinates of this world.[2]

Quotations and commentaries compiled in the initial stages of
the *Passagenwerk* are especially concerned with tracing the effects
of new technologies on the human sensory apparatus. Benjamin's
sketches of social experience illustrate how kinetic technologies,
such as trains, cars and aeroplanes, mangle and reformulate spatial
orientation, while new cultural technologies, such as photography
and cinema, assault chronology and produce contractions and
debunkings of temporality as traditionally conceived. Benjamin
explores how human subjectivity might correspond to the contemporary exigencies of existence and how technological art –
artworks that are produced by mechanical means and are
reproduced in numerous copies – translates and retransmits contemporary existence.[3]

Lukács' *Theorie des Romans* (1916), a study that was conse-
quential for a large number of intellectuals, insisted on a connection
between genre and history, invoking the historicity of aesthetic
forms.[4] The fragmentary structure of the novel, claims Lukács,
proves to be a legitimate form for the disclosure of truths about a
particular historical phase. In terms of form, the novel's non-

organic composition reproduces, as historico-philosophical necessity, the mirror-image of a world out of joint.[5] But for Benjamin, the novel is historically remaindered, due to the continuing commitment of its content to individual biography and its usability only for a solitary mode of reception. In a review of Alfred Döblin's *Berlin Alexanderplatz*, Benjamin argues that the novel can survive only if it adopts an epic, cinematic form.[6] Modern social experience, increasingly dependent on the mediations of impersonal social forms, demands new forms. The art historian Alois Riegl had espied the historically mutating organizations of perception that braced aesthetic forms, and his analysis of the historicity of perception is taken up into Benjamin's theory.[7] So too is Riegl's close attention to form – however it manifests itself – and form's relationship to history and truth. Riegl revered the ornamental forms of late Roman art which had been rejected by traditional art history as degenerate. In so doing, he teaches Benjamin to look for signs of coherence in artworks produced in non-classicist periods. And so Benjamin too was able frequently to employ the concept of decline (*'Verfall'*) positively, and to perceive in decay historical truth. Benjamin relishes the decline of all sorts of things: the bourgeoisie, aura, love and experience (*'Erfahrung'*), because all this degeneration is evidence of the initiation of an extensive overhaul of existence. In 'Der destruktive Charakter' (1931) or 'Erfahrung und Armut' (1933) there is revealed an ambivalent assessment of the political significance of social decay and decline. In 'Erfahrung und Armut', after various assertions of present poverty and barbarism, Benjamin demands 'complete illusionlessness in the epoch and nevertheless an unreserved acknowledgement of it'.[8] He stakes out meanings for the terms tradition, progress (*Fortschritt*) and decay (*Verfall*), all terms which recur in culture debates of the period. These terms had their communist inflection – but Benjamin re-spins them. Such a process of re-evaluation was consciously undertaken. It comes out in Benjamin's askance relationship to official communist positions, acknowledged in a response to Gerhard-Gershom Scholem's letter which had fulminated against Benjamin's possible membership of the KPD. Benjamin writes on 17 April 1931:

> If one is authoring counter-revolutionary writings – as you quite correctly characterize mine from the party's point of view – should one then expressly place them at the disposal of the counter-revolution? Should one not rather denature them, like spirits, make them – at the risk that they become unpalatable for everyone – definitely and reliably unpalatable for them?[9]

Benjamin's controlling objective is to produce material and concepts that cannot be used to shore up the enemy's rule. This might also make them generally disagreeable, but that was because thereby they exposed the similarities between faulty revolutionary and counter-revolutionary thought. Benjamin is conscious that he is the secret agent within, waging a war against bourgeois thought, for in the same letter he discusses his place of production, his 'writing factory'.[10] He lives in West Berlin, actually, the west of West Berlin, the most affluent part of the German capital, where he enjoys and utilizes the 'most modern culture'. This is his environment. His audience is the intelligentsia, his neighbours. And he knows how to speak to them, for he is one of them. In a letter to Brecht written in February 1931, he insists that it is necessary to show members of the bourgeois intelligentsia that the adoption of dialectical materialism is the only logical option, given their creative and material situation. That situation is the prole-tarianization of intellectuals.[11] To Scholem, that April, Benjamin indicates the desirability of a 'German Bolshevik revolution' from his point of view as writer. He states that a successful revolution would not change the party's attitude towards his present work, but it would enable him to write in a different way.[12] His material conditions of production would be altered, as would everyone's. In a letter to Max Rychner, written in March 1931, Benjamin outlines what he understands by materialist methods. He recommends that he be seen not as a representative of a dogmatic dialectical materialism, but as a researcher with a materialist 'attitude'. And he applauds the correspondence of Judaic teachings and his brand of non-determinist materialism, both of which assume that meaning and truth are won of speculation and research into a motile reality:

> And if I might express it in a word: I have never been able to research and think other than in a, if I may put it this way, theological sense – that is to say in accordance with the Talmudic doctrine of forty-nine levels of significance in each part of the Torah. So: in my experience, the most hackneyed communist platitude has more *hierarchies of significance* than contemporary bourgeois profundity, which only ever signifies apologetics.[13]

So he investigates the loaded language of tradition, progress, decline, degeneracy. This language of socio-cultural inquiry is not confined to the political left. The terms are more widely current. For example, the favourite word of German petit bourgeois ideologues would seem to be *Verfall*, with its intimations of decline, decay and dilapidation. Before the Nazi art and book burnings in 1933 (Benjamin's *Einbahnstraße* included), there were *Verfall-sausstellungen*, exhibitions of decay, chamber of horror displays of the degenerate culture of Jewish-Bolshevik Weimar Germany. In short, Benjamin's re-evaluation of the key terms in contemporary cultural debate involves a *détournement* of the concepts. For him, involvement with tradition means uncovering the tradition of the oppressed, not revering the weighty tradition of inherited, great literature. Progress is not construed as an inevitable, automatic, universal advance through history, but as a commentator's critical measure of actual social relations. Like the more orthodox communist Lukács, Benjamin analyses the social and political decay of the imperialist bourgeoisie by studying cultural manifestations. But, unlike Lukács, he does not necessarily condemn representations of decline and decay as decadent, degrading, subjectivist and designed by artists to elicit social impotence. Benjamin affirms the decline of the bourgeoisie, and along with it, the decline of aura, the decline of love, the decline of bourgeois potency with its concomitant decay of imaginative capacity and the decline of experience. And he perceives such decline to be outlined, for critical appropriation, in modern and modernist artworks. His insistence on the decline of the bourgeois individual, as subject of art and as art producer and consumer, intimates the Marxist terminology of capitalism's terminal decay. But, for Benjamin, every cultural product leaks intelligence about the make-up of its contemporaneous social world, no negativity is annexed to the idea of decline and no products of culture are irretrievable to meaning. There are no 'periods of decline' as such, for history uncoils unevenly. A statement in 'Konvolut N: erkenntnistheoretisches, Theorie des Fortschritts' in the *Passagenwerk* confesses that work's *esprit*:

> The pathos of this work: there are no periods of decline. Attempt to see the nineteenth century as thoroughly positively as I endeavoured to see the seventeenth century in the mourning play project. No belief in periods of decline.[14]

The task is redemption – to see things as positively as possible, and that includes seeing culture in decline as positively as possible. That may be by finding its utopian aspects and so rescuing decline from negativity. There is decline, then – if not periods of decline – but the cultural products in decline still reveal the world, and so it is no longer decline in the sense of being sterile and not worthy of attention. There are even 'epochs of decline' within certain procedures – conventional photography, for example, as the nineteenth century draws to a close and new technical forms struggle to be realized.[15] Such decline points out ways beyond itself, ways to make it good again. Benjamin advises that the contemporary degradation of experience be recognized in order to inaugurate the beginning of a new beginning, through a 'new positive concept of barbarism'.[16] Benjamin has understood the comment from *Das kommunistische Manifest* by Marx and Engels:

'All that is solid melts into air, all that is holy is profaned.'[17] It then continues: 'and people are at last compelled to face with sober senses, their real conditions of existence ...'. No talk here of modernity's endless evaporation and incessant perplexity, but rather of a stripping bare, a casting aside of all hocus-pocus and mystification: the possibility of seeing, for the first time, after the ruin of mythic apologia, truth.[18]

Judgement of art is a matter of technique and technology and the demands that they pose. Form is a technical issue, and technical forms lie buried in machinery like seeds yet to germinate. Forms are released through the innovations of technical change.

> After all, is it not so that all great conquests in the realm of forms come about as technical discoveries? The forms that will be decisive for our epoch lie hidden in machines, and we are only just beginning to suspect them.[19]

In an article from 1927 on Soviet film in general, and Eisenstein's *Battleship Potemkin* in particular, Benjamin states that important elementary progressions in art are not a matter of new contents (and so distances himself from the influential contentions of Panofsky's school). Nor are these progressions classified as new forms (as Wölfflin and his formalist pupils envisaged in their forecast of a requisite sequence of a creatorless and continuous evolution of forms and styles in an 'art history without names'). Revolutions in *Technik*, Benjamin insists, precede both content and form.[20] In these revolutions in *Technik*, which outcrop in a fracturing of artistic development, the political tendencies that inhabit every artwork are disclosed, since artworks are 'historical constructions of consciousness' ('*historische Gebilde des Bewußtseins*').[21] Technology-analysis, rather than psychoanalysis, is seen to bring hidden or repressed political tendencies to light. He sets about analysing a new technology capable of cracking apart art as received, and he considers the political tendencies that technology enables to surface. These research aims are carried out in 'Kleine Geschichte der Photographie' (A Short History of Photography), written for the journal *Die literarische Welt* in 1931.

Photographic Technologies

> When everything that people call art had got the rheumatics all over, the photographer lit the thousands of candles in his lamp, and the sensitive paper gradually absorbed the darkness between the shapes of certain everyday objects. He had invented the force of a fresh and tender flash of lightning which was more important than all the constellations destined for our visual pleasures.

Precise, unique and correct mechanical deformation is fixed, smooth and filtered like a head of hair through a comb of light. Is it a spiral of water, or the tragic gleam of a revolver, an egg, a glittering arc or a sluice gate of reason, a subtle ear with a mineral whistle or a turbine of algebraical formulae? As the mirror effortlessly throws back the image, and the echo the voice, without asking us why, the beauty of matter belongs to no one, for henceforth it is a physico-chemical product.

'Inside-out Photography', Tristan Tzara's 1922 preface to Man Ray's photograph album, *Les champs délicieux*[22]

In photography the beauty of matter is an issue for chemistry and for physics, which make the imprinting occur. As such, matter's beauty cannot be possessed, nor made transcendent, in the old ways. Material speaks – it is a found article. But it does not speak the sentiments it has been made to ventriloquize in the past – that being the articulation of a truth other than itself, a song of the spirit. Instead, this articulate material – a material that is not mute – is matter as ambiguity and puzzle – and art after art is its frame. Mechanically made and reproduced art will catch its secrets in a scientific process that is magical too. Photography has a direct, reflectional relationship to the external world. Photography promises its viewers objectivity – the English word lens in various European languages is some form of the Latin word *objectus* – in German, *Objektive*, in French, *objectif*, in Italian, *obiettivo*. This 'objectivity', a scientific by-product, is guarantor of historical faithfulness. Photography cannot fail to mirror external reality and, in mirroring it, provide accurate optic evidence of 'historical constructions of consciousness'. The foundation of photography's obdurate divulgence of truth is correlated to the fact that all photographs are analogical representations through their congruity at some level to an external given. There is an excess quantity in photography, absent in other art-forms.[23] A residue of non-art subsists in photography, an unsilenceable existence. Non-art steps outside of the representation and proffers something 'new and strange'.[24] Trace deposits of the real are summoned up by the technology of photography.

In 'Kleine Geschichte der Photographie' Benjamin hopes to show how photography is moving out of 'the realm of aesthetic distinctions to social function'.[25] Words such as 'social function' are the words that estrange his friend Theodor Adorno, who accuses Benjamin of instrumentalism, the result of a Brechtian contamination of categories. Through Lacis, Benjamin had met Brecht in Berlin at the end of the 1920s. Brecht's cultural-political practice presents Benjamin with a theoretical model of cultural production whose 'correspondence' (though not identity) with new technical forms, specifically filmic forms, suggests tactics for overturning current aesthetic relations.[26] Early in 1930 Benjamin wrote his first commentaries on Brecht's dramatic theory and practice. For Benjamin, the 'social function' of contemporary art is the disclosure of truths about the structure of a reality that is subject to historical change. The most important art does not disclose eternal truths, but particular, fixed, historical truths. The photograph, for example, is identified as the 'first image of the encounter between the person and the machine'.[27] The photograph, product of technical breakthrough, provides an image of something external to it. But the photograph represents more than just a simple image of what appears before the camera's lens. It images an experience of the encounter between people and world and people and machinery.

Photography renders two realities: the real, which has become historical after the moment of its recording, and the real, or moment, in which the photograph still exists. On the basis of an intervention of reality ('*Wirklichkeit*'), in the form of a 'tiny flash of coincidence', historical time resonates in the affiliation between image and viewer. There are connections between the idea of a chance photographic moment and ideas expressed in Siegfried Kracauer's 'Die Photographie' (1927), where the arbitrary photographic moment is seen to alienate for purposes of examination a sliver of nature from the tyranny of intention.[28] The photographic image elicits historically charged perception, dependent on traces of historical meaning in the image and the passage of time that places the viewer in history. Photography presents not so much the 'here and now' of a certain place and a certain time, a uniqueness such as is seen to accompany the experience of the traditional artwork. The important element is rather the connection made between the moment caught on celluloid and the moment of the perceiver. This 'here and now' – desired by the viewers – collides with the then of the photograph, the depiction of real pasts and 'long forgotten' minutes.[29] The future of the image's subject frozen in the lost moment of the photograph might be rediscovered in the clash between the presented moment of the past and the viewer's standpoint in the present. The viewer retro-predictively scans photographs for the history that will happen. Only photography can perform this function, because of its peculiar appeal to viewers. Its mechanical analogical basis captures a moment in time indexically-iconically and exports it into the future. Photography brings objects closer and lays them out for inspection. It is in this sense that photography may be a place to locate evidence, a '*Tatort*'.[30] This 'place of action' is where historical processes have actually taken place. Benjamin conjures up the languages of police detection and mysticism. The photographer is a descendant of the augurs and haruspices – and the photographer's task is to reveal guilt and point out the guilty in his pictures. Augurs are prophets or soothsayers, haruspices are Roman priests who practised divination, especially by examining the entrails of animals. The photographer provides an appropriately updated image for such forensic activity in a scientific age.

In 'Der Sürrealismus' Benjamin urged the exchange of the historical vista on the past for the political examination of the past.[31] This was suggested by surrealism's explosion of the accumulated weight of the past in the present moment. Old, outmoded objects, in this case nineteenth-century photographs, are made visible as origins. Historically remaindered objects, fragments of the past, are accosted as documents of cognition that detonate political significance once bombarded with knowledge from the present. 'Kleine Geschichte der Photographie' is an object lesson in exposing the 'historical constructions of consciousness' and the particular political disposition (of the users of the reproductive technology), displayed in the technologies and techniques of different epochs of photography. Benjamin's configuration of the 'essence' of photography aims to discover not simply a history of perception, but a politics of vision and visibility.

Through examinations of early photographs, late nineteenth-century studio photography and 1920s' avant-garde photography, 'Kleine Geschichte der Photographie' uncovers differing historical constructions of consciousness and political tendencies, whose perfect representational reflection is traced through differences in technique and technology. Benjamin reads historical consciousness both through the *mise en scène* of individual photographs and their aesthetic-technical attributes. The analysis of early photography asserts that an accurate picture is transmitted of the consciousness extant in the social world of the class represented there. The photograph fixes on celluloid a view of reality, held in the consciousness of a class when it imagines itself and the cosmos. Technological art is capable of tendering in ocular form the ideology of the self-representing class.

'Kleine Geschichte der Photographie' reflects on early photography's status as science. The first defenders of photography were utopians. They believed – as does Benjamin – in the power of photography to reveal the whole world. Arago's speech to the Chamber of Deputies in 1839 legitimates photography, not primarily as art-form, but in terms of its scientific applications. Arago lists a cosmic range of photographic subjects; from astrophysics to philology, from photographing stars to the idea of recording all the Egyptian hieroglyphics.[32] Expounding practitioners' initial sense of the 'actual scope of the invention', Benjamin draws out early photography as scientific, experimental and utopian in its breadth, and infers these as characteristic of the relationship between the mid-nineteenth-century bourgeoisie and its world. The expansive scope of legitimate photographic subjects allows Benjamin to label these bourgeois experimenters progressive and universalist in their aims. Photography, at this stage, is unencumbered by the profit dictates of its industrialization and the directives stemming from state intervention. Such directives attend the consolidation of bourgeois rule.[33] The bourgeois class imagines itself to be a universal liberator class, until that moment when it has conquered positions of power, at which point Benjamin descries a reactionary turn. Estimating the consequences of this change is crucial for Benjamin's analysis, as is made clear in an early note from the file on epistemology and the theory of progress in the *Passagenwerk*, where Benjamin endorses the 'politically essential' act of 'illuminating the bourgeois class situation at the moment when the first signs of decline appear'.[34] His analyses of individual images from the first period of photography assert that early photography mediates in visual form a specific comprehension of historical time as durable. It also conveys the future-oriented, continuing existence of the represented class in its given form. The mode of this mediation is technological. Early photographs emerge gradually on silver plates over a succession of moments. Time is spun out technologically in the drawn-out exposure, which forces long stretches of immobility. This eternalization of the moment is viewed by Benjamin analogously, relaying between technology and ideology, as sign of a sense of 'immortality' and permanence.[35] 'Aura' is mentioned in the article – introduced in the context of detailing an historical construction of consciousness. The appearance of aura in early photographs is read as a visual analogy of the represented class's ideology:

> There was an aura around them, a medium, which lends their gaze, even as it penetrates that medium, a fullness and a security.[36]

The short history of photography insists that the relationship of a technician to the technology is decisive.[37] Auratic pictures were taken by technologically literate photographers who perceived their customers' membership of an ascendant class and their possession of an aura that had nestled right into the folds of their suits.[38] Benjamin's graphic example of this is an image of the philosopher Schopenhauer, taken in about 1850. A photograph of the crumpled jacket folds of the *Naturphilosoph* Friedrich Schelling accompanied the study when it appeared in three instalments in *Die literarische Welt* in September and October 1931. The comfortable ambience of a rising bourgeoisie's sense of wealth and security envelops bourgeois subjects and exists as palpable, photographable component of their social reality, transmitted as the visual effect of a buffering, enveloping aura. Aura is socially occasioned by the conditions of existence of an aspirant bourgeoisie cushioned in the world. Aura as tangible effect or aesthetic manifestation is seen as technologically occasioned, reliant on a 'technical conditionedness of the auratic appearance' in early photographs.[39] This 'technical conditionedness' forms a 'technical equivalent' to the actuality of the representation. Benjamin recognizes the external, technical preconditioning of auratic manifestation. It is a mechanical-technical enhancement, whose reproductive proviso manifests itself in daguerreotypes as a delicate continuum of shading on the photographic plate, shifting from a bright central focus to darker edges. This compels photographic subjects to appear inside an ovoid, illuminated surface, a '*Hauchkreis*' that fades out into peripheral blackness.[40] Benjamin does not reject aura as a consequence of the limitations of a relatively primitive apparatus, but rather draws it into his theory of a potentially exact coincidence of *Technik* and object of representation, a sort of elective affinity. In an early moment of technological innovation, technology, its methods of representation and its products all combine in an amalgam of coincidence between technological possibility and representational accuracy. Benjamin also expresses the same point as a question of the relationship between technician and object of representation:

> In short, everything proves that Bernard von Brentano's supposition was correct: a photographer from 1850 stands on the same level as his instrument – for the first time – and for quite a while, for the last time.[41]

Technik and object of representation reciprocate each other and connive to offer a perfect re-presentation of historical actuality. Writing after aura's disintegration, Benjamin recognizes it as an actual historical component produced by certain forms of past consciousness. Truth reveals itself in the auratic appearance of the photographic object, but it is an historical instance.

A definition of aura, not as technical enhancement, but as experiential, perceptual relation, organized around the polarities of distance and closeness, is delineated late in 'Kleine Geschichte der Photographie'.

> What is aura actually? A strange weave of space and time: singular appearance of distance, however near it may be. Resting on a summer afternoon, following the line of a mountain on the horizon, or a twig, which casts its shadow on the viewer, until the moment or the hour takes part in its appearance – that is to breathe the aura of these mountains, of this twig.[42]

Aura is presented here as the fruit of the experience of someone who sinks into a panorama and forgets activity, adopting a con-

templative attitude to nature. Auratic perception is the vision of
someone who is submerged in a halcyon world. 'To breathe the
aura' means to experience perception in terms of a moment, a
'glance of the eye' ('*Augenblick*'), when subject and object seem to
be indistinguishable and united. Benjamin defines aura as element
of a perception that is defined in relation to objects in nature, yet
this definition is to account for an historical development, the
shrinkage of the auratic element in technologically produced art.
The connection between the two perceptions – the natural and the
historical auratic perception – is the sense – the conviction – of
serenity in the world.

Technological Decline, Decline of Aura

The middle section of 'Kleine Geschichte der Photographie' is set
in the time of Benjamin's childhood, and the history related is
distinctly biographical, subjective. A turn of the century ruling
class is shown to admit technology's fantastic productive power
only in armament pile-ups, which wait to defile nature, and the
expansion of commercial product. Though it may not necessarily
be members of the bourgeoisie who produce art, this hegemonic
class demands the means of its own self-representation, and enlists
artists to complete that task, specifically through the use of
photography. The commissioned photographs mediate the
perception, interests, values and historical actuality of the class for
which they have been produced: its historical construction of consciousness. The function of photography changes in alignment
with the changing social role and ideology of the culture-producing
class. First there were the visionary images of the experimenting
photographers' immediate environs. And also among the first
people who appeared as reproduced images were those who were
anonymous. Their status or class had no bearing on their representation. They were simply subjects for the camera's raptorial
glare. Photography, once beyond the cumbersome processes of the
daguerreotype, was, at first, a popular pursuit, native to the
fairground.[43] Later, it retreats to the parlours. Photography now
represents bourgeois faces, named and propertied individuals, and
their personal possessions – just as oil painting had done for
another class in another epoch. These photographs are stored in
thick, leather-bound albums on heavy, dark wood sideboards for
family possession and occasional viewing.[44] Benjamin's autobiographical descriptions of the conditions of his bourgeois childhood
teem with images of unhealthiness, crampedness, unfreedom and
dishonesty. He depicts the family home as a penal colony
populated by liars. The bourgeois interiors in which Benjamin
moves as a child are described as commodity-filled places where

photograph albums rest on tables, collecting dust in 'the stuffy atmosphere, disseminated by conventional portrait photography in the epoch of decline'.[45] Photography has entered an 'epoch of decline'. This decline is seen both to parallel formally and detail visually the decline of the bourgeois class as a progressive, universal, liberating force. Studio photography continues to reflect reality – but now this image is of a bad reality. Benjamin reconstructs its historical construction of consciousness, in order to demonstrate that in the 'epoch of decline' as well, photography, because of the mimetic cunning of its technological basis, reflects an accurate depiction of real conditions of existence, outside any intended ideology on the part of culture commissioners. In the 'epoch of decline' a politico-technological paralysis is visualized in photography. Photography communicates the truth of a material world in which private clutter signifies confinement and dishonesty, as well as the possibility of fantastic and compensatory dreaming.[46] Benjamin describes the studio portraits of himself and his brother, as well as one of Kafka, sad, young and tiny. He points out the artifice exuding from these pictures which have degenerated into the absurd and clichéd, their subjects forlorn, lost and inflexibly inhuman, amongst chunks of clutter, the luxurious, ludicrous junk of a commodity-producing society.[47] The lens, the objective, objectifies and absorbs on chemical plates the awkward poses of the alienated. A politico-technological paralysis is etched in this photography. These photographs record the truth of the absurdity and inhumanity of social relations in a Europe about to be consumed by fire. The synthetic nature of the studio props and the stiff stances of the subjects imprint on photographic materials the alienation of the Wilhelmine epoch. In spite of the dim lighting, Benjamin contends, 'a pose emerges more and more starkly in photographs, whose rigidity betrays the true impotence of this generation in the face of technical progress'.[48] Due to constraint exerted by the economic drive towards accumulation and the compulsion to enforce existing class rule through the reproduc- tion of current social relations, the ruling class is impotent in its interactions with the technology that it attempts to steer. Benjamin has observed the mimetic capacity of this objective recorder to capture truthful relations, but, in his accusation of technological failure, he introduces something else. The crime he has witnessed is the betrayal of the 'elective affinity' between humanity and technology.

'Decline' is visible. It sets in once the ruling class has secured political and economic hegemony. Benjamin suggests that relations of production block change, forcing the design of artistic productions in forms inherited from the old technology. The old relations of production act as fetters, impeding the growth of new art-forms. Decline derives from the ruling class attempt to retard the socialized development of the base and to sustain a class rule based on the contradiction between the continual revamping of the forces of production and the static maintenance of privatized relations of production. In 1935 Benjamin formulates this thought succinctly:

> The culture of the nineteenth century as a forceful attempt to stem the productive forces.[49]

The bourgeoisie's impotence in the face of technology has a parallel aesthetic reflex. This consists in the attempt to keep stable the extant network of aesthetic appearances. Photographers in this epoch stunt the technology they are commissioned to utilize, abusing the apparatus to produce photographs that sterilely mimic earlier styles. The traditional bourgeoisie, operating with 'an anti-technical concept of art', and threatened by the aesthetic crisis arising from the clash of *Technik* and art, are unable to come to terms with the possibilities of the new medium.[50] Benjamin describes incidents at the photographer's studio where he was dressed as an Alpine climber in front of a painted backdrop of the Tyrol, and, in another example, clothed as a neat little sailor, engulfed by studio props and fixed in a stiff pose.[51] These photographs are staged in studios that are described by Benjamin as ambiguous hybrids of torture chambers where executions take place and throne rooms where representation occurs.[52] Their set-ups are reminiscent of some of the first photographs from the 1840s. Technology impersonates the patterns of what has gone before because of a deadening incapacity to innovate within the medium and investigate its formal and aesthetic possibilities. The class that no longer progresses retreats and tries to lug technology behind it. *Technik* is not being used according to its essential determination. It is hampered, fettered, like the productive forces in general, held back by relations of production.

In an essay on Brecht's drama, written in the same year, Benjamin extends his advocacy of state-of-the-art technological practice to the non-technological arts. All 'progressive', that is, non-degenerate aesthetic forms, are necessarily aligned to forms pre-given by technology:

> The forms of epic theatre correspond to new technical forms, cinema as much as radio. It stands at the summit of *Technik*.[53]

The failure of photography to represent adequately in the 'period of decline' shows up as an imperfect realization of the idea of *Technik*. Benjamin's self-ascribed materialist scientificity measures against potential. Benjamin demonstrates the feasibility of perceiving visually the discrepancy between technological potential and actuality. Forcing together the technological realm and the socio-political realm, Benjamin discloses that improved technology has chased aura from photography, in the same way as the 'degenerate' imperialist bourgeoisie has chased aura from reality.[54] Any footing for arguing that aura forms a legitimate component of social reality has disappeared. Photographs need no longer record an aura in a doubled sense. First, they need no longer record it technologically, because of new inventions. A more advanced optical science of light-sensitive lenses banishes darkness and records appearances as in a mirror. The aura of a photograph is increasingly eliminated technologically, as transitoriness and repeatability become hallmarks of technologically-produced photographic art. Second, they should no longer record aura as a truth of bourgeois reality, because aura was historically bound to, and existed as aesthetic-technological correlation to, the cushioning ambience of a rising bourgeoisie's sense of wealth, security and technological experimentation. Likewise innovation in architecture relates to new modes of social experience. For example, the technical revolution in architecture stems from the introduction of new materials, especially glass and steel. These hold out the promise of a destruction of over-cluttered bourgeois interiors and the promotion of a spatial transparency. Benjamin elides such social transparency with the dawn of a social transparency and the lifting of social distinctions between street and home, individual and mass.[55] In the case of photography, aura, a quality bound up with the permanence and uniqueness of an experience, is banished simultaneously from the photograph and the world, sucked out, vacuumed. Describing Atget's photography, Benjamin writes that he cleanses photography's atmosphere, initiating the emancipation of object from aura. Atget looks for what is unremarked, forgotten, cast adrift and his photographs pump the aura out of reality like water from a sinking ship. In front of the lens, atmosphere, soul and aura wither. The end of auratic manifestation is connected to the end of a dreamy, contemplative and passive experience of the natural and social world and the possibility, made available by technology, of new forms of analysis based on viewer input – the activation of the viewer as photographer, and as photo-literate. In the 'period of decline', however, technology and object no longer coincide, but begin to diverge.[56] This divergence is signalled visually by the creation of a fake aura that betrays the reciprocity of elements, technology, representation and the real. Though mirror-exact image reproduction strips off the haze of aura, photographers, nevertheless, in the period after 1880 see it as their task to overturn the possibility of exact mirroring or the possibility of capturing the real. They smother their images in a fake aura, an artificially imposed obscurity, manufactured by the use of retouching and over-painting skills and certain modes of printing.[57] Benjamin makes the faking of aura evidence of the inappropriate ways in which a degenerate bourgeoisie utilize technology. The overlaid aura confirms a socio-economic process of technology abuse, but it also visualizes the ideological mystification that comes of the veiling and masking effects of commodity fetishism. Social reality is stripped of aura, but ideology suffuses reality with fake aura. The abandonment of aura reciprocates the possibilities of new technologies, as well as coinciding with an artistic-scientific, and political, compulsion to reflect the real.

New lens photography magnifies the structure of cell tissue, as well as unveiling aspects in material unseen before. The first photographs produced were unique and wondrously mysterious, but they were also immediately used as analytic, technical aids for artists.[58] Photographers in the 1840s were often drawn towards spiritualism. Daguerreotypes were seen to conjure up spirits in representation or exert inescapable supernatural forces on the sitting subject. Images were invested with magical powers, able to perforate the surface, to outstrip the visible and to reveal through the transcendental truth of magic. The scientistic discourses of photography, based in empiricism and documentary realism, both in the early years of social photography and in the 1920s, also, however, profess the same facility to penetrate appearances, illuminate essences and depict historical verity, whether through the apparent, unauthorized objectivity of the lens or through the formal properties of montage, which rely on juxtaposition, construction and dialectics.[59] The issue is not simply aesthetic or technological – it has its economic element. Benjamin notes that the contemporary, catastrophic economic crisis of the late 1920s makes questions of representation particularly urgent.[60]

Photographic Mimesis and the Construction of Deep Realities

In a comment on Antoine Joseph Wiertz, Benjamin observes that 'the theory of progress in the arts is bound up with the idea of an imitation of nature'.[61] In his earlier writings, Benjamin had speculated that originally the linguistic sign and the image had been combined in a mimetic correspondence between word and thing. After man's expulsion from Eden, the sign splits off from resemblance to the object and the mimetic function moves to become part of the remit of art. Later, his theory of politically progressive art-forms asserts precisely the desirability of a mimesis of reality in art. It is, however, Benjamin's definition of the constituency of reality, a reality accessible to technology, which forces him to reject the naturalism of surfaces. Photography accesses a differently constituted supercharged reality, a hyper-reality, with deeper, more detailed layers, layers that might be called unconscious, not available to the naked eye and only made perceptible by technological means. The camera dispatches a reformulation of the co-ordinates of the visible world, envisaging a realm previously invisible. It transfigures the possibilities of what can be seen. Mimesis in photography signifies the predisposition to access a nature different from the nature that avails itself to the eye. Benjamin introduces the term 'optical-unconscious' to describe a mode of perception made visible on celluloid and initiated by cameras. The 'optical-unconscious' details a reciprocity between human (un)consciousness and machinic perception. The first mention of an optical unconscious appears in an article on Soviet film, 'Erwiderung an Oscar A. H. Schmitz' (1927), in which Benjamin identifies film as a zone of debate between people and their environment. In film 'a new region of consciousness arises', through which people get to grips with the ugly hopeless world, comprehensively (*'faßlich'*), meaningfully (*'sinnvoll'*) and passionately (*'passionierend'*).[62] Photography and film, because of their indexicality to the world, reflect it, but in reflecting it, they also construct it as a world of extended temporality and fragmented space, a universe of 'synthetic realities'. As Benjamin puts it:

> These new synthetic realities can be viewed everywhere; the advertisement, *film reality*, etc.[63]

New technologies of reproduction display authentically the parameters of modern experienced reality as synthetic reality, technologically worked through. 'Kleine Geschichte der Photographie' details the 'different nature' available to machine-enhanced perception:

> A different nature speaks to the camera than speaks to the eye; most different in that in the place of a space interwoven by a person with consciousness is formed a space interwoven by the unconscious. It is already quite common that someone, for example, can give a rough account of how a person walks. But he would not be able to describe their position at the fracture of a moment of stepping out. Photographic aids: time-lapse, enlargements, unlock this for him. He discovers the optical-unconscious first of all through it, just as the drive-unconscious is discovered through psychoanalysis. Structural compositions, cell formations, with which technology and medicine deal – all this is more fundamentally allied to the camera than the atmospheric landscape or the emotion-seeped portrait.[64]

Whether we see better or deeper or just differently remains ambiguous. The worlds uncovered by photography may have existed before, but perhaps only in dreams. A 'scientific' way of appropriating new worlds seems to have been found. Photography allows the possibility of scientifically analysing reality through art for the first time. This possible condition of analysis becomes a necessary condition. Photography brings objects closer, exported across time, across space, available to microanalysis. It lays out the world for intimate inspection. Benjamin is enthusiastic about Bloßfeldt's plant photography. These extreme close-ups reveal the forms of ancient columns in horse willow, a bishop's crozier in the ostrich fern, totem poles in tenfold enlargements of chestnut and maple shoots, and gothic tracery in the fuller's thistle. The contemplative nature that provided the content of auratic experience is transformed and revealed as a supernatural zone of cultural activity. In Bloßfeldt's photograph album *Urformen in der Kunst* (1928) it seems that nature counterfeits technological forms for art, an excellently revealing synthesis. August Sander's photography, part of a huge project to photograph all the types in society, anonymous people – at each social level – also impresses Benjamin. Sander's portfolio of types collected together images of peasants, industrial workers, civil servants, intellectuals, artists, anonymous representatives of every social stratum and every walk of life. As Alfred Döblin put it in the project's prospectus, it moves from 'the peasant, the earth-bound man, takes the observer through every social stratum and every walk of life up to the highest representatives of civilization, and then back down all the way to the idiot'. He went further, explaining why, at this point, such classification of types might be necessary:

> Men are shaped by their livelihood, the air and light they move in, the work they do or do not do, and moreover the special ideology of their class ... The class structure is undergoing a revolution, the cities have grown enormously, some originals are still there but new types are already developing ... The divisions between youth and adulthood have become less clear, the dominance of youth, the urge for rejuvenation and for renewal, which has even biological effects, has become obvious. Whole stories could be told about quite a lot of these photographs; they invite us to tell stories. As subject matter, they are more stimulating and they yield more than many newspaper reports. These are my suggestions. He who knows how to look will be enlightened more effectively by them than by lectures and theories. Through these clear and conclusive photographs he will discover something of himself and others.[65]

Its sober approach unveils physiognomic, political and historical aspects in the material. In an age in which, Benjamin insists, people are increasingly judged according to what role they adopt or have thrust upon them, a photography book such as Sander's *Antlitz der Zeit* (1929) acts as a training manual or guide to the present day. Benjamin describes Sander's project as 'a tremendous physiognomic gallery' and it contains 'inexhaustible material for study' of the contemporary social world.

In contrast, but just as revealingly, Germaine Krull photographed the empty streets of Paris. Her photographs documented the strange life of the commodity – shop mannequins, the strange liveliness of shop windows, the poetry of advertising and commercial language, and the arcades. Benjamin collected her photographs, so often devoid of human figures. Its themes are similar to Atget's. Atget pictured Paris as emptied of human life, an alien zone, and subject to technological alteration. Photography's social function, the disclosure of truths about the structure of reality, also finds a form in surrealist practice, because this experimental avant-garde uses photography analytically. Benjamin is influenced by the surrealist assertion of an indexical relationship between photography and reality. Surrealist photographic practice is entranced by the indexical element, whereby the visible world imprints its traces on artistic products – sometimes quite directly. Man Ray's Rayographs are an excellent example of this. Yet more than catching the traces, surrealist photography delivers aesthetic expression for the wounds of human alienation, in order that they might be made amenable to a 'curative' analysis by the 'politically educated gaze' ('*politisch geschulten Blick*').[66]

But photography was modish, and already the sharp and glossy products of fast lenses were no longer appropriate to the age, insisted Benjamin. Mirror-like representations might become no more than sleek imitations of life, whose reality-effect is nothing more than a surface representation. In 1931, photographic practices, as Benjamin summarizes them, are varied. There is the work of photographic hacks who claim that the lens presents an objective '*Zusammenschau*' of life. There is creative journalistic photography, where the lens seeks interesting juxtapositions. This is a capitulation to fashion. The world is beautiful, it gushes, and it shows its skill by lavishing any soup can with cosmic significance, while unable to grasp a single one of the human connections in which it exists. These creations are like advertisements (and sometimes were advertisements), decontextualized and aestheticized.[67] This was the 'New Objectivity', 'Neue Sachlichkeit', the wrong type of surrender to thinliness. It was just the latest left-wing fashion, as Benjamin noted in his bitter attack 'Linke Melancholie', published in the same year in *Die Gesellschaft*. The left-wing intelligentsia had launched a number of 'intellectual booms', from activism to expressionism to new objectivity. All translated revolutionary reflexes, in as much as they appeared in the bourgeoisie, into objects of distraction, amusement, consumption. Expressionism raised its arm with a clenched fist, made of papier mâché. Then came new objectivity, in reaction to pure reaction, to expressionist ardour, it flaunted emptiness, its feelings flogged long ago.[68] In snapshots, the isolated frozen and disconnected moments are just so much material that turns 'experience into camera booty'.[69] Benjamin's history of photography rejects all these practices in favour of those who use photography according to the proper potential of the technology and, in so doing, create a critical and socially apt body of work. These people use photography to document social, collective practices physiognomically. Benjamin opposes the physiognomic to the individual, recalling his interest in the politics of the collective body. But he also proposes a new and appropriate photographic practice, a constructivist one. This involves a *'Beschriftung'*, a sloganing, making the photograph the site of a contradiction between word and image.[70] Such juxtaposition of text and image introduces politics into photography. This entails rupturing the image, as counterpart to the fracturing of the stability of the political order. The slogan also counters the intensification of the analogical, mimetic basis of photography, such as is essential to its naturalism. Two seemingly dissimilar things, word and image, are forced together in a montage, clashing and dialogically relaying back and forth. The photograph, supplemented by words, is a close-up from a scarcely recollectable angle. This unfamiliar perspective, as imagined by Russian constructivists, freezes the real, protecting it from habit and alienating the alienated. For photography to become a means of historical and political legibility, it needs to extend beyond mirroring into the constructive. The professional smoothness, the glassy impermeability and proto-commercialism of new objectivist photography refuses to admit the moment of production, the condition of being produced. All contradiction is wiped off. Montage, in contrast, is disruption – of the easy complacency of imagery and image-makers, of origin and originality, of categories of culture, and of fetishistically obscured conditions of social life that blankly manifest only the superficial appearance of things.

Benjamin's history makes three claims for photography. First, photographs are analogical representations that correspond to the experience of natural, optical perception; hence their access to the realm of truth – photographs as images of nature. Second, photographs capture something that is more intense than surface reality, be it an excess of historical duration that inheres in the image derived from the real or the exposure of the 'different nature' that offers itself to the camera-eye; hence their privileged access to something deeper than surface truth – photographs as images of different nature. Third, photographs are denaturalized. The 'optical-unconscious' hangs on an exploratory way of seeing, a microscopic incursion that slices up the intricate configurations of natural and social life. Mechanically reproductive technology operates such that it ruptures life's continual flow of images, blasting a fragment that has become a representation out of incessant movement into stillness for an instant of conscious reflection on its significance. In as much as they break beyond physical laws of spatiality and temporality photographs force open a gap for conscious reflection, depicting momentary relations – photographs as images of the anatural.

Towards the close of the article, Benjamin discusses a photograph of an A.E.G. or Krupps factory.[71] Now he casts doubts on the capacity of photography *on its own* to release any (political) information about the structure of the real:

> For the situation, Brecht says, becomes so complicated, that less than ever does the simple 'reproduction of reality' express anything about that reality. A photograph of the Krupps factory or A.E.G. reveals virtually nothing about these institutions. Actual reality has slipped into the functional. The reification of human relations, the factory itself, is not revealed. Something must indeed 'be constructed', something 'artificial', 'posed'.[72]

Referring to the social consequences of the thesis of commodity fetishism, Benjamin asserts that the relations and functions that are gaining in importance are not available to representations whose objective is a simple mirroring. The history of photography concludes that photography fails to represent the contemporary real, due to a temptation – offered by fast-lens technology – to rely on its simple analogism, now no longer appropriate. Recognition of photography's capacity for partiality in representation encourages Benjamin to turn to a new mechanical art-form. This art-form, he hopes, might avoid the dangers seemingly inherent in photography. He directs his attention to an infant art-form: film.

> Film: unfurling consequence? of all the notional forms, tempos and rhythms that lie preformed in today's machines, in such a form that all problems of contemporary art find their final formulation only in the context of film.[73]

In invoking a critique of photography, Benjamin begins to push beyond the analysis of celluloid imaging as a copy mechanism. Film organizes and reveals what is withheld from the unaided eye. His recognition of film draws upon ideas voiced by the avant-garde in the Soviet Union. Dziga Vertov, for example, had argued that the 'cinema eye' could be used as a research tool. Film is dislodged from copying by the incorporation into the narrative of shooting techniques.[74] Everything that constitutes the 'optical-unconscious', as worked out in relation to photography, can be seen to exist in film. And yet film as form allows a far more wide-ranging reformulation of spatial and temporal categories. Other theorists had already drawn analogies between film and the unconscious. Indeed, it is possible to surmise that in the initial formulation of the concept, an article on cinema, written early in the 1920s by an intellectual mentor Hugo von Hofmannsthal, had influenced Benjamin. Von Hofmannsthal writes of the masses of industrial workers who flee from the mechanization of their daily existence into the darkroom of moving pictures, in order to seek a substitute for the dreams that they can only allow themselves at night.[75] Movies as analogues of dreams play out the contents of a collective consciousness in front of a collective perceiver.

Before his next extended analysis of the artwork in the age of technological reproducibility, a treatise on the possibilities offered to political aesthetics by film, Benjamin looks further into the contents of the unconscious, memory and dreams, and he muses on the relation between dreams and unconscious impulses and experience and ideology. He does this through two fragmented autobiographical sequences – *Berliner Chronik*, from 1932, and *Berliner Kindheit um neunzehnhundert*, likewise begun in 1932.

CHAPTER 3

Berlin Chthonic, Photos and Trains and Films and Cars

Technical Aids

> Careful examination of the relationship of the optics of the myrioramas to the time of the modern, the newest. They must surely be registered as the base coordinates of this world. It is a world of strict discontinuity. The always-again-new is not old stuff that persists, or the reoccurring past, but is rather a one and the same, criss-crossed by countless interruptions. (Just as the gambler lives in the interruption.) Interruption entails that each gaze into space hits upon a new constellation. Interruption the tempo of film. And the result: the time of hell and the origin chapter in the baroque book.
>
> 'Pariser Passagen' 1 (1927–29)[1]

In his doctoral dissertation on Romanticism and art criticism, Benjamin indicated the early Romantics' use of optical prismatic metaphors in their *Naturphilosophie*.[2] Similarly types of opticality suffuse his philosophy of history. There are references to turn of the century optical gadgetry, and photography and film and all sorts of technologies of vision. Mimetically Benjamin commandeers technical forms for his thought-structures. He writes of his theory's montage principles of construction, and, in meditating on contemporary history, he ponders the affiliation of snapshots and moments. In the theoretical centre of the *Passagenwerk*, 'Konvolut N: erkenntnistheoretisches, Theorie des Fortschritts', Benjamin appropriates an allusion to technologized perception from Rudolf Borchardt's writings on Dante. The *Passagenwerk* should develop in its readership modes of seeing.

> The pedagogical side of this enterprise: To give our immanent image-forming medium instruction in stereoscopic and dimensional seeing into the depths of historical shadows.[3]

Benjamin had long been thinking of theory in terms of 'optics'. Reflecting on the 'optic' of surrealism – an ecstatic, romantic and occultist perspective – Benjamin demurs from its stress on the mysterious side of the mysterious. Surrealism snatches at

something outside itself, outside the world, to make and market its
weirdness. Benjamin conceives, in contrast, a 'dialectical optic', a
method of analysis that is drawn to but rejects the surrealists' fuzz
of Romanticism and their response to mystical phenomena such as
extra-sensory perception or mind reading. Benjamin's dialectical
optic indeed affirms the attractions of mystery – he too is drawn
to graphology and dream interpretation[4] – but, in opposition to
the surrealists, he insists that, in fact, there is nothing more extraordinary than the processes of thought itself – a mind-warping
narcotic if ever there were one – or the processes of reading – a
form of telepathy. What surrounds us – what we do now – is
already remarkable. This returns mystery to life, not to the other-
worldly. The 'dialectical optic' starts out from this, perceiving 'the
everyday as impenetrable and the impenetrable as everyday'.[5]
Marxist materialism is not immune to such poetry of the everyday.
Marx had said as much of the commodity form itself in *Das
Kapital,* where he describes the ordinary commodity as 'a
mysterious thing'. There is nothing stranger than this most banal
form invested with 'theological capers'. Marx writes of the fetish
commodity that there is no physical basis for the misapprehension. The peculiar character of the social labour that produces
goods produces it. Marx's work hoped, from the outset, to 'reform
consciousness' as he wrote to Alfred Ruge in 1843, and such
reformation 'consists *entirely* in making the world aware of its own
consciousness, in arousing it from its dream of itself, in *explaining*
its own actions to it'.[6] Time to wake up – to and from strangeness.
In Marx, such a process of negotiating ideology is related through
optical devices – the camera obscura of *Die deutsche Ideologie* or the
phantasmagoria that is mentioned in *Das Kapital.* Benjamin
likewise evokes optical devices or effects in the section titles and
thematics of *Einbahnstraße*: 'Imperial Panorama', 'Enlargements',
'Technical Aid' or 'To the Planetarium' where indeed telescopes
are likely to be found. This is not surprising, for, of course, *Einbahnstraße,* is all about Benjamin's own change of focus, and the
adoption of a new urban, political, modernist perspective, which
undertakes precisely the recovery of the extraordinary poetry of
banality – while defamiliarizing corrupt ideology, as, for example,
in the section titled 'Betting Shop' with its assault on privacy and
its class critique of erotics. A materialist analysis of ideology and
experience in the world is to be undertaken in full consciousness
of the mediating lenses that encroach on experience, framing it.
His dialectical gaze, equipped to penetrate the curious everyday,
is invoked repeatedly in the context of mediation, of lenses.
Objects, economy, love and experience of those things in life and
in dreams is the matter for analysis in this poeticizing of the
everyday. It figures a poetic action on materials because, in the

formalist sense, it hopes to renew, prolong and reawaken seeing. A section titled 'Optician' considers perception anew, remarking on the curious inconsistency of vision: how brightness or dullness draws or repels attention, how the final shape of actuality – the debris of a party – might expose the history of what has taken place in a space, or how, in wooing, the lover multiplies the self and is everywhere where the loved one turns. Seeing must itself be seen is Benjamin's formalist-modernist credo. Some of Benjamin's thoughts on perception – on the conditions of witnessing materiality – evoke Goethean-style considerations of the passionate and active role of light and dark in seeing.[7] It was, after all, the role of the eye and the role of the prism that made Goethe doubt Newton's objectivism. This is a materialism that refers back and forth between the physical-natural and the human world. It foregrounds the mediation of emotional attitude as much as of the physical world, of light, and of all those filters and lenses that convey experience to us. The presence of mediation – human and technical – does not make it any less materialist. Its emphasis on lenses is recognition of the historicity of seeing and of knowledge and the dynamics of comprehension.

Benjamin entitles one sub-section in *Einbahnstraße* 'Stereoscope', and so foreshadows a later piece in *Berlin Childhood around 1900* called 'Imperial Panorama', a description of his favourite optical entertainment device with its three-dimensional town views. The section 'Stereoscope' presents a description of everyday life in Riga. Benjamin had visited the city in November 1925 and saw the market, the steamers on the river, market traders, housewives, the red and white mounds of the apple-market. He is drawn to the shops. The shops sell corsets and hats, leather goods, coal, sugar and ironmongery. He observes how on signboards and walls each shop depicts its wares, but oversized. These giant wares are truly fetish commodities. The town, he tells us, is permeated with images.[8]

'Stereoscope' is an image of a town of images – the mundane is extraordinary, and motile. This is corroborated in the writing's construction of spatiality. There is a movement in the passage, turning textual strategies photographic, as the long view moves into close-up, and the close-up itself is superimposed and confused by the oversized character of the commodity signs. These filmic cuts, swift shifts of angle and scale, attempt to map a three-dimensional space, as the title 'Stereoscope' insinuates. This was appropriate, perhaps, for the hometown of montagist film-maker Sergei Eisenstein. Stereoscopy is exposed most dramatically in the split-view introduced in the final line of the piece. Speaking of the pictures that permeate the city, he notes that between them, however, rise tall, fortress-like desolate buildings bringing to life all the terrors of tsarism.[9] Here is signalled a bisected history of past and present – an example of Benjamin 'telescoping the past through the present' – whereby the horrors of tsarism become their own portentous memorial in new Riga. This perspective cannot be dissociated from Benjamin's ordeal in Riga. He had turned up out of the blue in order to surprise his lover Asja Lacis, only to find her absorbed in preparations for a play at the political theatre which she directed and which was subjected to frequent interference by the police. This new freedom is seen to be only a temporary interlude between old and new forms of surveillance. The 'telescoping the past through the present', opening up to potential futures, is just one instance of binocular vision at work here – one that cuts through time. Benjamin's dialectical glare accounts multidimensionally for the city in other ways. It shuttles back and forth from commodity to toy, adult view to childish perception. It catches nature and artifice, tourist and inhabitant, church and state versus human bustle and commerce.

Adorno, in his introduction to the 1950s' edition of Benjamin's writings, calls Benjamin's condensed mode of envisaging a 'micrological gaze'. This gaze is temporally aware, dialectical and objective, a 'micrological procedure', concentrating on the smallest thing, stilling its historical forces and turning it into image.[10] The impression, then, is of a close-up – a peering into material in order to record spatial, temporal and political dimensions. But this is no new objectivism. It is writing as montage image, an imaging cut through by time and tingling with the vibrating struts of social relations that underpin and traverse it. Stereoscopic and dimensional optics, then, are related in and through this vignette of Riga. Writing of Riga, Benjamin's double optic perceives things – the things for sale – in relation to their signs, the representations of the marvels of commodities, dreamlike, promising, fantastic, giant and childlike. Apart from the suggestion of commodity fetishism, the signs remind Benjamin of children's illustrated books, an indication to be taken seriously, for Benjamin was a connoisseur and collector of such material, and his interest in pedagogy led him to focus most specifically on the illustrated book as tool of education.

Benjamin's fragmented chronicling of urban spaces, *Berliner Chronik* (1932), is a return to childhood, and it is also a portrait of the betrayal of technological promise. Strikingly the memoir demonstrates how the characteristics of new technologies infringe on Benjamin's theoretical approach to material. *Berliner Chronik* uses formal criteria derived from film to illustrate, albeit contrariwise through the medium of words, an historical shift in perception. Construction, or montage, a central aspect of film is also the perceived characteristic of experience in the metropolis. City experience is filmic. Benjamin was drawing on a well-established convention. In Weimar Germany, the urban becomes not just a theme of the modern, but the very emblem of modernity. And the city seems best represented – actually and figuratively – by film, the most modern representational form. Film appears perfectly capable of re-presenting the city, of producing films that are set in cities and providing accurate portraits of lives in those cities. There exists a special intimacy between film as form, cinema as institution and city life as social phenomenon. The earliest films chronicled masses of people on the streets. Films of crazed chases through big city traffic, and glimpses into the metropolitan underworld soon followed these. The city reformulates human experience – and film provides a mode of cognizing this. Shock and stimulation of the nerves is the norm, and cinema reproduces these jolts. Cinema exploits the city-dwellers' desire to escape the rationalized industrial, technical world, and it does this by using a product of this world. Film records the complexity and fluctuating impermanence of city life, its speed, fracture and incessant movement. Experience in the city is montaged and discontinuous. Moholy-Nagy's film-sketch, *Dynamic of the City* (1921), was an image of a cityscape with building blocks, mathematical signs and graphic collage. It showed a junction with streams of traffic, and spanned from the top point of a radio tower down to the underground stations. The screenplay announces:

> Rows of houses on the one side, transparent, on the right penetrating through to the first house. Rows of houses fade to the right and turn again from right to left. Transparent rows of houses opposite each other, apartments moving in opposite directions and autocars moving even faster, creating a FLICKER on the screen.

As a traffic stream of alphabets whizzes past, the letters T E M P O are blasted forwards out of the blurring letter-chains. The film, never made, though an institute for cultural research had pledged funds, had no narrative moments, but was to be an aesthetic arrangement of graphic, photographic, mathematical signs.[11] *Dynamic of a City* was designed as a cartoon film of graphic images. It retransmits an abstract idea of a city. Others who likewise wish to affirm the modern experience of the city use the documentary genre, as practised by Walter Ruttmann in *Berlin: Symphony of a City*. But it was a form of documentary that emphasized the syncopation of montage. These avant-garde city-films made the city itself the subject of their films. In a simulation of new visual experiences, and imitating film's elevation of city to subject, Benjamin's autobiographical writings arrange fragments of Berlin in filmic analogues: scenes, sequences, edits, close-ups, details, moments montaged together. Possibly this filmic mode of presentation is even more remarkable in the subsequent autobiographical work *Berliner Kindheit um neunzehnhundert*. This later work built upon the material presented in *Berliner Chronik* and was written between 1932 and 1938. Like film intertitles, scenes elaborated in *Berliner Chronik* are given titles or heading slogans, once transferred to *Berliner Kindheit um neunzehnhundert*.[12] In the autobiographical writings, Benjamin depicts a series of experiences through a string of disconnected, non-chronological snapshots, a montage series of titled dissolves. Overlay, dissolve, superposition are rhythms that accord with the pace of modern life and the tempo of film. *Berliner Chronik* is organized around optical images and optical experiences. Reworkings in the later biographical writings interject acoustic elements, perhaps signifying Benjamin's recognition throughout the 1930s of the increasing importance of sound in film and the development of phonographic technologies.

Berliner Chronik, *1932: Technology, Memory, Experience*

> Superposition according to the rhythm of time. In connection with cinema and the 'sensational' mediation of news. In the context of the perception of time, 'becoming' no longer has any meaning for us, rhythmically. We subvert it dialectically in *sensation and tradition*. – Important to express these things analogically in the biographical.
>
> 'Pariser Passagen' 1 (1927–29)[13]

Before making preparations for suicide in 1932, Benjamin wrote a number of autobiographical sketches.[14] These recollected the past and theorized the act of remembering. The exercise was initiated at the start of permanent exile from a country in which everyday life inspired him with terror.[15] Some years later he looks back at the process. He discloses that he knew he was to undergo a prolonged, perhaps even permanent, leave from the city of his birth. For the purposes of 'inoculation' he conjures up images most likely to awaken homesickness in exile, those of childhood. He avoided nostalgia by 'limiting the examination to the necessary social irretrievability of the past, rather than the arbitrary biographical one'.[16] Evading sentimentality or individualism, he chronicles social history rather than autobiography. He dissolves himself into social spaces and relationships with things. In a city-portrait and review of Franz Hessel's *Spazieren in Berlin* from 1929, Benjamin claims the existence of a post-war Europe-wide intensification of the 'sense for reality, the sense for chronicle and document'.[17] Chronicle and document comprise Benjamin's own project. He displays a chronicler's concern with the processes of history and remembering history, and a documentary interest in assessing contemporary reality. *Berliner Chronik* formulates a theory of experience that hopes specifically to document past and present experience of urban technological modernity. The writings narrate explicitly how forms of experiences are mediated through technologies. *Berliner Chronik* constructs an autobiographical return to a specific historical past to display how new optical technologies are restructuring co-ordinates of experience in a crucial period of accelerated technological development. Technology's formative infringement on experience can be traced in the remaking of memory and subjectivity by new modes of technological representation. The structure and thematic of Benjamin's Berlin chronicling reacts to new technical ways of archiving for the collective through the employment of new media. Structurally and thematically it deals with the processes of memory-work. Benjamin traces both the emergence of new technologies and their role in modelling the processes of archiving and remembering. *Berliner Chronik* is a multi-layered transcript, with convolutions of place and moment, and a mélange of memory, fantasy, fiction, document and authorial self-reflexivity. Here Benjamin inaugurates a historiography that aligns the mechanisms of remembering with the processes of construction. He hopes to institute a political interpretation of past histories, through consciously selecting and intervening in the material and making connections between events in the past and in the present and in the future.

In 'Karl Kraus' (1930–31), Benjamin draws on commentaries by the Viennese satirist Kraus in order to criticize journalistic practices, especially in relation to war reportage. Kraus, along with others, had contended that, in the 1914–18 war, the mass media substituted itself for the individual action of remembering, resulting in an apparent overtaking of experience and memory by the representation of war in newspapers, photography and film. These representations comprise the superficial contents of a state-owned or state-supporting picture archive. The physical manifestation of the press, a series of phrases, is correlated by Kraus to the technology used to create copy.[18] The newspaper apparatus operates like a factory, demanding that a certain amount of information be created and rapidly prepared for machine processing. The mediation of the news event substitutes for the event itself and effects that sinister identity whereby it seems that events are reported prior to their performance.[19] Benjamin, following Kraus's critique, insists specifically on the decay of the spoken word in the post-war era, along with a burgeoning distrust in the word's ability to be adequate to the event. Benjamin intends to rescue memory and experience. He does not condemn the mediation of events – and the media's debasement of the word –

but rather, homeopathically, calls for an occupation of the site of media forms, for a strategy of re-broadcasting experience. Benjamin's elective affinity between the unconscious and technology, formalized in the 'optical unconscious', exerts pressure on his researches into recollection, enabling the supplementing of memories by the contents of the media archive, the substitution of *Technik* for human memory, and a modelling of the process of recollection on technological principles. When subjectivity becomes a matter of documents in the world and technological mediation it has become a social and a political issue rather than the preserve of the individual soul.

Benjamin's technical unconscious is born in the modern industrial society of the 1920s. A form of cultural representation based on the written word – novels, newspapers – switches to a new type of dominant representation or '*Anschauungsform*' based on the cinematic and photographic image.[20] In 'Kleine Geschichte der Photographie' (1931) Benjamin cited Moholy-Nagy's remark that the illiterate of the future will be the person who is unable to read photographs.[21] With this Moholy-Nagy indicated the axiality of the visual. The reproduced image insinuates itself into Benjamin's processes of recollection. He describes remembering as having more to do with brief moments – like snapshots – and with discontinuity – chance encountered images.[22] Recall results from a mental manipulation of space and time, a prioritization of temporary discontinuity over chronology: montage. Benjamin's model of memory also accords with the Freudian psyche. Freud insists that the unconscious knows no chronological time and experienced events are efficacious beyond the instant of their occurrence, passing into memory in trace-form. The non-linearity of memory, and the availability of the reproduced image as a spur to memory, prove integral to Benjamin's understanding of history and the method of presentation he begins to develop around the same time in the *Passagenwerk*. It is, of course, difficult to make pronouncements on the structure of the *Passagenwerk* as it is a bundle of index cards. 'File N', however, as the epistemological core of the project, offers certain methodological pointers on, for example, 'literary montage' and 'stereoscopic seeing', non-chronologies and the political significance of memory.

For many years, as he informs the reader early on in his Berlin memoirs, Benjamin thought of drawing a map of his life, a biographic representation plotting the social spaces between which he formed the relay.[23] This biographical gazetteer, drawn in the Parisian Café des Deux Magots and later lost, is reconstructed verbally in the Berlin memoirs. First, he imagines a city guide with highlights marked by little symbols, but then rejects this in favour of an ordnance survey map of the urban zone, designed for military purposes. The spatializing of life is coupled with an idea of a city topography that is not architectonic but 'anthropocentric'.[24] *Berliner Chronik* evokes the labyrinthine character of city spatiality, made analogous to the convoluted channels of the human psyche.[25] In 'Pariser Passagen' the dreaming collective of the nineteenth century is depicted sinking into the arcades as if sinking into the innards of its own body. A couple of years on and Benjamin's metaphor is now oriented to the unconscious rather than the physical.[26] Benjamin constructs underpasses of memory, arcades or routes leading to the unconscious of the city, and his conception presages the post-Second World War maps of the Situationist International. Elaborate and myriad entrances and tunnels enter into the interior. Such a presentation of modern experience or experience of the modern as social and subterranean has its analogue in the dream-induced 'loosening' of the ego, identified as a by-product of intoxicating experience in 'Der Sürrealismus':

> In the world's structure dream loosens individuality like a hollow tooth.[27]

Modern experience discontinues old lines of subjectivity. Emphasis on the endless proliferation of memories and the penetrable–impenetrable nature of city convolution leads to a denial of the possibility of autobiography in any commonly understood sense. Standard autobiography, Benjamin claims, has to do with time and sequence and all the things that make up a continuous flow of life.[28] It is also concerned with the recounting of an individual existence, from the beginning on and noting consecutively the focal points of a life. Benjamin instead folds personal detail into encounters with collective, generational and urban histories. Even when Benjamin describes events from his life, they accrue social significance.

The labyrinth of the city, especially the dives of low-life, uncharted streets, the underworld, underground – metro and otherwise – are transmitted to the reader through the naïveté of a childhood perspective. Around 1900 a world of wonder exists to be explored, for this child Benjamin too. In notes for the *Passagenwerk* Benjamin depicts the experience of youth as dreamlike, invested with possibilities and hope. Through children, each epoch maintains some stake in fantastic dreaming:

> The youth experience of a generation has much in common with the experience of dreams. Its historical form is a dream form. Every epoch possesses a side turned towards dreams, the child side.[29]

A review of Franz Hessel's *Spazieren in Berlin* elides the work of memory in the child and the *flâneur*, who both drift wide-eyed through the city.[30] Hessel is invoked in *Berliner Chronik* as one of the guides who taught Benjamin how to wander through the city and into the zones of the 'dreaming collective'.[31] In constructing or reconstructing collective histories or collective memories, Benjamin imagines a 'collective unconscious' and intimates a creative, utopian relationship between generations and their wish-investments in new technologies.

As Benjamin rewrites his childhood, European civilization is in tatters and mass destruction looms. This is the precondition for the fusion of disjunctive temporal elements in the viewpoint of childhood and the adult. Benjamin changes the temporal axis to make the autobiographical recollection a question of reflection from the present onto the past. Memory involves the associative 'capacity for endless interpolations into what has been'.[32] *Berliner Chronik* is written deliberately disingenuously. The places that Benjamin seeks out in the past all bear the traces of a future he knows will transpire.[33] Benjamin's memory-construction in *Berliner Chronik* forces the insertion of reminders of the present moment of writing into the text, a present that regards the past through the viewfinder of the intervening years, and is also intersected by the position of the writer, his class and status. Benjamin's history writing deliberately confuses chronology. There is no calendar of passing time – no 'chronicle' indeed – in his account of the history of a self and its spaces. Benjamin plays a trick with time. This trick has political ramifications. He pretends to be remembering the sense he made of the world when he was a child, when in reality he is a critic highlighting the trajectory he has witnessed. The curious temporality enables him to write of sunkenness in the spell of a deluxe middle-class origin. This remembered plush past contains in all its dusty, over-cluttered effects the first traces of the historical decline of the bourgeoisie. Illustrations of upholstered lumps of luxury and depictions of moments of class isolation fabricate a metropolitan topography that is lavishly replete with decay. In representations of the years preceding the destruction of the city by war, the adult-child's mock-prophetic inklings enable him to show how the city's foundations betray the fissures and fractures of an accelerating decomposition. The usage of the construct of the child or the as-if child is a way of returning to the past, in order to suggest a technique for envisaging and then breaking with that past. He is not writing of a singular and real childhood. In writing and remembering he envisages a possibility whereby the initial glimpse of a liberated relationship between child and the new technological cosmos provides an impetus for change. Writing from a position of knowledge of intervening events, Benjamin develops an odd gaze in which the role of memory signals a strategy for replacing historical continuity with political interpretation. Benjamin discloses a methodology, resonant with theoretical, political implications. The dialectical nature of the category *Technik* is mediated in the doubled presentation of what purports to be a descriptive, empirical history of *Technik* alongside an interpretive projection of technological potential.

A Descriptive History of Technik

> Now he accuses the town Berlin before the world court. My god, we, the maltreated tax payers, have the right to prosecute before any court this town, whose administration has staggered from one disgrace to another. How far we want to incriminate it before the world court, we have yet, however, despite everything, still to decide.
>
> Walter Benjamin, 'Ein Jakobiner von Heute' (1930)[34]

Berliner Chronik documents a history of *Technik*. It monitors an increasingly destructive usage of *Technik*. *Technik* appears initially as a liberatory force, but is shown to be used subsequently, due to the constraining effects of the relations of production, to destructive ends. An initial utopian period of technological development is insinuated in scenes aligned with early childhood experiences. Childishness is so important for Benjamin. When later, after the war, Adorno mentions Benjamin in *Minima Moralia*, he implicates him in the infantile, showing his analytical method to be one that can grasp underneath the official histories of heroes, to find knowledge and flashes of true experience in children's literature and puerile art.[35] An organic model of maturation organizes Benjamin's reflections on historical-technological change. In *Berliner Chronik*, and in contemporaneously written *Passagenwerk* entries, Benjamin establishes a paralleled past of individual childhood and social childhood. He recalls the infancy of an entire generation of the bourgeois class, cross-referenced with the epoch of socio-economic formation in which it lives. Benjamin's autobiographical return is staged analogically as the return to a childhood of technology and industrial capitalism. Overturning a simple evolutionism, Benjamin assumes a link between ontogeny and socio-historical phylogeny. The child's utopian perspective on the past hooks up with primitive moments of capitalist development. Merging two temporal planes, Benjamin appears to assert that the real potential of new technologies results from the fantastic projections of children, as well as from the experimental fantasies of early industrial progressivists. There may be a certain affinity here between Benjamin's conception and Marx's 'historical index of childhood'. Marx's idea of childhood communicates the normative character of Greek art, born in humanity's innocent infancy. In the draft introduction to his *Critique of Political Economy*, Marx asserts that it is impossible to deny that the naïveté of the child brings pleasure to the adult, and the adult attempts to reproduce the child's veracity on a higher level. Benjamin includes Max Raphael's 1933 French translation of the excerpt from Marx in 'Konvolut K: Traumstadt und Traumhaus, Zukunftsträume, anthropologischer Nihilismus und Jung' in the *Passagenwerk*:

> Historical index of childhood. In his deduction of the normative character of Greek art (as sprung from the childhood of humanity) Marx says: Does not each epoch see reborn, in the nature of the child, its own character in true and natural form?[36]

In the draft introduction's concluding remarks Marx also contends that cultural forms relate to technologies extant in the world at any one time. The modern technologies and technical products noted by Marx include self-acting mules, locomotives, electric telegraphs, gunpowder and bullets, newspapers and the printing press. Marx is particularly interested in the technological shifts that make Greek mythology redundant. For example, he asks rhetorically, what becomes of Vulcan compared with Roberts and Co., or Jupiter in the context of lightning conductors, or Fama side by side with Printing House Square. Both Marx and Benjamin exhibit a fascination with the fantastic energies of childhood for social imagination, and both recognize the imbrication of cultural forms and technological developments, albeit, in Marx's case, candidly enmeshed with a dialectical twist that affirms the nostalgic pull of ancient art. Marx locates a discrepancy between the base and the culture-producing superstructure, enabling the underdeveloped economic context of Ancient Greece to produce art that 'peaks' above later works produced in more advanced conditions. This is because its childlike charm speaks across centuries to our own utopian innocence and hope of escape from the modern cleavage of the social and the natural.

Benjamin writes of his childhood metropolis as a place that tenders unprecedented possibilities, types of wealth and stimulations. His father is a typical representative of a class of entrepreneurs and businessmen who had welcomed with puffed-up optimism the unfurling urban spectacle. Benjamin's childhood belongs to the end-of-the-century era of the first mass marketing of commodities. His child's city is a treasure trove, glittering with illuminations and sensations. As a young boy, Benjamin admits, he got to know the city as a 'show place of needs'.[37] The shopping arcade city, in which his father's purchasing power cut paths between shop counters, sales assistants and mirrors, is made of an unfathomable chain of caverns crammed full with piles of commodities. Instituting a return to a social childhood, impersonally concerned with spaces, places, objects, Benjamin glides back over the kitschy ruins and rubble of over-cluttered bourgeois interiors in Berlin's West End, writing less of people and more of the objects there and the spaces they occupy. Likewise, in 'Traumkitsch' (1926), Benjamin claims that the surrealists are 'less on the trail of the soul than of things'.[38] Benjamin sniffs out the thing-world. *Berliner Chronik* revisits the thing-world of his childhood. This thing-world is a sequence of spaces filled with the shards of urban bric-à-brac: telephones, chocolate machines, trains and railway stations, postcards, cluttered plush interiors, impressive stone and metal monuments that crown tree-lined paths or nestle alluringly in Berlin's cultivated Tiergarten. Interest in a material culture, perceived by Benjamin as supercharged with historical meanings, continues the half-magical, surrealistic approach to objective matter. Such an approach is fundamental to Benjamin's form of materialist diagnosis.

The thing-world, *die Dingwelt*, recurs in Marxian theory of the 1920s and 1930s. Lukács' term reification reflected on modern qualities of thingness and self-becoming-a-thing amongst the accumulations of fetishized commodity-junk. The thing-world in Adorno's essays was a zone where the self may capitulate to objectivity. Subjectivity is jeopardized in the thing-world. Benjamin, prompted by a surrealist-tinged relish for flea markets, antiquated technologies and detritus, collected an array of citations, clippings and cogitations on nineteenth- and twentieth-century paraphernalia, in order to sniff out social utopian investments. Combing through old and forgotten physiologies, booklets and reports, held in the archives of Paris's Bibliothèque Nationale, did Benjamin believe himself to be imitating Marx in the British Library, sorting through disjecta, accounts, invoices, tracts and tomes, in order to write his definitive guide to the secret and repressed history of the muck of the nineteenth century? Benjamin's hunger for details about junk and fashions and gadgetry disburses a context for modernist theorists' obsessive curiosity about things, furnishings and interior decoration. Material culture dwells in us as we dwell in it. It provides components for the personality, points of projection and the tabulations of taste back up the myth of the individual. Benjamin insists, surrealistically, on historical and social truths submerged in the objectivity of cultural commodities, especially those that have become outdated. Nineteenth-century culture is pervaded by a wealth of fantasies of material surfeit and future utopian schemas. Objects in the interior, this sediment of material culture might be the most socially symptomatic and legible, and, though indisputably in need of cashing in or redemption, definitely not to be disdained.

Industrialism's originally promoted pledge of widespread material abundance is reactivated in Benjamin's child-critic. The child succumbs to the magic and mania of street life, experimenting and delving for correspondences between subjects and objects. Benjamin's child-critic lingers and falters, enveloped in a haze of curiosity and invention. The happiest moments of a bourgeois childhood emerge in the description of the child as world-conquering micro-imperialist in the environs of the Potsdam summerhouse.[39] For the child, the city can be penetrated, its labyrinths examined. To be child-like is to be engulfed by the city, amalgamating with its glass and asphalt. One factor of infantile vision is that the child has a relationship to novelty based on its unfamiliarity with objects. The strategic importance of using the child's view as a way into an interpretation of history is that the child is seen to discover the new anew and, on this basis, brings novel technological worlds into the symbolic realm.[40] A child's creative perception of objects is seen to recollect the historical moment when new technologies were first conceived, moments described by Benjamin as 'for the first time' or from the 'too early' epoch.[41] In the memoirs, early technology – in its youngest days – is associated with the newly born. In one scene from *Berliner Kindheit um neunzehnhundert*, first published in early 1933, Benjamin depicts his father conducting business transactions on the telephone, inside of which is seen to slumber a newborn voice.[42] Images of birth, technological birth, perceptual rebirth, are coupled by an exclusion of death from the scenes of childhood. In 12 Blumeshof, the bourgeois home of Benjamin's maternal grandmother, the heavy furniture emanates a faith in an eternity that hopes to exclude misery and death.[43] Immortality and permanence are keywords in Benjamin's delineation of the self-comprehension of the progressive bourgeoisie, mediated in early portrait photography. But the solidity and permanence of this world which excludes death is undermined at various moments in the narrative. Cognizance's gradual crystallization is organized around the intervention of mortality into the narrative. The absence of death in 12 Blumeshof is contradicted by the death of Benjamin's childhood friend Fritz Heinle, whose suicide is provoked by the outbreak of world war in 1914.[44]

Benjamin returns to his remembered shards of the nineteenth century and the early twentieth century in order to engage antagonistically with history as it has been. He emphasizes the unredeemed promises of endless spectacular consumption and boundless technological production. The dialectical comprehension of *Technik* as an oscillating interplay between destructiveness and productiveness compels the outline of an urban scene that is utopian and dystopian. Dystopian moments are connected to the gradual realization of social and political exigencies. Benjamin links a perceived empirical decline of technology in the late nineteenth century to the constrictions and demands of the maturing, degenerating, capitalist organization of society. Technological decline tends to be presented analogically in the narrative with illustrations of Benjamin's entry into adolescence, with its disappointments and revelations. Benjamin acknowledges the fraudulence of capitalism's promissory ideologies. Within the course of the narrative of *Berliner Chronik*, the social implementation of the new technologies for military ends crushes the belief that technology will deliver abundance, permanent progression and eternal peace. Benjamin's memoir reveals his dawning awareness, in the years of the great carnage, that class barriers are not overcome in the modern machino-facture age, but are reinforced. Machine technology is not used to bring about utopia. Conjointly bourgeois ideology insists on maintaining restrictions. The limits experienced in adolescence are the walls of stuffy bourgeois interiors or the spaces informed and constricted by bourgeois morality, such as parents' drawing rooms, gratefully lent for an evening meeting, or rented furnished rooms where young men receive lady-friend visitors, conditional on their doors remaining unlocked.[45] Adolescence is a process of sexual awakening which is inseparable from recognition of class barriers and half-prohibited city-zones. Benjamin writes of the encounter between the prostitute and the client as the traversing of a threshold that delimits and confines his class.[46] The limits, barriers, uncrossable thresholds operate to separate the intellectual from the masses. Participation in the Youth Movement's useless headslamming against the walls of bourgeois society teaches him that 'no one can improve his school or his parental home without first smashing the state that needs bad ones'.[47] Attitudes cannot be altered without attacking conditions. Generational revolt mutates into political revolt. This cognizance is lashed to a focal event in the chronicle, the advent of the world war. The world war is a personal biographical and a generational experience. It is located in actuality at the point where Benjamin's childhood becomes adulthood. It functions to mark the moment when, due to the manifestation of a disenchanting and deadly knowledge of social actuality, technological innocence becomes manifestly technological guilt.

Heinle's suicide and that of his girlfriend, Rika Seligson, in response to the outbreak of war in August 1914, marks the moment of political awakening.[48] After their deaths the vain attempt to find a joint burial plot for the two young lovers makes Benjamin aware of the social, political and moral boundaries set in the city:

We felt them in the ignominy of only being able to find refuge in a dubious station hotel on Stuttgarter Platz, when finally, after the eighth of August 1914, days came in which we, who were closest to the dead couple, did not want to part from one another until they were buried. Even the cemetery proved to us the barriers that the town set down on everything that was dear to our hearts: it was impossible to obtain for the two who had died together one grave in the same cemetery. But these were days that made me ready for the insight, which I was to meet again later, and which convinced me that even the town of Berlin would not be spared the scars from the struggle for a better order.[49]

Exemplary moments from the time of Benjamin's adolescence provide historical evidence of the dawning corruptness of social, economic and political structures. Benjamin traces the negativity of capitalist development through a number of confrontations with class barriers in the city, the growing awareness of prostituted sex, and the disillusioning pain of military destruction with the human crises it unleashes. The autobiography slips into a melancholic decline which shadows the empirical decline of technological promise. The decline or degeneration of technology is flagged in the increasing divergence between possibility and actuality. Such an analysis, of course, threatens the term 'decline' with inconsistency – how is it possible to know the possibility in the first place? The possibility of knowing decline is indicated by the usage, for methodological purposes, of a type of theoretically constructed experience which might be described variously as utopian, fantastic, magical or redemptive. Through a depiction of *Technik*, Benjamin interprets the disastrous empirical record of modernity, manifest in the social betrayal of faith in technology on the battlefields of the Great War, in what he calls the 'time of hell', 'the modern epoch'.[50] Benjamin relates a history of technological development, marking out its process of decline, as it errs into what he terms 'untimeliness'.[51] A 1932 radio lecture for children, describing the collapse of the bridge across the River Tay in 1878, relates Benjamin's model of technology in miniature.[52] This radio lecture characterizes technological discoveries as either timely or untimely. 'Untimeliness' implies an inappropriate organization of relations of production, given the extant forces of production. Benjamin writes of 'too early' and 'too late' technologies. The file on iron constructions in the *Passagenwerk* notes that in the case of the arcades glass and iron came there 'too early' – and so the most brittle and the strongest material are both defiled – for in the middle of the nineteenth century people did not know how to use it, and therefore 'the day, glimpsed through the planes between iron supports, appeared so dirty and so dull'.[53] There is a moment for each technology – a moment in which it can be grasped, understood, used correctly and productively. The notions of timeliness and outmodedness, the 'too early' and 'too late', depend on the assumption of empirical *Technik*, those forms that have existed, and potential *Technik*, those forms that can and should, or could have and should have, come into being. To write of this assumes the validity of writing possibility into theory and seeing potential in actuality.

Remembering Berliner Chronik: *An Interpretive Projection of Technological Potential*

In *Berliner Chronik* Benjamin studies empirical history in order to show why and how technology has come to terrorize humanity. At the same time, his empirical tracing of a history of technological calamity is overwritten by attempts to establish technological potential, as counter-projection to the grim side of historical development as it has actually happened. Benjamin posits a dynamic in which the act of recreating the event is enstaged as a re-run for redemptive purposes. He uses the method of remembering as a way to open out a perspective on the past. He enacts a politicized interpretative method of representing history, in order to cast a critical gaze over the reciprocation of technologies in the modern era. *Berliner Chronik* insists on a multi-storeyed view of history, which, at each moment, contains the possibility of another, retrospective, corrective, disabusing re-evaluation of the past. His way of perceiving inaugurates room for a new evaluation of the missed, latent possibilities of *Technik*, and sublates the actual history of *Technik*. To expose technology's liberatory potential now, it is necessary to look back to the original moment of an object's appearance and to trace the bitter empirical history of its decline, while remembering the permanent possibility of an alternative, revealed in the perspective of the child *flâneur*. This evinces a structure, labelled by Peter Szondi 'hope in the past'.[54] Szondi's title and main theoretical point, 'hope in the past', is perhaps misleading. It is not so much a nostalgic-sounding hope in the past that Benjamin rediscovers in his return to childhood, but the promulgation of a way of seeing that will open out the missed possibilities of the past as tokens that might yet be redeemable. The traversing of the gulf that divides maturity from childhood, an interruption of a one-way continuity, does not mean that Benjamin gazes longingly at the lost past. He locates, rather, hope for the future in past potentials that did not materialize. Their presence, however, demonstrates that if these unfulfilled potentials are recognized, a sense of the potential inherent in our own historical moment might be uncovered. To revisit the past from the perspective of the now, with all the despondency that entails, is undertaken because a return to the past will determine for us what has been lost, what has been betrayed and also what is yet possible, given the resources of *Technik*. The empirical history of technological development is, then, joined by a 'mythic', redemptive and interpretative history of technological development, in which the act of interpretation, a reconstruction of what has been, formulates the possibility for change, by making the potential for transformation appear latent. This is a reiteration of what Benjamin links in 'Kleine Geschichte der Photographie' to the correct utilization of *Technik* and terms the 'politically educated gaze'.[55] His method of returning to the past with a child's eyes – setting up the theoretical construction of the 'for the first time' feeling – posits a technological innocence that the reader knows to have been betrayed historically. This salvages his inquiry into technology from the clutch of a pessimistic anti-technologism, and it ratifies his refusal to abandon technology as category or potential basis of a politics of liberation. A political encounter with the past involves the theoretical re-encounter with initially utopian and progressive tendencies contained within technology. These tendencies remain technology's enslaved potential and provide the foundation for a release from the disastrous present.

The attribution of filmic-photographic principles to the structure of memory, specifically in the explosion of chronology, enables Benjamin to intimate unredeemed possibilities within history. To cite one example: a scene in *Berliner Chronik* relates the death of an uncle, drawing analogies between memory and photography. The story is told twice at the end of *Berliner Chronik*. The first attempt is broken off, at the crucial moment, omitting still the missing detail, the forgotten piece that makes sense of the whole. The first narration is organized around a photographic metaphor:

> Anyone can observe that the duration for which we are exposed to impressions has no bearing on their fate in memory. Nothing prevents us from keeping more or less clearly in our memory those rooms in which we have spent twenty-four hours, and quite forgetting others where we spent months. It is not, therefore, due to insufficient exposure time if no image appears on the plate of remembrance. More frequent, perhaps, are the cases when the half-light of habit denies the plate the necessary light for years, until one day from a strange source it flashes as if from ignited magnesium powder, and a snapshot fixes the room's image on the plate. At the centre of these rare pictures we always stand. And that is not so curious, since such moments of sudden illumination are at the same time moments when we are outside of ourselves, and while our waking, habitual, daily self is involved actively or passively in what is happening, our deeper

self rests in another place and is touched by the shock, as is the tiny pile of magnesium powder by the matchflame. This sacrifice of our deepest self in shock is to what our memory owes its most indelible images.[56]

Habit is the enemy of memory – memory hits another spot, a deeper self, a self outside the 'self' of daily life. Benjamin dismisses outmoded photo-technology in order to evoke modern snapshot techniques for his equation. He introduces the notion of shock – habit's tormentor. Camera-like, consciousness records unconscious memories – this metaphor could be led back to Freud again, and his 'A Note on the Mystic Writing Pad' (1924), where the shock-absorbing psychic apparatus is said to operate just like this optical toy which retains traces of impressions on its wax underbody, while its celluloid upper skin wipes the slate clean again and again.[57] In terms of the psyche such erasure, repression of the impression, allows the normal continuation of daily life.

The second narration of his father's failed attempt to convey a sexual secret at the close of *Berliner Chronik* correlates shock and memory.[58] Benjamin's child-critic senses something forgotten lurking in his bedroom, and vows one day to return in his memory to the site in order to reclaim the lost fragment of meaning. He imprints photographically on to his memory each detail of the room's possessions, making an inventory of things. The suggestion of the possibility of reclaiming something 'forgotten' intimates that photography is more absorbent of reality than natural vision.

Memory images are also defined in this period in ways that evoke the curious temporality elicited by early auratic photography, as described in 'Kleine Geschichte der Photographie' (1931). They are constellations of past history and a contemporary engagement with that past. In the *Passagenwerk*, Benjamin writes of 'historical understanding as the after-life of that which is understood'.[59] Its pulse can still be felt in the present. Benjamin alludes to a proto-cinematic device in his short speech on Proust written in 1932.[60] This was written as a lecture, which he intended to deliver on his fortieth birthday. Various pieces of evidence point to the fact that this day had also been set aside as Benjamin's suicide date. Benjamin wrote in June 1932 to Scholem that he wanted to spend his birthday in Nice with 'a quite droll fellow' whom he had often met in his life. It seems that he was referring to death.[61] He planned to kill himself in a hotel. Instead of doing so, he chose to speak about memory and imaging the past. The lecture touches on mortality. Benjamin talks of dying and connects it to the cliché of a proto-photographic strip of images of a life whirring through a dying person's head. A celluloid self is buried in the unconscious or 'darkroom'. Memories are involuntarily summoned strips of montaged images. These flash past in rapid succession:

On the cognition of the mémoire involontaire: not only do its
images appear without being summoned; they are images never
before seen when we remember them. This is clearest in those
pictures in which – as in some dreams – we see ourselves. We
stand before ourselves, the way we might have stood somewhere
in a prehistoric past, but never before our waking gaze. Yet these
images, developed in the darkroom of the lived moment, are the
most important we will ever see. It could be said that our most
profound moments have been equipped with a little image, just
like those that come in cigarette packets, a photograph of our
selves. And that whole life, said to pass before people's eyes
when they are dying or are in mortal danger, is composed of just
these little images. They flash by in a rapid sequence, like those
booklets, precursors of the cinematographs, in which as children
we admired the skills of a boxer, a swimmer or a tennis player.[62]

The photographic metaphor of the darkroom of the lived
moment alludes to Bloch's utopian social philosophy. Bloch writes
of the 'darkness of the lived moment', indicating the instantaneous,
evanescent experience of a potential 'not-yet' reality which can be
glimpsed in the present, but is to be developed later.[63] This relates
also to a later image in the *Passagenwerk*. It combines the romantic,
the technological and the telescoped temporal. In a mixed
metaphor of chemical development and temporal perspective
Benjamin fuses critical concepts with a philosophy of history,
strangely synthesizing metaphors of the literary text and the photographic image:

> If one wishes to view history as a text, then it is valid to suggest
> what a recent author has said about literary ones: the past has
> deposited such images in them as can be compared with those
> that are caught on a light-sensitive plate. Only the future has at
> its disposal a developer strong enough to let the image appear in
> all its details.[64]

The proto-cinematic device, whose functioning is aligned by
Benjamin to the process of memory, appears once more in an autobiographical entry titled 'Das bucklichte Männlein'.[65] Alluding to
photography and the unconscious structured as a photograph,
Benjamin insists that the most important images in our lives are
those that develop later. The darkroom where this process of
development takes place is the darkroom of our subsequent lives,
the 'after-life' of the moment of the image. In the *Passagenwerk*
Benjamin, citing Bloch, lists fashion and architecture as instances
of objects in the collective's dream-consciousness. These objects
'stand in the darkness of the lived moment'.[66] The fantastic social
potentials at which these objects hint are as yet unrealized in

actuality because of the deadening constrictions stemming from power relations that constitute the economic base.

Experience and Poverty

Berliner Chronik theorizes memory and speculates on experience in relation to technological exigencies. Inescapable forces are exerted on contemporary experience by new technological forms. Experience with technologies, experience mediated through technologies, experience articulated by technologies, all coincidences of technology and humanity, contribute to a reconstruction of subjectivity. Benjamin argues that an entire reformulation of individuals and their perception has occurred, and points out the newly formed 'deepest needs' of a generation, articulated in film:

> On the rhythm of today that determines this work. Most characteristic of cinema is the play-off between the thoroughly fragmentary style of images, satisfying the deepest needs of this generation to witness the debunking of the flow of development, and the gliding music.[67]

Music smooths over the cracks and shocks that are so necessary for contemporary entertainment. There is a strict correlation between technical standards and changes in perception. This amounts to making experience an historical fact, and it obliges Benjamin to reject the category of empathy in historical research. Empathy, he contends, makes history abstract and is seen to negate irreversible historical changes in forms of experience.[68] Benjamin's historicity of the subject, who changes in complicity with the object world, prevents any fantasy of the possibility of reconstructing history 'as it actually was' ('*wie es eigentlich gewesen ist*').[69] Benjamin initiated his discussion of film in 1927, but his insistence on the importance of film, touched on in 'Zur Lage der russischen Filmkunst' and 'Erwiderung an Oskar A. H. Schmitz', is reiterated in subsequent years.[70] In ensuing work, Benjamin augments the model provided by mechanical visual effects into a model for existence in industrial capitalism. This is envisaged as habitation of the panorama, the phantasmagoria or the film.[71] Insistence on experience in the world as filmic asserts the foundational role of *Technik* in formulating the 'base co-ordinates of this world'.[72] Film takes on anthropic significance. It adopts a preemptive, training role, offering practice in modes of technological intercourse about to generalize imminently. Benjamin evokes structures of existence in the world, repeated in microform in these areas of image-production. The technical attributes of film correspond exactly to those identified by Benjamin as contemporary concerns of form in general. An entry in the *Passagenwerk* contends that film has taken over as the key representational medium, formulating 'all problems of modern formation as its technical question of existence in the shortest, most concrete and most critical ways'.[73] Film is assessed as an unfolding of notional forms, tempos and rhythms that reside in contemporary machines.[74]

'Erfahrung and Armut' (1933) is a succinct expression of how experience is transformed by technology. The short composition reflects specifically on the way that war, defined as a 'monstrous unfolding of technology', has altered experience and its transmission.[75] Benjamin writes of the now insufficient nature of the traditional idea of experience, tabulating the changed conditions of existence as they converge in the technological explosions of the 1914–18 war, as well as in their after-history at another critical moment when political reaction and the war drive set in. World war is the site of a mass encounter between people and *Technik*. This encounter overthrows what used to count as experience. Military technology has depleted the human capacity to retransmit experience. It is impoverished:

> No, this much is obvious: experience has deteriorated in value and that in a generation that from 1914 to 1918 went through one of the most monstrous experiences of world history. Perhaps it is not as curious as it appears. Was it not possible to notice at the time that people returned mute from the battlefields? Not richer but poorer in communicable experience. What was then forged ten years later in the flood of war books has nothing to do with experience that flows from mouth to ear. No, this was not surprising. For never have experiences been punished more severely by lies than strategic experience by the lie of the war of position (trench warfare), economic experience by the lie of inflation, corporeal experience by hunger, ethical experience by those with power. A generation that had gone to school in horse-drawn carriages, now stood beneath the heavens in a landscape in which nothing but the clouds had remained unchanged and in the middle, in a powerzone of destructive forces and explosions, was the tiny, fragile human body.[76]

'Erfahrung und Armut' announces the liquidation of experience. Once experience was coincident with wisdom and was passed down to children by their elders, through stories and folk sayings. It appears to be the very failure of the tiny human body to cope with the vast technological change, deployed in the service of destruction of nature, of human life, that leads to an impoverishment of the tenets of experience itself. All the utopias of technology's childhood are washed up on the beaches of northern France and muddied in the stinking black trenches of the 'new barbarism'.[77] Silent soldiers, crippled, shell-shocked, return from the front to another no mans' land. These soldiers are wooden, rigid marionettes, as silent as their ghostly siblings on the silver screen, and they act as woodenly too, having had thrust on them a mode of being that Brecht's alienation-effect would parody. They are rendered speechless by the incommensurability of the experience their bodies had suffered with the propaganda they received before, during and after the event. Experience, Benjamin argues, cheapens under the impact of the vast lie of colonial, imperial war. The individual is offered up as a vulnerable victim to a vast modern technology. The war of position is shown to be a lie, whose truth is the fighting inch by inch for muddy soil along front lines that edge painfully and slowly in the shape of mass body battalions backwards and forwards across a denuded terrain. The economic lie of wealth and expansion is exposed as the uncontrollable anarchy of inflation. The lie of good breeding is scorned by the blatant and brutal hypocrisy of the ruling classes. The idea of the sacred body is another myth. In reality, the body is blasted to flesh atoms on the field, pulverized in the crossfire of heavy artillery or torn on the rusting spikes of barbed wire frontiers. The experience that occurs on the battlefield is a trauma that issues in an inability to broadcast the experience in communicable terms. Technology itself, it would seem, has robbed the soldiers of utterable experience.

But the liquidation of experience is also the basis for a reconstruction of experience. Impoverished experience can be overpowered only if the fact of poverty is made into the underpinning of a political strategy of a 'new barbarism' that corresponds faithfully to the new realities of the constellation of *Masse* and *Technik*. These new realities are of anthropological significance. The contemporary person is 'a reduced person, a person kept on ice in a cold world'.[78] Benjamin's new anthropology responds to a perceived 'crisis' of the human, as he states in 'Theater und Rundfunk', an essay written in 1932:[79]

> It is the person eliminated by radio and cinema, a person, putting it rather too drastically, who is the fifth wheel on the wagon of technology.[80]

Reference to the fifth wheel is a way of saying figuratively to feel out of place, to be alienated. Alienation is inscribed in and by the new technological cultural forms:

> Film and gramophones were invented in the epoch of maximum alienation of people from one another, the epoch of incalculably mediated relationships which have become their only ones. In film a person does not recognize the way he walks, and in the case of the gramophone, does not recognize his own voice. Experiments prove this.[81]

Watching and listening to film and gramophone recordings, the broadcasting of self-estrangement, is a fitting activity in an era of alienation. The pessimistic edge of this insight is overridden by Benjamin's acknowledgment that a new type of techno-self is emerging. A previous concept of selfhood is historically remaindered. New cultural technologies exist in the context of maximum alienation of the self from self and self from others. But in establishing new modes of life and new types of interaction, these same technologies can be converted into the basis for an abolition of alienation, through a collective incorporation of technology into the self. Benjamin recommends recognition of experience's impoverishment, arguing that a model of experience appropriate to the now can be re-transmitted by the very machinery that impoverishes it. The value of technological means of reproduction lies in the opportunity they offer for an attempted reconstruction of the capacity for experience of the 'eliminated person'. This reformulation is a broadening of experience, an envisaging of new worlds and different natures. The suggestion of a largely visually explicit 'curative alienation' ('*heilsame Entfremdung*') in 'Kleine Geschichte der Photographie' (1931) is turned into a strategy for recapturing the full reality of contemporary experience, necessarily based on technological forms.[82] The conceptualization of experience as historically specific, subject to restructuring by new technologies is imported into Benjamin's programmatic aesthetic theory. In 'Erfahrung und Armut' Benjamin proposes that artists should not ignore or mourn experience's impoverishment, but re-transmit it, precisely by imitating the technology that gives rise to alienation. 'Erfahrung und Armut' specifies cultural producers who incorporate formally, in various ways, capitalism's alienating 'barbarism': Brecht, Klee, Scheerbart, Adolf Loos, Walt Disney with his Mickey Mouse character. Their artistic techniques are aligned to, or recognize, the state of technological productive forces, and are thus historically faithful and anticipatory of social praxis. They all incorporate candid reflections of the end of humanism: Brecht with his social-political dramaturgy, Klee with his constructivist abstractions and his modern angels, Loos with his unornamented modern buildings, Disney with his crazy animated world of lively beasts and technologies, Scheerbart with his utopian sci-fi fantasies which imagine how telescopes and aeroplanes and spaceships transform people, and how they might live new lives inside glass houses. Like Scheerbart's oddly, non-humanly named characters, the Russians also call their children by 'dehumanized' names such as October, *Pjatiletka*, after the five-year plan, or *Awiachim*, after an airline. Benjamin's aesthetic project from now on consists in a concerted effort to persuade artists of the need to assimilate into their work

– in some way or another – extant technological forms. This can be carried out literally by utilizing the newest technological inventions. But Benjamin does not simply recommend the use of technology to create art-forms that mediate technologically specific experiences. Benjamin argues for the employment of techniques able to produce effects redolent of those produced by new technologies. Guidelines for artistic praxis can be derived from the technological characteristics exemplified by the technological forms of film and radio, as is the case in Brecht's epic theatre. The technological restructuring of experience, specifically of memory and the unconscious, is seen to necessitate new models of textually and visually representing experience.

'Kleine Geschichte der Photographie' ended with the assertion of photography's inadequacy in representing the obscurity of modern relations. In one passage in *Berliner Chronik*, relating for a second time Brecht's rejection of naturalism, Benjamin aligns technological change and representation, maintaining that, historically, contemporary technologies are the appropriate media for illustrating the city at any one time. Certain technologies are seen to offer the means of an accurate and appropriate representation of the city, while others become outmoded. In *Berliner Chronik* Benjamin describes Sunday afternoon excursions to forgotten arcades, the Stettiner Tunnel, up by Wedding's A.E.G. factory, or the representation of Liberty in front of the Wallner Theatre. One of his female photographer friends was always there, snapping:

And it seems to me, when I think of Berlin, that the side of the town that we were chasing is the only side truly accessible to photographic recording. The closer that we approach its contemporary, fluid, functional existence, the more the region of the photographable shrinks: it has been noted correctly, that, for example, a photograph of a modern factory barely brings anything essential onto the plate. Such pictures could be compared to railway stations. In this era, generally, when the railways are beginning to age, they no longer offer the genuine entrance to the town. This nowadays unrolls on the motorists' approach roads through the town precincts, the outer suburbs. The railway station gives the order for a surprise attack, but it is an antiquated one that collides us with the old. It is no different with photography, even the snapshot. Optical approach roads open up to film the essence of the town such as those which lead motorists into the new city centres.[83]

The railway station, seen by Benjamin as a child through the foggy haze of distance and wonder, is shunted out of the way to accommodate the gleaming asphalt strips of a twentieth-century road.[84] In analogous fashion, static photography is displaced by film. The allusion to the photograph of the modern factory in 'Kleine Geschichte der Photographie' and the autobiographical piece makes manifest a connection in Benjamin's writings between strategies of representation of actuality and technological innovation. Benjamin asserts normatively that a stage has been attained at which certain possibilities have become available for the representation of today's fluid and faster world. Available modes of representation become necessary modes of representation.

CHAPTER 4

Dream Whirled: *Technik* and Mirroring

'Logically Consistent Developments'

Benjamin often uses the language of science and of technology. Perhaps he hopes to claim an authority derived from scientific method. Developmental tendencies in history and society dissolve aesthetics into a science and into techniques and technologies. The question of science and the claim to scientificity of Marxist method has long been contested. Benjamin's willingness to assert the form and language of science contrasts with Korsch's attitude towards science as a superstructural expression of class ideology.[1] It also diverges from Lukács' more dismissive approach to the scientistic conceptions of classical Marxist orthodoxy in *Geschichte und Klassenbewußtsein* (1923) and *Chvostismus und Dialektik* (1925). Lukács polemicized against the specious scientificity of positivist Marxism, fostered by Engels and displayed by Kautsky, Cunow and others. Translation of the methods of natural science to 'social science' distresses him. He writes:

> When the ideal of scientific knowledge is applied to nature it simply furthers the progress of science. But when it is applied to society it turns out to be an ideological weapon of the bourgeoisie.[2]

Lukács is allergic to the language of science in sociology. It is a fact, proclaims Lukács, that capitalist society, with its fetishistic objectivity, is predisposed to harmonize with scientific method. Benjamin, in contrast, wants to exploit the polemical power of the language of science, though he might concur that the natural sciences, as they exist, are complicit with capitalist ideology. It is necessary to admit the contradiction between contemporary productive forces and the private mode of appropriation, or between the development of science and industry, prerequisite for universal emancipation, and the capitalist prison inside of which this unfolding transpires. Presumably Benjamin's reliance on a technophilic, scientific discourse derives from his contact with Soviet cultural avant-gardism. Various artistic avant-garde movements of the time are immersed in the technical-technological. This is especially true of those avant-garde movements that are animated by events in the Soviet Union. The Russian formalist

Viktor Shklovsky gives a lead in statements which presume that technical rationality can crash through ideology: 'An engine of more than forty horsepower annihilates the old morality.'[3] For adherents of the revolutionary avant-garde, technology plays a crucial role in attempts to fuse art and everyday life, transforming art and life in the process. The avant-garde movements that lure Benjamin in the mid-1920s include constructivism, productivism and production art.[4] These movements broadcast a revolutionary commitment to art's powers of intervention in the daily lives of working people. The politicized avant-gardes in the years immediately following the 1917 revolution often discuss art in the language of science and industry. The image of the artist as engineer is rooted in Soviet avant-garde cultural practice as developed by figures such as Tatlin, Tretyakov and Rodchenko. In the 1920s, constructivist-productivist theorists and production artists, including Popova, Stepanova, Suetin, Sotnikov and Lavinskii, abandon art and enter the factories as designers. They are bolstered by Boris Arvatov's theoretical work, a series of articles written between 1921 and 1930, which eventually appeared in book-form under the title *About Agitational and Production Art*.[5] For Arvatov, production art, the work of the engineer-constructor, provides the model for the new Soviet society's form of creativity. One example of Benjamin's import of the language of science into his theory is his endorsement of experiment and his assumption that communist society is engaged in research into new forms of life. For example, in an article from 1927 on Soviet film, Benjamin writes:

> Allowing film and radio to influence such collectivities is one of the most fantastic mass psychological experiments presently being undertaken in that huge laboratory Russia.[6]

The Soviet Union is a testing ground for Benjamin's own researches in the guise of social or natural scientist. Soviet post-revolutionary conditions are seen to indicate both the potential direction and necessary drift of political development in Western Europe. The objective revolutionary thrust of industrialization, begun by capitalism in the nineteenth century, melds culture and technology in ways that apparently come to fruition in the Soviet Union. In the early to mid-1930s Benjamin undertakes a number of studies that are occupied with either tracking intersections between technology and culture in the nineteenth century, or suggesting models for a political aesthetic practice, drawn from perceived techno-cultural developments in the Soviet Union.

In the 1935 *Exposé* for the *Passagenwerk* Benjamin investigates how existence and consciousness are reformulated 'in the light of the new technical and social reality'.[7] New technologies appear as the material of a novel 'second nature'. Lukács, drawing on Hegelian categories, introduced the term 'second nature' into his social critique. Hegel had differentiated between, on the one hand, a pristine and paradisiacal nature of physical and biotic laws, forms and processes and, on the other hand, a 'second nature' made of the regulated social world of the market, the metropolis and culture. Over time, Lukács insists, 'second nature' becomes our only nature. Benjamin uses the term 'second nature' similarly, in order to counter the assumption that the cosmos is simply natural and static, non-social, non-historical. 'Second nature', in contrast, is technological, artificial, cultural, but, through use, it becomes part of the new nature, part of the given. Benjamin's overhaul of the human condition makes historical the natural and makes the natural subject to historical, technical pressures. Nature is technical nature. No absolute categorical distinction between nature and technology persists. Technology is socially and historically produced, but it always becomes part of a new nature. Benjamin phrases this in relation to art:

> One can formulate the problem of form in the new art bluntly: when and how will the worlds of forms that have arisen in mechanics, in film, machine construction and the new physics, and that, without our assistance, have emerged and overpowered us, make what is natural in them clear to us? When will the condition of society be reached in which these forms or those which have arisen from them open themselves up to us as natural forms?[8]

New cultural forms, he contends, signal a revolution in the relationship of art to technology and are an 'expression' of a new 'attitude to life'.[9] The new technical and social reality includes with technological art-forms, entertainment innovations, advertising, technical engineering and mass photojournalism. The 1935 *Exposé* of the *Passagenwerk* advises that communist culture will have to be built from the forms of technological media that exist in capitalism. Benjamin embraces a progressivist language. The development of forces of production 'emancipates' forms ('*Gestaltungsformen*') from art, just as in the sixteenth century 'the sciences freed themselves from philosophy'.[10] Even certain aestheticist art practices and *l'art pour l'art* are negatively informed by alterations in the socio-cultural environment. Art's desperate attempt to salvage the old aesthetic causes it to parade painterly technical abilities which photography and film cannot imitate. The industrial mode informs methods of distribution and the relations of production and consumption of art. Capital picks up instantly on technologically structured art's commercial potential as popular event, for example, in the form of panoramas or as cinema. Notes to the *Passagenwerk* and the 1935 *Exposé* trace preconditions for the communist transformation of culture to the process inexorably begun by capitalist methods of production. This process involves the industrialization of literature and forms of artistic production whose methods are in some way analogous to factory methods of mass production.[11] Further socialized development of technological cultural forms is, however, inhibited by their commodity status. Benjamin is also keen to point out the extent to which there is an ideological aim at work in nineteenth-century design. It masks 'technical necessities' by 'artistic aims', in order to aggrandize 'the worldly and spiritual rule of the bourgeoisie'.[12] Benjamin is calling to mind cladding, façading and the sort of ornamentation that had so infuriated the Viennese architect and critic Adolf Loos around the turn of the century. These practices led Loos to begin his campaigns against embellishment on designed objects. Loos contended that the 'march of civilization systematically liberates object after object from ornamentation'.[13] The title of his pamphlet 'Ornament and Crime', written in 1908, makes clear his view that decoration is a deceitful waste of labour, materials and capital. Benjamin's critique is less moral than Loos's, and rather more political-ideological.

In 1934 Benjamin intended to present a lecture on the author as 'producer' to the Institute for the Study of Fascism in Paris. 'Der Autor als Produzent' stresses the need to analyse relations of production, in order to suggest ways to bring them into line with forces of production. 'Der Autor als Produzent' makes recommendations for artistic practice in non-revolutionary Europe. Art can be prefigurative of social and technical relations to come. Prefiguration is important, for it indicates the extent to which Benjamin is convinced of a dynamic inlaid in technology and the forces of production. To pre-empt that development in art is to glimpse the potential (communist) future in the (capitalist) present, through an aesthetic negation of the social relations of capital. The movement between the aesthetic and the political realm, evinced in the assertion that aesthetic conceptualization can have political efficacy, discloses Benjamin's comprehension of reality as a totality.

In the real-existing communist present of the Soviet Union, contends Benjamin, unfettered forces and relations of production allow technological forms to unfurl. This is viewed as the 'logically consistent development of the means of production' (*'die folgerechte Entwicklung der Produktionsmittel'*).[14] Comparing technological development in capitalist societies and the Soviet Union, Benjamin hopes to establish that technology pushes 'logically' towards proletariat-friendly, socialized production relations. In capitalist countries this drive to realization must be pre-emptively enacted in art, as part of a critical artistic practice. Such pre-empting relies on the presupposition of a blocked dynamic of developing productive forces. In as much as the author uses art as a realm in which templates of new patterns of technical arrangements are generated experimentally, the author becomes a producer. The word 'author' in Benjamin's lecture denotes all sorts of culture producers who partake in acts of creativity. The producer relates to the forces of production, enabling their compensatory unfolding aesthetically. Technical forces push towards restructuring relations of production. Author-producers are asked to recognize and manipulate that drive.

In supplementary notes to 'Der Autor als Produzent' Benjamin asserts that the 'logically consistent development of the means of production' generates the breakdown of barriers between different forms of production and between producers and consumers.[15] Intellectual production is politically useful at the point when it forces an overcoming of separate spheres of competence, between genres, between specialists and lay persons, and between creators and recipients. This is, for Benjamin, the tendency of technological development *per se*. Tretyakov's art operations are mentioned in the lecture, for they demonstrate the direction of the development of art's new affinity with technology. The favoured forms include film, newspapers, radio and posters. Tretyakov's operative praxis is not formulated or comprehended within the terms of traditional aesthetics, such as rely on the traditions of particular genres. Rationalizing his fixing on Tretyakov, Benjamin writes:

> I have chosen the example of Tretyakov on purpose, in order to make you aware of how wide the horizon is, from which it is necessary to rethink ideas of form and genre in literature in the light of the technical conditions of our current situation, in order to attain those forms of expression that represent a starting point for contemporary literary energies.[16]

This was not just idle talk. In the years preceding the lecture, Benjamin had produced material for radio, amounting to an extensive body of work, both didactic and entertaining, and its intended audience was sometimes adult, sometimes young. The radio work was broadcast in the quite accessible media structures of Weimar Germany. Benjamin was convinced that radio produces new authors, new modes of communication and new audiences. 'Der Autor als Produzent' details Benjamin's own move out of the realm of critique into the realm of practice informed by theory. The circumstances of the lecture's production and intended reception indicate Benjamin's resolve to become more directly involved in open political debate and the promotion of recommendations for praxis. It was written for delivery at a Comintern educational institute.

In the sphere of political aesthetics, transforming the cultural and educational apparatus involves the organization of writers' workshops, artists' studios and staging popular theatre, as well as the active engagement of revolutionary intellectuals in literacy programmes and journalism. Benjamin sees the transformed role of the artistic producer realized in Tretyakov's work and also by the experimental wing of Soviet cinematographers. This process of recasting cultural forms occurs tendentially in recompositions in cultural formations in capitalist societies, brought about by developments in the forces of production and galvanized by the added impact of the market on art. The market has an impact for it acknowledges that technologically produced culture is viable, because it is profitable. The Soviet Union, however, with its new political system, is seen to speed up the 'logically consistent development of the means of production', by sanctioning and encouraging the development of a new set of relations of production for creative producers and consumers. Tasks are performed that were formerly not recognized as artistic. Culture is implicated in 'a huge process of recasting of literary forms'.[17] The merging of different orders of material, images and words for example, contests traditional segregations of form 'that hamper the production of the intelligentsia'.[18] Benjamin dramatizes this meltdown process in the lecture's confusion of forms of cultural production. He darts between photographs, novels, drama and film. Benjamin further complicates the historically developing realignment of the division of intellectual labour by exhorting critics to become photomontagists, authors to become critics, critics to become authors, practitioners to become theorists and theorists practitioners. The destruction of inherited artistic forms throws up new cultural forms in which workers participate directly, such as worker-newspapers or agit-prop films. Through a combination of new technological capacities and social recompositions, workers are able to engage in self-representation.

Curiously, Benjamin points to progressive tendencies in the Soviet Union at the same time as the official aesthetic position emanating from there rested on a popular frontist, class collaborationist rehabilitation of pre-revolutionary cultural models. Benjamin is perhaps, tactically, thrusting under the noses of Paris-based communists a memory of what was rapidly becoming repressed. Quoting himself, an anonymous 'author of the left', Benjamin diagnoses a 'literarization of living conditions' in the chaotic multiplication of literary copy brought about by technological development. In a dialectical twist the place where the word is most 'debased', the newspaper, is shown by certain Soviet practices to be the place in which it is redeemed, through an interchange between cultural producers and consumers which converts words into effective means of communication for workers.[19] New modes of communication initiate new forms of reception, once cultural production is demasked of its 'culinary character'.[20] Benjamin envisages a variety of cultural forms that extort new modes of reception. They insist on a labour of interpretation. New tasks for audiences coincide with what Benjamin terms the 'logically consistent development of political tendencies in the proletariat' (*'die folgerechte Entwicklung der politischen Tendenzen im Proletariat'*), and these lead it increasingly to claim and reform the means of production 'for its own purposes'.[21] These purposes coincide with the 'logically consistent development of the means of production' that is discernible under conditions of unfettered development. The logic of unfettered development, anticipated under capitalism only in the realm of art, turns worker-producers into authors, creative co-participants in the articulation of texts. This element of co-participation, made possible by, variously, technology and technique, determines the revolutionary status of a cultural object. He lashes out against a recent German intellectual fashion. The new objectivists, contends Benjamin, had claimed to want to destroy capitalist relations of production, but they had functioned as counter-revolutionaries because of their refusal to regard the relationship of the author to *Technik* politically. Benjamin's critical revolutionary art practice is not satisfied simply with using technology to produce art. The new objectivists use photographic technology to counter-revolutionary effect, through participation in the market-friendly logic of fashion and empathy. Crucial to Benjamin's rejection of new objectivist photographic practice is his refusal of its passive model of reception, a model that ensures the potential of technological culture for representing conditions of existence is converted into political paralysis.[22] It dissuades its audiences from active critical engagement with cultural artefacts, misusing technology to elicit contemplative responses. It is ignorant of the task of facilitating the 'logically consistent development of the means of production' and the 'logically consistent development of political tendencies' in the proletariat. The question of politics in artworks is not one of the political authority of an artwork's content. Nor is the class nature of art to be traced back to the class origin of the producer, for Benjamin presupposes the possibility of 'betrayal' of the class of origin on the part of the intellectual.[23] In 'Der Autor als Produzent' this idea of betrayal is not an exhortation to political sympathy with the proletariat, in the manner of Alfred Döblin, but is given, rather, a prescribed operative form as revolutionary-technical procedure that interrogates the artwork's quality as a

learning model for workers.[24] Audience activation by worker-
newspapers is one form. But also licensed by Benjamin's interest
in an enabling art-dialectics might be something such as James
Joyce's accessing of the unconscious through technical innovation
and his processing of street debris in *Ulysses* (1922), an example of
a peculiarly democratic and demotic art.

One draft of the lecture cited Trotsky. The quotation was later
dropped. Benjamin bowed to pressure and subjected himself to
self-censorship: the order of the day. Trotsky's words had been
included to attack intellectuals who claimed to be above the
messiness of material political struggle, but who thought they could
somehow challenge fascism with the power of rational thought.
The doomed mock-internationalism of the League of Nations was
promoted by just such a group of enlightened pacifists who insisted
on the ability of reason to counter the propulsion towards war, and
were unable to recognize the futility of such appeals in the context
of imperialist capitalism. The communist critique of the 'insincerity
and hypocrisy of social-pacifism' of the League of Nations had
been broadcast in the 'Twenty-one Conditions for Affiliation to
the Third International', presented at the Second World Congress
of the Comintern in 1920. Benjamin was closer to this hardline
communist analysis of imperialism and militarism. He wrote:

> Or in Trotsky's words: When enlightened pacifists undertake to
> abolish war by means of rationalist arguments, they are simply
> ridiculous. When the armed masses start to take up the
> arguments of reason against war, however, this signifies the end
> of war.[25]

In a very real sense, war was not about to disappear suddenly
because intellectuals were pointing out its irrationality. Kurt
Hiller's activism is typified as an idealist conscience-communism
for intellectuals, and is refused because of its antipathy towards
designing cultural models that foreground authors as producers
and producers as both authors and audiences. Conscience-
communism relies on moral guidance by the intellectual elite.[26] It
easily translates into forms of art produced by a privileged few and
providing dollops of moral guidance from on high. For Benjamin,
properly political art is predominantly concerned with reception
effects, generated by modes of production that provide conditions
for consumers to become producers or authors of an artwork's
meaning. Artistic production must have the character of a model
able to introduce other producers to production, by placing an
'improved apparatus' at the disposal of authors and audience,
bringing audiences into contact with the production process,
turning readers or spectators into collaborators.[27] Authors and
audiences alike become producers. Connections can be made to

Benjamin's depiction in his dissertation from 1919 of the romantic conception of immanent critique. Romantic critique 'can bring about the unfolding, the germination of the work's immanent core'. The incomplete romantic art production is unfolded and completed by the ideal and interactive receiver, the producer of criticism.[28] Intellectuals who claim to identify with the fostering of class struggle are encouraged to consider their place as producers within the conflictive ground of forces and relations of production. Benjamin's argument drafts the demand to change the production apparatus in ways that promote revolutionary authors as 'engineers' of an apparatus, rather than suppliers.[29] This apparatus is then used by its public, rather than consumed. Benjamin directs a series of questions at revolutionary artists. Do they succeed in promoting the socialization of the intellectual means of production? Do they have recommendations for the refunctioning of the novel, the drama and the poem? Do they perceive ways of organizing intellectual workers in the production process?[30] The final question is crucial, because it states unambiguous criteria for judging the effectiveness of revolutionary intellectuals. It questions their adeptness at mobilizing the 'organizing function' of cultural products.[31]

Benjamin's language echoes Soviet politico-aesthetic terminology with its use of words such as engineer, apparatus, production, function and organization. It is not always identical in sentiment, however. For example, the notion of 'organizing function' refers to the relationship established between artwork and viewer. This usage is not strictly the same as that of Rodchenko, Filonov and other constructivist-productivists in the Soviet Union who, in the debates after 1924, use the term 'organization' to refer to the demand for central state administration in the arts. Benjamin's scientistic, productivist conception of organization hopes to hold open a space for workers' self-activity, not policy dictatorship from above. Organization in artworks, organization by artworks are attempts to cleave a political space for the practice-oriented dialogism of productivist aesthetics. Benjamin is influenced by Korsch's attack on any materialist epistemology, such as reflection theory, which acts to neutralize or eliminate the critical significance of Marx's theory of practice. Benjamin read Korsch's *Marxismus und Philosophie* at the end of 1930.[32] In the same year Brecht and Benjamin collaborated on the idea of producing a journal called *Krisis und Kritik*. Brecht's 'teacher of Marxism', Karl Korsch, is listed in notes on this unrealized project as a possible contributor.[33] Benjamin, like Brecht, is influenced by Korsch's conception of production as a transformative practice, a disruptive activity. This conception fuses with left formalism's sense of artistic experimentation as a previewed transformation of the real, or probationary transmutation of subjectivity in relation to the real.

'Refunctioning' ('*Umfunktionierung*') is the transformation of instruments of artistic production by a progressive intelligentsia. It is part of a process of considering, in a 'truly revolutionary way', relationships of producers, as well as consumers, to *Technik*.[34] Authors are asked to recognize the dynamic of the forces of production, technology, by an engagement with *Technik* as technique.

Benjamin hopes to make artworks accessible to 'immediate social, and therefore, materialist analysis'.[35] For him, a concern with *Technik* is by definition concerned with the material practice of art, its production and reception. Through stressing the materiality of artistic execution, Benjamin attempts to understand not just how art relates to the world of production, but how it is itself a form of production, in as much as it is a reproduction of the real that then becomes part of the world. Representations of elements of reality in Brechtian praxis, a prototype for Benjamin's own deliberations, are treated as if they were part of an experimental set-up whose claims to reproduce the real are tested.[36] In Brechtian drama the interruptions of montage counteract the illusion of a completed reality that can be passively consumed and complacently acknowledged by audiences. Passive consumption is seen to be the mode of reception effected by naturalist theatrical mechanisms.[37] Brecht's aesthetic system, in contrast, conveys conditions that are actively 'discovered' through their startling analogies to the real, but are only consciously recognizable and ready for reconstitution in the perplexing moment of their estrangement.

'Der Autor als Produzent' was designed as an intervention into contemporary debates on aesthetics and revolutionary politics. Official communist art theory, broadly sanctioned by the lecture's facilitators, the Communist Institute for the Study of Fascism, appeared unable to break with a languid paradigm of reflection of class interests in artworks, querying only whether artworks are reactionary or revolutionary in their subject matter. Rejecting the standard materialist standpoint, which he classifies as preoccupied with 'great' and 'vague' historical lines of development and the representation of progressive subject matter, Benjamin is interested in specific artworks and their context. Benjamin had suggested this in two versions of a review entitled 'Strenge Kunstwissenschaft', written in 1932 and 1933. Drawing on the theorist Sedlmayr, he posits that research in art history should reject a model of continuous waves of formal innovation, resulting in general highpoints and lowpoints of artistic creativity. Instead, the critic must spotlight 'the investigation of the single work', considered in conjunction with its moment of historical emergence.[38] As Sedlmayer puts it, each artefact is like a 'little world', and so, in a sense, all the world can be found again within each art fragment. And each is in the world. For Benjamin, specific artworks are seen to exist not in a vacuum but within a socio-historical formation, 'in living social connections'. In 'Der Autor als Produzent' he exclaims:

> For the dialectical treatment of this problem, and here I reach the actual subject of the piece, the rigid, isolated object: work, novel, book, is of no use whatsoever. It must place it in living social connections.[39]

And he is concerned with patterns of reception, the 'relations of production' that artworks imply.[40] The artist is a producer but not a proletarian. Benjamin reformulates the problematic in terms of the animated category of agency and not the dormant sociologistic statement of class. But, in effect, it is not only the artist who is a producer, but also the viewer, the consumer of culture. A stance that considers the mode of reception as central to the question of the political nature of art contrasts with those theses on committed art that assume reception is not a theoretical issue and, consequently, that the factors, 'political commitment', technique and literary 'quality' have no dialectical relationship to one another.[41] In laying out his exercise in aesthetic criticism as scientific experiment, Benjamin hopes to prove that a proper debate on political literary criticism proceeds from completely different premises. He re-envisages the interrelationship between commitment and quality. Tretyakov has a comparable approach. He uses terms such as 'socioaesthetic tendency' – but, for Tretyakov, the enemy is custom, everyday life, preventing the shake-up of the psyche, the release of energy, the readiness to be equipped for new tasks and relations. Benjamin matches Tretyakov's rejection of the fundamentally undialectical opposition between form and content of an artwork.[42] For Benjamin, 'quality' or literary correctness, no longer defined as a qualification of aesthetic genius, is specified as a feature dependent on 'political tendency'. A political tendency that is 'correct' includes a literary tendency that is 'correct'. Literary tendency is disclosed as consisting 'in a progressive development of literary *Technik* or a regressive one'.[43] He explains the term 'progressive' later in the lecture as any act that is 'interested in the liberation of the means of production'.[44] In Benjamin's account, the progressive development of literary *Technik* or productive forces in art is a process that enables new relations of production and consumption. These new relations are innate, but impeded in new technological forms. Form is a social category. Benjamin's assessment of *Technik* in art is not a formalist argument about the renovation of the laws and forms of art, but connects with the place of *Technik* in the

social world. This is the key political significance of Benjamin's
Technik-Begriff, where *Technik* in art and technical experimentation gain directly efficacious roles. Benjamin's political cultural
recommendations attempt to compensate for deficiencies in the
social organization of *Technik*. Through the practice – that is,
production and reception – of art, relations of production and
consumption unfold, just as they unfold in the transition to
communism. By employing new forms of production in the
aesthetic realm, practice runs in new patterns of social existence can
be implemented. These patterns of social existence rely on the
mobilization of the elective affinity between technology and
humanity, and art is the realm where this elective affinity can be
played out. Political art permits the possibility of interacting
'adequately' with the forces of production, by offering a prefigurative training in relations of production that are potential in
technologies. Tretyakov's revolutionary-constructivism is similar in
that it considers form from the perspective of its social 'function'.
The revolutionizing of techniques coincides with revolutionizing of
reality and liberation into self-consciously organized production.
New forms lead to new ways of perception and thus to new
cognitions. A political tendency is thus unable to be severed from
technological and technical experimentation. This experimentation plays a role in emancipating the means of production by acting
as a training-ground in new modes of interaction between technologies and humans.

Fetishism and Realism

> Where does the boundary run between reality and appearance
> in the new?
>
> Notes for the 1935 *Exposé*[45]

Benjamin's aesthetic in 'Der Autor als Produzent' recommends
that artists should not assume the political progressiveness of a
reflection of appearances, be that the bald and glossy photographic
realism of new objectivity, or the reflection theory aesthetic
recommended by policy-makers in the communist parties, state-
sanctioned in 1934, and transmitted through the Comintern to
the international sections. Accompanying the reflection-aesthetic
is the disingenuous contention that the social reality so pictured is
a charmed one. Benjamin perceives a restorative, reactionary bias
in the new *Kulturpolitik* in the Stalinized Soviet Union. This new
Stalino-cultural politics demands reflection in artistic content of
social contents (that is, classes and class relations). In Stalinist
Russia the artist officially receives the classification engineer: 'the
engineer of human souls'.[46] The appeal to heroic Realism marked

a return to cultural tradition. Cultural tradition denoted the heritage of the nineteenth century, and the work of its rightful descendants. It betokened the promotion of classical values of harmony, heroism and grandeur. Stalinist aesthetics roll back the discoveries of the technophilic revolutionary avant-garde of the early post-revolution years. Though it draws in part on an avant-garde language inspired by machinery and mechanics, socialist realism ranks the intelligibility of content above form, and its images are cloying and romanticized, showing rosy-cheeked, happy peasants as often as they show smoke-billowing factory chimneys. Such content-focused techno-fetishism differs in this respect from the avant-gardist strains preceding it. The avant-gardists generally avoid images of machinery and are engaged, rather, in exploring the formal use of technology for the process of artefact and image-production. Techno-fetishism was widespread in the 1930s. As Meyer Schapiro, a Trotskyite art critic, reported in 1937 in an essay on abstract art, it was not confined to the Soviet Union:

> With the approach of the crisis of the 1930s critics like Elie Faure called on painters to abandon their art and become engineers; and architects, in America as well as Europe, sensitive to the increasing economic pressure, though ignorant of its causes, identified architecture with engineering, denying the architect an aesthetic function. In these extreme views, which were shared by reformists of technocratic tendency, we can see the debacle of the optimistic machine-ideologies in modern culture. As production is curtailed and living standards reduced, art is renounced in the name of technical progress.[47]

But something else was occurring alongside this promotion of the engineer in the powerhouses of totalitarian Europe. Simultaneously and strangely, in the Soviet Union in the mid-1930s, in a Stalinist *Diktat* stranglehold, and in Germany, now gripped by Nazism, the nineteenth century appears to return. In Stalinist Russia and in Nazi Germany, a restoration of former bourgeois cultural forms and relations is instituted. In conformist response, European Communist Parties' cultural sections fall into line. Johannes Becher pre-empts the official line with his contributions for the German communist side in the early 1930s, beginning with a commentary titled 'Unsere Wendung'. This piece on the 'turn' in policy is published in *Die Linkskurve* in October 1931.[48] The article marks a 'turning point' in the approach to culture, heralding a return to traditional literary models and re-instituting the notion of eternal scales of aesthetic value. The 'turning point' referred to a turn towards realism, also known as 'Great Realism'. In 1934 there is a Soviet Writers' Congress at which Socialist Realism is officially launched, and Karl Radek champions the realist novel while castigating Joyce's 'cinematographic' approach to everyday life rather than 'big events'.[49] The former surrealist Louis Aragon propagates similar sentiments at the 'Conference for the Defence of Culture' in Paris in 1935.[50] Aragon takes over the editorship of a communist cultural journal *Commune*, and soon changes its name to *Pour la défense de la culture*. In May 1936 he calls for the liquidation of various agit-prop groups who promote the self-organization of cultural labour. In August 1936 Aragon's 'Realism, the Order of the Day' attacks Léger's eclectic use of cinema, wireless, montage and advertising techniques in his art. Typically the communist aestheticians flaunt nineteenth-century paragons of realist style. One passage in 'Der Autor als Produzent' insinuates that, in reality, fascist aesthetic recommendations most closely approximate communist directives to writers to imitate nineteenth-century realists.[51]

Benjamin rejects a mimetic realism of contents and any intention artlessly to apprehend and record the real. The photography file in the *Passagenwerk* and the section 'Daguerre oder die Panoramen' in the 1935 *Exposé* examine how the invention of photography issued a challenge to painting and art.[52] A new philosophy of progress in art evolves, bound to the idea of imitation of nature ('*Naturnachahmung*'), defined in terms of the achievement of realistic effects.[53] The panorama, a popular technological art-form, attempts to imitate nature perfectly by means of technical artifices that emulate the changing light of day or the gushing of waterfalls. Benjamin notes that the panoramas mimic reality so successfully that David urges students to make studies of nature from them.[54] The panoramic portrayal of deceptively life-like transformations in nature foreshadows photography and sound-film.[55] For Benjamin, the imitation of nature in art, a naturalism of surfaces and effects, is an art suitable for a class keen to mirror superficial social contents for contemplative consumption. With their intensified chimerical power, new technologies of reproduction can mediate the seemingly real in the guise of the objective. Benjamin notes how the discourses of photography and film often imply that such sheer imitations of the natural world equal truth. This view appears self-evident to a bourgeoisie eager for its own reproduction and desirous of a means of reproducing an image of the world whose authority is gained from its claim to represent things 'as they actually are'. The mirror theory of art, which appears to form the basis of the aesthetic practice of naturalism, proves itself to be without secure foundation, either mirroring too dully or too flatly, or mirroring only nothingness or everything, without end or discrimination.[56] Acceptance of such a blank equation of reflected and external reality is a product of a 'naïve realism', a registration of surface, upon whose 'bourgeois character' both Benjamin and Adorno are later agreed.[57]

Lukács was speculating on these matters in his work on the historical novel, written in the mid-1930s. For him, too, the development of photographic technology was coupled to dilemmas about realism for a bourgeoisie in crisis. The flatness of photographic images kills history. Their monotony eradicates three-dimensionality, the full-roundedness that he reveres. Their fake objectivity creeps into the naturalist novels' deadening descriptions of objects. But Lukács can see no way out of the challenge to art posed by photographic technology: the 'principle of the photographic authenticity of description and dialogue' can lead only to a fetishistic 'archaeologism' of strange modern objects.[58] He condemns photography irredeemably, and turns his back on it, ever on the pursuit of 'the real principles of art'. Though he acknowledges the sudden and forceful intrusion of technological images, Lukács is not concerned with further investigating how photographic images may formulate – visually, analytically and legitimately – a shift in social relations. And he certainly refuses to entertain the idea that photography may produce, *in nuce*, shifts in social relations. In contrast to this, Benjamin engages with the problem of photographic technology and hopes to be able to acknowledge this technical shift and its ramifications, and formulate a beyond.

One file of the *Passagenwerk* is devoted to mirrors and their place in industrial society.[59] Benjamin describes a popular fascination with looking glasses, lenses and image stimulation. Such ocular passion marks the second half of the nineteenth century when mirrors were incorporated into strangely named machineries of image-production: kaleidoscopes, phantasma-parastasias, phanoramas, stereoramas, cycloramas, kigoramas, myrioramas and the like.[60] Benjamin's attention to the fascination with mirrors, and the technological gadgetry of representation that incorporates them, is not exclusively a study of new forms of representation in themselves but is part of a wider debate on epistemology and relationships between self and world. In the 'Mirror file' Benjamin considers the ways in which mirrors are deployed in the arcades to expand space into infinity, in defiance of boundaries and as a distortion of dimensions, causing disorientation and deception.[61] Benjamin identifies the essentially destabilizing function of mirrors, citing their movement of endless duplication that can never be overcome.[62] Bedazzling nineteenth-century Paris is reflected in a thousand eyes and a thousand lenses, intensifying the blinding brightness of illumination effects in shop windows, cafés, bistros, reflective façades and the 'glassy smoothness of the asphalt on the roads', all of which act as screens, reflecting subjects back to themselves as objects. In meditations on Paris, dubbed the 'looking-glass city', the crowd itself becomes spectacle and the mass seems to be reflected back to itself as a body of commodity-fixated consumers and not producers.[63] These producers, alienated from objects of production, now enter into intricate processes of exchange. Window-screens reflect a glimpse of the self amongst endless commodity chains of finished products, with price tags, smiling beguilingly. Here the figure of the *flâneur* is germane; for he is a figure who, while strolling the streets, sees himself reflected in windows, in other consumers, and sees fulfilment of his desires promised by the commodities on display that beckon him. The *flâneur* has been construed as the ultimate consumer, or, at the very least, a window-shopper. The *flâneur* is an observer – of the market.[64] But, as writer or journalist, he is also a supplier for the market.[65] Benjamin notes how the intelligentsia came into the market place as *flâneurs*. They thought it was to observe it – but in reality it was to find a buyer for their writing.[66] *Flânerie* turns into journalism – the writer as word-hack, the artist as illustrator. The musings on the crowd, the reflections on urban seductions have to be translated into hard cash. The *flâneur* is a vision of every-person who sells his or her self, for he is implicated in all facets of the universality of exchange in commodity society. The *flâneur*, like the worker, is subjected to the penetration of social relations by the market. For the *flâneur*, and to his degraded modern relation, the consumer, window-shopping, just looking, the reflections in the shop windows reflect back only the surface and screen out actual relations of production, relations that have indeed ensnared them too, as they search for custom. Class relations of production lurk behind the patina of the looking glasses. They must be brought out.

Descriptions of industrialized Paris and its glassy streets and commodity bodies dispense images primed to incubate Benjamin's way of seeing. Benjamin distrusts the mirror – the reflection in shop windows of the streets – and suspects any assertion that seeing is believing. A formulation in a file in the *Passagenwerk* entitled 'Traumstadt und Traumhaus, Zukunftsträume, anthropologischer Nihilismus, Jung', rearticulates the relationship of base and super-structure, indicating that Benjamin's approach emerges from an attentive reading of Marx's base/superstructure paradigm:

> On the doctrine of the ideological superstructure. At first it appears as if Marx only wanted to establish a causal relation between the superstructure and the base. But even the observation that ideologies of the superstructure mirror relations falsely and distortedly points beyond this. The question is this: if the base determines the superstructure, in what might be termed the material of thought and experience, and this deter-

mination is not a simple mirroring, how – irrespective of the question of how it arises – should it then be characterized? As its expression. The superstructure is the expression of the base. The economic conditions, under which society exists, are expressed in the superstructure; just as an overfull stomach, although it causally conditions the sleeper's dream content, does not find therein its reflection but its expression.[67]

The metaphor is bodily this time, and ardently materialist – it speaks of appetite. Benjamin hopes that the term 'expression' ('*Ausdruck*') will avoid a simple causality and sever his materialism from a mechanistic reflection model. But, given Benjamin's insistence on the centrality of the forces of production, it is clear that he does not completely relinquish causality. The category '*Ausdruck*' allows for the familiar model of a base expressing itself in the superstructure. However, this is no simple reflectionism. Benjamin's idea of expression draws on the notion that there can be various modes of manifestation of an essential reality. It insists that no upended reflection of contents inheres in the superstructure, but rather a reflex determined by, yet not identical to, economic forms. This theory of a formal expression of the base in the superstructure militates against a political art practice rooted in direct reflection theory and combats an art criticism that takes the degree of meticulous and convincing surface reflection of social contents as its measure.

In *Die deutsche Ideologie* Marx mentions the camera obscura. The reference has been interpreted along the lines of reductive, mechanical materialism. It has been used as epistemological booty to bolster reflection theory. The camera obscura is a darkened chamber which captures events in the external world on a mirroring surface inside the instrument. The optical toy inverts the image. Metaphorically, the camera obscura proposes a base that determines and a superstructure whose illusory 'reflexes' and 'echoes' are directly determined. This posits an inverted relationship of reflection, a direct correspondence between object and representation.[68] Claiming authority from the camera obscura extract, various materialist analyses imply that social beings apprehend reality by receiving a topsy-turvy imprint in their minds of the economic substructure. The materialist philosopher capsizes the reflections of ideology to execute a representation that eludes the workings of ideology. Art practices based on this model of ideology could reasonably profess the supremacy of an aesthetic of reflection, resolute that it is possible to represent and know the real by upending apparent reality. The camera obscura metaphor tallies with the false consciousness thesis suggested in Benjamin's review of Kracauer. This presents the broadcasting of misinformation about the social structure as a case of ideological mismanagement by the owners of the means of mental production.[69] Art by and for the bourgeoisie is envisaged as an ideological conspiracy and the revolutionary artist need only inlay extant forms with true contents.

Benjamin turns to other specular inventions concerned with perceptual innovation. He scrutinizes phantasmagoria, photography and film and investigates their formal and aesthetic properties, in order to assemble other models of ideological discharge. The phantasmagoric machine, mentioned by Marx in his discussion of commodity fetishism in *Das Kapital*, is a nineteenth-century visual spectacle which projects a parade of ghostly figures before its spectators' eyes. It does this by inverting painted slides.[70] The origin of their convincing illusioning nestles not in subjective errors of perception – it is not the eye that deceives the viewer – but in the phenomenal form of reality presented. Such fantasies and illusions, such misappropriations of the real, as generated by the phantasmagoric machinery, rehearse how people perceive daily the contents of their social worlds. Benjamin alerts us to the ideological mystification inlaid within the economic structures of capitalism. It is an objective fact and not a wilful deception produced and disseminated by capitalists. Marx indicates as much in relation to fetishism. He says that, in capitalism, the labour of the individual is realized as an act of exchange between products, and so, for the producers, the relations connecting the labour of one producer with that of the rest appear, not as direct social relations between individuals at work, but as they really are, in fetishized form, as thing-like or material relations between persons and social relations between things.[71]

The *flâneur*'s female counterpart is the prostitute, who also has been quite ruthlessly inserted into commodity relations. The effects of such an insertion are multiple; providing the basis for a revolutionary change in family relations, as well as an involvement in an absolute and deathly exploitation. This is the contradictory, at once revolutionary-Futurist, then reactionary-restorative drive of capitalism. In Benjamin's Paris writings this contradiction is vividly imaged by the whore, who sells her sex by selling her body, the worker who sells labour-power, and the mannequin, a super-consumer who models on her body the constricting grip of the commodity. Women and girls especially model the congealed substances of the commodity – the attractive surface of capital. Modernity's time, according to its own chroniclers, is a time of repetition, repetition of the new in the guise of the ever same. For Benjamin, it is, above all, gamblers' time and girls' time, because both play it most compulsively, one obliged to presage the next winning move, the correct selection from a limited palette, the others hitched to its tempo as beat out by fashion, '*Mode*'. Fashion maps the time of modernity – as much publicized permanent change, the single eternal, but, in truth, more like a shuffling round of elements. Fashion in the *Passagenwerk* is never far from death; for what always changes is always expiring too. Fashion draws the girls deep into the material world of the inorganic-anatural,[72] turning women into explorers – as well as display vehicles – of a new continent of artifice. This continent is a realm of commodities, an enterprise zone of manufactured beauty, comprised of congealed commodity substances – cosmetics, permanent waves, hair tinting, adornments and gemstones.[73] Benjamin projects fashionable urban womanhood catching a glimpse of her self in reflective shop windows. Sometimes her self fuses with the unbending bodies of mannequins, whose appealing, commodity-draped forms commingle with her dream-ego, providing an unblemished role model. But, says Benjamin, because fashion beats out, of needs, a brisk and compulsive tempo, the fashionable girl's 'permanent efforts at beauty' are like a never-ceasing punishment meted out in hell: a Sisyphusean labour.[74] This appears corroborated by one glance at the Paris hairdresser Emile Long's monthly dispatches from the frontline of fashion from 1910 to 1920, from the 'Decline of the Turban Headdress' and Marcel Waving through chignons and postiche and 'The Ears Are Now Being Uncovered' to 'A Variety of Evening Coiffures to Counteract the Chinese Styles'. These missives were written for an English trade journal, and their dictation of trends appears to be a type of passive 'botanizing on the asphalt' to see what is in vogue, almost as if these phenomena were part of the natural world, while, at the same time, being good for business in its profitable engendering of this season's do's and don'ts.

Those who are constantly at pains to keep up are identified as more than types subjected to the capitalist tempo – theirs becomes rather an historicist practice – a frantic attempt to make history appear in an era without history, or an era in which all history appears as permanent reiteration. Fashions quote the past, past events, past fashions. This idea of quoting is glossed elsewhere in the *Passagenwerk* with the word 'resuscitation' (*Belebung*).[75] Fashion is a barometer of social actuality and an agent of ideology, though Benjamin also claims that its tuning into economic structures indicates that it may also be predictive. Fashions substitute for lost history, or unredeemed promises, in homogeneous, empty time. They replace the genuine experience of history, turning it into representation, a costume drama. The flip-side to this is Benjamin's observation that in Russia of the post-revolutionary years, a period that is chock-a-block with genuine and rapid transformation – rather than surface rearrangements – fashion can no longer keep pace.[76]

In the *Passagenwerk* Benjamin records how, through fashion, woman is dissected, fetishistically in actuality, symbolically in allegory. She becomes a thing-strewn landscape, historical because commodified.[77] Homicidal clues scar the commodity-body, now inorganic, consumed and humanly devalued. This is not a body that brings forth life, nor should it be in this technical life-world. The file 'Malerei, Jugenstil, Neuheit', 'Painting, Art Nouveau, Novelty', in Benjamin's *Passagenwerk* is headed by a quotation from the second part of Goethe's *Faust*, written in 1831: 'Old-fashioned procreation we declare to be vain folly.'[78] The line is spoken by Wagner, Faust's former student, stumbled upon by Mephistopheles in a medieval alchemist's chamber filled with cumbersome apparatus designed for various fantastic purposes. There Wagner is synthesizing a homunculus, a manikin, a little man, in a glass tube. Wagner makes new life – in this case it is particularly intelligent and sprightly life – without the intercession of woman. Life is to be made technically and rationally. Wagner continues with his incantation:

> The beasts may still enjoy that sort of thing,
> But human beings, with their splendid talents,
> Must henceforth have a higher, nobler source.
> Look there, a flash! – We now can really hope:
> If we compound the human substance
> By mixing many hundred substances
> The mixture is what matters – carefully
> And seal it tight with clay in a retort,
> Then re-distil it properly,
> Our secret labours will be finished
> It works! The moving mass grows clearer,
> And my conviction the more certain:
> What's been extolled as nature's mystery
> Can be investigated, if but Reason dare,
> And what she used to let be just organic
> We can produce by crystallizing.

The manikin, his first words 'is daddykins all right?', is the result of a fantastic synthesis of Enlightenment reason and medieval necromancy, indicating that even the new might be generated out of the assumedly superseded or past (which is something dear to Benjamin's concerns when he spoke, in his short history of photography of the difference between technology and magic as a thoroughly historical variable[79] and which might be another way of speaking about non-synchronicity in any time slice).[80] But Wagner's generation of new life is a spillover from the key motif in Goethe's play – Faust's pact with the devil, a transaction motivated by intoxication with the superbly productive powers of new knowledge and skills, acquired by whatever perilous means. The pact's context is more concrete than that of devilish bargaining; it is more broadly a reflection of the apparently bewitching productive powers of capital and technology. Marx cites Goethe's *Faust* in *Das Kapital*: 'money is now pregnant' – 'Geld hat Lieb' im Leib' 'Money begets money', so it would seem, when it turns into interest-bearing capital, and its investments in productive technologies yield yet more return. The message is clear: that which is dead can reproduce, as if by magic; the past arrested in congealed substance can issue in the future. There is a spatial analogue here too: what is buried can generate effects on the surface – as Mephistopheles shows in his plan to convert the exhausted Imperial land where he and Faust are guests, from gold currency to a paper money-based system. Once this is done they may develop productive forces in the coastal area, mobilizing the workforce and exploiting them massively. Lethargic wealth hidden under the ground – and only putative – is to become animate, released by the dynamism of capitalist development. The fluid of exchange is all; the material that backs it is as fugitive as value itself has become. Economics is never more clearly presented as alchemy – and alchemy is also what is involved in Wagner's cooking up of Paracelsus's recipe. But this is alchemy quickened by the novel energies of capitalist potency, and 'Old-fashioned procreation' – the natural way – is declared to be 'vain folly' when technologies of making the new anew present themselves. Of course, Mephistopheles is obliged to add: 'One who lives long will have seen much, and nothing here on earth is new for him.' Whatever the case, the upshot for mortals such as Wagner is: what use breeding, creation or procreation, when reproduction is better as a technological matter? This must indeed be a dream of things yet to come, as well as of times past. Wagner's lines are surely positioned there at the start of the file on 'Painting, Art Nouveau, Novelty' to pre-empt one of the motifs of *Jugendstil*, the new art, *art nouveau*, an art tendency separated from Goethe's *Faust* by a period of 70 years, which brought to Europe, and beyond, the 1848 revolutions, the retrenchment of reaction and advancing industrialization. The motif, phrased variously in the entries that follow in the bundle of notes and quotations, involves Jugendstil's curious relationship to pre-pubescence, the denial of fruition that is evident in its look and themes, its young girls, its hollow forms, its stylized, artificial flowers and sunbeam circles, aura-halos made metallic, its typical lines appearing like nerves on show, in turn a semblance of so many electrical wires. This look, these themes, Benjamin characterizes as a result of a curious and particular synthesis of technology and nature. The last theme indeed signalling the 'Cult of Nerves' of the *fin de siècle*, suffered by many among the sensitive middle classes, including Strindberg's second wife, and Benjamin shows it to be a projection of the newly discovered autonomic nervous system conceived as a border form between the world of the organism and that of technology.[81] Benjamin notes in the 'Painting, Jugendstil, Novelty' file that:

> The high point of the technical arrangement of the world lies in the liquidation of fertility. The ideal beauty of Jugendstil is represented by the frigid woman.[82]

Later, in the same file, Benjamin notes:

> On the motif of infertility in art nouveau: one thinks of conception as the least worthy style, the animalistic side of creation.[83]

The *art nouveau* woman, or girl – typically a girl carrying plucked flowers – whom Benjamin claims is to be found also in Nietzsche's 'Among Daughters of the Desert' in *Thus Spoke Zarathustra*[84] – appears pre-sexual, unfecund, in Jugendstil's artistic concoctions, which eschew any traditional association of womanhood with living and fertile nature. It is another version of Wagner's brewing of a new man in a glass vial, evading the natural physicality of procreation through manipulation of the magic of science. But its tone is more desperate, the more woefully appears the refusal of maturity and maternity in Jugendstil, youth style's projected fusion of adolescence, technology and technique. In Benjamin's eyes, Jugendstil is a rejoinder to various threats, albeit repressing those fears – most notably these are technology's imperilment of art, capital's disastrous assault on nature and technology's war-bound drive.

In the trends of realism, in the 1860s, there is an attempt to reconcile technology and art.[85] In this case, the artists were, for the first time, unsettled by the new procedures of reproductive technologies in art, and so, says Benjamin, they imitated its methods, devising, according to the photography historian Gisèle Freund, an impersonal attitude towards nature, whereby they insisted that the same scene could, or should, be painted ten times and identically.[86] Relaying an episode from Kafka's *The Trial*, Benjamin derides this Realist programme, and sets it in its place: an analogue vision of 'modernity'. Repetition characterizes modernity – and the new is fundamentally suspected to be another version of that which has already existed. In *The Trial*, the painter sells K. pictures of a landscape: 'Do you not want to see another picture that I might be able to sell you?' The painter pulls out from under the bed a pile of unframed pictures, all covered in dust. One is of a tree surrounded by dark grass and, in the background, a multi-coloured sunset. 'It's pretty', says K. and buys it. Immediately the painter pulls out what he calls a 'companion piece' – but it is, in fact, identical. K. says he will buy the two and hang them in his office. 'You like the motive' remarks the painter and pulls out yet another. K. buys a third, and on it goes until all of the identical landscapes have been foisted on him, for, says the painter, K. has revealed his taste to be that of one of those who like a sombre vista.[87] Once niched, the consumer will no longer be able to elude the biddings of the market and the confusion of a momentary desire with perpetual susceptibility. The consumer is now a target for the market, and prey for everything that is 'just in' or 'just out'.

Kafka's anecdote serves Benjamin to illustrate the spent creativity of art at a particular moment and its enslavement to technological compulsion. There is a particular moment when what Benjamin describes in *Zentralpark* as the 'paralysis of social fantasy' sets in.[88] Its first symptoms are quite clearly diagnosed by Benjamin, the onset coming quickly after 1848. They become only more evident retrospectively, the other side of war (Kafka's *The Trial* is written through the years of the Great War) and, in fact, rooting in the endless materials of the Paris archives, Benjamin amasses plenty of evidence to prove that nothing is more reiterated than the sense of this insensibility. The idea of the new, the next thing, as only endless repetition surfaces as itself a cliché informing modernity's temporality in general. The possible reproduction of reality (or saleable segments of its optical field) appears to mutate into the reduplication of events, the reproduction in reality itself. This sensibility is exposed in the first quotation of Benjamin's 'Painting, Jugendstil, Novelty' file. Maxime du Camp, the photographer and traveller, notes in his study of Paris, its organs, its functions and its life in the second half of the nineteenth century: 'History is like Janus, it has two faces: whether it regards the past or the present, it sees the same things.'[89] Du Camp, the discoverer of new continents and new worlds opened up by science and communications, fundamentally doubts whether there can be anything new in the world. Baudelaire dedicates a poem to him in *Les Fleurs du Mal* called 'Le Voyage' wherein a voice says:

We have seen the stars, waves, and also sand; And, despite shocks and unforeseen disasters, we were too often bored, the same as here.

And later the voice moans 'So much for what is news around the globe!' to which Baudelaire's rowdy closing riposte is:

Once we have burned out our brains, we can plunge into the abyss – Heaven or Hell, what matter – deep into the Unknown to find the *new*![90]

The new is not here on earth, but may be elsewhere, buried, latent, undiscovered, longed for but probably fatal. Some time after this 1861 outburst of worldly ennui and tragic sense of redundancy – defined by Benjamin as already a pre-emptive strike from a precocious analyst *against* the genre in formation[91] – the new art appears, again.

Art nouveau, Jugendstil is the second attempt of art to confront technology, says Benjamin. Its attraction to sterility turns out to be a thematic by-product of the renewed attempt to 'incorporate' technology into art. Jugendstil girls' infertility, their unreproductiveness, is matched by technology's evermore marked excessive productivity – most specifically noted in terms of technology's reproductive powers, but also in relation to technology's sheer presence in the environment. In a little piece called 'The ring of Saturn or something on ironwork' Benjamin presents the nineteenth century as a battle between new-fashioned architects, engineers essentially, happy to work with current technologies and scientific mathematical formula, and artist-architects of the old school who thought in terms of styles. As at the turn of the century the engineers triumphed, Benjamin notes a tendency, a reversal – 'the attempt to renew art by using the form-treasures of technology'.[92] Though it repressed the threat of technology as competitor and clutched more obviously at technical motives, it was no less motivated by fear of the threats that technology posed, particularly in the realm of reproduction. And so, we are told, it hoped to 'sterilize' technology by making it part of ornament.[93] Benjamin notes Jugendstil's obsession with the hollow form, mirrored in literature – the example cited is *Zarathustra* – by pauses.[94] This obsession with emptiness rather than plenitude is identified as a stylistic moment in ironwork and technical construction as much as in Jugendstil.[95] The new, new life, new form, new art, emerges not of woman, not of nature, not of organic bountifulness and not of a respect for technology's capabilities, but of the uncomfortable and unnatural coupling of sterilized and 'stylized' technology[96] and decrepit art, still clinging to its aura.[97] Benjamin couples *art nouveau* with Futurism, another 'reactionary attempt to dissolve technically conditioned forms from their functional context, turning them into natural constants'.[98] The new is a defensive reaction, a symptom; which means it is trapped in the skeleton of what went before, repeating somewhat the time duplicated in Kafka's anecdote[99] and manifest in myriad archived fragments, a time discerned as the underpinning of modernity, a 'time of hell'.

But, Benjamin tells us, in the time of modernity, the experience of time, of new and old, is uneven. Again we are returned to the synchronicity of the non-synchronous. The new and the old coincide in time – just as Marx observed that various modes of production coexist at once – and even what is new can retain its newness for a longer or shorter time, particularly if its usefulness is not spent. In the file on Baudelaire, in the *Passagenwerk*, Benjamin explains how fashion is always a masking; the self-proclaimed new is always conditional. He writes:

> For the materialist dialectician discontinuity is the regulative idea of tradition of the ruling classes (that is to say, primarily the bourgeoisie), continuity is the regulative idea of tradition for the oppressed (that is to say primarily the proletariat). The proletariat lives slower than the bourgeois class. The example of its fighters, the insights of its leaders do not age. Or in any case they age far more slowly than the epoch and the great figures of the bourgeois class. The waves of fashion break on the compact mass of the oppressed. In contrast to this the movements of the ruling class once it has achieved power have a fashionable streak. In particular the ideologies of the rulers are more changeable by nature than the ideas of the oppressed. For they have not only, like the ideas of the latter, to accommodate themselves to the particular social situation of struggle at the time, but also to misrepresent things as a fundamentally harmonious situation. This business can only be carried out eccentrically and haphazardly. It is in the fullest sense of the word 'modish'.[100]

This discontinuity is a rhythm of the ruling classes; girls and gamblers dance to their beat. Discontinuity, then, is the overriding feature of the new, as detailed by Benjamin, and as relayed by the many plotters of modern experience whose aperçus he collates. He quotes Georg Simmel's characterization of modern sensitivity, a sensation-seeking that cuts out the substantial middle, enjoying only beginnings and endings – Simmel's evidence includes the substitution of the cigar by the cigarette and the desire to travel often, sign of an addiction to departures and arrivals.[101] Or a fixation on what is in and what is out, what has value today and not tomorrow. Benjamin quotes Paul Valéry from 1935 on 'the absurd superstition of the *nouveau*'.[102] A modern fixation with 'sensation' – with novelty and its sudden shocking debasement – is instituted through the most banal of forms. Benjamin finds it significant that in the middle of the nineteenth century it becomes the case that, while a well-worn coin loses nothing of its value, a postmarked stamp is devalued. 'It is,' he supposes, 'the first sign of value whose validity is undetachable from its newness.' Further, he notes, the recognition of such value immediately coincides with its devaluation.[103] Value, far from being an eternal, has become a matter of a moment, and subject to cancellation and renewal. This new type of value might be linked to the increasing predominance of exchange-value.

The prostitute provides a 'dialectical image' of social relations in capitalism's hell time of stop–start and annulment. Benjamin discusses prostitution as aura-annihilating – an assault on mysteriously sourced value. The 'revolutionary character of *Technik*' presents itself in prostitution as an aura-annihilating symptom of the 'decay of love'. Mass society's forms of entertainment commodify desire. Economic fantasies are transmuted to the erotic sphere, reforged as the love of another who has been touched by the magic wand of monetary value and technical anti-nature. The desire for multiples becomes part of the sexual drive of the city inhabitant. Degraded love fixes sex and sexuality in an economic girdle. The love-illusions that drape romantic fictions of sexuality are exposed in prostitution.[104] It reveals. Prostitution shows sex denuded, disruptive of the myth of harmony at the core of love. Its blatant honesty rips apart the current unreasonableness of love between a woman and a man. The political economy of the prostituted body, accepting payment for love, exemplifies modern love's reality. A study of the mechanism of prostitution divulges knowledge of the alienated existence of humans. The performance takes place behind a veil of money. This weave of economics drapes itself like a thin metallic shield across the whorish body, glossing over the shame of the client. It stamps out in hard brass a symbol of fetishized relations.[105] The woman-for-sale is drawn and draws others into death; that is into relationships between things. The client identifies with the woman-as-thing, with exchange-value.[106] Such a relationship is exemplary of alienated social relations in capitalism. Marx makes this observation, in the Paris economic and philosophical manuscripts of 1844: 'Prostitution is only a *particular* expression of the *universal* prostitution of the *worker*, and since prostitution is a relationship which includes not only the prostituted but also the prostitutor – whose infamy is even greater – the capitalist is also included in this category.'[107] A new holy trinity: the pimp, the prostitute and the client. These three are just a particular form of capitalist, worker-commodity and consumer – admittedly one that most excites 'the sexual fantasies of the bourgeoisie'.[108] Prostitution conglomerates sexuality, commodity fetishism, labour and capitalism. Benjamin uses the whore as synedoche of the oppressed and as exemplary victim of exploitation and, so, a worker. The double commodity of the whore – as worker and ware – exposes a correlation between sex for money and the misery of toiling: both forms of prostitution.[109] Indeed, there is a general deterioration in the quality of sex as industrialism reveals itself as punishing force. Sex as work, sex for money, money and sex. The body and its pleasures suffer, as suggested in a comment in the *Passagenwerk*. Benjamin suggests that, with the Saint-Simonians, industrial labour appears in the light of the sex act. The idea of joy in work is conceived according to the image of the desire to procreate. Two decades later the relationship has been reversed: the sex act itself stands under the sign of such joylessness as crushes the industrial worker.[110]

Marx insisted that the fetishized experience of social relations is not incorrect, not an ideological delusion, but is a correct experience of a defective actuality. Circumstances appear to people 'as they really are'. Marxist criticism faces soberly the conditions of life as they appear to experience. It acknowledges the existence of reified relations, and then sets out to explain and overturn them. This suggests that ideological illusion about social commodity relations is a faithful perception of the self-representation of things.[111] The phantasmagoria illustrates this in its proposal that representations, rather than being upturned reflections of the objective world, are telecasts of the objective world's mediated expression in illusive form.

Marx wrote *Das Kapital* during a period when photographic equipment and optical machinery were inundating the market and implanting themselves in a burgeoning techno-culture industry. As these machines were fabricating enormous quantities of images, the signs of things appear to displace the things themselves. Oversized advertisements, stars of stage and screen – all these sign-things are fetishes, fetishes of fetishized commodities. All acquire an occult power over producers and consumers and are animate, larger than life, more animated than we, who, in relation to them, are mere things. To conceive seeing as believing, in this context, appears patently absurd – or rather ideological. Fetishism is actual, things are more animate and powerful than workers, but to stick with this point is to succumb to fetishism itself. The point, however, is criticism of that state of affairs – and so a return to the material relations of production in order to equip the word power with new meaning. So Marx suggests, the commodity object has no connection with the physical nature of the object itself. Seeing, Marx explains, is a physical relation between physical things, whereby light is really transmitted from one thing, an external object, to another thing, the eye.[112] But the perception that attaches to the commodity fetishized thing turns it such that the thing seen is in fact a screen that obscures the material process of the object's production. Marx describes the ordinary commodity as 'a mysterious thing'.[113] There is nothing stranger than this most banal form invested with theological caprices.[114] It is strange because 'there is no physical basis for its fetishized misapprehension. The peculiar character of the social labour that produces goods produces it'. That labour needs to be historicized in theory and structured anew in practice.

In the 1935 *Exposé* of the *Passagenwerk* Benjamin cites Marx's analysis of commodity fetishism. According to Benjamin, phantasmagoric commodity fetishism reaches its acme in the spectacular technological displays of the world exhibitions.[115] Here it seems as if things have more personality than their anonymous makers. From 1935 this new slant skews Benjamin's research for the *Passagenwerk*. In a letter to Gershom Scholem, written in May 1935, Benjamin argues that the project has found a solid theoretical underpinning in the Marxist theory of commodity fetishism. Increased contact with Brecht is one factor that accounts for Benjamin's deeper engagement with Marx's writings and the project's usage of a frankly Marxist terminology. A letter to Adorno, dated 31 May 1935, imparts the story of Benjamin's intellectual formation over the previous decade since beginning the *Passagenwerk*. First there had been Aragon and his *Paris Peasant*, and fellow arcade-fanatic Franz Hessel's endless conversations. Then had come hard debates with Adorno and Horkheimer, Gretel Adorno and Asja Lacis. These debates broke Benjamin from his romantic rhapsodizing. After this, there followed 'the decisive meeting with Brecht' and that brought with it 'the high point of all the aporias of this work', which Benjamin then confronted.[116] Scholem judged this decisive encounter with Brecht negatively. He labels the acquaintance 'disastrous', 'catastrophic'.[117] Adorno too feared Brecht's influence on the project. For Benjamin it brought into focus the theoretical challenges that he had to face. These challenges involved a productive wielding of Marxism and Marx's analytical tools, in full knowledge that some 'orthodox' Marxists would protest at his method.[118] And perhaps he was also aware that some other less orthodox radicals – his friends – would baulk too. So continues the inconvenient life of a perverse intellectual in a gruesome climate.

Mimesis

> Art should not be a mirror, but a hammer.
> Soviet constructivist group *Lef* [119]

Benjamin bids for a new understanding of mimetic practice in art. He insists that 'political' art conceive itself as reflecting social practices not social contents, and so switches to questions of agency and experience. Mimetic impulse intent on imitation is ill conceived because it engages in the futile venture of bridging the gap between image and object by cloning the object. In contrast, Benjamin's realism is not principally concerned with the representational relationship between sign and referent. His approach to mimesis has philosophical precedents. In the *Kritik der Urteilskraft* Kant makes a distinction between two types of imitation: '*nachfolgen*' and '*nachahmen*'. The first type of imitation is creative, the second merely reproductive.[120] Another precursor is Nietzsche, who recognizes two forms of mimesis. In addition to the reproductive function of imagination Nietzsche postulates a productive imagination. This works in coalition with judgement and he maligns a pathological form of mimesis with its undertones of dependency and forfeiture of self-motivation. Benjamin's realism no longer refers to an identity between *Scheinobjekt* in art and *Objekt* in the real, but extends to experience, activity and actuality.

Benjamin commends the incorporation into art of fragments of lived experience. These shards comprise art's 'authenticity'. Or rather they break with traditional notions of art and undercut representation by spurning representation in favour of the presentation of actuality. He favours art that risks emulating extant actual and potential modes of activity and experience in the world, covered by the category of 'testing'. Benjamin illustrates his argument with Dada, an initiator of montage practices. Advocates of socialist realism who discourage montage aesthetics scorn Dada. Attacks on montage techniques hit high pitch at the Soviet Writers' Congress in 1934. For Benjamin, the 'revolutionary strength of Dadaism' lies in its 'testing art for its authenticity' (*Authentizität*).[121] The same word was used in 'Kleine Geschichte der Photographie'. Benjamin uses the Latin-derived word *Authentizität* to underscore the indexicality of the photograph, its chemical fixing of a photic actuality, capturing a moment in time and exporting it into the future. The photograph brings objects closer for inspection, providing an imprint of the world.[122] It reveals traces of the objective modern world. In Dada, the public, confronted by framed fragments from the material world, learns that 'the smallest authentic fragment of everyday life says more than painting'. This authenticity rests on the incorporation into art of real-life fragments – cigarette stubs, cotton reels, bus tickets. His category of 'authenticity' enables him to champion Dada as a realistic art practice, because of its incorporation into art of fragments of reality: cigarette stubs, bus tickets, pieces of material, commodity labels, and so on.[123] Dada turns refuse into art, spilling out the everyday real into the sacred space of the aesthetic. Here, then, Benjamin grounds his modernist realism on the incorporation into art of real contents which form part of the actual material of experience. Montage and slogans counteract the limitations of a natural *Optik* through interference with the naturalistic surface of the image.[124] When Benjamin espouses the cause of Dada for its manipulation of scraps of rubbish and its immortalizing of the ephemeral, he urges that such remnants ripped from actual life act to retard momentarily, for the purposes of anti-art critique and interpretation, the swirl of commodity production and annihilation. A realism constituted from reality fragments is a critique of art's framing and of art's commodification. Rubbish made into art nods to its social human equivalent, the excluded *lumpen*. In a short, unpublished review from 1925, in defence of illustrated magazines, Benjamin had legitimated popular journals, calling this time not on their 'authenticity' but on their '*Aktualität*', 'actuality', 'topicality'. Their 'documentary character' consists in pandering to a type of metropolitan curiosity. The magazines incorporate various fragmented aspects of everyday life. Benjamin writes of them:

> To show things in the aura of their topicality is more worthwhile, is much more fruitful, even if indirectly, than showing off the rather, in the final analysis, petit bourgeois ideas of education for the masses.[125]

The magazines' photographic representations and passages of street talk render an actual metropolitan experience. This experience is significant and unpretentious.

Art is not absolutely autonomous from the social world, nor is it simply a class-determined reflection of the ideology of specific groups. For these reasons, the technique of montage is endowed with 'special, perhaps even total rights' as a progressive form.[126] Montage provides an example of a truly political art because it reflects the conditions of production themselves, mimicking the structure of the relationship of workers to the technologies that they operate and retracing the techniques of industrial production; but with an important proviso. Under capitalist relations of production, workers have no control over the products that they produce. Through the ingression of technology into art, the structure of production that is mimicked artistically gives back that option of control in the aesthetic realm. Montage is thus both a reflection of the real and a construction of potential.

Benjamin is particularly interested in film's relationship to the real. Film is an expressive mimetic medium which is formally adequate to a sense perception refurbished by industry. Benjamin is not so preoccupied with the iconic nature of film. He is attentive rather to the way that a shock-imbued, disjointed form of unconscious perception, habitual in modern daily processes of work and leisure, is duplicated by the conscious perception required by film. Benjamin correlates specifically the dislocating fractures of Taylorized work processes to the filmic principle. Routine to both the situations of work and the filmic principle is the flittering past of discontinuous images and objects in a continuous stream. Taylorized work practices and film are seen as products of a similar technological axiom.[127] The conjunction of technological equipment (film apparatus) and technical principle (montage) guarantees a certain type of structural mimetic capability; a mimesis of active, labouring being in the world.

Class, Technik, *Dreams*

> The rulers wish to secure their position with blood (police), with cunning (fashion), with magic (splendour).
>
> *Passagenwerk* (pre-1935)[128]

In a letter criticizing the 1935 *Exposé*, Adorno comments on Benjamin's over-valuation of machine technology and machines. He notes that this over-valuation has always been peculiar to bourgeois theories wherein 'the relations of production are concealed by an abstract reference to the means of production'.[129] But Benjamin's notes show Adorno's accusation to be misplaced. In notes for the 1935 *Exposé* Benjamin outlines the political dangers of technocracy in a remark connecting the infamous nineteenth-century technocrats to contemporary fascist stabilizers of the system.[130] The 1935 *Exposé* assaults the conceptions of the Saint-Simonians. The Saint-Simonians projected visions of the industrialization of the earth and the development of the world economy, but they ignored the factor of class struggle.[131] Benjamin understands the stakes of a one-sided technocratic promotion of the machine in isolation from social relations of production. His dialectic of the modern age criticizes precisely the unmediated identification of technological change with social improvement. Ideologies and propaganda surrounding the technologies of industrialism feign to eliminate class divisions. The world expositions, with their displays of machine technology and art, military canons and fashion, objects of business and pleasure, present a phantasmagoric politics whose basis is the identification of industrialization with progress. Industry and technology are presented as capable of bringing forth future peace and class harmony. In actual fact, those 'wish-symbols', the promises of industrialism, are turned into junk and rubble by the skewed development of the productive forces 'even before the monuments that had represented them had crumbled'.[132] In the *Passagenwerk* and the 1935 *Exposé*, Benjamin portrays Second Empire Paris as a prototype, the '*Ursprung*' of capitalist bourgeois civilization. The politically contemporary relevance of his historiography is found in that civilization's vanishing point in the here and now. Benjamin grasps back to the visioning of images of devastation uncovered in his work on seventeenth-century baroque tragedy. Baroque allegory mounts up images of ruins to lament ruefully the experience of failure and history's lack of achievement. Benjamin writes that it is Balzac who first speaks of the ruins of the bourgeoisie, and surrealism that first allows its gaze to wander uninhibitedly across the ruination that the capitalist development of the productive forces leaves in its wake.[133] The technological rationality that nurtures various systems of capitalist domination celebrates its first triumphs in the nineteenth century. This *'Zerstörungswerk'*, executed by Haussmann in his expansive boulevards – disadvantageous for street struggle – and metropolitan destruction for the benefits of the bourgeois class, is proof of the hellishness unleashed by capitalism's inhibition of the development of relations of production to match forces of production. Aesthetic-technical recommendations in 'Der Autor als Produzent' serve as an attempt to foreground the importance of consideration of the relations of production – the context of culture – while the 1935 *Exposé* and the *Passagenwerk* begin to analyse the political significance of technological 'wish symbols'. The Paris studies form a riposte history of the nineteenth century, a 'dialectical' Marxian re-narration of a 'fairytale', in which Sleeping Beauty is finally awoken from the nightmare sleep of capitalism's commodity phantasmagoria by the deafening alarm of class struggle. Benjamin's original title for the *Passagenwerk* was *Eine dialektische Feerie*, a dialectical fairytale, but this title was abandoned because of its impermissible lyricism.[134] But in these studies class struggle appears as phantasmagoria of dreamy tussles about the possibilities of *Technik* and its reception. Such fantasies of technical alternatives conjure up surrealism's games of city-sights conversions and urban bouleversement.

Technik as reflected in imagination bares a utopian countenance to the collective. Recognition of the potential ability of *Technik* 'to relieve the human lot' is inherent in the collective fantasy.[135] Wish-images and fantasies about bountiful usages of new technologies are contained in this collective fantasy. The products of technology are entrusted with latent utopian contents. In this context, Benjamin returns to the base superstructure question. In notes for the 1935 *Exposé* Benjamin remarks:

> The reflections of the base in the superstructure are inadequate, not because they have been consciously falsified by the ideologues of the ruling class, but because the new, in forming itself graphically, always combines its elements with those of the classless society. The collective unconscious plays a greater part here than the consciousness of the collective.[136]

In these notes Benjamin mobilizes the unconscious for his metaphor. And he wants to assert its role in political discourse, that is its relevance for political motivation and political desire. Harbouring ontogenetic and phylogenetic memories of a non-oppressive social arrangement, the collective unconscious provides the images of technical potential, traces of the configurations of utopia.[137] In the 1935 *Exposé* he writes instead of the 'collective consciousness', and expresses the compensatory role of this collective imaginary:

> In the collective consciousness images, in which the new is intermingled with the old, correspond to the form of the new means of production, which to begin with is still dominated, by old forms (Marx). These images are wish images, and in them the collective attempts to transcend as well as to transfigure the incompleteness of the social product and the deficiencies of the social order of production.[138]

The 'collective consciousness' strives, through conjuring up rhapsodic images, to compensate for underdevelopment of the social ordering of production. Benjamin refers in the *Passagenwerk* to Ernst Bloch's social utopian philosophy of the momentary, fleeting experience of a potential not-yet reality that can yet be glimpsed in the present. [139]

An entry in the 'Mirror file' of the *Passagenwerk* comments on connections between Freud's paradigm of the individual unconscious, replete with repressed sexual contents, and a consciousness of the collective with its 'repressed economic' contents.[140] Benjamin's reference to a 'collective consciousness' is stimulated not only by Freud, but also by Marx. The motto for 'file N' of the *Passagenwerk* is lifted from Marx's 1843 letter to Alfred Ruge:

> The reform of consciousness consists *entirely* in … arousing the world from its dream about itself.[141]

Marx insists on awakening the world from the dream. In 'Pariser Passagen' Benjamin repeats Marx's thesis about a bourgeoisie unable to come to consciousness and enmeshed in dreams or mystification about the social order.[142] But he is ambivalent about dismissing dreams entirely. Dreams may contain clues to the better order, or detail hopes and aspirations of the not-yet real but potential. It is not so much a question of awakening from the dream, but making the dream come true.

Adorno criticized Benjamin's concept of 'collective consciousness' as it appeared in the 1935 *Exposé*, claiming that it did not integrate a class moment. See, for example, this quote:

> Permit me here to risk an aperçu: that the Marxist objection against the constitution of such a collective consciousness as undialectical, i.e. does not contain in integrated form the class moment, probably coincides with another objection which I would pose quite differently: that is the demand that the

dialectical image may under no circumstances be transposed to consciousness or unconsciousness.[143]

But a class-inflected moment is integrated, albeit in indirect form. Benjamin desires to make conscious and make actual an inherent will to utopia through the release of the potential of technology. Technology must be made to work for social transformation rather than enforcing the soporific dream state. The bourgeoisie sustains the dream state by conserving the relations of production in which technology is entwined. These effect a fetishized relationship of subjects to objects. Benjamin tags the bourgeois collective, the sleeping, half-dreaming collective. The proletariat is caught up in the same 'collective consciousness' but, importantly, as a class it possesses the ability to revive collectively, through a realization of class-consciousness. This realization is coextensive with the actualization of the potential of *Technik*. Through class struggle, and spurred on by utopian investments, the proletariat strives, in an enactment of reciprocity, to harmonize with the designated patterns of relations of production mapped out by *Technik*. Fetishized 'collective consciousness', filled with the utopian dreams common to all classes, specifically dreams about technological and social utopias, is broken open only by the proletariat with its special relationship to *Technik*. This relationship endows it with the capacity to use technological media to realize the dreams.

CHAPTER 5

Murmurs from Darkest Europe

1934–38: Benjamin and the Unpopular Front

Exiled in Paris in 1934, Benjamin drafted 'Der Autor als Produzent' and continued to collect snippets for the *Passagenwerk*. That February there was turbulence on the streets. The political Right was especially clamorous in these riotous demonstrations. Battles on the Place de la Concorde on 6 February left 15 dead and well over 1,000 wounded.[1] The French parliament warned that a fascist putsch loomed. Benjamin watched events from his central Paris hotel room at the centre of the commotion. The rowdy events on the streets and the increasing authority of the fascists and royalists forced a unity on the French left, as they sought ways to resist the belligerent right. Until now, the official Communist Party policy had been one adapted to the 'third period', a concept that was product of ultra-left lunacy. In the third period social democrats were dismissed as social fascists, representing the 'moderate wing of fascism'.[2] Communist Party doctrine insisted that the third period acknowledged impending economic catastrophe, the precondition for revolution. The main enemy was social democratic 'social fascism', a promotion of the lie of reformism, seeding illusions, and so impeding the revolutionary development of the proletariat. The analyses of the third period and social fascism were first mooted in 1924 at the 5th Conference of the Comintern. They became part of official doctrine from 1928, once Stalin was firmly in control of the Comintern. Trotsky was critical of these concepts, insisting that total condemnation of the reformists split the working-class movement. He called for a united front of social democrats and communists.[3] Communist Party policy metamorphosed during the giddy early months of 1934. In France the call for a general strike in February brought the Communist Party-controlled trade union federation, the CGTU, together with the main trade union federation, the CGT. The Socialist Party and the Communist Party combined forces in a demonstration.[4] New alliances formed in response to fascism's European triumph. Though few would admit it, Trotsky's policy was – belatedly – adopted.

On 6 May 1934 Benjamin responded to a letter from his friend Scholem. Contemptuously, Scholem had contested Benjamin's commitment to the credo of communism. Benjamin's reply protests that a credo is the last thing to which his communism resorts, arguing that the practical affirmation of communism in his writings 'leaves the theory (the credo if you like) a much greater freedom than the Marxists suspect'.[5] Benjamin wishes to differentiate between the content of the terms Marxism and communism. Marxism is a body of orthodox theory, aligned to nineteenth-century social democracy and Comintern directives. Communism represents a praxis-oriented set of intellectual outlines for socio-economic critique and a paradigmatic space in which to think a presently unredeemed 'right' to control over intellectual means of production.[6] Benjamin's communist affiliation was rooted in his historical experience. His communist sympathies were distant from orthodox party conceptions. He describes communism as a 'lesser evil', in comparison to everything else that 'surrounds' them, and it is to be supported in its 'practical, fruitful form', but not in its dogmatic 'unpractical and sterile form'.[7] Perhaps Benjamin was impressed by the practical activity on the streets of Paris – the *de facto* alliance between socialist and communist trade unionists and militants, as yet unsanctioned by the dogma from Moscow. It was not until June 1934 that a united front agreement between socialists and communists in France was forged formally, overturning the Communist Party's third period-social fascist analysis.[8] In October 1934 the bloc of resistance swelled to include radicals, and, in July 1935, the policy of popular frontism was made official and sanctioned in Moscow.[9] So many class stand-offs turned into so many polite handshakes. According to the definition by Dimitrov and Togliatti, like a vanishing target, the conglomeration of capitalist interests that fascism represents contracted. This made possible an extremely broad cross-class coalition of anti-fascist elements in the anti-Hitler alliance. The Popular Front had a plastic concept of who could be allies, and an extremely concentrated idea of the enemy. Two hundred families of finance capitalists were perpetrating the Nazi nightmare. The popular front's programme vowed to fuse workers' demands with patriotic loyalty to the state. An impossible pact. In fact, it meant that class politics was out, national defence was in. Trotsky denounced the Popular Front in France as a betrayal of the French working class to imperialism.[10] The Popular Front slate won the 1936 elections. Soon afterwards strikes broke out in the city. Communist and socialist trade union officials and the Party leaderships refused to join the strikes and chose to make accords with anxious business leaders. By June, one and a half million workers were on strike. On 9 June Trotsky indicated that he was sure the French Revolution had begun.[11] Blum's Popular Front government seized the Trotskyist newspaper, *La Lutte Ouvrière*, which had published Trotsky's call for the establishment of revolutionary French soviets. The government alerted the *gardes mobiles*. Communist, socialist and radical leaders branded the strikes and factory occupations illegal actions. The wave of militancy waned as employers plotted their own offensive, encouraged by the government's initiatives against a militant working class.

Benjamin spurned the co-joining of communism and social democracy in an alliance with liberals. This pact served to double-cross the supporters of both communism and social democracy. He followed political developments in France, and noted his observations in correspondence, often in letters sent to his Christian communist friend, Fritz Lieb. In a letter to Lieb written in July 1937, after a radical-led government had taken over from the fallen socialist-led government, Benjamin writes:

> Hope for improvement is postponed; what, however, can't be put back are the rising prices. Do you remember the 14th July we spent together? How perceptive that disgruntlement which we then half dared to voice now seems. If you want to further expand your view of the politics of the popular front, then take a look in the French left press: they all cling solely to the fetish of the left majority, and they are not concerned that this majority executes a kind of politics which, if it were being done by the right, would provoke insurrections.[12]

Strikes and factory takeovers, led by the fascist Doriot movement during the following December, were evidence of confusion in French class politics. Benjamin blamed the confusion on the leadership of the working-class movement who spent their energies on smothering all possibilities of escalation. A letter to Lieb, written in San Remo at the end of December 1937, reasons that, over the past two years, the leadership had succeeded in robbing the workers of their elementary sense of instinctive action. It had destroyed their infallible sense of when and under what conditions a legal action must give way to an illegal one, and when an illegal action must become violent.[13]

1937 was the year in which claims to represent the people were travestied visually and spectacularly at the Great Universal Exhibition in Paris. At the grandiose spectacle of national splendour the pavilions of *völkisch* Hitler Germany and the people's Stalinist Soviet Union stood side by side, vying with each other for greater monumentality. Speer's *Deutsches Haus*, designed, according to the official 1937 guidebook, to reflect 'the strength and personality of the entire nation', was massive and fortress-like, and its gladiators and spread eagle stood for the Aryan ideal. Inside it flaunted signs of *völkisch* community and technological optimism refracted through Race, Blood and Spirit.[14] Boris Iofan's Soviet

Pavilion afforded a tall pedestal for Vera Mukhina's industrial worker and collective farm girl, holding aloft their hammer and sickle, and immobilizing in concrete and steel the onward march of the Soviet populace. The word 'people' was on the lips of leaders in the 1930s. The people, according to Hitler, drew sustenance from ideas of national and racial community, a supersession of class antagonism in the nation of one race. Similarly, the Soviet people, according to Stalin, were living in a country where class struggle had been decreed a thing of the past. Artists and writers formed a cadre in the service of the 'people' (kulaks and dissidents excluded). And the citizens of the European Popular Front were to be nourished by a national-bourgeois vision of the populace, embodied in the cult of the Great Revolution. The Popular Front in France, each 14 July for three years, championed the 'great' bourgeois revolution of 1789.

A fortnight after the election of the Popular Front government in France in July 1936, the Spanish Civil War began. By 2 August Blum had hatched a plan of non-intervention, despite the Spanish republican government's urgent request for aeroplanes and *matériel*. In Spain the Popular Front policy meant the subordination of the proletariat to the Spanish bourgeoisie. It eventually led to the liquidation of militants.[15] The war ended in the victory of Franco's fascist troops in 1939. Victor Serge, in *Memoirs of a Revolutionary 1901–1941*, relates how the outcome of the Spanish collapse provoked a catastrophic moral collapse in France, as the state and its organs repelled and insulted the dispossessed Spanish refugees. Many were interned in concentration camps, while the bedraggled, bewildered partisans of the left, according to Serge, did little to help.[16]

On the other side of Europe the Nazis were annexing Austria. A laurel-crowned Hitler entered Vienna in the middle of March 1938. This was an easily executed invasion and the first episode of *Gleichschaltung*. The subsequent plebiscite in Germany and Austria gave the Nazis more than 99 per cent of the vote. Foreign governments voiced little opposition.[17] Benjamin's letter to Karl Thieme in March 1938, taking note of events in Austria and Spain, voices despondency:

> As far as I am concerned, I can hardly conceive any longer of suffering or death still making sense. What seems terrible to me, in the case of both Austria and Spain, is that the martyrdom is endured not for the actual cause itself but rather for a compromise proposal, be it the compromise of Austria's precious ethnic culture with a despicable economy and state, or that of revolutionary thought in Spain with the Machiavellianism of the Russian leadership and the mammonism of the local leadership.[18]

Leadership in these dismal European days is corrupt and compromising. Perhaps Benjamin foresaw the Ribbentrop–Molotov pact between the Soviet Union and Nazi Germany, sealed in August 1939. There are no alliances that cannot be forged – except for the right ones.

Eavesdropping in Brecht's House

At Brecht's homes in exile in northern Europe Benjamin transcribed his conversations with the playwright. These exchanges chronicle a shared interest in the retrogression of the Soviet workers' state. They quip grimly about the state that refuses to wither away.[19] On 24 July 1938, Brecht shows Benjamin a poem. It was called 'Der Bauer an seinen Ochsen'. The poem is a coded death ode to Stalin, but Stalin is not yet dead. Benjamin writes:

> Brecht, by the way, is not prepared to offer a more enthusiastic form of honour; he says he's sitting in exile and waiting for the Red Army. He follows the Russian developments; and Trotsky's writings as well. They prove that there is cause for suspicion; a justifiable suspicion, which demands a skeptical consideration of Russian affairs. Such a skepticism stands in the tradition of the classical writers. Should it be proven one day, one would have to fight the regime – publicly. But unfortunately or thank god, as you will, this suspicion is not yet a certainty. To derive such a politics from this situation as the Trotskyists do would be unfounded. That, on the other hand, in Russia itself, certain criminal cliques are at work, is not to be doubted. One can see it from time to time in their misdeeds.[20]

Suspicion is the motto of this period of purges. The factions are forming, but whom do they represent? Benjamin and Brecht monitor the Marxist cultural theory emerging from the Soviet Union or voiced by its fellow travellers. But discussion of literary theory and aesthetics is briskly deflected into discussions of cultural policy and then discussions of politics in general. In late July 1938 Benjamin records:

> The publications of Lukács, Kurella et al. are giving Brecht a good deal of trouble. He thinks, however, that one ought not to oppose them at the theoretical level. I then put the question on the political level. His formulations pull no punches there either. A socialist economy does not need war and that is why it cannot tolerate war. The peace-loving nature of the Russian people is an expression of this and nothing else. There cannot be a socialist economy in one country. Rearmament has inevitably set the proletariat back a lot, back to stages of historical development that have long since been overtaken. Among others the

monarchic stage. Russia is now under personal rule. Of course only blockheads can deny this.[21]

And, a few days later, again of Lukács, Gabor and Kurella, the leading communist literary critics: 'With these people,' comments Benjamin, 'no state can be formed.' Benjamin transcribes Brecht's reply:

> Or *only* a state, but no communality. They are simply enemies of production. Production gives them the creeps. It cannot be trusted. It is unpredictable. One never knows what will come out of it. And they themselves do not want to produce. They want to play apparatchiks and control others. Each of their criticisms contains a threat.[22]

Brecht cuts to the quick, specifying the bureaucratic mind-casts of the Stalin-friendly hacks who defend the centralized control of industrial production as much as they dictate the forms and contents of cultural production. Self-activity scares them. Self-activity implies workers' activity. Autonomy unbalances the hoped-for sureties of the five-year plans, and disrupts the resumption of class society. In a conversation about the new novels in the Soviet Union, Benjamin admits that they no longer follow what is published because of the deterioration in literary quality. Cultural work has gone to ground in the Soviet Union. In revolutionary times, revolution infiltrated every literary question. Now there is no longer anything of aesthetic-technical interest. Bourgeois models are imitated; bureaucratic control insists that the only legitimate subject for art is hero-worship. Cultural production turns on a pinhead. In June 1938 Benjamin notes:

> Then we talk about poetry and the translations of Soviet Russian poetry from various languages that flood *Das Wort*. Brecht thinks that the authors over there have a hard time. It is seen as a deliberate provocation if in a poem the name Stalin does not appear.[23]

Benjamin and Brecht cautiously admit the defeat of the workers' movement. Their thoughts twist and turn as they acknowledge, then disavow, the magnitude of the failure. The reluctance to concede defeat is more perceptible on Brecht's part. In August 1938 Benjamin records Brecht's bet-hedging position:

> In Russia a dictatorship rules *over* the proletariat. We should avoid disassociating ourselves from this dictatorship for as long as it still does useful work for the proletariat – i.e. so long as it contributes towards a reconciliation between the proletariat and the peasantry, giving prime recognition to proletarian interests.[24]

A few days later Brecht labels the Soviet Union a 'workers' monarchy', and Benjamin 'compared this organism with certain grotesque gambles of nature such as are dredged up from the depths of the sea in the form of horned fish or other monsters'.[25]

In a letter to Gretel Adorno, written in July 1938, Benjamin chastised the intellectual poverty of Johannes Becher's party-line journal *Internationale Literatur*. He was appalled by the journal's equation of his work with Heidegger's philosophy, on the basis of an extract from an early piece of writing.[26] In the letter Benjamin confirmed Brecht's view that the theoretical line imposed by Russian cultural politics spells catastrophe for everything that they had been defending for the last 20 years.[27]

The evidence is incontrovertible. On 26 July 1938 Benjamin notes Brecht's comfortless verdict.

There can't be any doubt about it any longer: the struggle against ideology has become a new ideology.[28]

CHAPTER 6

The Work of Art in the Age of Unbearable Capitulation

The 'Artwork Essay': Three Different Versions

Initial notes for the essay 'Das Kunstwerk im Zeitalter seiner technischen Reproduzierbarkeit' were written in the autumn of 1935. The first version was completed at the close of 1935.[1] The second version was a partial and extended rewrite, completed in February 1936,[2] and contains material and various theoretical formulations excluded from the final version. The second version is the one on which Adorno based his critique in a letter dated 18 March 1936.[3] Pierre Klossowski translated the second version of the 'Artwork essay' in the spring of 1936, but he made of it a shorter French version called 'L'Oeuvre d'art à l'époque de sa reproduction mecanisée'.[4] The French translation, which appeared in the *Zeitschrift für Sozialforschung* in 1936, was without the first thesis and omitted other references to Marxism. Executing his task with the Institute's full backing, Brill, a supervisor allocated to Benjamin in Paris in order to prepare the piece for translation, had attempted to efface traces of Marxist theory from the second version of the essay. Brill cut the entire first thesis. This thesis set the 'programmatic work' within a Marxist framework. Much to Benjamin's dismay Brill insisted upon a number of other cuts. That something was at stake in the differences between the second German version and the French version might be discerned from the following event. In December 1936 Horkheimer tells Benjamin that Jay Leyda wants a German copy of the 'Artwork essay', so that he can translate it into English for the library of the Museum of Modern Art in New York. Horkheimer instructs Benjamin not to comply, in order to avoid the admission of differences between the German and French versions. Divulgence of discrepancies could lead to 'discussions'.[5] The differences are political. In the French version not only are references to Marx cut out, but also all topical political references and passages that divulge political positions. Horkheimer insists on the removal of lines that betray 'political allegiance' or use a 'politically topical formulation'.[6] Horkheimer introduces a new set of references. It is informed by liberal impulses, although at times this language coincides with

t discourse – references to fascism are substituted
:otalitarian states, all allusions to communism are
:ndorsement of 'constructive forces of humanity',
ire becomes modern warfare or modern war, the
:he present social order' is replaced by 'for a true
:onverted into expressions of American liberal pro-
)pular Frontist class collaboration, whatever the
 revolutionary language is expurgated. The essay
ilate 'revolutionary demands in the politics of art'
anu aisu tu represent a catalogue of political analyses with 'infor-
mational value for the French avant-garde'. Given this, Benjamin
argued that all the omissions, forced upon the text by the executive
at the *Institut der Sozialforschung*, had rendered the text incompre-
hensible.[7] Contrary to his protestations and insistence on the
critical, engaged character of the writings, Horkheimer's editorial
suggestions prised Benjamin's contributions away from leftist
political debate and direct political intervention, no doubt as a
genuflection to the exiled Institute's American hosts.[8] He writes:

> We must do everything within our power to preserve the journal
> as scientific organ from being drawn into political press
> discussions. This would represent a serious threat to our work
> in this and perhaps other areas.[9]

At every stage of its production the 'Artwork essay' is dogged
by miscellaneous battles over terminology and content. Conflicts
about Benjamin's work were habitual at the Institute. Very few of
his submissions appear in the *Zeitschrift für Sozialforschung* in their
originally intended form. In 1933, as a response to proposed
amendments to his essay 'Zum gegenwärtigen gesellschaftlichen
Standort des französischen Schriftstellers', Benjamin insinuates in
a letter to Scholem that his editors at the *Institut der Sozialforschung*
operate an editorial policy that butchers his work through deletions
and distortions. He compares the editors' proposed changes with
the advance of fascism in Europe.[10] Editorial interventions do not
end with the 'Artwork essay' débâcle. The next major work, 'Über
einige Motive bei Baudelaire' (1939), once it appeared in the
Zeitschrift für Sozialforschung, was subject to erasures. Eradicated
was the opening discussion of Marx's evaluation of professional
revolutionary conspirators in the 1840s, references to proletarian
struggles on the barricades and the politics of putschist Blanqui –
all elements that Benjamin had included in his original draft 'Das
Paris des Second Empire bei Baudelaire'.[11]

The third German version of 'Das Kunstwerk im Zeitalter seiner
technischen Reproduzierbarkeit' was begun during the translation
of the second version and was still described as a 'work-in-progress'
by Benjamin in 1938 and again in 1939.[12] The third version enjoys

a canonic status as the final, definitive version. The third version includes some material not previously used in the other two versions, notably references to Brecht's *Der Dreigroschenprozeß*, and a selection of quotations from Paul Valéry, Alexandre Arnoux, Rudolph Arnheim and Georges Duhamel. In some senses it might be said that the Brechtian elements are amplified, perhaps as an act of defiance against Adorno and his terror of Brecht's sun refusing to sink beneath exotic waters. But other formulations and ideas central to the second version disappeared.[13] It was this third version that was translated into English as 'The Work of Art in the Age of Mechanical Reproduction', and so gained widespread notoriety and inclusion in numerous art history and cultural theory compendia. Benjamin's title translates into English as 'The Work of Art in the Age of its Technical Reproducibility'. This literal translation may seem to suggest only elusive differences, but it implies conceptual parameters for any interpretation of the 'Artwork essay'. The wider idea of technological-technical, rather than the limited notion of mechanical, situates the essay more directly as part of Benjamin's ongoing investigation into the dialectic of *Technik*. The idea of reproducibility shifts the emphasis of the essay onto a study of the impact of reproduction on all forms of art and creative practice, once those technologies that make mass reproduction a possibility or potential have been developed.

In a letter to Werner Kraft, sent in late October 1935, Benjamin claims a unique status for the 'Artwork essay'. He describes it as an exemplary set of materialist axioms of art theory.[14] The essay, he insists, represents a formalization of conclusions reached during the course of ten years' engagement with materialist poetics. Organizing a new model for the discussion of cultural production and cultural analysis, the second version of the 'Artwork essay' establishes a number of categories, including 'first *Technik*' and 'second *Technik*', semblance ('*Schein*') and play ('*Spiel*'), which are seen to work together with further categories such as 'cult value' and 'exhibition value'. The loss or marginalization of the categories 'first *Technik*' and 'second *Technik*', semblance and play from the final version of the argument, disrupts its intricate dialectical-theoretical framework.

At the beginning of the series of theses on art and technology, Benjamin claims that the various formulations that he has introduced into art theory are unlike usual concepts in art discourse because they are unusable for fascism.[15] They are unusable for fascism because they unmask the ways in which fascism manufactures its confection of false representation. In the essay's epilogue Benjamin explains how the fascists use new technological art-forms. Technological art-forms have emerged because they are demanded by the newly proletarianized masses, who respond to the teleology of *Technik* and the development of the forces of production. Fascists participate in this aspect of technological modernity. Not for usage by fascists is Benjamin's critical breakdown of *Technik* into component parts, and the indication of various facets to *Technik*, facets that can be weighted and manipulated by practitioners. It is on this basis that Benjamin grounds a strategy for a critical political practice that utilizes technology in a 'truly revolutionary way', that is, in a way that reinvents the relations of aesthetic production.[16] Analytical scrutiny of *Technik* hopes to open up potential for a political-aesthetic strategy useful for the political left.

Actual Potential

Benjamin's letter to Horkheimer of 16 October 1935 places his theses on twentieth-century art in a continuum with his studies of nineteenth-century Paris. These studies trace the 'fate' of art in modernity.[17] The 'Artwork essay' tracks the 'vanishing point' of Benjamin's historical construction of the nineteenth century in the present moment. Outlining nineteenth-century cultural forms is not simply an historically reconstructive exercise, but a gesture towards explanation of what art has become, is becoming and might become for contemporary readers, 'for us'.[18] A remark on Marx's methodology in the opening thesis of the 'Artwork essay' notes that Marx goes back to the 'basic relations of the capitalist mode of production' ('*Grundverhältnisse der kapitalistischen Produktion*').[19] The phrasing suggests Marx's working out of the abstract laws of capitalism as they exist in basic form, but also the sense in which Marx is seen to map out an historically embryonic form of capitalism as it was originally, 'at its beginning'. In one phrase Benjamin intimates a methodology that broaches the fundamental composition of relations in the present, as well as the historical nature of the past. Marx is said to work out these 'basic relations' in order to give 'prognostic value' to speculations on future economic formations. Setting past, present and future in planarity, Benjamin assimilates Marx's method into his own intricately connected temporal telescopage. He interprets Marx's model as one that seeks information about the configuration of future production forces and relations in an analysis of present forces and relations. Benjamin's description of the temporality of his methodology in the letter to Werner Kraft employs the device of a telescope whose line of sight cuts through time to envisage a fantastic image of the previous century. This anticipates the way that modern astronomers study the origins of the cosmos by observing events at many light-years distance – an idea that returns us to the nineteenth century when photographers attempted to

photograph the stars.[20] Benjamin claims that his study depicts the
mirage of the nineteenth century, seen through a bloody fog, in a
future, liberated and non-magical condition.[21] This visioning of
the past in a future condition introduces a split between the actual
fate of art and the potential direction of art in the twentieth century.
The double reading of actual and potential developments in art is
contingent on the completed supersession of superstructural misalignment with the base. Intensifying exploitation of the proletariat,
through the siphoning off of surplus value from increased productivity, relies on maintaining exploitative relations of production.
Simultaneously, Benjamin assumes, the conditions for transcendence of class exploitation through the abolition of capitalism are
made possible by the collectivized development of production.

While working on the preliminary stages of the 'Artwork essay'
Benjamin began a study of the communist, and erotica enthusiast,
Eduard Fuchs. Here Benjamin remarked upon Fuchs' early
derivation of implications from the constellation of *Masse* and
Technik. Fuchs was a member of the illegal SPD in the late 1880s.
After opposing the war, he founded the Spartakusbund and the
KPD. Later he joined the KPD Opposition. He wrote various
cultural histories between 1905 and 1923, on caricature,
pornography and etiquette, amongst other things. In 'Eduard
Fuchs, der Sammler und der Historiker' (1934–37) Benjamin
insists that technology be seen as a product of history and not
purely a natural scientific factor. Positivism is a failed intellectual
project, according to Benjamin, because it is unable to understand
the importance of the social conditions of production in any
evaluation of technology.[22] The positivists recognize only the
progress of natural science, and not the regressions of society which
result from a capitalist organization of the social. Positivists are
oblivious to the destructive side of technological development,
signalled in the mushrooming fabrication, under exploitative
conditions, of fetish commodities and vicious weaponry. Benjamin
writes of the 'threshold' at the turn of the century. After this
threshold has been crossed the massive energies generated by the
development of technology become wholly destructive and used
most strikingly for the waging of war and the propaganda of war.
Technologies are used to speed up production and massively
multiply information in ways that, Benjamin claims, 'outstrip
human needs'.[23] This is a fact that the social democrats have been
unable to discern, let alone act upon politically. The demand for
a detailed specification of *Technik* carries over into 'Das Kunstwerk
im Zeitalter seiner technischen Reproduzierbarkeit'. In its epilogue
Benjamin reiterates the need to organize the relationship between
technical forms of production and social agents of production,
familiar from 'Theorien des deutschen Faschismus' (1930):

If the natural utilization of productive forces is impeded by the property system, the increase in technical devices, in speed and in sources of energy, will press for an unnatural utilization and this is found in war, whose destructivity is proof that society was not mature enough to make *Technik* its organ, that *Technik* was not well enough cultivated to master elemental social forces. Imperialist war is determined in its most monstrous features by the discrepancy between powerful means of production and their insufficient utilization in the production process (in other words, by unemployment and the lack of profit sources). *Imperialist war is the revolt of Technik. This recovers, in the form of human material, the claims to which society has denied its natural material.*[24]

In Nazi Germany technology is embraced in order to expand the productive base. At the same time, by ensuring the stabilization of the relations of production, partly through ideology and partly through physical violence and the dismantling of proletarian organizations, the Nazis negate the masses' 'right' to transform those property relations, the legal form of social relations.[25] The impediment of the 'natural' utilization of productive forces erupts in war. War is a diversion, a means to quash the material reality of class struggle by summoning supra-class goals. It is the only way that people can be mobilized not as classes but as masses, and the only way the advance of modern *Technik* can be contained without endangering property relations. This use of *Technik* sends further out of kilter any electively affinitive co-ordination between forces and relations of production. The opening section of the 'Artwork essay', indicating an intensifying pace of technological development, presupposes a discrepant relationship between forces and relations of production. A change in conditions of production makes itself noticeable in the cultural relations of production, subject, however, to a time-lag.

Artistic production is subject here to the same tensions as production in general. But Benjamin twists the specific Marxist category of exploitation into a more general concept of abuse or misuse. Marx too had written about the misuse ('*Mißbrauch*') of *Technik* in *Das Kapital*, and specifies such abuse as both the apprehension of the technical apparatus as a thing, and the use of *Technik* to generate decadent forms.[26] For Benjamin, there is an increasing 'abuse' of art, occasioned by the maintenance of conditions of production, supplemented by the opposing drive towards the self-abolition of art. A technological dynamic pushes for art's dissolution. Benjamin charts a dialectical development of art, depicted as both a possible and a necessary direction for art, in which a quantitative shift in the type of art being produced, due to new conditions of production, turns into a qualitative shift in the nature of art. One statement in a series of preliminary theses noted during the first stages of work on the 'Artwork essay' contends: 'The technical reproducibility of the artwork leads to its obsolescence.'[27]

The artworks favoured by the bourgeoisie abuse the inherent drive in art to be produced according to new concepts, or, rather, they abuse art's drive towards self-abolition and development into something other. Continuously relations of production institute a countervailing movement to keep art as art, ordered around traditional categories.[28] The superstructure tries to hold back and counter changes in the base, and so attempts to avert the abolition of art that has been facilitated by the changes in the relationship between producers and public. At that moment there were a number of Marxists debating the meaning of base and super-structure in relation to artistic production. Marx's draft introduction to his *Critique of Political Economy* had recently been made available. Max Raphael was one who pondered its implica-tions for art history and theory, and Benjamin was acquainted with his deliberations. Benjamin wanted new thoughts to match a new epoch. Contemporary artworks are conceived by critics and artists in terms of outmoded concepts, such as creativity and genius, eternal value and mystery, 'concepts whose uncontrolled (and at present almost uncontrollable) application leads to a processing of data in the fascist sense'.[29] The obliteration of art is repudiated by a fixing of capitalist relations of production in the art world and, specifically, the film industry. The political evaluation of the rela-tionship between classes and film cannot be possible before film has released itself from the chains of its capitalist exploitation. The capitalist film industry violates new social needs, as does fascism. See this passage:

> It is therefore valid both for film capital specifically and fascism in general that an undeniable need for a new social order is secretly exploited in the interests of a possessing minority. The expropriation of film capital is for that reason alone an urgent demand of the proletariat.[30]

Art's commodity status re-envelops 'emancipated' art and its 'shrinking aura' in fetishized notions of its conditions of production and disempowering modes of reception. The star cult, promoted by the capitalist entertainment industry through fan clubs and spectacles, conserves the magic and rotten shimmer of the artifi-cially boosted commodified star personality. Its complement, the cult of the public, a corrupt concept of mass or '*Volk*', attempts to substitute for class.[31] Charismatic stars and swooning masses are common to fascism and the capitalist entertainment industry. Fascist artworks, part of a continuum of artistic production under capitalist conditions, are used to legitimate 'exploitation' of the proletariat and art. They misuse the 'legitimate demands' of the proletariat, supplanting its political representation with its artistic representation. The idea of art, the *an sich* of art, is negated in the given reality of fascist dictatorship and its impact on social relations, including aesthetic ones.[32]

Benjamin is most interested in artworks that are situated at 'the crossing point of three lines of development'. These he designates as 'formed', due to their having kept in line with changes in the base.[33] 'Formed' artworks are anticipatory, allowing prognosis, because of their supreme sensitivity to the telos of *Technik* and, occasionally, they have pre-empted in art wider technological change. The telos works towards new modes of reception in art. Benjamin highlights the example of the Imperial Panorama moving-picture show, displayed to an amassed, though not yet collective, public. The panoramas of the nineteenth century were a popular art entertainment for the masses.[34] Inherited products of technologically and socially motivated staleness and untimeliness are blasted out of meaningfulness by new popular models lurking in the artificially lit alcoves of the city. 'Formed' art is responsive to the telos of *Technik* artistically, functioning as a testing ground for effects such as will be effortlessly executed in the future by new art techniques. Benjamin's example is the Dadaist attempt to generate certain effects on audiences at Dada events. These effects will later be achieved easily in Charlie Chaplin's films. 'Formed' art is responsive to the telos of *Technik* technologically, working out specific forms through artworks. The example given is automatic mutoscopes or photo-books, flicked by the thumb to produce a rapid succession of images. Such forms materialize as technological pre-emptings of the filmstrip. The technological forms that shadow the transfigurations opened up by artistic forms appear as part of a continuous entelechic unravelling. The illustrated newspaper, according to Benjamin, is virtually hidden in lithography. Sound film is hidden in photography.[35] The products of any present moment are contained in proto-form in preceding technologies. Future developments in art, human evolution and technology are predicted and almost realized in new forms.

Until the advent of technical reproduction, pictures had been made by hand, parallel to the manufacture of goods before the development of industrial machinery. Technical reproduction in art, beginning with woodcut technology, advances intermittently, but with accelerated intensity, until it reaches a qualitatively new stage in lithographic reproduction. Lithographic duplication allows for mass quantities and rapidly changing forms. The invention of photography induces a further speed-up effect, basing reproduction not on the pace of a hand that draws, but on the seeing eye and the machinery of the lens. Film is the culmination of a process that accelerates the activity of perception reproduction, such that it eventually occurs simultaneously with speech.[36] Drawing on Kracauer's film studies, Benjamin asserts that film's tendency drives at an ever more 'faithful' 'reproduction of reality', or 'the most exact reproduction of nature'.[37] In an essay written in 1936, 'Pariser Brief II', use in art is defined as that which aids an under-standing of reality.[38] He reports on the painter André Lhote, influenced by Cézanne and Cubism, who declares that every new *Technik* entails a new optics. New ways of seeing are necessitated by increasingly complex engagements with reality. For Benjamin, the photographic basis of cinematic representation offers a seemingly unmediated doubling of empirical reality through its iconically asserted surface resemblance. A more complete and swifter reproduction of the perceptual constituents of reality is achieved. Photography and film negate the idea of autonomy in art, because they are more and more directly determined by external reality. *L'art pour l'art*, a 'negative theology of pure art', contemporaneous to the first trials in photosensitive art-forms, is a reaction to the photographic threat to art. *L'art pour l'art* attempts to underscore the autonomy of the artist in the face of a crisis in autonomy claims for art.[39] Autonomy claims are threatened in another sense. Benjamin insists that the commodity status of art counters the appearance of artistic autonomy, because the artwork becomes inextricably reliant on the vicissitudes of the market.[40]

In film the artwork is technologically reproducible en masse, and the subject matter, reality, is also technologically reproducible. Benjamin's film theses parallel contemporary Marxist polemics on realism in art. Cultural policy in the Soviet Union insisted on artistic representation of what purported to be actual lived proletarian reality. Under Stalinism, realism is emerging as state-favoured aesthetic mode. Stalinist realism finds theoretical formulation in Andrei Zhdanov's pronouncements on socialist realism. Though the premium is on realism, Soviet socialist realism, given to be the accurate, naturalistic effect of reflection of the social world, exceeds the documentary demand by mirroring an invisible immanent tendency towards the unstoppable victory of the proletariat.[41] In the 'Artwork essay' Benjamin likewise stresses the importance of dense ties between artistic representa-tions and the matter of external reality. In contrast to the short history of photography, Benjamin is less anxious to counter the analogue in representation through recommendation of slogans and juxtaposition. But he is keen to negate the illusion of a direct correspondence between the real and its mediation by film. He stresses rather that film's mediation has the look of the real, but is in fact a second order reality.[42] Crucial to the filmic operation is that the filmic product appears to be a simple analogical reflection of reality. The masses are 'entitled' to this rendering of the real. This reflection constitutes the basis of their enjoyment of art. But there is a paradoxical trick. Playing film off against painting, Benjamin comments:

> *Thus, for the contemporary person, the filmic representation of reality is incomparably more significant, since it ensures an aspect of reality, which is free of all apparatuses, precisely because of the intensive permeation of reality by the apparatus. And that is what the contemporary person is entitled to ask from a work of art.*[43]

This reflection is already highly mediated by technology in a secret way. The secrecy lies in the fact that the various technologies of production are invisible once the film is projected. Film, especially sound film, at its moment of shooting, its moment of production, offers a perspective that has never before been conceivable. In the theatre, Benjamin contends, it is possible to conceive that what happens on the stage is an illusion. Unmediated human display is the obvious counterfeit. Film's relationship to illusion and reality is more complicated. At the moment of production the filmic process does not allow the spectator to adopt a viewing point that would exclude extraneous accessories such as lighting equipment and crew. At the moment of production the illusionary nature of the event is manifest, discounting an exceptional moment of technological and human harmonization when 'the position of the viewer's pupils coincide with the position of the recording apparatus'.[44] Later, when projected, film can appear as convincing illusion of reality – albeit a montaged, speedy reality that induces a spectating that is mobile. This is result of post-production. The illusion of reality is a second order manifestation, dependent on the re-intervention of technology.

> Its illusionary nature is a second order nature, a result of cutting. That means: *in the studio the apparatus has penetrated so deeply into reality that its pure aspect, freed from the alien substance of equipment, is the result of a special procedure, namely, shooting by a specially adjusted camera and montaging the shot together with other similar ones.* The equipment-free aspect of reality has become the most artificial; the vision of immediate reality has become a blue flower in the land of technology.[45]

Projected film relies on a secret technology that ensures, if the film-makers so desire, a continuity of lighting and reconstructed chronological time. Film appears persuasively as a completely unmediated objectivity because of its accurate surface recording of reality and because of the effect of gathering its resources for the construction of a realistic look. The complexity of the photographic artefact resides in its ability to mediate the hoax of presence, through its correspondence to external reality. A comment in the *Passagenwerk* points out the productive confusion between the lens and the objective fabrication of reality in art, whereby the presentation of the immediate is seen as a presentation of the actual. The invention of the lens sends artistic production into crisis.

> On the rise of photography – communication techniques decrease the informational merits of painting. And anyway a new reality is furnished, in the face of which no one can take on the responsibility of a personal position. The lens (objective) is appealed to. Painting, for its part, begins to emphasize colour.[46]

For Benjamin, photographic objectivity cuts two ways. The new technological means of representing external reality draw an authority from their copy relationship to the world that they reproduce as 'the image of a total reality'.[47] But Benjamin cautions that, in fact, the manufactured image of a total reality is 'smashed up' by formal means. Acknowledgement of this prevents the misunderstanding of film as flat reproduction of the real. Any aesthetic practice that remains content with an idea of the authority of reflection must be rejected, due to its inability to cut into the real, to jut into it, to interrupt its reproduction, or be cut by the real itself, in the way that bus tickets and cigarette butts introduce reality fragments into Dada art.

Not all film-makers aimed to project moving life-like pictures. Film cameras were developed to break down and cut up the movements of humans and animals, and used then to re-present those movements in continuous single frames. These experimenters, the inheritors of Eadweard Muybridge's horse-stepping dissecting gaze, were interested less in the fluid representation of movement and more in its analysis. Early film is frequently more concerned with the divisible, than the simply visible. Benjamin emphasizes this potential of film, the capacity for subjecting actuality to analysis. The ruination of physical laws, a devastation roamed over by the camera eye, provides raw material for analysis. An eye armed with a camera can 'test' the world.[48] It reveals unsuspected aspects of reality. Film manufactures the possibility of unsuspected representations of reality that are humanly accessed only by extreme modes of non-normal consciousness. Benjamin reiterates his surrealist approach to reality and draws film into the picture. In the two earlier versions of the 'Artwork essay' Benjamin locates objective camera vision in the actual subjective human perception of non-rational types, psychotics or dreamers. The amazing fact of film is that it makes an individual – idiosyncratic – perception into a collective, mass one:

For the manifold aspects that the recording apparatus can win from reality lie for the most part only outside a *normal* spectrum of sense perceptions. Many of the deformations and stereotypes, the transformations and catastrophes, open to detection by the world of optics in film, are actually found in psychosis, in hallucinations, in dreams. And so those methods of the camera are practices, thanks to which collective perception appropriates the individual ways of seeing of the psychotic or dreamer.[49]

It is not just a question of being able to analyse reality scientifically, but also of perceiving structures of reality in alternative ways. The strange visions of dreamers and psychotics are recreated in cinematic techniques. The fragmenting, allegorizing, destructive effect of cinematic devices tends to cut through the natural appearance of the everyday landscape like a surgical instrument, counteracting film's capacity to reflect the surface. Camera operators penetrate their apparatuses deep into the material of reality, executing a technologizing of the look, a dissection of the 'total'. Translated into aesthetic terms, this indicates a rejection of simple reflection theory in favour of a new way of representing actuality in its multiple potential modalities. The image becomes 'a multiply fragmented thing, whose parts reassemble themselves according to new laws'.[50] Montage, as avant-garde procedure, acts to eliminate the organic totalities of art categories. Organicism champions the inability to recognize the fact of construction. The montaged avant-garde work proclaims itself an artificial construct, an artefact that draws attention to the strange fact that it is made up of reality fragments. Writing at the same time his polemic on film, the former Dadaist, Hans Richter, extolled the way in which from the early days of cinematic recording:

> Everything that happens on earth has become more interesting and more significant than it ever was before. Our age demands the documented fact.[51]

But, at the same time, Richter propounded montage practice and technological intervention. His *Film Enemies of Today – Film Friends of Tomorrow*, written in 1929, construed film's basic nature as the deployment of the camera tricks of slow motion, speed-up, superimposition, lens distortion, animation.[52] Richter's kind of analytical practice is not the mainstream of film production and Benjamin is more concerned to speculate on popular cinema.[53] But all film relies on the technological principle of structuring through editing or montage. This is its thorough permeation by technology and the technical. This permeation necessitates its analytical attitude towards the construction of the real. Film is a synthesis of artificial, constructive procedures and organic resembling operations. Its synthetic nature makes it a perfect realm for the exercise of modernist realism.

In a fragment written in 1934 Benjamin describes how Dada, operating in the context of a perceived crisis of art, had 'stressed the authentic: combated the illusion'.[54] Negating illusion means in the case of Dada to incorporate, as part of art, the actual matter of social existence. In film everyday social matter, presented on screen and arranged through editing, is alienated from its normal positioning in life. In this act of estrangement film both negates the illusion of the real and represents external reality, extending the comprehension of actual scientific and social 'necessities that govern existence'.[55] Apart from depicting the realm of necessity which is intrinsically a part of the actual physical world, film also tests the limits, pushing back and exploding scientific and natural laws in a utopian gesture, proving that while film is bound up with representing the actual, it does not entirely relinquish the traditional artistic function of representing an ideal real. Film in its movements, twists of time and space, liberates perception through the dynamiting, dynamic power of the fractioned second.[56] Filmic technology mediates the experience of spatiality and temporality by attacking any seemingly natural re-presentation of space and time. Benjamin sees film as presenting a new cognitive potential. In the newly discovered celluloid continent of the 'optical unconscious', minutiae appear, amongst which it is possible, in the moment of viewing, to be free from all constraint. All those actual imprisoning interiors are blown apart by film's stretching of laws of physics and geography. Space and time and movements through space and time are elastic. The possibility of transformation is represented graphically on screen. As Benjamin indicates, in the second and third versions of the essay, using an insight from the film theorist Rudolf Arnheim, film's array of technical tricks allows the revelation of new structurations of material. For example, Arnheim points out, spinning out time technologically through slow motion does not simply slow down movements, but makes movements appear gliding and ethereal.[57] Montage in film, the normal filmic process of editing, reflects back to workers a view of the world as experienced by themselves, but also, simultaneously, a view of the world as malleable. Representation on film does not just mime the reified world. Film is mobilized as that realm where actual constraints are superseded. Film is politically significant, because potential realities are realized actually, but within the realm of representation. The new image world of the camera becomes a new play-space for humanity, authentic but also provisional and blatantly manipulated. Benjamin scissions the heart of the film into two parts: reflection and construction. Reflection refers to the actuality represented in film; construction is concerned with possibilities offered up by film.

Benjamin allocates three roles to film: film as authentic representation of surface reality; film as research tool, for the probing of invisible physical and scientific laws of the real; film as a medium through which to present potential and utopian transformations of current social and physical reality. Each of these angles is also considered in its relation to audiences, in terms of its 'educative value' ('*Lehrwert*') and 'consumption value' ('*Konsumwert*').[58]

The 'Artwork essay' speaks of art in relation to social function. The oldest artworks were made for ritual purposes and were believed by their users to be imbued with magic power. The function of objects that operate within ritual is bound up with their existence and not their visibility.[59] Accessibility to these ritual objects is restricted and their worth lies in their sheltering of mystical powers. The emancipation of the artwork from its ritual function leads to increasing opportunities for exhibition. Exhibition art is defined as author-fixated and it elicits contemplative responses. Artworks accrue new value through their ability to be exhibited to increasing numbers of people. People, alone or in small groups, stare at pictures by great artists in galleries. With the perfecting of reproductive techniques, art enters into crisis. A third category emerges – political art. Art based on politics denies authenticity, authorship and contemplative reception. Art grounded in politics does not conspire to disempower individuals or collectives. Politics, true politics, is the dialogic space between subjects and objects or individuals or collectives. Photographs and film are exemplary forms of political culture. They reverse art's traditional function, basing its 'praxis' on a structure that enables the possibility of collective human intervention in both production and reception. Films are not artworks in any traditional sense, Benjamin states, categorically. Through film, art can potentially end. Benjamin's assertion touches on Heine's extension of Hegel's analysis of 'the end of art'. Heine had demanded cognizance of a new relationship between art production, science and politics as part of his critical suspicion of idealism. Benjamin responds to this demand. A binary division within each block complements his sectioning of artistic production into ritual art, exhibited art and political art. This schism attributes shifting emphasis to a series of dialectical polarities at the core of artworks. The polarities are cult value and exhibition value and semblance ('*Schein*') and play ('*Spiel*').[60] The role and relative weighting of these polarities in any particular artwork determine the character of relations between producer and perceiver. Benjamin complicates the status of these polarities by pointing out that they do not function as mutually exclusive. This intricate structure of shifting and provisional values at the core of the artwork is necessary for Benjamin to keep in play a flexible approach to actual products of cultural activity within capitalist relations of production. The analysis of any artwork involves evaluating a play-off between its structuring values, cult value and exhibition value, and formal modes, semblance and play. To take one example: exhibited art has not entirely excluded cult value from its core and can summon up its fetishized characteristics under specific social circumstances.

In preference to the traditional idealist philosophical opposition between appearance and essence, Benjamin's core antagonism is between play and semblance. The second version of the 'Artwork essay' differentiates between traditional and technological art according to their relationship to these polar categories of semblance and play. Cult value 'pupates' within semblance. Semblance is bound up with auratic perception.[61] Benjamin summarizes idealist aesthetics' theoretical formulation of the conjoint existence of auratic perception and beautiful semblance ('*schöner Schein*'). He defines semblance in identical terms to aura; it offers up the presentation of a veiled artwork, enveloped in a shell or shroud. Semblance is connected to idealizing representations. In a note for the second version of the 'Artwork essay' Benjamin remarks:

Where it ceases to seem, it ceases to be beautiful.[62]

Semblance is countered by play. That Benjamin is well versed in the idea of play can be seen in his evocation of play, games and toys in various contexts, as well as in his frequent references to childhood and children's experience. He was also an avid collector of toys.[63] Semblance's retreat, equivalent to the shrivelling of aura, is compensated for by a gain in space for manoeuvre or playroom ('*Spielraum*').[64] Exhibition value counters semblance and begins opening up spaces for play around a de-auraticized relationship to the object. Semblance is further challenged by mass reproduction:

The widest room for play has been opened up in film. In film the moment of semblance has retreated completely to the advantage of the moment of play. Because of this, the positions that photography has gained in respect of cult value are now extremely secure.[65]

Film enacts art's dialectic of semblance and play, interplay of resembling reflection and playful construction. The moment of play dominates. Resemblance, in retreat in film, is not absolutely negated, because of the analogical basis of filmic recording. Film enables the constructed presentation of vast and previously unimagined spaces for manoeuvre and play in ideal and educative form, as it includes the possibility of alteration and provides provisional images of reality.[66] Film is not a medium for beautiful semblance, but utopian representations of a transformed real inhere in film's reliance on play and provisionality.

Reproductive techniques and the perceptual and reception strategies that they enforce start off the decay of cultic and auratic factors. The uniqueness of the ritual artwork is connected to its embedding in the context of tradition.[67] The definition of aura repeats virtually word for word the phrasing from 'Kleine Geschichte der Photographie'.[68] There Benjamin traced aura to the structure of production of early photographs. In early photography the photographer, immersed in a slow and difficult process, is more like a skilled artist, customarily producing unique prints. The discussion of aura in the context of the 'Artwork essay' once more revolves around the notion of uniqueness ('*Einmaligkeit*'). A secularized form of aura in the cult of beauty taints much art produced for exhibition. The definition of aura in 'Kleine Geschichte der Photographie' stipulates that the aura apparent in early photographs results from the authentic representation of the represented subject, a comfortable and confident bourgeoisie. It is a socially and technologically prompted physical haze on an artwork. Early photographs incorporate moments of individuality and authenticity, both auratic categories. Their character of reality as analogous representation of the real preserves individuality, the person, the moment photographed. Benjamin reiterates this point in the 'Artwork essay', affiliating the presentation of beauty to cultic, subjective investments in individual personalities on the part of the viewer.[69] But here aura is not a materialist description of an objective attribute, but rather a relational position, an attribute of perception, produced or denied by the interaction solicited between viewer and art object. This sense of aura, located as an attribute of an historically determined perception, is underscored by its definition as illusory appearance.[70] An artwork may be said to have an aura if it claims a unique status based less on its individual qualities than on its real or metaphorical distance from the viewer. The auratic artwork is not immediately accessible to perception, but hidden, removed from the viewer, distant and separate. This distance need not necessarily be a physical space between viewer and painting, but the creation of a psychological unapproachability. Auratic perception involves a response to an authority that has been claimed on the basis of the artwork's position within a tradition or in a social order. Auratic works emanate withdrawal and an unbridgeable absence, undetachable from ritual. Benjamin details both a technological basis of the contemporary decline of aura and a social basis of the contemporary decline of aura, related to the increasing growth of urban masses and the connected intensity of their movements.[71] But aura or auratic perception is not necessarily negated by photography if certain subject matters continue to be represented and if certain social relations continue to obtain. Aura is permanently in a position to reappear. Non-auratic photographs, such as those made by Atget, depict collective experience or social environments. The new politicized photographer sets out to produce the non-auratic. But, Benjamin points out, intention is not the only factor. Technological developments in themselves bear certain implications for aura, the reproduced object, producer and consumer. Photography, made mass and quick by technological progress, sheds the auratic envelope. The maker of a technologically produced image is no longer an artist, but rather a functionary who acts as a catalyst of a technical production process. A chemical process set off by a catalyst necessarily should produce non-auratic imagery.

Aura atrophies alongside social and technological change – not just advances in photographic science, but in concert with more general technological change. For example, Benjamin mentions that gas warfare is a new means of abolishing aura.[72] Like an out-evolved organ, aura 'withers away'. Aura's historical obsolescence is symptomatic of tradition's propulsion into crisis. But it is not automatic, and it is all too easy to generate a fake aura, unless efforts are made to counter this. The essay's images detail objects active-consciously prised from their shells, veils stripped away, smashed up aura. The rending of the veil is metaphorically the same activity as montage's disruption and tearing, sometimes quite literally, as, for example, in the case of Kurt Schwitters' 'Merz', a name procured by ripping strips from an advertisement for the Kommerz- und Privatbank.

Strictly, it is technology that releases the object from tradition. The reproduced artwork can be reproduced over time identically. Its historicity is continually remade. This is tantamount to a repudiation of history. Film signals 'destructively', 'cathartically', the liquidation of the traditional value of the cultural heritage.[73] Technical reproduction negates uniqueness, defined as the original and singular existence of the artwork in one place at one time. But these terms are anyway undercut. Uniqueness and its pendant genuineness, claims Benjamin, come into being only at that moment when they are faced by the copy and the fake. When historical testimony is jeopardized, the authority, the traditional weight of the object is affected. It is not solely the traceable historicity, a singular uniqueness that the print denies formally. Benjamin uses the example of history films to contend that history as content becomes homogenized and liquidated and embroiled in the logic of standardization and 'the sense of the equality of all things in the world'.[74] The reproduced artwork shatters tradition, but this shattering is a manifestation of wider socio-historical processes. It is a result of contemporary crises of political and economic organization and the formation of new political mass movements, equivalent to a 'renewal' of humanity.[75]

Benjamin's discussion and demotion of the value of tradition for a critical aesthetics is an oblique political intervention. To talk about tradition in art at this moment had particular significance for communists. In various programmatic statements on literary policy from 1930 onwards there were disputes about the appropriation of tradition – Brecht, Lukács, Ernst Ottwald all took part. Official communist literary politics was busy recuperating into the canon great artistic monuments created by a rising bourgeoisie. Benjamin is contemptuous of alliances with traditional culture and its representatives. Just such an alliance structured the popular frontist conception of art. The Popular Front strategy was based on class collaboration, and the assimilation of liberals into the ranks of communists. All men of good will, opposed to the extremism of fascism, were to join together, while, in the interests of a common front, patching up any differences between them. Famed individuals, notable artists and writers, had to be attracted, to lend well-bred weight to the movement. This meant recasting slogans and modifying the analysis of just who the enemy is. In order to attract grand intellectuals, flattery was necessary. Culture's value was reasserted by the communist parties, as they turned inwards to seek alliances, rather than to cleave class-wise. Through such nationally focused mobilization the communist parties tightened their grip on national political structures, and were able better to dispense with, by demoting, working-class militants who advanced class demands.

In a letter to Alfred Cohn, written in July 1935, Benjamin alludes to the Congress for the Defence of Culture, the popular front effort to bring together respectable, liberal bourgeois artists and Party members.[76] The conference celebrated the sealing of a mutual assistance pact between France and the Soviet Union. Prior to the conference André Breton had baulked at the idea of defending the abstract notion of 'culture'. It signified only the booty of the bourgeois enemy. And the alliance proposed by the conference brought together simply representatives of that enemy and defenders of the purges and trials of Soviet activists and intellectuals in Moscow. The surrealists sent a letter to the conference organizers, denouncing

> touching declarations such as those of André Malraux, Waldo Frank and Boris Pasternak – nothing but warmed-over platitudes, childish ideas, and boot-licking. Those who claim to be saving culture have chosen an unhealthy climate for their activities.[77]

Benjamin tells Cohn that he considered his meeting with Brecht the only pleasant one at this meeting designed to bring together anti-fascist intellectuals. Benjamin and friends, with their cultural formulations and intellectual suspicions, were stepping out of line. Their theoretical ventures were not wanted. In another letter to Alfred Cohn, written at the beginning of July 1936, Benjamin evoked the resistance to 'Das Kunstwerk im Zeitalter seiner technischen Reproduzierbarkeit' on the part of émigré writers who were members of the Communist Party.[78] Benjamin had presented ideas from the essay in lecture form. Writers in the audience who were party members, he notes, attempted to block debate, but then fell into silence. Benjamin attributes this behaviour to their instinct for self-preservation. The writers felt their own well-practised literary activity to be under attack, but Benjamin is confident that they were also not up to the debate. He also remarks that the founding of the journal *Das Wort* in Moscow led him to fear that literary policy for the Communist Party would consist in the promotion of belles-lettres.

Great Realism and great artists go hand in hand, writes Romain Rolland. Such a return or restoration of a bourgeois past was accompanied by the reconfiguration of the traditional division between author and public. Culture becomes a heritage and the artists and their administrators expect 'the people' to salvage it. Culture is expensive clutter evacuated and stored in museums. It is the past. It has value for it is special, unlike people. This is illustrated most startlingly by Picasso's message, in late December 1937, to the Second American Artists' Congress, a Popular Front beano. Picasso, the giant of European modern art, was lending his support to the Popular Front, and his statement to American artists made clear just who was expected to save what for whom and at what cost. The grand man of art intoned:

> I am sorry that I cannot speak to the American Artists' Congress in person, as was my wish, so that I might assure the artists of America, as director of the Prado Museum, that the democratic government of the Spanish Republic has taken all the necessary measures to protect the artistic treasures of Spain during this cruel and unjust war. While the rebel planes have dropped incendiary bombs on our museums, the people and the militia, at risk of their lives, have rescued the works of art and placed them in security. It is my wish at this time to remind you that I have always believed, and still believe, that artists who live and work with spiritual values cannot and should not remain indifferent to a conflict in which the highest values of humanity and civilization are at stake. No one can deny that this epic struggle for democracy will have enormous consequences for the vitality and strength of Spanish art. And this will be one of

the greatest conquests of the Spanish people. Convinced of our triumph, I take pleasure in greeting the American Democracy, as well as those present at this conference. Salud – Picasso speaking.[79]

The people were to prostrate themselves before national cultural legacies, perhaps sacrificing themselves to art in the process. All of this countered Benjamin's ideas of self-organization, of workers' participation in art, and of the reinvention of cultural practice.

'Das Kunstwerk im Zeitalter seiner technischen Reproduzierbarkeit' does not outline the shape of proletarian art after the seizure of power or in the classless society. Benjamin focuses rather on what is to be done now. Dismissing any interest in partisan affiliation at the level of content, and also any concern with setting up ahistorical models of literary value, Benjamin insists that to analyse the political significance of an artwork, its technical structure must be considered. Celluloid art is created with an eye to mass reproduction or reproducibility and conditions of large-scale distribution.[80] Photographic art fulfils the double criteria of being both reproducible and incorporating the fact of reproduction into its formal make-up. In technically reproduced art there is no longer a significant notion of an originality that is valued for its inviolate authenticity. The reproduction of an object on celluloid stands as a copy of itself, an object of mass reproduction, and no longer a unique representation. Benjamin discusses the effect of technological reproduction on the landscape. The mediated landscape possesses an odd quality of depreciated presence. This can be contrasted with Benjamin's example of the unmediated experience of nature as the experience of aura. Its quality of authentic and singular existence in one place at one time is disparaged.[81] Reproduction loses what Benjamin terms the quality of 'here and now'. Technical reproduction can put the copy of the original in multiple new contexts of reception. The copy is favoured over the original, because of its provisionality, its unfixedness from a singular existence and a limited access. Process copy reproduction can continually alter and improve upon the format of 'the original'.[82] Art as was can no longer be in the face of reproduction, and artistry moves from isolated and unique production to a sort of scientific production in front of a number of production experts. These experts intervene ('*eingreifen*') in the new artistic product.[83] This contrasts with Brecht's view of theatre as the realm of the ever improvable and dialogic. As such it is dissimilar to film. Film is fixed and immutable once made. Brecht focuses more precisely on the object than the object in production or reception. Audiences become experts, because they critically measure film against the daily reality that they experience and because they learn to assimilate new scenarios of potential social and physical ordering.

Benjamin claims that technologically reproduced art meets its viewer halfway, in a situation determined not by tradition but by the viewer. The viewer 'actualizes' the reproduced object. Responding to newly forced modes of reception the public is authorized. Contemplative and distanced observation is vetoed. Film negates distance, demanding a reception that is not a form of contemplative submersion in faraway, immutable events, but a more casual, 'distracted' mode. The ground of art is moved from a place of stasis ('*Standort*') to a place of action ('*Tatort*').[84] The masses are described as a matrix or womb out of which traditional behaviour towards artworks is reissued as newborn. These masses demand a bridging of distance between themselves and the objects they produce and consume. A passage from pre-1935 notes in the *Passagenwerk* formulates the importance of this 'bringing closer':

> On the political significance of film. Socialism would never have come into the world had one only wanted to enthuse the workers for a better regulation of things. Marx's understanding that they would be interested in a world in which they had it better and which appeared to them to be fair accounts for the strength and authority of the movement. But it is exactly the same with art. At no time, not even the most utopian moment, will it be possible to win the masses for a higher art, but only ever for one that is closer to them.[85]

It is not just the artwork that mutates, but also the relationship of viewer to artwork. The burgeoning quantities of proletarian culture-viewers have grown such that a critical mass is reached: quantity has transformed into quality.[86] For Benjamin, the mass appropriation of art is literally a manhandling of cultural products. The copy can be manipulated. It is 'tactile'. Exhibition, the ability to see and be seen, tactility, the ability to touch, are sensuous concepts that relate new art to the physical presence of the collective receiving body. Benjamin negates any idea of artistic autonomy in his version of art as embodiment of corporeal, material nature. His conception of aesthetics includes categories such as 'tactility' and shock – forces that act on the body. It is dislocated from a bodiless idealist aesthetic based on illusion, the imaginary and fictitiousness. Bourgeois idealist conceptions of art are wound into a narcissistic ideology that argues art is born from itself. Benjamin's approach reinterprets the ground of aesthetics sensuously. For Adorno, such a move is characteristic of Benjamin's behaviouristic anthropological materialism. Adorno labels it a positivism that takes its measure from the human body.[87] Locating sensuous perception as the root meaning of the Greek notion of '*aisthesis*', aesthetics and art are related to the development of the human sensorium, as well as existing in relation to the proximity of revolution and the re-innervated collective.[88] This idea is echoed in Marx's education of the senses through liberation. In the Paris economic and philosophical manuscripts of 1844 Marx discusses sensuous experience and its curbing under the rule of capital. The man who is starving, says Marx, knows no human form of food, only its abstract form. That is to say, he knows only its crude, restricted form. The man with worries has no fine sense for drama's represented traumas and joys. And 'the dealer in minerals sees only the commercial value, and not the beauty and peculiar nature of the minerals; he lacks a mineralogical sense'. The dealer in minerals sees only money, another hard, inhuman substance, when he views his jewels. But Marx insists that, in freedom, there will be a vision of jewels and minerals that discerns their beauty and their specificity truly and above all. The culinary sense, the aesthetic sense, the mineralogical sense, have all been restricted under capital's dominion. And yet they hold out a promise; the very notion of restriction implies a countervailing force that strives to realize itself. The stony monetary value of minerals coupled with their glorious aesthetic value – their pleasure for the eyes and joy to the touch – reside side-by-side in the object. Abstract – commodity – forms must be filled with sensuous, aesthetic, human meaning.[89] This meaning is a meaning for the senses five. The extent of corporeal delight is the measure of social, human liberation.

Benjamin's re-evaluation of '*aisthesis*' insists on tactility, the haptic, as part of the new techno-enhanced perception. In some sense the physico-spatial 'bringing closer' is a re-approximation and reformulation of pre-bourgeois folkloric spatial relations. Crucial to earlier epic tradition is a reliance on the proximity of a collective of listeners. Industrial capitalist relations erode the oral communicability of experience, but technical reproduction compensates for that change by instituting new potential for a familiarity between receivers and producers, once more in the form of collectivized experience: through mediated mass produced things, such as newspapers or films.

Technology and techniques broach the distance. Closeness, tactility, sensuousness are not to be interpreted as literal presence. In some ways, corporeal disappearance is precisely what is at stake in technological art. In the first two versions of the 'Artwork essay' Benjamin emphasizes the function of filmic reproduction as aesthetic expression of the alienation of self.[90] In all three versions of the essay he examines the role of the actor as depicted by Pirandello:

> The film actor, writes Pirandello, feels himself to be in exile. Exiled not only from the stage, but also from his own person.

With a dark uneasiness, he senses an inexplicable emptiness. It arises from the fact that his body becomes a cancelled manifestation, the fact that he evaporates and is robbed of his reality, his life, his voice and the noises caused by his moving about, in order to be transformed into a dumb image, flickering for a moment on the screen, and then disappearing into silence ... The small apparatus plays with his shadow in front of the audience; and he must content himself with playing in front of it.[91]

The film actor becomes a shadow on the screen, only eerily present in a transmission that occurs in a different time to real time. Actors become props and props become actors (people seem like things, things like people).[92] There is an uneasy loss of presence and embodiment involved in the translation of the person into a material object for film. This loss of the human, also a decline of aura, is paralleled by the presentation of an increasing consciousness of alienation in the world. The attempt to close distance between self and object is interpreted as both enabled by new technologies, but also as an ideal resolution of real contradictions. In notes for the 'Artwork essay' Benjamin writes how the 'passionate' inclination of contemporary masses to 'bring things closer' and bridge the distance between themselves and objects may be only the reverse side of the sense of an increasing alienation from things and from the self.[93] In this way, loss of aura becomes a precondition for political action, because it both signals and makes possible a clarified understanding of the alienated relationship of people to things and to themselves.

Film imprints on celluloid the alienated existences of humans. Simultaneous to the forfeiture of aura and the loss of presence of the 'here and now', a sense of a shattered totality of personality is promoted by the stage actor. At the level of production the film actor does not play a coherent role, but rather a disjointed series of fragments, a number of efforts and essays.[94] The camera operator stands in the same place as a supervisor who overlooks recruits in a factory or office. The film apparatus is structured similarly to the mechanism that supervises the work process daily. This mechanism is responsible for ensuring that the overwhelming majority of people working in offices and factories are 'alienated from their humanity'. In the evening the same masses go to the cinema to watch actors take revenge on the apparatus in their place, not only by asserting, in the face of the apparatus, their humanity (or what appears to the audience to be their humanity) but by making that apparatus serve the actors' own triumph.[95] Aesthetic practice carries the scars of human self-alienation. It is a remedial process, the 'curative alienation' of 'Kleine Geschichte der Photographie' (1931) reworked as filmic therapy:[96]

Through representation by the apparatus, the person's self-alienation has found a highly productive utilization.[97]

The rebirth of the new collective technoid body emerges out of the complete self-alienation of the representation of the self in front of the apparatus and in front of the mass. Marx's technical anthropic notion of the modern human-machine construct is an influence. Marx, for example, describes the machine as a mega-subject whose human operators 'are conscious organs, co-ordinated with the unconscious organs of the automaton, and together with the latter subordinated to the central moving force'.[98] Film re-enacts the drama of alienation and reification. In some of his notes for the 'Artwork essay' Benjamin concentrates less on the representation of alienation and more on the possibility of sublating alienation during film production through the 'liquidation of the difference between mental and manual labour', the root of alienation. In film production the actor is a sensuous representation of mental reflexion and the operators undertake highly mental efforts. Film functions to counter the trauma of social alienation, in part, by its actual methods of production.[99]

Benjamin assumes the continuous evolution of human senses. Not only does he identify a change in methods of technological reproduction of external reality, but also a change in the structure of human perception itself. The reproduction of reality alters the way reality is envisaged, production in the workplace alters human perceptual organization and necessitates new forms of reproduction of reality. The organization of human perception is determined not only by nature but also historically. That is to say it is determined in line with technological innovation. Film, as representative of a transitional moment in the history of perception, makes clear the historical contingency of vision. New forms of art are compelled by changes in the human perceptual apparatus. Human perception reacts to modern urban life and its scattering of shocks. This necessitates an intensified presence of mind.[100] The moment of legitimacy is essential in Benjamin's identification of a correlation between the subject's demand of both art and social experience: the legitimate demand for forms of entertainment appropriate to actuality and retransmitting actuality. Benjamin posits the iconicity of the filmic artwork's representation of the real, but this is complemented by another borrowing from the world of the real, the structural homology between technological production methods and film's methods of production. Crucial to Benjamin's analysis is the way that, in its organizing principles of mass reproduction and standardization, modern industrial processes inhabit the technologies of cinematic reproduction. An instance of elision between construction in engineering and construction as the technical-formal principle of film is given in an entry in the *Passagenwerk*. Benjamin writes of the 'awakening sense in the century for construction'. This first manifests itself in the arts in Cubism.[101]

Film appropriates the structure of contemporary working-class reality in its technological organizing principle. In film 'discontinuous images supersede one another in continuous succession'. This rapid sequence and tactile thrust of its sounds and images allows cinema to rehearse in the realm of perception what the conveyor belt imposes upon people in the realm of production.[102] Benjamin points out that conveyor belt and filmstrip appear in virtually the same historical moment and the social significance of one is dependent on the other:

> the moving belt, which plays such a decisive role in the production process is, more or less, represented in the consumption process by the film strip. Both appeared around the same time. The social significance of one cannot be completely understood without the other.[103]

Benjamin couples the dislocating ruptures of early machinofacture and Taylorized work processes with the filmic principle. Through the representation of movement and the activity of the scanning eye as it scrutinizes the edited image, film reproduces reality as evanescent traces of fragmentary perception, a form of receptivity routine for the urban mass. In the cinema and on the conveyor belt, discontinuous images fly past in a continual flow. Benjamin describes this play-off of discontinuity and continuity as the dialectical basis of film. Film corresponds mimetically to the shocking, abrupt, discontinuous external environment of the street and the factory, banal reality.[104]

In an essay titled 'Über das mimetische Vermögen' (1933), Benjamin describes the 'mimetic capacity' as an adaptation to the environment and to the methods of working with objects in that environment in a relation of acculturation, affinity and reciprocity. Mimesis refers to a flexible interaction with another. Benjamin's understanding of mimesis contradicts Adorno's pessimistic sense of the mimetic capacity as the compulsion exerted on culture consumers to conform to the culture industry's images of themselves.[105] For Benjamin, mimesis is denoted as the original impulse of all creative activity.[106] In the second version of the 'Artwork essay' Benjamin determines a polar impulse in mimesis.

> In mimesis slumber, tightly bound up in each other like cotyledons, the two sides of art: semblance and play.[107]

Art is semblance and play – both of these are mimetic. The training school for mimetic behaviour is child's play. The child imitates all products of its social environment. Rather than art as just a naturalistic mimesis of contents, Benjamin affirms mimesis in practical play.[108] Film's impulse to imitate surface reality, and the way that film is also mimetically aligned to methods of production in its structure, comprise its doubly mimetic existence. In film mimesis as play assumes a critical and corrective function. Film acts as a site of training in order to cope with new perceptual co-ordinates by imitating them and letting audiences practice them.[109] Mimetic reception of the external world in film can be enabling, because of its objectification and presentation of productive processes. This contrasts with the defensive mimetic reflex in the factory, whereby workers co-ordinate their movements to the machine and are protected from shock only at the price of benumbing their reflexes. Contemporary mimetic techniques in film tutor the collective in employing this faculty effectively, as defensive shield against the trauma of alienation. Benjamin does not ignore the dangers of mimetic adaptation to the film object. Technicization of imagery can, he warns, conjure up mass psychosis by eliciting tensions in an unconscious struggling against assault by film shocks. But Benjamin values the collective laughter inspired by slapstick comedy and Disney cartoons as an 'antidote', a 'therapeutic detonation' of technologically created mass psychoses. This indicates that 'mimetic capacity' can also be used as a release.[110] The mimetic capacity permits revision of experience in new and befitting ways.

First Nature, 'Second Nature', 'First Technik', 'Second Technik'

> Becoming (!) Nature which arises in human history – in the act of engendering human society – is the *real* nature of people, and therefore nature, as it exists through industry – even if in *alienated* form, is true *anthropological* nature.
>
> Karl Marx, quoted in 'Konvolut X: Marx', in the *Passagenwerk* (1935–37)[111]

Man, 'the negative being who *is* only to the extent that he suppresses Being', is identical to time. Man's appropriation of his own nature is at the same time his grasp of the unfolding of the universe. 'History is itself a real part of *natural history*, of the transformation of nature into man' (Marx). Inversely, this 'natural history' has no actual existence other than through the process of human history, the only part which recaptures this historical totality, like the modern telescope whose sight captures, *in time*, the retreat of nebulae at the periphery of the universe. History has always existed, but not always in a historical form. The temporalization of man as effected through the mediation of a society is equivalent to a humanization of time. The unconscious movement of time manifests itself and *becomes true* within historical consciousness.

Guy Debord, para. 25, Society of the Spectacle

One of the important social functions of film, states Benjamin in the two earlier versions of the 'Artwork essay', is to establish an 'equilibrium' ('*Gleichgewicht*') between the person and the apparatus.[112] This notion of equilibrium necessarily invests the apparatus with some sort of subjectivity or agency. Benjamin could be accused of fetishism, an anthropomorphization of the apparatus, as he attempts to accredit it with equal rights to human beings. The process of a fetishistic endowment of the machine with subjective power is accentuated by an extension of the 'making human' of the apparatus. This transpires through the notion of the 'optical unconscious'. The 'optical unconscious' substitutes a space consciously penetrated by people for an unconsciously penetrated space seen by the camera eye.[113] A 'new region of consciousness' is conjured up by film, developed only in collaboration with technology:

> Space expands in the close-up, slow motion extends movement. The enlargement of a print does not simply render more precise what was already visible but unclear: it reveals rather entirely new structural formations in the material. So too slow motion not only presents familiar qualities of movement but reveals in them entirely unknown ones which, far from looking like retarded rapid movements, give the effect of singularly gliding, floating, supernatural motions. Thus it becomes obvious that a different nature speaks to the camera than speaks to the eye.[114]

The new technological nature that opens up to the camera is an augmented nature. It includes not only the creaturely and physical, but also the man-made, cultural and historical. The nature that exposes itself to the camera is unlike the unmediated (first) nature that displays itself to the eye. The technology of the camera and film, its movements and its editing, substitutes increasingly for human gesture and interpretation. The contents of the psyche become externalized in technological effects. Technology acts to pre-interpret the material on show. The succession of images in film forecloses meaning, because in film the meaning of each single bit is informed by the sequence. Film offers up to the viewer a closure without holes. There are no gaps offering to the viewer snug resting places amenable to contemplative nestling. The machinery dictates the pace and point of view.

One can compare the screen on which the film plays with the screen on which the painting appears. The image on one of them

changes, the image on the other does not. The latter invites the
viewer to contemplate; in front of it the viewer can abandon
himself to a chain of associations. He cannot do this in front of
the film recording. Barely has he grasped it with his eye when it
has already changed. It cannot be fixed. The chain of associations of the person watching is immediately interrupted by its
transformation.[115]

The intertitle in film or the slogan in the illustrated magazine
heighten this effect of pre-interpretation by the apparatus.
Benjamin writes of 'directives' that rein in the gaze and make
meanings more precise, predetermined, refusing to leave the image
free-floating.[116] Any interpretation of a filmic image must, then, be
based on collusion with the technological apparatus that mediates
it and an acceptance of the machinery's superior consciousness.
This endorsement of technological consciousness is the basis for
a harmonization or dialectical interpenetration of the person and
technology in a techno-consciousness. In the first version of the
'Artwork essay', and in notes for the second version, this interpenetration is interpreted as a realignment of relations between
humans, as first nature, and 'second nature'.[117]

Lukács' model of reification had presented the idea of 'second
nature'. Lukács' idea of reification implies a politically crippling
disarming of the senses and intellect of a humanity confronted by
'second nature'. An uncontrollable domination is permanently
threatened by 'second nature'. In the first version of the 'Artwork
essay' Benjamin elaborates in detail the way that technology,
instead of liberating humanity from myth, confronts it as an uncontrollable force of 'second nature', just as overwhelming as the forces
of a more elementary nature in archaic times. Technological
productions of 'second nature', despite the fact that technology is
now severed from ritual and no longer in the service of magic, still
remain uncontrolled and uncontrollable, alienated from
management by those who make them. War and economic crisis
demonstrate that technology, or 'second nature', is not working
in harmony with humans or nature.[118] In Benjamin's contemporary situation, for example, 'second nature' is seemingly subsumed
back into (first) nature in the Nazi mythology of 'blood and soil'.[119]
The mythology of 'blood and soil' appears to rest on natural
categories, but is, in fact, just the discourse that legitimates an
actual abuse of nature by technology ('second nature').[120] Their
relation to utopia testifies that these technological forms are
abusive. Utopias – for Benjamin their devising is a constant in
history – always appear as in the form of fantasies about the
deployment of technology to humane ends. The Nazi 'blood and
soil' ideology transposes utopias of both first and 'second nature'
in perverted form. 'Blood', as pure untouched Germanic essence,

negates the utopia of (first) nature. The utopia of first nature would use medicine as a disease-eliminating testing-ground for microbes, in an effort to improve the human body. 'Soil' offends the utopia of 'second nature', whose corrupt Nazi realization is the man who uses technology for military purposes to climb into the stratosphere in order to aerial-bombard the ground.[121] Benjamin is insistent that people need to learn how to use technology or the productions of 'second nature' to work in harmony with nature. The alternative is the permanent substitution of utopia by war-driven, life-denying dystopias, such as the substitution of power stations by human power in the form of soldiers, or the substitution of human transportation by weapons transportation.[122]

Having established that 'second nature' always threatens to run out of control and endanger nature, Benjamin considers its character further. In so doing he hopes to be able to suggest a political strategy for ensuring human parity with 'second nature'. 'Second nature' can adopt potentially what Benjamin terms a 'play-form' ('*Spielform*').[123] Communism is a political form that engages in a playful encounter with 'second nature'. Through play-form, reciprocity and training, efforts can be made on the part of humanity to act out its elective affinity with technical 'second nature'. In notes for the second version of the essay revolutions are identified as attempts to control 'second nature' or 'social elemental forces'. The emphasis here is less on equilibrium and more on a notion of expertise gained through practice, on the part of the collective.[124] The shift in the terms of debate towards ideas of play and training compels a new language. Benjamin abandons the concept of 'second nature' in the reworked second version of the 'Artwork essay', replacing it with 'second *Technik*', a form of *Technik* that is categorized as possessing an open character and a built-in affinity with play.[125] The new category of *Technik* aims to enable a detailed discussion of art production and reception, as well as technological development in general. Benjamin asserts that a 'world-historical battle' with political consequences is fought out between 'first *Technik*' (a category that replaces first nature, suggesting that nature is always already worked upon and so is non-natural) and 'second *Technik*'. Replacing nature by *Technik* emphasizes the extent to which, for Benjamin, increasing distanciation from nature is teleologically inscribed in social development:

> The origin of second *Technik* is to be sought there where the person, for the first time and with unconscious cunning, set about taking a distance from nature.[126]

For Hegel, reason works its way into history through the desires of unconscious historical subjects. Benjamin identifies a similar unconscious process in social development as humanity imagines more elaborate technological utopias which are capable of removing humanity from sites of danger. In listing a number of characteristics typical of the two forms of *Technik*, Benjamin appears to be suggesting that technology itself possesses agency, interests and demands. 'First *Technik*' is connected to archaic cultures and is fused with ritual. The productions of 'first *Technik*' are rooted in fixed space and repetition in time, and yet seem to be unique ('*einmalig*'). 'First *Technik*' denotes a specific form of interaction between humans, nature and technology. In 'first *Technik*' humans react to nature's overwhelming powers by abusing it, signifying also a form of self-abuse. 'First *Technik*' is concerned with the domination of nature. 'Second *Technik*', on the contrary, adopts rather a mediating role, allowing play between nature and humanity.[127] 'Second *Technik*' is a form of machine/human interaction, in which humans are empowered to actively control and determine the ways that technology is used, while respecting its essential nature. One difference between 'first *Technik*' and 'second *Technik*' consists in the fact that 'first *Technik*' exposes the person to risk of death, that is, the ravaging of nature, while 'second *Technik*', in a humane gesture, liberates people from vulnerability in the face of nature and protects them from risk:

> The great technical deed of first *Technik* is, to a certain extent, human sacrifice. The great technical deed of second *Technik* lies along the lines of remote controlled airplanes that do not need a crew. Once and for always is relevant to first *Technik* (it has to do with mistakes that can never be rectified or the eternally substituted sacrificial death). Once is as good as never is relevant to second *Technik* (it deals in experimentation and a never-tiring variation in the conditions of testing).[128]

The political importance of technological experimentation grounds any understanding of the concept 'second *Technik*'. The opposition established at the core of artworks, semblance and play, is aligned to the two forms of *Technik*. 'First *Technik*' is connected to semblance, and also cultic magic. 'Second *Technik*' is connected to play and scientism:

> Semblance is the most removed, but therefore also the most lasting scheme of all the magic processes of first *Technik*. Play is the inexhaustible reservoir of all the experimental methods of proceeding of second *Technik*.[129]

Play and experimentation are the principles that predominate in technological art, by definition closely connected to 'second *Technik*'. Film is the perfect realm for the activity of play and experimentation. The socially decisive function of contemporary art is that it exists potentially as a zone of practice in a co-operative game between the three terms, humanity, nature, technology, due to its capacity to encourage the aspect of play. Benjamin gropes towards an idea that has its roots in Schiller's *Über die ästhetische Erziehung des Menschen; in einer Reihe von Briefen*. Art as a form of play is the sphere where a reconciliation of tensions is practised.[130] Film exercises people in playful apperception and reactions necessitated by the new apparatus.[131] Intercourse with the new apparatus teaches the person that liberation from enslavement will occur only once the constitution of humanity has accommodated itself to the new productive forces opened up by 'second *Technik*', by establishing new social relations and new techniques of intercourse.[132] This was an idea of shake-up well rehearsed by Tretyakov.[133] Film can be slotted into an educative role, whereby practice with technological co-ordinates through art begins to destroy inherited patterns of production and reception, while at the same time, in creating a human-technoid being, recreating the corporeal sensorium. The human being is in the process of adapting itself physically and psychically to new Tayloristic conditions of existence. Industrialization sets in train anthropological effects. The political meaning of the idea of 'play' becomes apparent in relation to the evolutionary adaptation of human social relations to new productive forces. The imaginative connotations of play cancel out any tainting of Benjamin's concepts by a harsh anti-humanist industrial fetishism. Revolutions are intimately connected to the process of syndicating humans and technology. In a footnote to the second version of the essay Benjamin comments on the aim of revolutions to accelerate the accommodation of human beings with 'second *Technik*'. Revolutions are described as innervations of the 'new, historically primary collective'. This collective finds its organs in 'second *Technik*'.[134] The fusion of the collective and technology into a new techno-body is expressed by the concept of 'second *Technik*':

> For it is not only second *Technik* that states its demands to society during revolution. Precisely because this second *Technik* wants to go beyond the drudgery of work to achieve the increasing liberation of the person, the individual suddenly sees its room for play [manoeuvre] expand to an unforeseeable degree. The individual does not yet know its way around this play space. But it registers its demands. The more the collective makes second *Technik* its own, the more individuals in the collective will be able to feel how little the previous *Technik*, when they were under its spell, had been theirs.[135]

'Second *Technik*' exposes the alienated nature of first *Technik*, where, in the context of different forces of production, the domination of nature coincided with human sacrifices. What becomes clear, with this new techno-structure, is how little belonged to humanity when it was subjected to technological processes. The 'demands' posed by 'second *Technik*' spring neither from humanity alone nor technology, but from both in collaboration.

Benjamin's comprehension of materialism is literal. It acknowledges the materiality of bodies, and the materiality of the culture they produce and consume – and also the historical nature of sensuous perception. At times, Benjamin's interest in thinking about bodies might appear as matterism, rather than materialism. He develops a technical anthropology of historically mutable nature. Anthropics itself becomes a matter of technics: reorganizable, transformable. That this reconstruction must be arranged around the new co-ordinates of existence, transmitted through new technologies and ways of operating those technologies, is made explicit in a statement in the 'Fourier' file of the *Passagenwerk*. Even revolution becomes a utopian stimulation of the 'technical organs' of the collective, its sensuous faculties. That his materialism or matterism is not simply mechanical, but concerned with human activity – innervation of the body – is indicated in this little sketch, illustrating a common idea in his own and Fourier's politics:

> Fourier's idea of the spreading of the phalanstères through explosions compares with two ideas from my politics: that of the revolution as an innervation of the technical organs of the collective (compare with the child who, in attempting to possess the moon, learns how to grasp), and 'cracking open natural teleology'.[136]

Technology causes social, human and political change and new technologies have initiated a disintegration of traditional criteria. This move cannot be revoked. But, at the same time, Benjamin demonstrates that consciously organizing art around the new opportunities opened up by 'second *Technik*', represents only one possible way of organizing art.[137] In the second version of the 'Artwork essay' Benjamin introduces a further opposition between 'seriousness' ('*Ernst*') and 'play' ('*Spiel*') or, in other words, 'strictness' ('*Strenge*') and 'non-compulsoriness' ('*Unverbindlichkeit*').[138] These oppositions appear in every artwork, though with varying weighting. All art is connected to 'second *Technik*', in as much as it can be received playfully, and it is connected to first *Technik*, in as much as it is received seriously. A note for the second version of the 'Artwork essay' further connects seriousness to fascism and play to communism.[139] Benjamin implies that all artworks have the capacity to promote fascism or communism, depending on the mode of reception that is enabled. Such an assertion negates what has been often construed as the apparent contradiction of

Benjamin's essay: that technological reproduction in art leads necessarily to communist revolution. Such a claim renders the epilogue senseless. Even technological art, deeply marked by all the categories thrown up by 'second *Technik*', such as play, experimentation, science, is still also informed by first *Technik* and cultism, magic and semblance. This is key in Benjamin's discussion of technologized Nazi art. Nazi film uses technology to promote predominantly the characteristics of first *Technik*.

Epilogue: Aesthetics and Politics

> Even though the masses bring it into being, they do not participate in conceiving the ornament. And as linear as it may seem: no line protrudes out of the tiny segments to determine the whole of the mass figure. In this it is similar to the *aerial pictures* of landscapes and towns, for it does not emerge from the interior of a given reality, but rather appears above it.
>
> Siegfried Kracauer, 'Das Ornament der Masse' (1927)140

In the epilogue to the 'Artwork essay' Benjamin writes about the Nazis' recording machine projections. In these the masses seem to look themselves in the face. The latest technological forms are used by the Nazis to produce representations of the masses. The human/machine interpenetration, the industrialized eye, is not abandoned in Nazi propaganda practice, despite their reinvention of a nostalgic nineteenth-century aesthetic in the realm of high art, and their ideological promotion of rural values. Fascist monumental culture is forged for the masses and out of the masses, and it deploys technology to mediate images of these moulded masses. News reports such as the Nazi *Wochenschau* productions, with their bird's eye, dictator's eye, god's eye view, emphasize the vast size of the spectacular shows, the Nazi rallies and sportive-military displays. The dictatorial camera eye surveys the surface areas of the productions, cruising above and across the dramaturgy and tightly controlled choreography of the event. The camera eye transmits aerial views of specific regimented shapes made out of 'human material'.[141] These shaped, ornamentalized masses are bearers of a structure that they do not compose, but into whose order they are made to slot.[142] The references are martial. The mass body is a disciplined material, a phalanx. In the Nazi ornament the mass looks itself in the face, but it is dominated by an authoritarian order that is external to it:

> *Mass reproduction complies well with the reproduction of the masses.* In the huge rallies, the monster meetings, in mass sporting events and in war, all carried out these days in front of recording machines, the masses look themselves in the face. This process,

whose import cannot be emphasized too much, is closely connected to the development of reproductive or recording technology. Mass movements appear more clearly to the apparatus than to the human eye. Hundreds of thousands of cadres are best seen from a bird's eye perspective. While this perspective is just as accessible to the human eye as it is to the apparatus, the image that the eye carries away with it is incapable of enlargement, unlike the photograph. That means, then, that mass movements, and, at their pinnacle, war, represent a form of human behaviour that is especially fitted to the apparatus.[143]

War and mass ornamentalism have found an appropriate means of representation in new technological forms. But it is a use of technology that draws only on the characteristics identified by Benjamin as inherent in first *Technik*. These representations use technology as a means of incapacitating receivers. They substitute active receivers, who participate in the production of their own representation, with a deployment of 'human material' by a dictatorial authority. This authority is fixated with the aesthetic patterning of collectives. The representation of regimented collectives demonstrates that those collectives are not called upon to choose their own formations and associations. Nazism super-imposes a decadent aesthetics on the political sphere.

Technik is used in Nazi aesthetics to cancel out a number of 'rights'. These 'rights' or 'demands' are derived from 'second *Technik*'. Benjamin establishes various 'rights' in the 'Artwork essay': the 'right' to transform property relations, the 'right' to view cultural products that present an accurate vision of reality, the 'right' to be filmed. In the Nazi *Wochenschau* productions a political and a perceptual discourse are skilfully elided, in order seemingly to carry out these 'rights'. Fascism hopes to remain in power by giving expression to the masses in terms of visual representation, but not in terms of their 'right' to political representation. The public satisfies its modern thirst for representation, but in a hollowed-out fashion. This representation is a mockery of revolu-tionary will. The Third Reich places the executors of its art, as much as the recipients of it, under a paralysing spell.[144] The mass ornaments are staged in order to be represented. The reality reflected back at the masses by the machine provides a presenta-tion of people deployed in scenarios designed for the act of reproduction itself. Representation without 'self-understanding' or self-organization on the part of the masses, is representation of a cult without sense, an expression without right and a body of the collective without the rationality of the collective.[145] Fascism par-ticipates in modernity. Its aesthetics respond to the changes in perception wrought by new technologies. Fascism acts upon the new machino-anthropos. It uses film and radio, technologies of the masses. But it bends these forces of production into an aesthetic form that demands contemplative attitudes. Nazism offers only mimetic representation, not political representation. In (visual) representation without (political) representation, humanity, once an object of contemplation for the Olympian gods, is now an object of contemplation for itself, rather than a self-consciously acting, playing and innervated collective. The incapacitated subjectivity, formed in the process of fascist subordination (to the spectacle, to the violence of executive organs), is, according to Benjamin, so alienated from itself, that it derives aesthetic satisfaction from war. Estranged humanity experiences its own death 'as an aesthetic pleasure of the first degree', states Benjamin, referring to the nihilistic consciousness generated by the unsuccessful reception of *Technik*.[146] An abortive reception of *Technik* always issues in the destruction of human life. Destruction and annihilation become important components in the masochistic fantasy of the class that occasions the devastation. In one entry in the *Passagenwerk*, part of the file of quotations on the themes of antique Paris, catacombs, demolition and decline of Paris, Benjamin writes:

> Fantasies about the ruination of Paris are a symptom of the fact that technology was not received. From these speaks the dull consciousness that with the great towns the means grew to flatten them to the ground.[147]

The technological fantasy, hazy from thoughts of ruination, goes hand in hand with a secret inkling of the miserable nature of the organization of production. The modern ruin at the nucleus of capitalist civilization gives birth to a consciousness that is still draped with the vagaries of the mythic reception of technology. Benjamin's study of Eduard Fuchs evaluates the destructive consequences of ill-received *Technik* in the twentieth century. The effects are both military and ideological:

> The energies developed by *Technik* this side of the threshold are destructive. They foster primarily the *Technik* of war and that of its journalistic preparation.[148]

Benjamin insists on the possibility of a misappropriation of *Technik*. Such misappropriation is shown in fact to be the actual reality of capitalism, and it is continued in the fascist version of capitalism. Technological misappropriation is manifest in varying ideologies, such as petit bourgeois rejection of technology or rarified futuristic-fascistic celebrations of machinery.[149] Benjamin repeats the claim made in 'Theorien des deutschen Faschismus' (1930). Fascist art rests on an aestheticism that brackets out the rational human.[150] The techno-body of the collective, visually represented but paralysed when it comes to self-determined political action, is abandoned to the clutch of danger. It is forfeited to war. War finds perfect aestheticized representation in film, as the *Wochenschau* and countless feature films attest. A telling anecdote: on 2 February 1933, immediately after Hitler had been appointed chancellor, Ufa released *Morgenrot*, a film about a submarine in the 1914–18 World War. The new cabinet, including Hitler, Hugenberg and Von Papen attended the première.[151] Even at play their technological imaginary was serious.

Benjamin's interest in the ornamental and organized spectacle of fascism coincides with the analysis of pre-Nazi body culture offered by Siegfried Kracauer in 'Das Ornament der Masse' (1927).[152] Kracauer's article appeared on the *feuilleton* pages of the *Frankfurter Zeitung* and it discussed synchronized dancing troupes and acrobatic displays. In his article he argues that the fetishized spectacle of numerous seemingly identical bodies acting in concert, like cogs in a machine, exists as simulacra of the entire logic of the socio-political order. The marshalled body extravaganzas re-enact the alienation of humanity from nature, transmitting evidence of the debilitating grip on the collective of a reified 'second nature'. Such a modern, rationalized organization of bodies and the social body is well represented through new technologies, in aerial and panning views. In the first two versions of the 'Artwork essay', Benjamin suggests that the filmic representation of alienation and rationalization may be curative.[153] It would seem though that the Nazi technological representation of alienated subjectivity is qualitatively different. Benjamin specifies Nazi technologized art as the art practice that debilitates supremely. *Technik* itself, as utilized by the Nazis, exerts a devitalizing grip, precisely due to its misuse. Technology is mis-deployed in the Nazi spectacle. Modern technologies of film and radio are misused in forms that repeat the disempowered relationship of spectator to art-object, familiar from certain trends in bourgeois aesthetics. In the last version of the essay Benjamin stresses the cultic, ritual basis of Nazi ideology, and aligns it with technology-abuse in art:

> The rape of the masses, who fascism, with its cult of the Führer, forces to their knees, has its counterpart in the rape of an apparatus that is pressed into the manufacture of cult values.[154]

Benjamin argues that it is through the employment of aesthetic means, by redirecting the technical apparatus to the production of cult values, that fascism displaces the contemporary 'drive' to revolutionize relations of production and property relations. This is backed up by an ideological discourse that promotes flattery of the existing economic order by ahistorically insisting on its eternal features. Fascist art and politics demonstrate the re-entry of cult values, the re-entry of semblance into representation and a repression of playful production and reception. Fascist aesthetics is the ultimate aesthetics of semblance. Fascist politics is the ultimate politics of semblance. Fascist practice denies the interplay between first and 'second *Technik*'. It negates the functional value of art as training ground for a harmonious machine/human interplay within a socialized productive apparatus. The crucial final formulation in the 'Artwork essay' insists that technology's destruction of tradition and reorganization of space and time is symptom of a crisis. The crisis must culminate in either the rejuvenation of humanity, marked by humanity's adoption of a political relation to art, or its complete destruction, signalled by an aestheticization of politics.

There is a connection made in the 'Artwork essay' between tactility, the quality of having been brought close to the masses, inherent in political art, and tactic, as mode of political operation. Benjamin presupposes that to theorize and make recommendations for artistic practice is also to make theoretical recommendations for actual political practice. Just as alterations in technological and social conditions of production have forced traditional notions of artistic activity into contradiction with inherited relations of production, so they overturn traditional notions of political activity. A footnote details Benjamin's comprehension of class consciousness and his analysis of KPD practice.[155] Adorno believed this passage to be one of the 'most profound and most powerful' pieces of political theorizing since Lenin's *State and Revolution*.[156] Benjamin's point concerns the dialectic of reactivity and activity. This dialectic also informs the terms first *Technik* and 'second *Technik*'. Benjamin establishes an anti-vanguardist critique of the party and stresses the necessity, for successful leftist politics, of self-active masses. As soon as the proletariat engages in class struggle it becomes active, rather than reactive.[157] The revolutionary leader is not a leader in the traditional sense. He is someone who 'does not draw the masses behind him, but lets himself be continually included in the masses, in order to be one of hundreds of thousands for them'.[158] In fascist technologically reproduced scenarios it is specifically the 'compact masses', an abstraction borrowed from Le Bon, who find representational form. Benjamin insists that the quality of the class-consciousness of the proletariat, labelled by him 'the most illuminated', and the proletariat's participation in class struggle, act to loosen its composition as a grouping of compact masses. Because of this, the proletariat's representation in the fascist *Wochenschau* is clearly unsatisfactory. Only reactive compact masses find satisfactory representational form in these productions. Compact masses are the homogenized Nazi fabrication parading in the *Wochenschau*. The petite bourgeoisie is precisely such a collection of emotional and reactive compact masses, particularly susceptible to panic. Fascism, shouldered by the panic characteristics of the petite bourgeoisie, understands and exploits for political ends the reactive elements of the mass. These petit bourgeois 'compact masses' form an antithesis to the active cadres of the proletariat who are obedient to a collective ratio, and are also conversant with technology. Benjamin contends that communist tacticians, presumably Marx and Lenin, argued for the necessity and possibility of 'winning the petit bourgeoisie' to the side of the revolutionary proletariat. In revolutionary situations, shaken up by their own political reaction and thrown into upheaval by action, the petite bourgeoisie can become radicalized and join a revolutionary movement. Benjamin is criticizing third period theory and practice, which argued for the working-class purity of the vanguard party and, states Benjamin, produced a form of politics which 'promoted illusions that were fateful for the German proletariat'.[159] But, by the time of the essay's first public appearance – in French in 1936 – Communist Party tactics had mutated into Popular Frontism. In any case, this passage was dropped, and Benjamin moved on to a broader, more fundamental critique of the historical and philosophical bases of Marxism.

CHAPTER 7

Time for an Unnatural Death

Puppets of History

The experience of our generation: that capitalism will not die a natural death.

Passagenwerk (1937–40)[1]

Only *that* historian will have the gift of fanning the spark of hope in the past who is firmly convinced of this: even the dead will not be safe from the enemy if he wins. And this enemy has not ceased being victorious.

'Über den Begriff der Geschichte' (1939–40)[2]

'Das Kunstwerk im Zeitalter seiner technischen Reproduzier-barkeit' (1935–39) is not just a piece of art criticism. It sets out an analysis of *Technik* in general and its marking of social maturity. If society accommodates *Technik* sufficiently, then *Technik* and humanity coexist in 'harmonious playing', and *Technik* will not revolt destructively in imperialist war. Imperialist war cashes in its claims on 'human material', because society has withdrawn its 'natural material'.[3] Benjamin's last writings persist with this theme. The last entries in the *Passagenwerk* (1937–40), 'Über einige Motive bei Baudelaire' (1939) and 'Über den Begriff der Geschichte' (1939–40), digress from examination of cultural applications of technology and artistic social relations to an examination of the social relations of *Technik* in the labour process. His assessments voice mordant criticism of social democracy, which is seen to commit the positivistic, technocratic fallacy of accenting material relations of production at the expense of human relations of production.

Benjamin's last jottings look at the nightmare of industrial labour and how so much destruction has become possible amidst such productivity. The next bloody massacre colours these formulations. Benjamin hopes to relate history in ways that do not reinforce the sense that such history as has happened was inevitable. He wants to suggest that the rulers who have ruled need not always rule. It need not go on like this. It must not go on like this, for *this* is hell. Progress, the continuation of business as usual, is catastrophic:

The concept of progress is founded in the idea of catastrophe. That it continues like this, *is* the catastrophe. It is not what stands before us at any one time, but rather this situation now. Thus Strindberg in *To Damascus*? -: hell is not what awaits us – but this life here.[4]

How to understand the connection between progress and catastrophe is the task of 'Über den Begriff der Geschichte'. In letters to Max Horkheimer and Gretel Adorno, Benjamin emphasizes the unsystematic character of these historical-philosophical 'theses'. He claims that his series of graphic and anecdotal vignettes have the 'character of an experiment'.[5] 'War and the constellation engendered by it', Benjamin admits, form the seedbed of the theses.[6] The disjunction of history and theory, the shock of fascism, the horror of militarism, mean that to stop the recurrence of the nightmare new modes of thought must be written and new modes of practice developed. The theses intervene in the present.[7] The imminence and immanence of catastrophe, indicating the necessity for new thoughts and new histories – in order even to understand how we have reached this moment – is suggested by a phrase in 'Kommentare zu Gedichten von Brecht' (1938): 'namely that even tomorrow could deliver destruction of such vastness that we might see ourselves separated from yesterday's texts and productions as if by centuries.'[8] Benjamin's friend Scholem later determined many interpretations of the theses, branding them a product of Benjamin's shocked awakening to the reality of Marxism, at the moment when the Hitler–Stalin pact was signed.[9] And so Scholem fixed an image of Benjamin as a naive, disillusioned utopian. Scholem's deciphering cancels out Benjamin's own account of the theses' motivation in a letter to Gretel Adorno. They represent well-pondered thoughts, for the theses, he divulges, had been germinating for 20 years.[10] That is to say, from 1939 back two decades to 1919 – when, perchance, the seed of the thoughts is planted by the final, fatal struggle of the one political group enthusiastically cited in the theses, Luxemburg's and Liebknecht's *Spartakus*, revolutionary challenger to social democracy, and those two cut down with its tacit approval.[11]

Some preparatory writings note Benjamin's intention to fuse historical work and contemporary political analysis. He expresses the desire 'to formulate a theory of history from which fascism can be viewed'.[12] The theses voice, essentially, a bitter critique of political doctrines – vulgar Marxism and reformist social democracy included – whose theories of history and political praxis are united by forms of inevitabilism or secular forms of fatalism. The implication is that from their theories of history the victory of fascism was unforeseeable, and their political practice was inadequate:

The objects given by monastic discipline to friars for the purpose
of meditation were designed to turn them away from the world
and its affairs. The train of thought that we are pursuing here
emerges out of similar considerations. It intends to free the
political worldling from the ensnaring nets of those politicians
in whom hope had been placed that they would be opponents
of fascism, but who in this moment lie flat on their backs,
affirming their defeat with the betrayal of their cause.[13]

The social democratic reformists are implicated in betrayal. They
had been so convinced of progress and their mass base, under any
circumstance, that they had engaged in complicitous deals with
the political establishment. The social democrats' dogma holds
faith with the permanently progressive yellow-brick road of history,
lined by ever-developing forces of production, interminable
technical progress and the cheering crowds of a mobilizable mass
base. But there were other traitors and acts of betrayal to account
for, such as the Ribbentrop-Molotov pact, signed on 23 August
1939. It took effect immediately once signed and contained the
following clauses: Germany and the Soviet Union resolve not to
attack each other or aid any third party assault on the other. Communication and consultation on issues of common interest are to
be maintained. Each party is not to align with powers who plan to
threaten the other signatory. The pact was to hold good for ten
years with an automatic five-year extension, unless one party gave
the other notification of termination one year in advance. It
contained a secret clause: Poland and eastern areas were to be
divided between Germany and the Soviet Union. The Soviets
hoped to gain Bessarabia, Latvia, Estonia, Finland and Poland
east of the Vistula and San rivers. The pact once signed, policy
began. Germany invaded Poland on 1 September 1939. The
Soviets invaded eastern Poland on 29 September. Non-aggression
went alongside a trade treaty and arrangements for extensive
exchange of raw materials and armaments. This vile alliance of the
vile stemmed from the Communist Party's attempt at double-
dealing. In this instance, the political worldlings are the European
proletarians and the betrayers are the politicians who affirmed a
supposed anti-fascist tactic. This tactic resulted in the Communist
Party welcoming Hitler as Stalin's ally. The Communist Party
leadership called for capitulation before the Nazis. Prior to this
accord, Stalin had agreed to withdraw International Brigades from
Spain and had reduced aid to the Republican government. The
fascist General Franco finally defeated the young democratic
government in March 1939. This was not foreseen in the line. In
the third period Comintern orthodoxy held that fascism was one
stop along a road of collapse that led to an assured destination:
the termination of capitalism. The classless society is always just

around the next corner. Sections of the German Communist Party contended that Nazism represented a bourgeois counter-revolutionary movement, a purely defensive step against an insurgent working class, close to revolutionary victory. However, in actuality, the working class is on the defensive by the time fascism kicks in. It is under attack and it is 'corrupted'.[14]

After Benjamin's death Gerhard-Gershom Scholem coins an influential interpretation of 'Über den Begriff der Geschichte'. He brands it a melancholic final piece of work, composed after a sudden and startled awakening to the nature of communism. Scholem's rendition insinuates that the theses move away from politics in order to leap into transcendence.[15] In Scholem-influenced studies of Benjamin's effective testament the theses are again and again construed as the offspring of a theological messianism. Such messianism is seen to break definitively with the political philosophy of Marxism, a creed that propounds inevitable progress in history. But there are obstacles to too eagerly propounding the theses as testimony to the ultimate triumph of theology. The pointers to Benjamin's salvage operation for Marxism are too multiple to be ignored, even if, as Brecht and Adorno recognized, this operation remains allusive, because of its insistence on outlining potent and memorable *images* for revolution and for thought.[16] For Benjamin, Marxism is a matter of images. Benjamin writes that Marx correctly secularized the representation of the messianic age in the image of the classless society.[17] The classless society is an image, an analogy for the messianic age. Such an image, argues Benjamin, benefits the revolutionary politics of the proletariat, in a sense reminiscent of Sorel's positive evaluation of the image of the general strike, worked over by Benjamin in 'Zur Kritik der Gewalt' (1921).[18] 'History breaks down into images not stories,' he notes.[19] His correction to historical materialism insists:

A central problem of historical materialism that should finally be realized: whether the Marxist understanding of history must necessarily be bought at the cost of its vividness? Or, in what way is it possible to combine increased vividness with the execution of the Marxist method? The first stop along this path will be to carry the montage principle over into history. That is, to build up the large constructions out of the smallest, precisely fashioned structural elements. Indeed to detect the crystal of the total event in the analysis of the small, individual moment. To break, then, with the vulgar naturalism of historicism. To grasp the construction of history as such. In the structure of commentary.[20]

Perhaps this discloses why Benjamin devotes so much attention to assessing visual mediations of reality in photography and film. The notion of vivid history hopes to inject imagination and vision into history telling, visuality, graphicness, a life-like realism, a human history, but always conscious of technical mediations.[21] Benjamin unfolds Marxism in images as a result of his evaluation of the significance of the image for political praxis: the filmic image or the philosophical image that snaps thought into being. He is trying to re-imagine revolutionary politics; a small gesture with vast implications in desperate times.

'Über den Begriff der Geschichte' and the preparatory work for the theses present vignettes like picture puzzles. The first image, the opening thesis of 'Über den Begriff der Geschichte', recounts an anecdote about a chess-playing automaton. This is a mechanism able to match each competing chess-player's turn with a winning move:

> The story is told of an automaton constructed in such a way that it could respond to each move in a game of chess with a countermove that ensured him victory. A puppet in Turkish attire, with a hookah in his mouth, sat in front of a chessboard placed on a large table. A system of mirrors created the illusion of a table transparent from all sides. Actually a hunchback dwarf, who was an expert chess player, sat inside and guided the puppet's hand by means of strings. One can imagine a philosophical counterpart to this device. The puppet known as 'historical materialism' is always supposed to win. It can easily be a match for anyone if it ropes in the services of theology, which today, as the story goes, is small and ugly and must, as it is, keep out of sight.[22]

This mechanical form, judging by appearances, is always superior to human intelligence. In fact, Benjamin reveals, the autonomy of the machinery transpires to be a fake and the machine's success rests on a dwarf inside the mechanism who, disposing over an ingenious mirror-system trick, combines his intelligence with the capacities of the technology to produce such successful gaming. Benjamin's disclosure of the illusioning function of the chess automaton's mirror, when imported into political theory, could intimate the fallacies of positivist accounts of politico-historical dynamics. From a philosophical and epistemological perspective, the image insinuates the world of difference between reflecting, presented as obscuring, and reflecting upon, comprising a complex understanding of mechanisms in total. Benjamin extends the image of the chess automaton and dwarf to an analogy with political philosophy. The automatic doll, always 'supposed to win', is associated with historical materialism and the hunchback dwarf is linked to theology.[23] Historical materialism is first introduced within quotation marks. These are subsequently dropped. This establishes a differential status between the one version of historical materialism and the amended version conceived and recommended by Benjamin. The theological dwarf pulls the strings of the materialist puppet, and yet it would seem that materialism is in charge, because it wins.[24] There figure religious motifs drawn from various theological traditions, not just Judaism. Benjamin is not concerned with developing or interpreting religious doctrine in any sense. That was more the work of Scholem.[25] Religious motifs are one part of a versatile montage strategy, rather than evidence of ardent religious commitment. It is more significant to try to identify what theology as figure or image might represent. It might be like this. Theology's antithesis, the theoretical prognoses of contemporary historical materialism, has traditionally been too concerned with the automaton, expecting that the development of this machinery will on its own automatically guarantee the truth of historical materialism, manifest in the victory of the proletariat. In bringing the theological dwarf who makes the expert moves into play, Benjamin reminds historical materialists of a crucial moment in the revolutionary equation; the mediation of practice through a class of operators. The dwarf, theology, might represent a moment of *Geist*, or consciousness. The dwarf is animated, its activity signalling something other than automatic technological development. Benjamin's rendition of an historical materialist comprehension of historical movement is suggestive of a reciprocal co-articulation of technology and the operator who disposes over the technological mechanism. This raises the question of Benjamin's own form of determinism. Benjamin foretells the success of the doll (historical materialism). It is 'supposed to win', but it can only win if the class recovers enough to 'master' its technology. In this sense Benjamin also recognizes that the working-class revolutionary movement is capable of losing.

Second image: using the example of the train, Benjamin challenges a metaphor often present in socialist political discourse. A parable in preparatory notes for 'Über den Begriff der Geschichte' revokes Marx's image of historical movement, and reflects on the process of history in terms that rebuff any notion of automatically assured revolutionary progression:

> Marx says that revolutions are the locomotive of world history. But perhaps it is quite different. Perhaps revolutions are the grasp for the emergency brake by the human race travelling on the train.[26]

Benjamin uses the image language of trains and socialism uncon-
ventionally. Such use of arresting imagery harks back to his interest
in Aragon's surrealist practice, whereby imagery disrupts destructively the accepted order of things by not appearing conventional,
and by overturning expectations.[27] Benjamin's image detracts from
notions of progress assured through technological development
and conveys a plea for a conception of politics based on class-
conscious activity. In this image revolution occurs as an
interruption, motivated by conscious intervention on the part of the
travelling collective. The classless society is not the terminus or
telos of progress, but rather is consequent on the interruption of
progress.[28] The language of Benjamin's image implies rejection of
any Marxian concept of progress without interruption, exemplified
in Plekhanov's promise: 'We, indeed, know our way and are seated
in that historical train which at full speed takes us to our goal.'[29]
Revolution as interruption in the continuum of history dovetails
with Marx's idea of revolution as the end of the prehistory of
humanity and the beginning of true human history. Benjamin's
image is similar to an image of class society in Engels' *Anti-Dühring*
(1876–78). This image likewise invokes the image language of
locomotion. The bourgeois class, unable to control the energies
of the forces of production, is 'a class, under whose leadership
society is racing to ruin like a locomotive whose jammed safety
valve the machinist is too weak to open'.[30] Engels' image suggests
the potential barbarism that will arise if the status quo of
production relations is not suspended. It poses the question of
control of policy and control of the technical apparatus. For
Benjamin, *Technik* is not simply the hardware, but also a set of
relations of production. The question is one of control. The image
of halting the greatest technological invention of the nineteenth
century, the railway train, derails technocratic conceptions of an
automatic relationship between changes in relations of production
and technological evolution towards the classless society. It
counters the almost religious fetishization of the technological. In
'Eduard Fuchs, der Sammler und der Historiker' (1934–37),
Benjamin mentions Du Camp's vision of the locomotive as the
saint of the future. Maxime du Camp was a photographer and
traveller, that is to say, traverser and reformulator of nineteenth-
century time-space, who must have sensed that his voyages over
land were immeasurably improved by this swift new mode of
propulsion. And Benjamin quotes, with irony, Ludwig Pfau: 'It is
quite unnecessary to become an angel, he wrote, and the railway
is more valuable than the most beautiful pair of wings!'[31] These
two, and the Saint-Simonians, articulate the defective, fetishized
reception of technology.

Benjamin's theses propagate a politics through images. Their cryptic, poetic references derive a language for thinking when language has failed. Like poems, they are intended to say so much with few words. The politics of images rewrites the terms of historiography, disciplines, thought. To think differently means to recast the available components. What else is Marxism? But Marxism must be something else than what it has become. Quotations from Korsch's *Karl Marx* manuscript in the *Passagenwerk* affirm Marxism, in as much as it provides 'a completely undogmatic guideline for research and practice', as understood most clearly, Benjamin suggests, by Sorel and Lenin.[32]

The Failure to Progress

> Les choses ne peuvent ne pas s'arranger.
>> Jean Jaurès on the eve of his assassination
>> and the outbreak of world war in 1914[33]

Benjamin assaults vulgar-Marxism's misconception of *Technik*. He underscores Marx's emphasis on the socio-economic consequences of the division of labour, the division of the proletariat into skilled and unskilled workers, the mythologization of industry by the bourgeoisie, and the Marxist categories of alienation and commodity fetishism. The social by-product of commodity production is the endowment of labour with supernatural powers. These act to naturalize the relations within which labour occurs. These naturalized relations include the enslavement of the worker, who possesses only labour-power, to the class with the power to organize labour conditions.[34] Under these economic relations, labour is measured quantitatively. Scientific social democratic socialism also relies on the objectivity of materially quantifiable things: technology, machinery, economic statistics and productivity. Benjamin claims that the social democrats remain bound to a quantitative fixation on productivity and omit reflection on how the quality of the labour process and social relations affect the worker. Focus on the quantifiable, Benjamin argues, results in a technocratic ideology. Factory labour is promoted by social democracy as a welcome result of technological progress, and in itself a 'political achievement'.[35] The stubborn belief in progress and trust in a mass base is founded on social democracy's fetishization of quantitative accumulation in all its forms.[36] This connection between the stubborn belief in progress and faith in a mass base is further identified with the political will for 'servile inclusion in an uncontrollable apparatus'.[37] Benjamin noted Marx's 'Randglossen zum Program der deutschen Arbeiterpartei'.[38] According to Marx's critique, the 'Gotha Programme' stayed economically within the

framework of the capitalist economic form and practically within
that of the bourgeois-democratic state, since the social democrats
envisaged the persistence of capitalist society for some time. For
example, they harboured illusions about Bismarck as the workers'
friend. Not only economy and politics, but also technology
remained tied to capitalist organization. Benjamin emphasizes the
class implications of the technical apparatus – the relation of
production. This is in contrast to social democrats who believe it
is possible to inhabit the apparatus without significantly changing
its form.

Karl Korsch influenced Benjamin.[39] Korsch identifies the
importance of the division of labour, that is the structuring of class
society, insistent that this too, along with nature, technology and
science, is to be recognized as a productive force. Benjamin cites
Korsch on Marx, fragmentedly:

> Concept of productive force: Marx's concept of social productive
> forces has nothing to do with the idealist abstractions of
> technocrats, who imagine they can determine productive forces
> in society ... purely natural-scientifically and technologically ...
> Certainly, according to ... Marx, the ... technocratic sensibility
> is not enough ... to remove ... those material obstacles that ... the
> dumb violence of economic relations ... sets up against any trans-
> formation of present circumstance.[40]

In the *Passagenwerk* Benjamin notes the 'murderous idea of the
exploitation of nature', dominant since the nineteenth century.[41]
The exploitation of the proletariat is traded off against the exploitation of nature, regarded as separate from it. Benjamin alludes to a
leading social democratic theorist, Josef Dietzgen, who appears to
assume that nature exists gratis.[42] Writing of the vulgar-Marxist
conception of nature, Benjamin restates a formulation from
'Eduard Fuchs, der Sammler und der Historiker' and extends it in
order to link social democratic philosophy and fascism:

> It only discerns progress in the mastery of nature and ignores
> the retrogression of society. It displays the technocratic features
> later encountered in fascism. Among these is the concept of
> nature that differs ominously from the one in the socialist utopias
> of *Vormärz*. Labour, as it is now understood, amounts to the
> exploitation of nature, which, with naïve complacency, is
> contrasted with the exploitation of the proletariat.[43]

Benjamin, in his counterblast, follows Korsch in substituting for
pure nature, preceding all human activity, a vision of nature as
produced, mediated and reformed by human social activity. Nature
is transformable social material.[44] And labour must turn into play,
if it is to be revolutionized. Benjamin so revives the thought of the

utopian socialist Charles Fourier, as well as recalling Marx's early conceptions of labour in the 1844 manuscripts: work as a form of self-realization. In a situation of highly developed productive forces work can turn into play. Benjamin figures another, better byway to socialism: Fourier's playpen versus Dietzgen's commuter haul. Labour accomplished according to the model of children's play is not oriented to the production of exchange values but to an improvement of nature. In the late 1930s Benjamin completes some notes on the architect and science fiction writer Paul Scheerbart's *Lesabéndio* (1913). These notes affirm Scheerbart's utopian conception of a highly technologized, but non-exploitative relationship to nature.[45] Technological destruction of nature is disastrous and, importantly, avoidable once labour relations have been reorganized. A society no longer reliant on economic exploitation remoulds the relationship between humans and nature. It is non-exploitative, not least because humans are a part of nature.[46]

The concept of progress becomes a dogma at that moment when it is no longer a socially critical concept, but has become a *Geschichtsphilosophie* which measures the bad infinity of 'the tension between a legendary beginning and legendary end of history'.[47] Benjamin craves a critical concept of progress that is a 'measure of specific historical transformations'. Progress begins, in actuality, only at that moment when revolutionary class-conscious activity is instigated in order to mutate forms of production. Benjamin deciphers similarities between bourgeois historicist and evolutionist social theory and the social democratic belief in infinite, continuous, automatic progress. The abstract, universalistic notion of progress – prevalent in bourgeois social theory – is promoted by Darwinist theory:

> The theory of natural selection had a decisive significance for this process; because of it the opinion became widespread that progress would occur automatically.[48]

Darwinist theory, once transported to the social realm, is central to the project of evolutionary socialism promoted by Second International Marxists. In the work of party philosophers, such as Dietzgen and Kautsky, historical materialism is interpreted as an extension of Darwinist evolutionism applied to human history. Benjamin comments in the essay on Fuchs that it makes a difference whether revolutionary optimism relies on the capacity for decisive action of the working class or on an alteration of the circumstances in which they act. Social democracy tends towards the second option.[49] Benjamin's complaint in the theses on the philosophy of history concerns social democracy's confusion of the progress of specific skills and knowledges with the progress of humanity itself.[50] For Benjamin, a specific progress might be

gleaned in this concrete process of the development of knowledges
and skills, but this turns into an abstracted notion that empties out
politics and history from the concept of progress when applied as
a measure of the progress of humanity. Benjamin endeavours to
break up abstract ideas of the universal, be they universal history
or universal humanity. This is consistent with Marx's methodology,
which refers to a concrete universal, saturated with content and
conceptually developed by a process of abstraction and
mediation.[51] Benjamin distinguishes between a formalist notion
of progress and a critical theory of history, a 'concrete consideration of history', sensitive to varying levels of regression and
progression.[52]

The *Passagenwerk* includes an excerpt from a letter sent by
Hermann Duncker to Grete Steffin. Duncker reports that Marx
and Engels were ironic about any absolute belief in progress.[53]
Marx's taboo against an undialectical fetishism of concepts led
him to suspect and avoid the word 'progress'. Progress is typically
asserted to have value for the totality when, in fact, it has meaning
only for particularities.[54] Benjamin likewise turns his attention to
disintegrating the notion of progress historically and politically. A
late entry in the *Passagenwerk* states that, as the bourgeoisie
conquer positions of power, 'the concept of progress increasingly
renounces the critical function that originally belonged to it in the
nineteenth century'.[55] Benjamin diagnoses class inflections in the
dominant ideology of progress. As the bourgeois class secures
economic and political power, progress, a cardinal strand in
Enlightenment political rhetoric and social theory, unfolds in
actuality its class inflections as economic and social progress for
one class, presented ideologically as the universally significant
progression of humanity itself. Such a concept of progress relies
on a celebration of the progression of technological development
and advancement in the technical domination of nature. In
bourgeois terms, technological advancement and technical
domination of nature are signs of intensified alienation and more
effective exploitation of the operators of technology and the raw
products of nature. The easy identification of technological
development with progress overrides questions of social form or
production relations. Technology is extricated from the circumstances of use and refashioned as *per se* a guarantor of progress.
This connects with an assertion made in the unfinished methodological addendum to 'Das Paris des Second Empire bei
Baudelaire', written in June 1938. The methodological addendum
sets out a statement of intent for a non-reductive historical
materialist critique and against Moscow-inspired historico-cultural
criticism which extracts social products from their past and present

position within production relations, and is thus unable to analyse materialistically.[56]

There are various modulations of the ideology of progress in social democracy: Darwinist evolutionist determinism, blind optimism and the dogma of the inevitable and necessary victory of the party. Benjamin argues that social democrats base their political practice on the notion of a social and technological motion of endless and inevitable perfectioning. Progress is never to be concluded and is seen as essentially unstoppable, a continuous straight or spiralled line. The idea of the classless society is made into an 'ideal' and becomes thus an always postponed, endless task. Historical time is seen by the ideologues of progress as a sort of endlessly functioning clockwork mechanism. Such time has its tempo beaten out by the machinery of incessant production. Benjamin draws an image: empty and homogeneous time for the social democrats realizes itself in space as an antechamber where subjects wait more or less calmly for the commencement of better times, their whole existence oriented towards the future. Benjamin's move challenges every theory of history that assumes improvements come in time, in a world where each day is better than yesterday. Such an attitude cannot begin to speak about fascism. The social democratic faith in progress in history, guaranteed by technological advance, is one of the reasons for its 'later collapse' politically once confronted by fascism. It had, of course, already shattered once before when it complied with the nationalist horror of world war. To be shocked that fascism can occur in the twentieth century is a wrong-headed result of the belief in linear and cumulative progress.

Repeats: Bourgeois Thought

> Definitions of basic historical concepts: the catastrophe – to have missed the opportunity; the critical moment – the status quo threatens to remain in place; progress – the first revolutionary measure.
>
> 'Konvolut N: erkenntnistheoretisches, Theorie des Fortschritts' in the *Passagenwerk* (1937–1940)[57]

One entry in the *Passagenwerk* quotes this passage from Marx's *Der achtzehnte Brumaire des Louis Bonaparte*:

> Marx on the second republic: Passion without truth, truths without passion, heroes without heroic deeds, history without events; development whose only motor appears to be the calendar, exhausted by continual repetition of the same tensions and slackenings ... If any period of history is painted grey on grey, it is this one.[58]

Marx's comments on the disastrous emptiness of history after the failure of the 1848 revolutions are adopted by Benjamin to characterize another, later epoch of failed revolutionary hopes. The repetition occurring in Benjamin's time is twofold: for the second time in a half-century humanity witnesses preparation for military destruction. The other repetition is the endless iteration of mass commodity production. These two facets are flung into relation. The link between deskilled production and the increasing importance of the military, between production and destruction, is expressed in this footnote to 'Über einige Motive bei Baudelaire' (1939):

> The shorter the apprenticeship of the industrial worker, the longer becomes that of the military. Perhaps it is part of society's preparation for total war that training is migrating from the practice of production into the practice of destruction.[59]

Commodity production depends on a logic of obsolescence. The logic of obsolescence relies on an economic system that reproduces itself and its contents while perpetually eradicating its specific surface traces. The fashion industry is the key cipher of this process.[60] Benjamin debunks the propagandistic fiction of ever-novel commodity productions as a series of superficially differing regurgitations, materializing from a fixed organization of production relations. This monotonous rhythm of production for accumulation is labelled by Benjamin (after Nietzsche) 'eternal return'.[61] In 1938 Benjamin incorporates into the *Passagenwerk* files and into writings on Baudelaire notes on Blanqui's *L'éternité par les astres*. He uses the tract as an example of a critique, albeit resigned and fatalistic, of the 'ideology of progress', for its final formulations note how the new is always old, the old is always new. The number of our doubles is infinite in time and space, and these doubles are flesh and bone, with breeches and jacket, crinoline and chignon. They are not at all phantoms, but are the present eternalized, and they are 'vulgar re-editions, redundant reproductions'.[62]

Blanqui was a hero of repeatedly abortive insurrectionary movements in 1839, 1840 and 1870, and spent half his life in prison as punishment for his revolutionary activism. His cosmological speculation was written during a period of incarceration, after the failure of the Paris Commune and the massacre of 6,000 communards, according to Maxime du Camp, or Lissagaray's 17,000 or Louise Michel's 30,000. Whatever the numbers, Blanqui's speculations in its wake etch a social nightmare of catastrophic and eternal returns of crises, while the citizens of the nineteenth century are depicted as damned ghostly apparitions.[63] These spectral personalities dwell in a world segmented by infernal, mechanistic natural sciences.[64] Benjamin credits Blanqui for his penetration of the 'phantasmagoria of progress', but notes that the nineteenth-century terrorist remains unaware of the economic source of the fantasy of this 'eternal return of the ever same': that is, 'the accelerated progression of economic crises'.[65] Benjamin unmasks the eternal return as an ideological reflex connected to economic and technological formations. And while, in one sense, Benjamin allows prophetic power to the theory of eternal return, calling it a 'dream of the amazing discoveries yet to come in the area of reproductive technology',[66] it is also the complement of a crisis-ridden capitalism, in which what is true is truly the unconscious acknowledgement that there is nothing new to come, because no future can be imagined in the context of the current economic order. Eternal return is incapacitating:

> Life under the influence of eternal return guarantees an existence that does not emerge from the auratic.[67]

Eternal return is an emblem for the underlying economic structure of capitalist commodity production. Labour, an eternally returning, eternally demanded expenditure of energy – performed in vain under atrocious conditions – emerges as a Sisyphusian task. A quotation from the *Passagenwerk* draws together labour, mythology and eternal return:

> The essence of mythical occurrence is return. In it, inscribed as a hidden figure, is futility, such as is written on the faces of various heroes of the underworld (Tantalus, Sisyphus or the Danaides). Thinking through eternal return in the nineteenth century again, Nietzsche makes it the figure whereby mythical fate once more takes place. (The eternity of hell's punishments has perhaps taken the worst sting out of the antique idea of eternal return. It substitutes eternal torture for the eternal circuit.)[68]

Endless torture is mythology's worst figment and it has a modern guise. The division of labour necessitates a mechanical measure of labour time. This is the empty, homogeneous time of manufacture. In a section of *Das Kapital* Marx illustrates this division of time – reflexively – through the example of watch-making.[69] The work process, especially the one endured in the factory, deskills operators and forces learning by drill and repetition. Industrial work processes form an 'automatic operation', wherein each act is the exact repetition of the previous one. Work is a reactive and reflective process. At work the activity of the worker, like the unlucky gambler, eternally recommences from point zero.[70] In 'Über Einige Motive bei Baudelaire' Benjamin writes:

Marx had good reason to stress the great fluidity of the connection between segments in artisanal labour. This connection appears to the factory worker on an assembly line in a detached, reified form. Independently of the worker's volition, the object being worked upon, comes within his range of action. And it moves away from him just as arbitrarily. Every kind of capitalist production ..., writes Marx, has this in common, that it is not the workman that employs the instrument of labour, but the instrument of labour that employs the workman. But it is only in the factory system that this reversal for the first time acquires technical and palpable reality. In working with machines workers learn to coordinate their own movement to the uniform, unceasing motion of an automaton.[71]

Capitalist instruments of labour make use of the worker, and factory machinery gives this transposition a technically concrete form. Machinery turns animate; humans become adjuncts to the machine.

The study of industrial labour, its first formations in the nineteenth century and its arrangement in the twentieth, reaffirms Benjamin's notion that *Technik* has assaulted the human body. *Technik* has motivated a 'crisis in perception'.[72] Furthermore, *Technik* has submitted the human sensorium to a complex training.[73] In the last *Passagenwerk* entries and writings on Baudelaire Benjamin extends his anthropology of industrialized humanity by introducing the neurological category of shock into discussion of the experience of work. From the factory to the battlefield the experience of shock, physical and psychic, constitutes the norm.[74] Technology dictates a syncopated, dislocating rhythm. Workers must permanently react to this rhythm. Citing Marx, Benjamin described how in the factory system workers learn to coordinate their 'own movement to the uniform and unceasing motion of an automaton'.[75] But such adaptation was more widely demanded. The city itself is a cauldron of shock-effects. These shocks daily assault the dismantled individual. The Lunapark fairground, site of cosmic '*Erfahrung*' in Zum Planetarium, is described in 'Über einige Motive bei Baudelaire' as the place where workers become accustomed to the drill of the factory.[76] Photography is one of the most significant instances of shock-experience, Benjamin contends in 'Über einige Motive bei Baudelaire':

> Amongst the various gestures of switching, inserting, imprinting etc. the photographer's snapping has been the most conse-quential. One press of the finger is enough to fix an event for an unlimited time. The apparatus delivers the moment, so to say, a posthumous shock. Haptic experiences of this kind were joined

by optic ones, such as are supplied by the advertising pages of a newspaper or the traffic of a big city.[77]

Optical experiences and haptic, tactile ones are the stuff of modern urban life. They are all forms of assault on the body. Invoking Freud's *Jenseits des Lustprinzips*, Benjamin presents shock as a necessary prophylactic, a psychic shell of consciousness that protects the organism against stimuli and the threat of excessive energies. Shocks that are registered on this shell are seen to be less traumatic, since it is able to act as a buffer. The modern unskilled worker, claims Benjamin, is sealed off from experience as '*Erfahrung*'.[78] Such experience is now atrophied – it is *Erlebnis*. *Erlebnis* is experience as a series of shocks, it is disruptive – and where once, in the nineteenth century, it appeared as the experience of the adventurer, now, in Benjamin's time, it appears as fate.[79] A comment in the file on idleness reflects on the conditions of succumbing to the ultimate in total '*Erlebnis*', military experience – a 'total experience' that is enmeshed with death, that is to say, 'fatal'. Its motto is the military code: 'I was born a German and therefore I must die.' Perhaps it has become possible, reflects Benjamin, because the mechanisms of exchange, and the fetishism of commodities, make contemporary experience empathy or iden-tification with the objective:

> Is it empathy with exchange value that makes people at all capable of 'total experience'?[80]

Shock as a component of experience is complemented by the motif of numbness – its opposite in a sense – and equally as con-stitutive of the psychic make-up in urban industrialism. Numbness – the shock repeated until it becomes no longer a shock but the norm – causes insensibility, an effect of the psychic necessity to parry the blows and of the repetitive nature of labour. The human being transformed into an automaton – or machine appendage – is an extreme example of the novel social condition(ing): displaying simultaneously an alertness (a preparedness to perform) and a numbness (an emotional disinvestment). Living bodies have been transformed historically into deadly armatures, scaffolds, machines for work. It is this that Baudelaire has understood, as Benjamin comments in 'Zentralpark' (1938):

> Machinery in Baudelaire becomes a cipher of destructive forces. Such machinery is not least the human skeleton.[81]

Flâneurs, Class-fighters, Conspirators

Machinery is a force that sucks up human labour. Because of this, strategies of resistance to the capitalist organization of labour –

idleness, non-productivity, dandyism, *flânerie* – intrigue Benjamin. He devotes a file of the *Passagenwerk* to idleness – '*Müßiggang*'.[82] Marx too recognized that idleness, more than anything else, was the most effective form of resistance in the age of manufacture.[83] What else is the strike? Benjamin studies idleness and the *flâneur*, a dawdler who appears to be capable of protest, through his torpidity, against the eternal, homogeneous pace and tempo of production in the nineteenth century.[84]

In *Der achtzehnte Brumaire des Louis Bonaparte* (1851) Marx recounts the cultural and political abdication of the republican bourgeoisie.[85] He describes how the bourgeoisie destroys its own institutions and values, and also its expressive forms. Through its fawning to the president, its vilification of parliament, its suppression of the press, the bourgeoisie invited Bonaparte to overpower and annihilate its speaking and writing section, its politicians and its *literati*, its platform and its press. With the crushing of the 1848ers' revolutionary movement now complete, the victorious section of the bourgeoisie, supportive of 'a party of order', sought to take its 'cause' away from the most articulate artists. They called upon Napoleon III

> to destroy their speaking and writing segment, their politicians and literati, so that they might confidently pursue their private affairs under the protection of a strong and untrammelled government.[86]

It severed its own hands and gagged its mouth so that it might pursue its private affairs, confident that a strong and untrammelled government would protect it. This led to a schism within the bourgeois class. In the methodological addendum to 'Das Paris des Second Empire bei Baudelaire', Benjamin remarks that the theory of *l'art pour l'art* assumes decisive importance around 1852, at that time when the bourgeoisie sought to take its cause out of the hands of the writers and poets.[87] The *literati* become redundant, no longer spokespeople for a just cause and a virtuous class. Benjamin cites Marx's depiction of the suicided bourgeoisie and uses this context to account for the emergence of a critical bourgeois bohemian type obsessed by consumerism, urbanity and supersensitivity. Modernism begins in this period of coerced marginalization. Benjamin's studies of Baudelaire decipher the conditions of emergence of the avant-garde. Dallying on the streets, observing the spectacle become forms of defiance against the philistine segments of the class who no longer request brave formulations and orations. It is also a secret token that these bourgeois artists cut off from actual power or social innovation have time aplenty for distraction and just looking.[88] Hence their painterly and literary reproduction of spaces of leisure and consumption, such as parks and lakes, cafés and boulevards.

The *flâneur* assumes importance as an identification-figure for the poet or journalist who disappointedly comes to realize that conditions for the production of words are dictated by the market. As Benjamin relates it, the *flâneur*'s position is unstable, indicative of a crisis unleashed by the organization of production. The *flâneur*, who longs to be a free-floating intellectual, is in thrall to the market. The instability of the *flâneur*'s position in the late nineteenth century – at least as constructed in Benjamin's project – issues from changes brought about by industrial capitalism. His life-style, in as much as it is leisurely, is threatened by urbanization in general, and Taylorism specifically, with its factory system of mass production demanding universal speed-up and standardization in all areas of life. Benjamin notes how 'Taylor popularized the watchword "Down with dawdling!"', and this slogan becomes part of a general cultural war against lassitude.[89] The *flâneur* is on the losing side of a class struggle over the pace of life and autonomy of action.[90] His livelihood – for Benjamin's *flâneur* gets by as a *homme de lettres* or journalist, a poet of everyday life, supplying the *feuilleton* press – is permanently under threat, because of his subservient relationship to the anarchic and selective market. Benjamin argues that eventually the *flâneur* becomes a wage-slave, his last incarnation being the sandwich man, condemned endlessly to tramp the streets.[91] The sandwich men H. E. L. Y. and 'S., who snake their way through James Joyce's cinematic modernist epic *Ulysses* (1922), donate an apt image. These street walkers are stripped of individuality, reduced to initials, not even their own, but spelling out the home of commodities. Such restriction of the personality to the barest alphabetical clue relates to another image in the *Passagenwerk*. In 1935, Benjamin notes, there was a female fashion for wearing little metal initial badges, pinned to the jumper or coat.[92] This signifies, he suggests, an increasing restriction of the private sphere, and the commodification of the self, as part of love-ritual. Everyone has a price. Everyone has a label. Everyone is for sale.

On 24 January 1939 Walter Benjamin wrote a letter to Max Horkheimer.[93] It is one of Benjamin's literary round-ups, a few snapshots of the current Paris literary scene, along with considerations on war and fascism in France and Germany. The theme of this slice through Parisian intellectual life is betrayal, on the part of the bourgeois vanguard and avant-garde alike. Paul Nizan's novel *The Conspiracy* is discussed at length. Nizan was a friend of Henri Lefebvre and together they had been involved in the 'Philosophies' circle in the mid-1920s. *The Conspiracy* is a story of a circle of super-intelligent young bourgeois men, attracted to revolutionary thought after the Russian Revolution. They seek the authentic life of risk and rejection of their philistine families. Treating revolution as a posture, they hatch two fatuous conspiracies – one military, one industrial – to try to force the pace of change. Benjamin speaks of how in the 1920s, 'when the youth were still carried by a revolutionary wave', comrades from the bourgeoisie were approvingly called 'traitors' by such as Louis Aragon. These young men are 'traitors' to their class. Nizan's story, Benjamin surmises, might be about the Surrealists who also exchanged Rimbaud and Lautréamont for Hegel and Marx.

The Conspiracy is a critique of the dullness of everyday life – voiced by the bourgeois intelligentsia, bourgeois boys with that fatal combination of time to play, an inheritance to spend, and an excessive intellect that magnifies social constriction. For brief moments their cause is identified with the proletarian cause – but it falls away – says Benjamin – because of the isolation of the proletariat.[94] That is an old story. Benjamin had written of it before. A radio lecture in 1931 on the Bastille, the French state prison, had identified the original bond of political activists and artists making common cause to overturn life as it goes on.[95] The Bastille was a place of incarceration for people who had contravened against state security. There were two classes of prisoner held there; those who were accused of conspiracy and treason, and those more numerous inmates who were writers, engravers, book dealers and binders, all people who had propagated books that offended the king or his favourites. Peopled by conspirators and seditionaries, and governed by an obfuscatory command structure, it was no surprise that the Bastille was rife with rumours. None of the inhabitants was quite certain who else lodged there behind the screened windows that stopped the prisoners from seeing the governor's strolling visitors and musicians. Systems of communication were developed, tapping information in code between cells. Prisoners disappeared from between its walls as swiftly as they had appeared, subject as they were to the whims of the powerful. The storming of the Bastille, home at that moment to just 16 prisoners, was the first visible act of destruction in the French Revolution, and it occurred, insists Benjamin, because of the arbitrariness of its punishments. Seemingly released then into the French post-revolutionary cosmos was a ragged band of writers, artists, artisans and conspirators. In short, a low-life bohemia of gossip-mongers, art-pedlars and revolters, who dispersed into the fertile air of a new class rule. Having occupied the same space of confinement, they forged a bond that bore offspring. For it was from their ranks that the avant-garde was born, as Clement Greenberg noted in 'Avant-garde and Kitsch' (1939).[96] No longer 'at home' in the prison, these homeless rebels agitate and aggravate from inside the vaster prison of the bourgeois world; opposed to that world, but inside it, they figure a place apart.

Marx and Engels wrote about this clique in 1850, in a review responding to two books: Chenu's *The Conspirators* (Paris 1850), and de la Hodde's *The Birth of the Republic* (Paris 1850).[97] It is a milieu of bohemians; critics, seditionaries, anarchists, putschist types uncomfortable with both the old order and the new as it is turning out. Marx includes amongst these bohemians full-time professional conspirators, and those who are occasional or part-time, reliant on pimping and dealing. For them all, existence is uncertain, chance-filled, and their only fixed points of call are the taverns. Their conspirators' business consists of jostling on the process of development of the revolution, artificially pushing it to crisis, plucking a revolution from out of thin air without preparing the conditions for a revolution, their critics charge. For them, the only condition of revolution is the sufficient organization of their conspiracy. They are 'alchemists of the revolution' and like alchemists they are fixated, obsessive, and champion the vaporization of ideas. The conspirators embrace wild schemes and phony science. Marx and Engels remark:

> They embrace inventions that are supposed to perform revolutionary miracles: fire bombs, destructive machines with magical effects, riots which are to be the more miraculous and surprising the less rational their foundation is.[98]

Marx and Engels scold these anarchistic spontaneists. The revolutionary conspirators have no purpose other than the overthrow of the existing government – and they deeply despise the theoretical explanations of the workers' parties, with their laborious assessments of class and economics. And, furthermore, they detest the fact that they need to take money from the '*habits noirs*', the 'black coats', 'the suits', the more or less educated representatives of the revolutionary party. They are tied to the party, but their revolt hopes to float free of its seemingly sensible mundanity. Such an attitude of ceaseless rebellion, and such a precarious existence, is carried over into the artistic milieu. Art is not so much inspired, as conspired. An avant-garde emerges whose techniques are modelled on the activities of the conspirators with whom they often times cavort – trouble-making, 360 degree critique, pranksterism, destructionism, tract and manifesto-issuing, and the like. Theirs is a critique of everyday life. The everyday must be blasted apart. It is not so far from Marx's view. A critical concept of the everyday is present in Marx. And in *Capital*, volume 3, Marx indicts this 'religion of everyday life' as the zone of the bad common-sensical, of the fetishised realm of appearance.[99] In *Value, Price and Profit*,

Marx speaks of everyday struggles, a constant class war. This is the constant encroachment of capital on daily life. That it goes on like this is the catastrophe. It throws up guerrilla fights – articulated as reformist demands – but these ceaseless skirmishes will never overturn the system that generates the tension in the first place. But nor will conspiracy, confusionism and terrorism.

These actions come from a dislodged and disaffected class fraction who thought it would rule through sheer intelligence, yet finds itself superfluous. Everyday life – that is the life of the street, low life – is a catalyst for their creativity. In a 1929 review of books by Pierre MacOrlan, Benjamin observes a fascination for the milieu of the lumpenproletariat, whores and petty criminals. This began, he says, with Flaubert and the emergence of a vague revolutionary hatred of the bourgeoisie and an intensified sense of erotics. From then on a 'subterranean communication of the intelligentsia with the yeast of the proletariat' materializes, as the 'free' intelligentsia declines, for the bourgeoisie is no longer strong enough to maintain the luxury of a 'classless' intelligentsia who once represented their interests happily and for the long term. The word avant-garde, drawn from a military or naval context – the avant-guard, the foremost division of an advancing force – crossed over from the military to politics ending up in art, in Paris, by the 1850s, just as Napoleon III elects himself emperor and secures an authoritarian rule with harsh and swift economic-political change. From then on, the relationship between avant-garde art and the vanguard party is fraught. But trickier still is the relationship between the avant-garde and the bourgeoisie.

Class politics are thrown awry after 1848 and the failure of the revolutions in Europe. The bourgeoisie is cleft, politically split. The workers' movement is knocked back. Artists scurry to the margins, representing no one clearly, and certainly not officialdom or a heroic ascendant class. It is in this atmosphere that the avant-garde militates; scuttling between factions, susceptible to influences, ideologically wed to no one force, spurning conformity in all its guises, lurching between destructive nihilism and constructive re-ordering. For the second time an intellectual front is formed, exhibiting a raw, military discipline. The first had been the front of 1789–1848, a bourgeois class on the offensive, its intellectuals in the front ranks. Marx speaks of this period, in his *Eighteenth Brumaire*, as one in which 'men and things seem set in sparkling brilliants, ecstasy is the everyday spirit' but it is 'short-lived' and 'a long crapulent depression seizes society'. The second front is defensive and the intelligentsia finds no place. It seeks therefore the romanticism of classlessness, of slipping through the ranks, to join the lumpens. They imitate them without being connected to them at all. This, notes Benjamin impatiently, has been going on for 50 years and has led to much confusion.[100] Some hitch their criticism to the fortunes of the revolution. When it goes down, so do they.

Baudelaire was a good case study for Benjamin. His existence was akin to that of the conspirators, disaffected, but dependent on money-suppliers, be that those in the market or on the left. Baudelaire, archetypal modern hero, lives off extremist politics and rebellious attitudinizing. Benjamin notes this:

> Professional conspirator and dandy fuse in the figure of the modern hero. This hero imagines himself to contain a quite secret society within his own self.[101]

Super-narcissist, at home on both sides of barricades,[102] Baudelaire epitomizes what Benjamin terms 'the metaphysics of the provocateur'.[103] In Belgium Baudelaire was regarded as a French police spy. In France he oscillates between backing the revolution of 1848 and supporting clerical reaction. For Benjamin, Baudelaire is a 'secret agent' in another sense. The class's fault-lines run through him, for he is 'an agent of the secret discontent of his class with its own rule'.[104] For him, the revolt is all, even the revolt against the revolt – hence his swift shifts of allegiance. But what matter that in a situation of such confusion that police spies, as if they truly were the rebels they imitate, fall on the barricades of Paris.[105] And where art for art's sake, as a 'negative theology' of art, mutates into a political gesture. Baudelaire's artistic attitude hinged on rumour, conspiracy, provoked scandal, and played with irony and macabre humour – as displayed in the vicious but arch prose poem *Let's Beat Up the Poor (Assommons les Pauvres)*.[106] It was, notes Benjamin, just such a milieu that produced Napoleon III, who sustained the techniques of bohemia in his rule of the Second Empire, deploying 'surprising proclamations and mystery-mongering, sudden sallies, and impenetrable irony'.[107] Avant-garde confusionism turns into the impenetrable murk of bourgeois power tactics. Scuppered by the rollback of social revolution, the avant-garde surrenders its palette of advanced techniques to the class that rules over it.

The dénouement of Nizan's *The Conspiracy* is set in the winter of 1931, when one of the characters, the poorest of the clique with the least to lose, becomes a police spy. Benjamin notes that his decision happens at the same moment as the French Communist Party is curbed, accused of planning a vast conspiracy to bring down the state. The informer justifies his action of changing sides, because he – and not just he, but his conspiring comrades too – always had to back the winning side and where once Marxism had promised the victory of the proletariat, now it was clear that the party of order would win out. That is the force of history, he says.

Its trend cannot be bucked: 'the man who wants to trick history is always tricked, nothing can be changed by petty means. Revolution is the opposite of policing.'[108]

Benjamin outlines how in the period of reaction, the avant-garde gets tangled up in economic tendrils. Of the hero of modernity, Baudelaire, *flâneur* and artist, Benjamin writes: 'He parades the concept of purchasability itself.'[109] The avant-garde exits from the dim milieu of seedy conspirators. Emerging from the underworld to snoop upstairs, the *flâneur* seeks the anonymity of the crowd, while longing to stand out.[110] Hence the immersion in everyday life, but simultaneously the desire to explode it.[111] Like the sharp-eyed political pundit or a canny consumer, he is an advance-guard researcher into capitalism. His knowledge is the secret science of booms and crashes. He wants to be in the game and ahead of the game, and he has to cheat. As *flâneurs*, the intelligentsia, artists and critics, come into the marketplace – looking for buyers. Benjamin explains: in the middle of the nineteenth century, as the avant-garde emerges, the conditions of artistic production change. Art is the commodity form that faces a mass market, and like any other commodity, it is in competition with others.[112] Citing the particular organization of poetry, he writes:

> It is important that Baudelaire came up against the relationship of competition in poetic production. Of course, the rivalries between poets are ancient. But since 1830 it was a case of rivalries being played out on the open market. This, not the protection of nobles, lords or clerics, was to be conquered. For lyric poetry, this condition was heavier than other forms of poetry. The disorganization of its styles and schools is the complement of the market, which opens before the poet as a 'public'. Baudelaire was carried by no style and had no school. It was truly a discovery for him when he found that individuals confronted him.[113]

In 1846 Baudelaire had expressed the view that the schools of art and the associations of emancipated workers confound atomisation.[114] Later, though, he had come to the recognition that art too is about commerce, and originality no mark of authentic genius, but of the good scam, the thing that will sell. The artist of modern life is permanently under threat, menaced by market rebuff. The best artists are those who get to know the market and so work it to their advantage. Internal competition is stiff. Benjamin notes how art's commodity nature is heightened by the advent of photography, for photography can pull other objects into the process of circulation, realising capital from saleable segments of the optic field – and this is most peculiarly demonstrated by art itself as the photographer Disdéri gains a state monopoly on all postcard reproductions of things in the Louvre.[115]

And that is why Benjamin concedes that technical and formal progressions may occur in advertising, that cunning by which the dream forces itself on industry. Preparing to migrate to the frames of pictures hanging in dining rooms, Benjamin tells us, are advertisements for schnapps, cocoa from van Houten, jams from Amieux.[116] Later, asserts Benjamin, the surrealists simply make this fact of commodity aesthetics explicit when, in their poetry, they treat words like names of firms and their texts are prospectuses for firms that are not yet established.[117] They have absorbed the everyday poetry of commerce into their work – or they have invented commerce as poetry. Either way, a new market of the market opens up – which returns us to Benjamin's letter to Horkheimer. The surrealists crop up several times in the letter. It is through them that Benjamin introduces his final snapshot of the Paris scene, dedicated to discussion – not of an autonomous literary creation – but a pamphlet for the jeweller's Cartier, written by the former avant-gardist Paul Claudel. It is Claudel who is mentioned in Nizan's *The Conspiracy*, when the police informer, in his testament to his former co-conspirers, reels off a list of special writers, a boast that he associated with the truly revolutionary and the truly brilliant; Claudel, Rimbaud, Valéry, Proust.[118] Benjamin notes how on 1 July 1925 the surrealists had put out a leaflet called 'Open Letter to Mr Paul Claudel, ambassador to Japan'. They wrote:

> For us there can be no talk of balance or great art. The idea of the beautiful has long gone to roost. Only the moral idea remains incontestable – for example the knowledge that one cannot be French ambassador and a poet at the same time.[119]

Benjamin feels vindicated. The jewellers Cartier have produced a little book called *Mystique of Precious Stones*, written by Claudel. It is not for sale, but is available at jewellers, and it does not seek to educate readers about the mystique of precious stones through history, but rather to be an ambassador for stones in order to sell them. Its language is high-flown. And like the patron in old pictures, Cartier appears in the book. Claudel calls him a merchant, such as is praised in the Gospel. He delivers the sea of its mystical fabrication – the pearl. Claudel tells how a poor blind and deaf man finds the pearls by scooping in the depths, in order that he, Claudel, might now hold in his hand this angel-made, holy nothingness. Benjamin is clear – this is where the poetry of advertising language has ended up, in a botched avant-gardism that adds up the elements incorrectly. Though the image of the advert-speak betrays a truth: the merchant has his place in the shadow of the gospels. The proletariat – blind and dumb from labour – suffers under the curse of work, and finally there is the consumer, the one to whom this new beatitude is directed. And the pearl is the mystical mustard seed of the Gospel. For Matthew, it is the smallest seed but once grown it outstrips all the others. What happens to it is child's play compared to the miraculous deeds of the pearl in economic life. Benjamin quotes Claudel:

> The pfennig has its exchange value, law prescribes it, but justice guarantees it. But the pearl, product of the duration and fruit of the sea, has no other value than its beauty ... Its appearance on the market devalues all other goods; it changes their price; it brings disquiet to the banks, it threatens the balance of all transactions. For it carries with it an element that is absent from any number: I am speaking of that spiritual covetousness which comes from contemplation.[120]

'Value' is the unavailable mystery. So speaks a diplomat – also one of the first to order luxury spectacle frames from Cartier in the 1930s, together with Henry Bernstein, Francis de Croisset, Jean Cocteau, Colette, Gaby Morlay, Gabrielle Dorziat. His words are well wrought, embellished enough to glorify the everyday world of commerce. The surrealists meet their nemesis. Out of a seedy milieu of rebels, putschists, conspirators, and nonconformist types, it would seem that the law of the market, and the failure of social revolution, spawn a hardened hoard of hacks and cops and dispossessed, flushed out of the underworlds and pulled into commodity worlds, and many of them are bought up then to render surveillance functions and broadcast conspiracy theory in a darkening world. In 1938, Benjamin notes how Baudelaire once wrote in a diary: 'A fine conspiracy could be organized for the purpose of exterminating the Jewish race.' By the time Benjamin wrote this, far more powerful conspirators and snoops were in charge in Germany.

Consumers: Empathy and Fetishism

In a letter to Horkheimer, written in August 1938, Benjamin notes the importance of Marx's concept of commodity fetishism.[121] The mechanisms of 'commodity fetishism confuse the genuine categorization of history'.[122] They exude an ideological effect. Benjamin attempts both to depict and unravel the ideological confusions in the categorization of history. Society's repression of production, because of the form of fetishized production, makes its representation of itself fetishistic. This thing that the bourgeoisie calls its culture is phantasmagoric.[123] It is a fantasy, a projection, a fabrication that hopes to deny its fabricated provenance. In the

1939 'Exposé' of the *Passagenwerk* the concept of the phantas-magoria becomes a key methodological concept.[124] Benjamin's idea of the phantasmagoria particularly disturbs Adorno when he encounters it in 'Das Paris des Second Empire bei Baudelaire'. He finds it an insufficiently objective category and indicative only of the 'vision of social characters'.[125] The category of phantasmago-ria indicates, for Benjamin, a lived relationship to experience on the part of a class that does not recognize itself as class but as mass, because the organization of production encourages it to overlook actual relations of production. The structure of the commodity economy reinforces the phantasmagoria of existence.[126] Such phantasms exude an intoxicating effect. Benjamin insists that as long as existence is structured by phantasmagoria humanity will be delivered up to mythical angst. The human face of the collective can only emerge once the enchanted, commodity-seduced mass is expunged. The century has been unable to align a new social order to the new technical possibilities and so the 'deceptive mediations of old and new gain the upper hand. This is the core of its phan-tasmagoria'.[127] Such phantasms are structurally occasioned, but Benjamin's political recommendations demand a break from the sway of phantasmagoric fictions. To consumers, commodities seem autonomous, ahistorical and discrete from human production. Traces of production in objects of consumption are repressed, so as to disguise the fact that the person who exchanges commodities did not make those goods, but appropriated the work contained in them. Under capitalism, social labour appears in the form of the exchange of objects as equivalents. This has implications for the nature of ideology: social relations appear in the form of things and what is social and historical is mistaken for natural and eternal. Social atomization impedes the development of class-conscious struggle. Facsimiled in the endless reflections of mirrors and shop windows in cities, the crowd, claims Benjamin, is recast as spectacle. It watches itself walking, wanting and buying. The mob of the nineteenth century has been domesticated and disciplined. It is now a consumer crowd, individuals in the mass who are encouraged to forget their role as producers. The mass of mass society, those swelling ranks of customers, audiences, producers, visible from the late nineteenth century, is located in the department store, at the sites of consumption.[128] The process of amassing of individuals across class – in the theatre, in the army, in the city – is boosted massively by the free market.[129] The total-itarian states make the mass society their model.[130] The *Volksgemeinschaft* tries to expel everything that prevents individuals melting into a customer mass. Benjamin brings the phantasmagoric consciousness and its glossing over of the reality of class difference into connection with both commodity fetishism and totalitarianism, forming a span between his study of nineteenth century Paris and his meditations on Nazi Germany:

> The connection that this has to the modern is demonstrated perhaps best of all by the *flâneur*. The semblance of a crowd motivated by itself, containing its own soul, is what satisfies his thirst for novelty. In fact this collective is nothing but semblance. This crowd, on which the *flâneur* feasts, is the hollow form, into which seventy years later the *Volksgemeinschaft* was poured. The *flâneur* who prides himself so on his alertness, on his self-sufficiency, was also ahead of his contemporaries, in that he was the first to fall victim to a delusion that has blinded many millions since then.[131]

Benjamin insists that the chimeras of consumption and the mass consciousness (substituted for class consciousness) of the crowd conceal the reality inherent but obscured in the experience of production. Capitalism issues from the social relation between monopoly capital, whose agent is the state, and wage labour. As such it is a relation of exploitation and struggle. The reality of class struggle reveals the illegitimacy of fictions about the social order.[132] Benjamin writes of the proletariat: 'it dispels the appearance ('*Schein*') of the mass through the reality of class.'[133] Recognition of the reality of class is permanently in danger of being eclipsed. Identification with commodities and the act of shopping threatens to shatter any solidarity between producers. Not only the relationships between person and commodity and between person and person are fetishized, but also the relationship between worker and means of production. Benjamin goes so far as to assume that the danger exists that the producer of things empathizes with the manufacturing machines, with 'its fetishistically driven objects', so as to supplant itself as their 'soul'.[134]

It transpires that ideas of endless perfection and the idea of eternal recurrence are not disconnected from one another. The belief in progress towards an endless perfectibility and the idea of an eternal return are complementary antinomies, both mythically grounded or beyond the scope of any possibility of human intervention. Both are examples of a 'flat rationalism' that excludes any appeal to the evidence of human experience.[135] Benjamin construes capitalist acculturation as training in a distanced and debilitated seeing. He details his category of 'empathy'. Empathy spans both the relationship between people and the past and the relation between people and products, in commodity-producing society. Empathy is promoted between the mass and ruling class ideology and between producer-consumers and exchange value. The self adopts the position of the commodity. Consumers sympathize with commodity objects. Consumers empathize with the turning of subjects into objects.[136] Benjamin insists that the lesson of the world exhibitions – 'where the masses in consuming learnt empathy with exchange value' – is 'look at everything, touch nothing'.[137]

Anti-sympathy, Pro-modernist

Historicism is the enemy. Historicism uses an 'additive' procedure, presenting a mass of facts to fill up empty and homogeneous time where history passes by without human input, a tale of great men, like us but not quite like us little people. Benjamin uncovers a central strand in historicist philosophy: the conception of a continual progressive course of history as a pile-up of event after event. Historicism, claims Benjamin, is happy to establish causal connections between moments in history, threading together sequences of events as if they were the stringed beads of a rosary.[138] Historicism deals in empathy with the version of the historical past presented by the ruling class. This past is closed to re-evaluation from the perspective of the oppressed. In a preparatory note for 'Über den Begriff der Geschichte' Benjamin points out how historicism depends on recounting the antics of glorious heroes of history in monumental and epic form, and is in no position to say anything about the 'nameless':[139]

> It is more arduous to honour the memory of the nameless than that of the renowned. The celebrated, that of poets and thinkers is no exception. Historical construction is devoted to the memory of the nameless.[140]

Obstructing the loudly professed endless perfectibility of humanity, Benjamin wishes to construct a re-visioning of the past, wherein the historian bears witness to an endless brutality committed against the 'oppressed'. This he understands to have been Marx's task in *Das Kapital*. *Das Kapital* is a memorial, an anti-epic memorial, pulsating in the present, impacting on the relation between the present and the past, insisting on redress. Marx's depiction of the lot of labour is presented as a riposte to the vacuum of historical experience. Marx memorializes the labour of the nameless, whose suffering produced 'wealth' in the vast accumulations of commodities.

Benjamin's favourite Bolshevik slogan from the Russian revolutionary years was: 'No fame for the victor, no pity for the vanquished' (*Kein Ruhm dem Sieger, kein Mitleid den Besiegten*).[141] The phrase raises the question of remembering concretely the revolution that spawned it. How to mark an event where word is that the heroes are not great individuals, but a class acting for itself. What the Bolsheviks did is of interest here. Lenin's secular 'Plan of Monumental Propaganda', was presented to Lunacharsky in

1918. Lenin evoked *Civitas Solis* by the Renaissance utopian, Campanella. In Campanella's ideal town, the walls were adorned with frescos, dispensing an optic education in natural science and history. Lenin declared likewise that short, expressive inscriptions be positioned in significant sites, on suitable walls or on special constructions. These inscriptions were to contain the most basic Marxist principles and slogans and tightly worked out formulations evaluating historical events. But more important than these slogans, he asserted, were 'statues – be they busts or bas-reliefs of figures and groups'. They would not be 'of marble, granite and gold incised lettering' but 'modest, and let everything be temporary'.[142] The concept of monumental propaganda was deleted in the presentation of the ephemeral and contingent. The past was preserved and cancelled at the same time, in conceptually complex, but visually direct street scenes – such as the encaged statue of Alexander III on Uprising Square, detourned and decorated by Ivan A. Fomin in Leningrad, in 1927. Some designers took revolutionary concepts into the realm of abstraction. The task they posed themselves was how to formulate visually and tightly, but without glorification of individuals, the events that were occurring. A concise solution appeared in Nikolai Kolli's building-sized structure, a constructivist object depicting a red wedge cleaving a white bloc. It commemorated the first anniversary of the Revolution and was erected on Revolution Square.[143] This was a concrete blow against an historicism whose bastions Benjamin outlined: the strongest being the 'empathy with the victor', which always suits the current rulers. In its stead the monument posed an intellectual abstraction. Another bastion of historicism that it overturned was the idea of a universal history – that is, the idea that history is a history of the human race, composed of nations. This monument presented the case of class solidarity, class cleavage and internationalism. Another historicist position that the monument smashed was the notion that 'history was something that could be narrated', that history presented a linear story whose events could be threaded and fingered one after another like beads on a rosary.[144] Instead it offers a moment of splitting, a revolutionary idea. With this point, Marx's methodology enters into the frame. Benjamin outlines what he understands of Marx's methodology several times in the notes, though it does not appear in the final transcription of the theses:

> In a materialist study epic continuity is abandoned in favour of constructive conclusiveness. Marx recognized that 'the history' of capital is represented only as the steely, widespanned scaffold of theory. It grasps the constellation into which his own epoch has entered with quite specific earlier moments of history. It

contains a concept of the present as the now-time, in which are exploded splinters of messianic time.[145]

A version of the last sentence appears in the appendix to the published theses – but the reference to Marx was cut. A similar sentiment exists in note form:

> In a materialist study the epic moment is blasted unavoidably in the train of construction. The liquidation of the epic element is to be taken on as Marx did, as author of *Capital*. He realised that the history of capital is only to be constructed in the steely, widespanned framework of a theory. In his theoretical outline of labour under the domination of capital, which Marx lays down in his work, the interests of humanity are better preserved and transcended than in the monumental, ponderous – at root leisurely – works of historicism.[146]

Benjamin's point is that Marx's *Kapital* provides the model for a materialist history, that is, a modernist history – a history that sets out in full theoretical self-consciousness. For the dialectic of theory and practice, historical reality is constructed out of categories, essential concepts that work back on the history that is recounted. To be explained are the mediations between the moments of capital. External temporal continuity is less relevant. History breaks down into images not stories – it is the flash, not the continuum that is important. Precisely, it is the continuum that is to be arrested. Its method counters historicism at each move. It refuses continuity, linearity, in favour of a synoptic glare, in which each element of the whole is unfolded from each other element. An entire system of global exploitation is unfolded from its smallest, yet at the same time most inclusive, element, the commodity.

Instead of empathy, anti-heroes and cleavage, blasting significance from the fragments that bear traces of the whole. Marx's introduction to *Grundrisse*, first published in 1939, the year that Benjamin composes the theses, has a similar perspective:

> Bourgeois society is the most developed and the most complex historic organization of production. The categories which express its relations, the comprehension of its structure, thereby also allows insights into the structure and the relations of production of all the vanished social formations out of whose ruins and elements it built itself up, whose partly still unconquered remnants are carried along within it, whose mere nuances have developed explicit significance within it, etc.[147]

Marx continues:

> It would therefore be unfeasible and wrong to let the economic categories follow one another in the same sequence as that in

which they were historically decisive. Their sequence is
determined, rather, by their relation to one another in modern
bourgeois society, which is precisely the opposite of that which
seems to be their natural order which corresponds to historical
development.[148]

This casts economic and social relations in a new light. No
longer to be related is a tale of unfolding history – for history read
progress – but rather a snapshot of now with its contradictions
intact, with its histories still pulsating in the present.[149] This is
what Benjamin means by introducing a theoretical structure, rather
than an epic sweep. History as unfolding is supplanted by an inter-
rogation of time, viewed in capitalism, as empty, homogeneous,
rather than as it might be, filled, or fulfilled. Time, for Marx, is
the question to which 'all economy ultimately reduces itself'.[150]
The quality of time-experience is to be replaced in the project of
comprehending social relations. Benjamin describes the historical
subject, whose critical situation the materialist is to recall. The
historical subject 'is not transcendental but the fighting, oppressed
class in its most exposed situation'. Historical knowledge comes to
it alone, but it comes in flashes, moments and involuntary
memories, which prove the liquidation of the epic mode.[151] The
lightning flash, the profane illumination, the dialectical image has
no truck with melancholy, with slowness, repetition and contemplation.

'Über den Begriff der Geschichte' imports modernist theory into
historiography, in order to prepare the way for new and different
histories – of the past, present and future. History writing is
allegorical and filmic, based on fragmentation, montage and construction. In a letter to Gretel Adorno of April 1940, Benjamin
draws specific attention to the seventeenth thesis, stating that it is
this one that best reveals the hidden but conclusive methodological connection of these considerations with previous writings.[152]
The seventeenth thesis outlines Benjamin's 'constructive' historical
method.[153] In it Benjamin posits another construction, incorporating a different vision of historical time:

> History is the object of a construction, whose site is not that of
> homogeneous and empty time, but one filled with now-time.[154]

Unlike historicism, materialist historiography arrests a moment
of time and illuminates each historical trace, so providing a 'revolutionary chance in the struggle for the oppressed past'.[155] The
sentiment is doubled: an allegorical, constructive methodology
imparts the past of the politically repressed and the repressed past.
Even universal history, condemned as the bad historiography of
historicism, is acceptable, indeed messianic, if it is organized
according to a constructive principle.[156] 'Über den Begriff der

Geschichte' transmits formally, as well as thematically, discontinuity, fragmentation and a catastrophic structure of history. Such
characteristics, Benjamin insists, are closer to the actual experience
of history. One technique is the use of allegory. From *Ursprung des
deutschen Trauerspiels* (1923–25) through to the 'Baudelaire file' in
the *Passagenwerk* Benjamin associates the allegorical method with
the dialectical method. Allegory's fragmented and manifold articulation forces an active mode of reception on the audience.
Allegory ties together disparate things in vivid images, shooting
across a total picture, blasting into meaning significant parts. The
totality appears to us, fetishistically, in fragments. In the late
writings on Baudelaire, Benjamin focuses on the notion of allegory
as a literary-technical means to present the complex epistemology
of the now. An allegorized approach is seen to be historically
appropriate, in that it represents the actual stakes of the historically real as experienced in commodity capitalism.[157] Allegory is
a disfiguration of social disfigurement.[158] It has two important
technical properties: the anti-symbolist ability to disrupt aesthetic
illusions of the real, and the forcing together, through montage or
image pile-ups, realms that are seemingly discrete, but actually
connected. One example of this is the allegorical relationship of
prostitute and worker. Allegory is a technical means to retransmit
discontinuity, fragmentation and a catastrophic structure of
history.[159] In 'Zentralpark' (1938) Benjamin writes: 'Majesty of
the allegorical intention: destruction of the organic and living –
extinguishing of semblance.'[160] The allegorical intention expels
the 'false semblance of totality' of the organic by shattering it into
fragments.[161] Benjamin's organicism, in contrast, always relates
to the technical. Allegory exerts technical effort on the organic. To
write allegorically, for Benjamin, is to shatter fetishistic fallacies of
natural appearance and false totalities – a homogenization that
plugs critical distanciation. The allegorical method, like film, rips
up the manifestly natural context of things, snapping open the
apparent continuity of nature and history and prising apart space
for reinterpretation and transformation. Allegory makes clear the
dependence of the image on the action of interpretation. The
interpreter of allegory is as capacitated as Benjamin's film spectator
or the theatre-goer at a play by Brecht or the activist poring over
a photomontage by John Heartfield. Allegory and film and montage
are capable of transmitting a broken vicious misery now, as well as
relaying the possibility for critique of that brokenness. Film had
promised to heal the scars of alienation by representing that
alienation. Allegory works similarly:

> Allegory struggles against this deceptive transfiguring of the
> commodity world by disfiguring it.[162]

The critical impact of aura-annihilating objects resides with Benjamin's readiness to take illustrations of negativity – death, corpses, *Unmenschen*, destructive characters – as tokens of 'redemption'. It is from this perspective that Benjamin takes pains to incorporate the energies of hate into class struggle.[163] Hate is a distrustful, debunking and vengeful attitude. Hugo Fischer, in *Karl Marx und sein Verhältnis zu Staat und Wirtschaft*, a book used by Benjamin for his researches into Marxism, states that Marx's politics are born mainly out of hatred.[164] Benjamin approves this. In a capitalist world it is necessary, maintains Benjamin, to use a certain violence to rip through the myths of concord. Benjamin found this, in unsystematic form, in Baudelaire: 'Baudelaire's allegory bears traces of the violence that was necessary to tear apart the harmonious façade of the world around him.'[165] The trouble with social democracy, according to Benjamin, is its lack of hate. Liberation is to occur in the name of future generations. Benjamin notes:

> This training made the working class forget both its hatred and its spirit of sacrifice, for both are fed by the image of enslaved ancestors rather than that of liberated grandchildren.[166]

In notes for the theses on history, Benjamin registered his motivation for recasting notions of recording the past. He claimed that:

> an idea of history that has freed itself from the schema of progression in an empty and homogeneous time would at last lead back into the field the destructive energies of historical materialism that have lain paralysed for so long.[167]

The first purpose of the theses, then: the redemption of historical materialism. The Bolshevik slogan 'No fame for the victor, no pity for the vanquished' (*Kein Ruhm dem Sieger, kein Mitleid den Besiegten*) is understood to mean that solidarity must be expressed with dead brothers, rather than with future generations.[168] Again, then, the stress falls on redemption, redeeming knowledge of the past, in order to act in the present. This Bolshevik slogan closed thesis XII in the first completed version of the theses on the philosophy of history.[169] Later versions of the theses were written most consciously with an awareness of possible censorship issues, if the theses were to pass through the postal system.[170] At one stage 'historical materialism' became 'historical dialectic', 'class struggle' became 'the struggle in antagonistic society' or 'conflict', the 'oppressed' becomes the 'subordinate', 'vulgar Marxist' becomes 'vulgar', 'fascism' becomes 'the totalitarian state order'.[171] Traces of Marx in the theses were smudged, secreted only in remaining half-sentences.

Techniques of History Writing

we have other jobs than to aid governments which are subjectively reactionary (such as the United States and England), that is accomplices of the enemy, and objectively the playthings of historical necessities which they don't understand. We have our own jobs and it is only in doing these without compromise that we will contribute to the downfall of the Nazis – never in becoming conformist.

Victor Serge: 'What is Fascism? The Discussion Continued', January 1940[172]

Benjamin perceives writing about the past as a form of avenging. He alludes to the kaleidoscope of concepts that click into new patterns according to the priorities and exigencies of the ruling class at each moment.[173] Revolutionary political practice demands that the kaleidoscope of concepts must be smashed. From the ruins other configurations emerge. The losers, not the victors, get their chance to form patterns. Benjamin posits a historiography based on the flash of the dialectical image, a sudden memory that emerges replete at the instant of danger.[174] It is a sort of interruption in the continuity of historical narrative. This irruption arrests activity, constituting a 'revolutionary chance in the struggle for the oppressed past'.[175] This memory can be inserted in the place left vacant by the evacuation of memory in capitalist daily life.[176] In cracking open the idea of the pastness of the past, the 'once upon a time' attitude, and in wresting the past away from the single ruling-class narrative of history, construction of a dialectical concept of historical time is made possible.[177]

In a letter, written on 16 March 1937, Horkheimer challenged Benjamin's view of the 'uncompletedness' of history. The crimes that have been committed against the oppressed, and the pain that has been suffered, are irreparable. Benjamin affirms this from a scientific perspective, but rejects it as a one-dimensional conception of historiography. Constructing history is not only to be seen as a task contained by a scientific discipline, but also, suggests Benjamin, transposing romanticism's conception of the after-life of artworks to social life, as a form of 'remembrance'.

> What science has determined, remembrance can modify. Remembrance can make the incomplete (happiness) completed and the completed (suffering) incomplete.[178]

This is what is called theology. Theology emerges as the moment of transformational possibility. Theology is, here, the moment of outstripping the given. Transforming the interpretation of the past opens the field for the transformation of the future. The representation of history is an impetus for political action. 'Fulfilled

time' is the time of remembrance of past time, which is simultaneously part of the consciousness of present historical action, as
thesis XII displays. It is the space of reinterpretation and the space
of re-intervention in the past. Philosophy is not capable of changing
the world, but of changing the image of change and, in so doing,
clearing the way for the forces of change or, as Benjamin modestly
puts it, improving our position in the fight against fascism.[179] Bad
historiography transmits only conformist ideology, claims
Benjamin, although it imagines that it retransmits the past 'as it
actually was'.[180] Benjamin insists on the construction of past, lost
possibilities from the viewpoint of the oppressed.

One vignette in 'Über den Begriff der Geschichte' is based on a
watercolour by Paul Klee. Benjamin wanted to collect art by Klee,
and, if he had been wealthy in later years, he might have acquired
several items. In April 1921 Benjamin went to a Klee exhibition in
Berlin, and at end of May he went to Munich and bought a
watercolour called *Angelus Novus*. The new angel, affixed above
his desk wherever he lived, fluttered through his life. It provided
the name for a critical journal he wished to found. He wrote about
it as example of the childlike aesthetic at the core of the modernism
he prized. The picture seems to detail history's doubled capacity
for progression and regression.

> There is an image by Klee called Angelus Novus. On it an angel
> is depicted who looks as if he is about to distance himself from
> something that he is staring at. His eyes are wide-open, his
> mouth is agape, and his wings are spread. This is how the angel
> of history must look. He has turned his face towards the past.
> Where, in front of *us*, a chain of events appear, *he* sees one single
> catastrophe. This unrelentingly piles rubble on rubble and flings
> it at his feet. He would really like to stay, awaken the dead, and
> repair the smashed pieces. But a storm is blowing over from
> paradise, and it is tangled in his wings and is so strong that the
> angel can no longer close them. This storm forces him irresistibly
> into the future to which his back is turned, while the pile of
> rubble in front of him grows skyward. This storm is what *we* call
> progress.[181]

The storm that blows the angel away from the mounting
wreckage and into the future is the storm of progress. The angel
stares at the skyward-growing junk pile of debris, dreadful historical
events, wasted lives, futile objects. The angel, like Benjamin, wants
to gather up the rubbish and the rubble on the ever-growing junk
pile. But the angel's optic – his eyes are staring, his mouth is open
– is one of impotence. Touch, intervention into the catastrophic
unfurling, is what he cannot achieve. Collecting the rubbish
together, mending it all, would be the act that could renew the

hopes for progress through technology, raised in the nineteenth century and so horribly betrayed at the beginning of the twentieth. It marks that 'hope in the past', hope encapsulated in the arc between past and present, or the '*weak* messianic power' with which each generation has been endowed.

In a radio lecture on Brecht and commitment, delivered in 1962, Adorno insists that Klee's angel is the angel of the machine. Adorno tracks a direct line from Klee's First World War cartoons of Kaiser Wilhelm as inhuman iron-eater to the Angelus Novus.[182] If Benjamin's *Angelus Novus* is likewise seen not only as an angel of history, but also as an angel of the machine, the full force of ambiguities of the machine's role in Benjamin's social theory can be unpacked. The new angel is impotent witness to a continual destruction, and yet still asserts its desire to heal. It wants to 'pick up the pieces', but it cannot because of the logic of the dynamic that has ensnared it. In order for salvation to occur, a subject must be activated. This subject must have historical knowledge, and be one who takes full cognizance of the memories of past brutalities that have actually affected the body of the proletariat. This subject must be capable of action in the face of the continuing historical catastrophe. Benjamin hopes to enable a politics based on a historiography that takes into account the role of historical subjects. Important here in this idea of subjective activity is the idea of the leap. This comment appears at the close of thesis XIV:

> The French Revolution viewed itself as Rome reincarnated. It quoted ancient Rome the way fashion quotes costumes of the past. Fashion has a flair for the topical, no matter where it stirs in the thickets of long ago; it is a tiger's leap into the past. This leap, however, occurs in an arena where the ruling class gives commands. The same leap in the open air of history is the dialectical one, which is how Marx understood revolution.[183]

The leap is a name for the grasping at historical transfiguration. This word leap evokes Lenin's reading of Hegel's *Logic*. C.L.R. James enthuses about this moment:

> In reading 'On Quality in the Doctrine of Being', Lenin writes in very large writing:
>
>
> LEAP
>
> LEAP
>
> LEAP
>
> LEAP
>
> This obviously hit him hard. He wanted it stuck down in his head, to remember it, always.[184]

James goes on to explicate the importance of this jump in Lenin's thought. He quotes from Lenin's notes, scrawled while reading Hegel's *Logic*.

> Look at this remarkable note on Observation 3. Movement and self-movement (NB this. An independent (*eigenmächtige*) spontaneous, *internally necessary* movement), alteration, movement and life, principle of every self-movement, impulse, (drive) to movement and to activity – opposite of dead being – who would believe that this is the core of Hegelianism, of abstract and abstruse (difficult, absurd?) Hegelianism. We must uncover this core, grasp it, save, unveil, purify it – which Marx and Engels have also accomplished.[185]

For James, it means a new recognition on Lenin's part, his own political, theoretical leap. During the war years, in Zurich, as his previous categories break up with the self-immolation of the Second International, Lenin breaks through to an essential revolutionary precept: leap equals spontaneous activity equals self-movement. Benjamin demands the leap on the eve of a new world war.

Benjamin's call for an interventionist moment demands actors: 'man enough to explode the continuum of history open'.[186] Who is man enough? What the angel is incapable of carrying out becomes the job of both the 'historical materialist' who remembers past dismemberment, and the 'subject of historical knowledge', the 'fighting, oppressed class itself' who is Marx's revenging class, not the social democratic redeemer of future generations.[187] The concept of history itself becomes a medium of class struggle. Benjamin writes the perspective of the classless society as possibility into the theory of history itself.

Benjamin's earliest notes describe one aim of the *Passagenwerk*: to formulate a dialectical philosophy of history that can overcome the ideology of progress in all its aspects.[188] 'Über den Begriff der Geschichte' is a late attempt to write a dialectical philosophy of history that denounces the content of inherited ideologies of progress. This occurs in part by separating the category of *Technik* into forces and relations of production, and arguing that development in both realms forms the only correct basis for measuring progress. Once more, as in 'Der Autor als Produzent' (1934) and elsewhere, an interest in uncovering a dynamic of *Technik* is supplemented with an interest in intellectual *Technik*, that is experimentation with modes of expression, including manipulating ways of disrupting ideologies of continuity and progress and inherited modes of reception. This politics of form has been a long-term undertaking. In a sense by reframing conceptual models, he introduces a moment of experimentation into historiography. Benjamin works on modes of presentation in order to incorporate the possibility of revolution, theoretically. Such deliberation on conceptual models could be interpreted as a sign of defeat, an exiting from practice. Of course, at the time of drafting the theses on the philosophy of history and the late Baudelaire writings, effective revolutionary practice has become immeasurably more difficult, and, for that very reason, more critical. Benjamin's gesture is not simply idealistic. Mindful of the reflex between theory and practice, he sets out to redraft ways of conceptualizing revolution, in order to provide a corrective to practice.

In 'Über den Begriff der Geschichte' Benjamin struggles to come up with a Marxist materialist theory in a tremendously violent world, during the grisliest moments of objective defeat of the working class. The class's impotence is matched by the impotence of the exiled author. His critique of vulgar-Marxism and social democracy is certain that the proletariat is at this moment not the fighting, recognizing class. The German working class has indeed been corrupted by the opinion, promoted by social democracy, that it is they who 'are swimming with the current' of technological development.[189] Social democracy has abetted the lethal cutting of the veins of the working class. The disfigurement of the class is the most compelling reason for despair.

From his first experiments in materialist theorizing Benjamin engages in a critique of *Technik* as part of a political fight to bring to view a system in which forces and relations of production are consonant with one another. But his project has a greater urgency in these final moments, precisely because the temporary victory of the enemy occurs in the context of a debased working class, existing in a mystified relationship to its technologies. Ultimately, the only thing left at this moment is for the theorist to follow Benjamin's prescriptions and be 'man enough' to use theoretical techniques that try to counteract the depravity of the German working class; techniques that must be introduced into a materialism gone awry. The theorist is the last subject left to break up the continuity of catastrophe as theoretical gesture. If the theorist is heard, and the conceptualization of politics (and with it theories of technology, class and history) correspondingly altered, then theory moves into the realm of practice. Theory might then become a material force as soon as it is gripped by the masses.

Benjamin is clear: 'Not man or men but the struggling, oppressed class itself is the depository of historical knowledge.' He goes on to remark that in Marx it appears as the last enslaved class, as the avenger that completes the task of liberation in the name of generations of the downtrodden.[190] Benjamin's emphasis is on the intimate connection between struggle, historical practice and knowledge, theory. Such a formulation recalls an earlier set of theses that may well have provided the Benjamin's model, Marx's 'Theses on Feuerbach', written in 1845. The 'Theses on Feuerbach' were, according to Engels' notes, which accompanied their first publication in 1888, 'written down quickly, absolutely not meant to be printed, but invaluable as the first document, wherein the brilliant seed of the new world view is planted'.[191]

In 1917 Lenin also penned, in isolation, a series of theses, characterized by Zalezhski as 'an exploding bomb',[192] which would turn the drift of thought into revolutionary action. In remarks on Hegel, from 1915, arguably the necessary philosophical study that made the revolutionary-pragmatic concepts in his 'April Theses' possible, Lenin comments:

> We cannot imagine, express, measure, depict movement, without interrupting continuity, without simplifying, coarsening, dismembering, strangling that which is living. The representation of movement by means of thought always makes coarse, kills, – and not only by means of thought, but also by sense-perception, and not only of movement, but every concept.
>
> And in that essence lies dialectics.
>
> And precisely *this essence* is expressed by the formula: the unity, identity of opposites.[193]

Lenin notes thought's forcing of a discontinuity on actuality. He emphasizes the moment of interruption of thought, the splitting of concepts, suspending movement in order to make thought possible, just as Benjamin too claimed: 'thinking involves not only the flow of thoughts, but their arrest as well.'[194] The essence of dialectics is in this arrest, this splitting. It nestles in its very name. *Dia* means splitting in two, opposed, clashing and *lectics* comes from logos, the word for word or reason. The concept must be split.

Marx's theses and Lenin's theses and Benjamin's theses all propose a break with former dominant modes of thought on the left, and a new visioning of the relationship between thought and practice. Indeed, it is possible to say that such visioning is precisely the talent of the thesis form. Theses work on the cusp of theory and practice, twisting thought into practical action. In this sense, theses cannot but be dialectical. The 'Theses on Feuerbach', the 'April Theses' and 'Theses on the Philosophy of History' break with old modes, which compounds their difficulty. They compose new concepts, in order to shift the space of thought and action. The theses strive to hold open a space for the possibility of revolutionary political activity in the darkest years of the century, but simultaneously, in Benjamin's case, they represent the climax of the alienation and marginalization of the German intellectual who speaks in tongues to the few who listen. But the chances of these recommendations – written on the run – being taken on were slim. Indeed the theses were not even intended for publication. In a letter to Gretel Adorno, written in April 1940, Benjamin discloses:

> I don't need to inform you that I have not the least intention of publishing these notes (and certainly not in the form in which they have been presented to you). They would open up the floodgates to enthusiastic misinterpretation.[195]

Does Benjamin assume misinterpretation will arise from these cryptic formulations, as they struggle to break with previous modes of expression and thought, or is it that his scrambling of the political map that traditionally divides left and right, reformist and revolutionary, is only conceivable with difficulty and meaningful to so few? When Brecht first read the theses one year after their composition, recasting Benjamin's fears expressed in the letter to Gretel Adorno, he commented that the number of those willing even to misunderstand them was too few.[196]

Benjamin's Finale: Excavating and Remembering

Photography and Book Jackets

There is so often a photograph of Walter Benjamin accompanying editions of his writings or writings about him. Few authors are so excessively imaged in this way. It is usually a photograph taken by Germaine Krull in 1938.[1] Occasionally the pictures used are by Gisèle Freund, whose theoretical writings about photography deeply impressed Benjamin and contributed to his sociology of the image. Sometimes a sombre and frumpy image of Benjamin taken in 1939 is used.[2] Another image by Freund, snapped in 1937, has also illustrated book jackets.[3] Freund provided some incidental images of Benjamin. She used him as an extra in a photo-series on the libraries of Paris. This appeared in a magazine in 1937. An excerpted image of Benjamin from this series forms part of the jacket design of *Benjaminiana*.[4] On other occasions Charlotte Joel is the photographer. Her pictures stem from the late 1920s. These mechanical image-makers were all women – perhaps that signalled to Benjamin the progressive aspect of photography, as cultural form and historical technology, compared to painting. Another photograph favoured as garnish for the book commodity is an anonymously authored image from 1916, with Benjamin shabby-looking in a crumpled suit.[5] Dora, his future and then former wife, is customarily cut out of the picture. A second photograph by Germaine Krull also appears occasionally.[6] This was taken in 1927. Susan Sontag opens her introduction to an English collection of essays by Benjamin with a tender description of this photograph.[7] She then goes on to describe three more photographs, emphasizing how Benjamin's eyes are always shielded, his glance averted. Sontag's semiotic analysis of this Benjaminian gaze reveals a profoundly melancholic hero, caught up from early on in a disastrous biographical unfolding. All these images, such atmospheric portraits, appear staged to cash in on just that status of the photographic portrait detected by Benjamin in 'Das Kunstwerk im Zeitalter seiner technischen Reproduzierbarkeit' (1935–39). Portrait photographs provide celluloid evidence of 'the cult of remembrance of loved ones, absent or dead', wherein nestles the last glimmer of that disempowering structure called aura.[8] Photographs possess cult value. Benjamin's cultic being, apparently inextricably entwined from way back in the fatal logic that steers him to his suicide, seems graphically, indexically displayed in these tragic photographs of the hero. Perhaps such a reading of the photograph is set up by Benjamin's own analysis, in 'Kleine Geschichte der Photographie', of an early photograph, an image of Dauthendey and his wife. A high-contrast, stilted image of the photographed photographer, catching the eye of the viewer, while his wife looks aslant into a fateful distance, appears to Benjamin to contain clues to her future slashed-wrist suicide.[9] However, in Benjamin's case when it comes to the business of academic illustration, the excessive deployment of the image of the author seems to reinforce precisely what Benjamin criticizes in the same article, when he attacks conventional bourgeois portrait photography. The photographs are strongly contextualized to confirm the myth of Benjamin as a solitary, lonely, melancholic intellectual. True to his film fascination, Benjamin attempted a type of thinking in images. For example, some of the theses on history, such as thesis IX on the Angel of History, describe a kind of film-montage – the description of Paul Klee's *Angelus Novus*, the analogy between this and the angel of history, and at one and the same time, our picturing of the identical scene that the angel sees. Such image-thinking presents a concentration of data, an allusiveness that breaks open too secure a reading, throwing the act of interpretation back onto the reader. But his own image has worked back on him. There is a strong identification forged between the image and the man. Benjamin, in interpretations, has become the embodiment of reduced versions of his images – sometimes the aloof *flâneur*, but most often sad Benjamin, the impotent angel of history, unable to fix things, avatar of brokenness as virtue. The book jacket photographs and article illustrations undergird a myth of individuality and personality. Benjamin had deemed this myth highly inappropriate in a mass age when, as Brecht's anti-romantic dictum put it: the self is the last bit of rubbish you have to get rid of. Commercial portrait photography, as Benjamin asserts in 'Kleine Geschichte der Photographie', displays instead the greatest self-indulgence. Bourgeois photography is a vehicle for the ruling ideology. It flatters the individual who in reality is dissolving or recomposing in a mass age. Portrait photography bolsters a fantasy of personality and value, and, used to elevate the author-individual, inscribes hierarchical relations of power and underlines the reification of the individual as commodity. In 'Kleine Geschichte der Photographie' Benjamin betrays his disgust with a photographic practice that relies on what he calls the 'they're looking at you of animals, people and babies, which so distastefully implicates the buyer'.[10] Benjamin rails against the commodification of the person, while acknowledging it as process. Benjamin wants to smash such photography, by proving simultaneously – if seemingly paradoxically – its outdatedness, technologically, and its suitability to bourgeois ideology, but unsuitability for a mass proletarian politics. In 'Kleine Geschichte der Photographie' he constructs a history of photography, since its beginnings, in technological and ideological terms, and concludes with an argument in favour of analytical, surrealist and montage photography, new photographic practices, appropriate to a mass age. Benjamin had learnt his lesson from Alexander Rodchenko, the Soviet photographer, who had claimed in his 1928 *Novyi Lef* essay 'Against the synthetic portrait, for the snapshot' that only the serial portrait makes sense. There Rodchenko writes:

> Modern science and technology are not searching for truths but are opening up new areas of work, and with every day change what has been attained. Now they do not reveal common truths – 'the earth revolves' – but are working on the problem of this revolution. Let's take:
>   aviation
>   radio
>   rejuvenation, etc.
> These are not mere platitudes, but constitute areas that thousands of workers are expanding in depth and breadth, thanks to their experiments. And it is not just one scientist, but thousands of scientists and tens of thousands of collaborators. And hence there will never be eternal airplanes, wireless sets and a single system of rejuvenation. There will be thousands of airplanes, motorcars, and thousands of methods from rejuvenation. The same goes for the snapshot.[11]

Photography must be on the side of the moment, countering art's purchase on eternity. The notion of the 'true' image has been blasted apart – to use Benjamin's words – by the dynamite of the split second. No snapshot is an absolute resemblance – Rodchenko uses the example of Lenin to make his case – there are only moments and coincidences. No one photograph summarizes the essence of Lenin, for there is no essence, there is no synthesis, only a shifting subject who moves through time, modifying history, being modified.

Benjamin's own choice of book jacket illustration – for the 1928 edition of *Einbahnstraße* (One Way Street) – contrasts starkly with those for volumes of his work produced posthumously. He commissioned from the photomontagist Sascha Stone a dynamic, chaotic urban array of street furniture, vehicles, crowds and advertisements: a modernist scene for a book of fragments. For his own books, a Benjamin-inspired usage of photography might provide a reflexive commentary on the ubiquity of the mass-reproduced image in the modern age, or might detourn an image in order to serve as a warning about the dangers of the fake cult of intimacy with the charismatic star, promoted in the age of mass communications. Not a hero in sight, but crowds, city slipstreams. These philosophically motivated design decisions were not adopted by the Benjamin industry. Books in the capitalist culture industry tend in the end to become gravestones, and, as in some kinds of burial etiquette, a singular trace of a past moment once lived finds its way into the frame. The blow-up of the genius-individual in the frame occupies the whole space, pushing off-camera the work's purpose as political critique.

Present-day book jacket designers or their directors are not deterred, determined that the appeal of the author will translate into the appeal to the consumer. The photographs of Benjamin, when they appear on the covers of his books or in coffee table editions for fetishists, though not used in a Benjaminian way, do reveal something about the status of the author – in a commodity capitalist age. The commodity status of art and artists acts to re-envelop 'emancipated' art and its 'shrinking aura' in fetishized notions of its conditions of production and incapacitating modes of reception. The star cult, promoted by the capitalist entertainment industry through fan clubs and spectacles, conserves the magic shimmer of the artificially boosted commodified star personality. Benjamin is bathed in auratic light. Photographs of a man caught with his eyes unfocused behind moon lenses appear poised to conjure up fantasies of immediate knowledge of the author and a romantic empathy with his mortal suffering. Photo-frozen Benjamin, alone and pensive, renders an image of the outsider who 'makes a home of his homelessness'.[12] The image seems perfect for someone who dies in a no mans' land.

The past has a claim on us – Benjamin was convinced of that. The book jackets, the books themselves, the articles, the artworks, the memorial stones to Benjamin all make demands on the present, forcing re-readings from the perspective of now. The book jackets, the artworks, the memorial stones, these shards of recollected Benjamin recall the demand voiced by Benjamin in 'Über den Begriff der Geschichte': 'The past carries with it a temporal index by which it is referred to redemption.' That is to say, for a Benjaminian Marxist, there is no point in viewing the past – including, that is, viewing a passed away Benjamin – unless it is from the perspective of lost opportunities, now potentially viable. For Benjamin, the costly task of the historical materialist is to redeem the past, make clear and put aright past oppressions, in order to set the record straight. The first publication of Benjamin's

'Theses on the Philosophy of History' was a small attempt to compensate for the passing that came too soon. In 1942, two years after Benjamin's death, a hectographed volume, *Walter Benjamin in Memoriam*, was issued by Adorno's Institute for Social Research in Los Angeles. The volume was a special issue of the *Zeitschrift für Sozialforschung*, a journal in which Adorno had sometimes published Benjamin, albeit always after thorough censor's penwork. As well as the theses on the philosophy of history, it contained a bibliographic note on Benjamin's writings, two essays by Max Horkheimer and an essay by Adorno. In an unpublished introduction to the theses, Adorno noted that, though not intended for publication, 'the text has become a legacy'. Adorno and Horkheimer, co-editors of the volume, wrote:

> We dedicate these contributions to the memory of Walter Benjamin. The historical philosophical theses at the front are Benjamin's last work.[13]

Now a posthumous Benjamin was allowed to speak from beyond the grave. But this voice from beyond the grave was only the beginning of what became a voluble jabber. The Benjamin industry – with its multi-volumes and endless speculations – ensures that little of Benjamin's work is lost for history. But in his theses on the philosophy of history, Benjamin adds that, while this acts in accordance with a truth – nothing should be lost for history, no matter how large or small a thing – it is only 'for a redeemed humankind that the past becomes fully citable in all its moments'. In other words, the layers, the events, the people whose visioning may be obscured by class-skewed lenses become discernible only with revolutionary effort. The historical materialist knows that images of the past are permanently in danger, threatening to become a tool of the ruling classes. For this reason he writes:

> In every epoch the attempt must be made anew to wrest tradition away from a conformism that is about to overpower it.[14]

If such a wresting of tradition from conformism fails, Benjamin notes, *even the dead will not be safe from the enemy if he wins*. This statement holds true for the illustrious dead, held up by fame, not passing through into forgetting – that is to say, it holds true for Benjamin.

Melancholy, Personality and Monuments

Walter Benjamin has been liked so much by so many. His name, footnoted not least for its 'celebrated opacity', good for lending a cachet of intimidating intellectualism, functions as a signifier of blamelessness.[15] His immunity from guilt rests on his status as ultimate victim. It resides also in his lack of taintedness with party politics, so the story goes. Benjamin was an anti-fascist, but he was never a Stalinist.[16] And he died too soon to make those post-war commitments that marked down his contemporaries, such as Brecht or Bloch, who reappeared in the German Democratic Republic, and so were tainted by their complicity with Stalinism. Benjamin shines forth as an acceptable embodiment of dissidence, from everything.

Benjamin's gracing of contemporary theory is often as an incarnation of scholastic detachment from actuality. The love of this victim-critic on the part of intellectuals is consummated in the sentimental popularity of the figure and his biography. Often his theory is only sketchily evoked, frequently in the epigrammatic form of the eternal return of this or that quotation. There have been moments when it was not unusual to find in any *feuilleton* section of the broadsheet press or journal some quote from Benjamin somewhere: a torn fragment, vindicated theoretically as part of the 'mimetic delirium' gripping those who write about him.[17] Benjamin's 'posthumous fame' endures.[18] All this in spite of Ralf Konersmann's disenchanted petition: 'why we should perhaps stop quoting Benjamin'.[19] Benjamin's method, ripping quotations out of context, brushing other authors' writings against the grain to make new constellations, seems turned back on him. Benjamin had been attracted in Brecht's theory to the notion of plagiarism, quotation and sabotage of contexts.[20] This recontextualizing is pursued so far that even the practice of book production and consumption becomes, for Benjamin, the collection and reconstitution of data into fresh contexts that startle through their newness. Ripping, breaking up and recontextualizing has taken place with a vengeance to Benjamin's corpus of writing. It is torn limb from limb, and divided up into pre-Brecht-influenced writings and post-Brecht-influenced writings, pre-Marxist writings and post-Marxist writings, aura-destroying essays and aura-preserving essays, Leninist Benjamin versus surrealist Benjamin versus Heidereggerian and Schmittian Benjamin. Ultimately, Benjamin appears not only cut off from consistent adherence to any specific movement, but also divided against himself.

Benjamin as tragic hero, torn apart by melancholy and the difficulty of existing, becomes detached from the political history in which and against which he was engaged actively, and is made a passive victim of a sorrowful fate. There is a danger of memory as disempowerment, as sweet melancholy. Benjamin notes the tendency for memory and memorials to fetishize the act of remembering and not the remembrance of acting. In his *Passagenwerk*, Benjamin sketches the 'brooder', the pre-eminent melancholy subject, who dwells on fragments, clouded by a tormented sense of occluded significance indwelling in insignificant things. Benjamin is always more interested in what he calls, after Proust, involuntary memory, which rejects the conscious application of subjective meanings upon the range of experiences presented to consciousness. Involuntary memory provides an unexpected shocking link between a concrete experience in the present and its cognate in the past. It is a deliverance from temporality. It produces a shock, a waking up, albeit to the power of something like a dream. In contrast to the endless task of memory and mourning, history-telling becomes, for Benjamin, especially in his theses form – a writing that tends towards action – a type of praxis, a grasping, a *Begreifen*, which produces the history it reports, by theorizing, not narrating, and so making history, not writing it, as does Franz Mehring when he wrote *The Paris Commune in Memoriam* in 1896. Benjamin quotes from Mehring's article in the *Passagenwerk*:

> The history of the Paris Commune has become a great testcase for the question of how the revolutionary working class must order its tactics and strategy in order to attain the final victory. In the case of the commune the last traditions of the old revolutionary legends have collapsed forever: no benevolence of fate, no courageous heroes, no martyrdom can replace the clear insight of the proletariat into the imperative necessity of its emancipation. What was valid for revolutions by minorities, carried out in the interest of minorities, is not true ... for the proletarian revolution ... In the history of the commune the seeds of this revolution were overgrown by the creepers that grew out of the bourgeois revolution of the eighteenth century into the revolutionary workers' movement of the nineteenth century. In the commune, the solid organization of the proletariat as a class and the principled clarity about its world-historical role were missing. That is why it failed.[21]

This is history as critique. Mehring was a crude Marxist, but he can at least write history as critique, as pushing towards action. He makes history happen in writing it. This is what Benjamin wished for too.

However, many instead see Benjamin as a man wishing to escape history, seeking to disappear into the folds of convoluted time, having embraced only his melancholic destiny, and that from the very start.[22] As the theorist Zygmunt Bauman phrases it in his version of the mythologization, demonstrating a remarkable insensitivity to political and historical forces:

> If Benjamin invites the attribute of intellectual more than any other thinker or writer it is because he made that general fate of the intellectual, with its grandeur and misery, hope one cannot

do without and blunders one cannot escape, into his consciously embraced private destiny; into his life programme. Benjamin's life, and Benjamin's death, were about the refusal (or was it incapacity?) to be fixed.[23]

Bauman wields Benjamin in a sweeping thesis about intellectuals and their ontological refusal of closure and fixity. Yet a glance through Benjamin's public and private papers shows that Benjamin did not escape into the solitude of exile, like some lone-rider intellectual, moving for the sake of moving. Benjamin's moves were as calculated as his moves in the exhausting games of chess with Brecht and Korsch in Denmark.[24] He abandoned Berlin permanently soon after the Reichstag fire in March 1933, though he departed with heavy heart, a demeanour that can be retraced in the autobiographical returns to the city – described as an 'inoculation' against homesickness – in the 1930s.[25] In his correspondence, he explains the terror he experienced in Berlin and his fear of walking the streets or breathing the repressive air clogging Nazi Germany.[26] Exile is not a case of voluntary non-fixity by intellectuals. One reason for Benjamin's hasty retreat was precisely the knowledge that there were intellectuals aplenty who were fixed, tenured firmly and cushion-cosily to chairs in illustrious German universities, ready to rally enthusiastically behind the Nazi polity. Benjamin is a casualty of a specific constellation of political and social forces that excluded him, along with other critics of the capitalist system, especially in its specific guise as fascism, at various turns (from the university, from money-making publishing, from Germany, from France, from Spain), forcing him on towards frontiers, which, as Brecht stated, would eventually become traversible in one direction only.[27] Benjamin died in a no mans' land, darkened by the shadow of fascism, in the process of escaping from Vichy France and Nazi-occupied France, through Spain, to America. He was refused right of passage over the border and was threatened with deliverance to the Gestapo, to whom Benjamin was already known, his German nationality having been revoked. Suicide seemed preferable to murder by the enemy.[28]

Benjamin's monument, conceived by the Israeli artist Dani Karavan, was erected in 1994 near where he died on the Franco-Spanish border, at Portbou. The monument is formed from a cramped iron passageway. This narrow corridor arrests the visitor behind a thick windowpane, enforcing the metaphor and the actuality of the impossibility of passage. The visitor is stranded and directed to feel as Benjamin did in September 1940, a tiny, fragile figure suspended above a vista of the perilous swirl of the sea below. For the monument's visitor the tangible forces responsible for Benjamin's death are symbolized by a spectacle of nature, and in the restaged empathetic moment, historical reference is depleted, political specificity evaded.[29] The monument is perhaps less an effort to memorialize the specific historical and political significance of Benjamin's life, death and theory, but functions rather as a most fitting monument to much recent reception of his work. Many explications of Benjamin seem to cower in the shadow of the monument.

Bauman, already before the fall of the wall a polemicist against communism, drags Benjamin from the jaws of Marxism, also known, by him, as the jaws of dogmatism. Benjamin used this figure of speech in a reference to Scholem's negative attitude to his philosophical positions. Benjamin writes to Kitty Marx-Steinschneider from Skovsbostrand in 1938 that, on a visit to Paris, Scholem seemed to have perceived him 'as a man who has made his home in a crocodile's jaws, which he keeps prised open with iron braces'.[30] Benjamin is reforged by Bauman into the top metaphysician of liberalism: the philosopher of possibility. Possibility, for Bauman, connotes a vague notion of openness, rather than critical potentiality coiled in the now. For Bauman, the evidence of Marxist influence in his work becomes just one more testament to Benjamin's undecidability. In an escapade, says Bauman, Benjamin tried to be called a historical materialist. He wanted, it is said, to belong. But it was just another label for him. Finally, Benjamin had to reject Marxism because Marxism rejects possibility. Bloch and Lukács had been seduced by a promise called Russia, a chance to invalidate one man-made nightmare by another one. But Benjamin came to his senses. Possibilities, Benjamin understands, are also mortal. History is a mass murderer, and materialism its weapon. Historical materialism is described as another room that Benjamin leaves. And Benjamin, bathed in the mystique of a life under the sign of a legendary suicide, becomes the talisman of modern melancholics who indulge in the aestheticization of suffering.[31] In 'Der Erzähler' (1936) Benjamin writes:

> It is a dry material on which the burning interest of the reader feeds. What does that mean? A man who dies at the age of thirty-five, said Moritz Heimann once, is at every point of his life a man who dies at the age of thirty-five. Nothing is more dubious than this sentence – for the sole reason that the tense is wrong. A man, so says the truth that was meant here, who died at the age of thirty-five appears *to recollection*, at every point in his life, as a man who is going to die at the age of thirty-five. In other words: the statement that makes no sense for real life, is indisputable for remembered life.[32]

Benjamin describes the mythologized way that characters are grasped in textual remembering. Retrospectively, death becomes the starting point, indeed the point of it all. He alerts readers to violence done to lived experience in the novel. The mythic memory of life closes down experience, faking a literary illusion of fate. Characters are turned into simplified representatives of their own fateful destinies whose lives gain meaning only by their deaths. Benjamin falls victim to this mechanism – one he had admitted in his thoughts on recollection and its reinvention (of the past, of objects), in his attempts to open up history to potential and reconstruction. Remembered life, in Benjamin's writings, reveals a truth that could only develop its full form later, so the photographic metaphor goes. But his life, remembered by others, sets something else in motion. Rather than the opening up of the meaning of a life to memory and to the forces that were blocked, the tendencies that won out – Benjamin becomes the main protagonist in a tragic and often recapitulated biography of the theorist whose theory is in every point the theory of a man who kills himself in 1940. Reports on his theory lock him into his thanato-biography.

Bauman regurgitates the line of Benjamin's friend Gerhard-Gershom Scholem, further perpetrating the myth of the necessity for isolation on the part of the intellectual: 'You are endangered more by your drive for community ... than by the horror of loneliness that speaks from so many of your writings.'[33] This misses what the real historical-political source of danger was for Benjamin. Contrary to the line, common amongst contemporary intellectuals, which sees Benjamin as embracing death willingly, a tragic figure, an ill-fated man of letters, Benjamin's demise has to be seen in conjunction with the devastating political capitulation of the period. His fate was not the unique destiny of an ill-fated saturnine incompetent. His death, and most importantly his theory, must be brought into constellation with the actual mounting rubble-heap of history.[34] The nature of Benjamin's critique of the murderously twinned histories of Hitler and Stalin as a form of active engagement with that history, that is, a political judgement of it, is too often missed. Scholem's railing against Benjamin's drive for community also ignores the productiveness of the ensuing intellectual exchanges. Community resulted in important collaborative encounters with, for example, Franz Hessel, Brecht, Asja Lacis, Ernst Bloch, Wilhelm Speyer and the Institute for Social Research. The motivation to community issued in correspondence with diverse characters, including Adorno and Gretel Karplus, Scholem, Lieb, Kracauer, Florens Christian Rang, von Hofmannsthal. Benjamin's motivation to community also issued in travel – to Moscow, Ibiza, Denmark, Capri, Paris and elsewhere. These were all places where he threw his ideas into new public realms. Benjamin's legendary personal loneliness and intellectual isolation underpin the pervasive myth that his work was virtually unpublished in his lifetime.[35] The notion of community is linked to the idea of social and political commitment. If, as Bauman says, to describe Benjamin is to describe the archetypal non-committal intellectual, then all Benjamin's work written from the late 1920s onwards is mocked, because it is precisely about the politically urgent task of reformulating the notion of the intellectual in terms of community and commitment. Benjamin's project is prescriptive, redrawing the intellectual. For Benjamin, the intellectual becomes a politically engaged intervener into social and cultural crisis. He criticized intellectuals who saw scholarly labour as the pursuit of ambivalent, non-committed positions, supra-political commentary and the vague class-unspecified project of freedom and a new human order. Reviews from the 1920s and 1930s mark a contribution to Benjamin's increasing self-understanding as a contemporary cultural critic who comments on what he has identified as a crisis of the social and the political. Benjamin regards his critical contributions as salvos in an intellectual civil war. In connection with this bellicose role for the intellectual, Benjamin considered issuing a journal with Brecht in 1930. It was to be called *Krisis und Kritik*, and was to concern itself with the understanding of contemporary culture and society as both in permanent crisis.[36] Thus it was planned as a critical journal in both senses of the word. The crisis was identified as an interconnected crisis of both the social and the political, and a crisis in intellectual critical response. In addition, bourgeois self-understanding has mutated. It has now to negotiate the new social mapping out of the metropolis. Benjamin asks where the space of the intellectual may be. Modernity thrusts on the intellectual an awareness of the limits of a severed and private position. Intellectuals had now to come out on to the streets and experience the exigencies of the public zone.[37]

Benjamin had little choice but to jostle on the streets and in the marketplace. He was not able to take up a position in a university – because of his Jewishness (there was an unofficial ethnic-religious numerus clausus) and his unconventional scholarship. Probably unbeknown to Benjamin, Horkheimer helped to fail his *Habilitation* thesis on baroque mourning play, which was submitted to the university in Frankfurt. This qualification was a prerequisite for any teaching position. The preface to Benjamin's failed postdoctoral thesis, written in 1925 and unpublished, retells the fairytale of *Sleeping Beauty*, asleep in her thorn bush and awoken by the cook's noisy and violent attack on the kitchen boy in the castle. Benjamin claims to be the brutal master chef, assaulting with an earsplitting ferocity the cosy presumptions of the academy. But he also claims for himself the role of Sleeping Beauty, a poor and wounded waif, who has tried to break in to the old-fashioned academy:

> I would like to tell the story of Sleeping Beauty a second time: she is sleeping in her thorn bush. And then, after so and so many

years, she awakes. But not to the kiss of a Prince Charming. It was the cook who woke her, when he smacked the kitchen boy; the smack resounded with all the pent up force of those long years and re-echoed throughout the castle. A fair child sleeps behind the thorny hedge of the pages that follow. The last thing to come near her should be a Prince Charming in the shimmering garments of science. He would be bitten as he kissed his betrothed. It is left to the author in his role as master chef to wake her up. For too long now we have been waiting for the smack that must resound ear-splittingly through the halls of science. Then too will awaken that poor truth who pricked itself on an outmoded distaff when, despite prohibition, she wanted to weave for herself, among the tattered rags, a professor's robe.[38]

Benjamin retells the fairytale as part of a bitter attack on the academy. It will not be the passionate clasp of the ruling classes that sends shock-waves through the (collective) body, inspiring it to revolt – for that after all has only ever been a soporific tranquilizer. It will be rather the crude and ferocious and impulsive activity of the oppressed, spattering out years of pent-up energy. As the *flâneur* recognizes, the streets are more vital than the academic institutions.

A Short History of Benjamin Studies

Reflection on Benjamin and his relationship to the disastrous events of twentieth-century history can be reversed in a look at history's relationship to Benjamin and his writings. Benjamin points out that the reception of an artwork or a theory is historical, and a history of that reception might be more fertile than analyses of texts.[39] The history of the reception of Benjamin's writings is a history of academic fashions. To retrace what has happened to Benjamin's project is to encounter the dumb violence – ordered by fashion – of which the academy is capable.

The Anglo-American reception of Benjamin was marked by Hannah Arendt's selection of texts and her contextualizing introduction to the Schocken edition of *Illuminations* in 1968, a piece that first appeared in *The New Yorker*. The writings chosen by Arendt for the collection mostly reflected Benjamin's literary concerns. As she stated in the closing editor's note: 'The chief purpose of this collection is to convey the importance of Benjamin as a literary critic',[40] or an '*homme de lettres*'.[41] She also introduced, as philosophical cousin, Martin Heidegger.[42] The story in Europe was different. In Germany, in the years after 1968, there was a poster of Benjamin which depicted him with a joint in one hand (because of his writings on hashish) and a Soviet machine gun in the other. For a while a New Left rehabilitates Benjamin in the very zones where he had previously been marginalized: academic institutions, the Frankfurt School. And then, in 1970s Britain, when 'Der Autor als Produzent' (1934) and 'Das Kunstwerk im Zeitalter seiner technischen Reproduzierbarkeit' (1935–39) were first made available in English, a brief and fragmentary interest in Benjamin flared up amongst leftist cultural theorists, and resulted in an influential television series and book, *Ways of Seeing*, by John Berger.

In their bibliographic survey of Benjamin scholarship, Markner and Weber argue that, in the 1980s, attempts were made to invert the 'development' of Benjamin's thought. Markner and Weber catalogue a critical 'reversal of the direction of development of his thought and neglect of the struggle over his orientation'.[43] It is evident that Benjamin studies have embraced a powerful tendency which refuses to place Benjamin's work historically, and attempts, by snatching motives from here, there and everywhere, to extract a philosophy, while dodging the task of situating Benjamin's writing *within* the context of his dialogues with left politics. In an essay on the place of Benjamin in the discipline of Cultural Studies, Angela McRobbie argues that the resurgence of interest in Benjamin in the 1980s was due precisely to the fact that Benjamin offers a critique that is not formulated around the Marxist fetishes of the 1970s: the working class as an emancipatory force, the notion of history moving inexorably towards socialism, the belief in social progress.[44] For those who detached Benjamin from leftist political critique two academic lines in Benjaminology surface from this point, influenced largely by postmodern, anti-materialist philology. One line reinvents him as a proto-poststructuralist, cut off by slippery signifiers from the concerns of Marxism. The other line reinterprets Benjamin as a Jewish thinker, reforming his whole work around the unvoiced central project of Judaism.

Scholem has been most influential in asserting a Judaic version of Benjamin's theory. Scholem's Judaic version belittles or bemoans the encounter with Marxism. He described Benjamin as 'a theologian marooned in the realm of the profane'.[45] Scholem read Benjamin as if he were one of the kabalistic masters, immensely perceptive but vulnerable to 'self-deception', 'delusion' and suicidal self-destruction, especially when politics was at issue.[46] Scholem also claimed to be the only person in the world qualified to comprehend Benjamin's work, and this was despite the fact that he disregarded Benjamin's Marxism, dismissing it as an emanation only of a superficial jargon which acted to conceal a profound religious sensibility. Scholem was convinced that Benjamin used communist 'phraseology' to mask the discrepancy between his 'actual' and his 'alleged' thought processes.[47] He accused Benjamin of fighting in disguise.[48] Scholem perceived Benjamin first and foremost as a metaphysician of language, absorbed in mystical accounts of linguistics, in the tradition of Hamann and Humboldt.[49] This recognition draws in large part on Benjamin's early philosophical forays. In a rejection of mechanical, bourgeois enlightenment secularism, and its narrow conception of experience, Benjamin had developed a fascination with the epistemological foundation of a higher, deeper, broader concept of experience, in opposition to Kantianism's debasement and division of experience.[50] In a letter to the literary critic Max Rychner in March 1931, Benjamin reflects on his early writings. He mentions *Ursprung des deutschen Trauerspiels*:

> Now this book was certainly not materialist, even if it was dialectical. What I did not realise when I wrote it has become clearer to me subsequently: that a connection exists from my rather peculiar linguistic-philosophical position to dialectical materialism's mode of conceptualizing – even if it is tense and problematic. But there is not one to the boom of bourgeois thought.
>   Cur hic? – Not because I was a disciple of the materialist view of the world; but because I strive to direct my thought towards those objects in which at any time truth appears most concentrated. And today, that is not eternal ideas or timeless values.[51]

Benjamin's reflection on his former method attempts to read in an embryonic political intent. The German 'bourgeois-idealist' literary establishment had ignored his book on baroque mourning plays.[52] This study establishes an historically bound theory of allegorical language. Allegorical discrepancies and ambiguities between sign and thing in these plays signify the failure of human language to arrest and steady signification. The baroque form of allegorical expression disrupts the connection between being and meaning, and so captures historical truth in the seventeenth century when systems of domination and belief are in crisis. This is quite unlike the procedure of the classicist symbol, insists Benjamin. The classicist symbol falsifies historical experience, by presenting itself as a stable, material embodiment of timeless, transcendent perfection. In the study of baroque mourning plays Benjamin mobilizes a 'mystical' theory of language for a socio-historical and dialectical understanding of *truth*. This quest for truth marshals a politics of aesthetic form.

But in the 1980s Scholem's linguistic mystical reading best suited fashionable literary theory. Poststructuralism continues the linguistically weighted version of Benjamin's work first insinuated by Arendt's reference to Heidegger. In her introductory essay on

Benjamin, written in 1968, Arendt united Benjamin and Heidegger by arguing that Benjamin reveals the arbitrariness and intentionlessness of language, making his thought akin to Heidegger's.[53] Paul de Man later persists with this line. He offers an allegorical reading of Benjamin's work. This imputes to Benjamin's linguistic theory the notion that all language is wholly devoid of intentional significance, generating meaning-effects that function in a realm apart from human agency. Language is thoroughly contingent.[54] The poststructuralist, literary approach treats the political as a black hole at the centre of Benjamin's work, and hopes that identifying such a void helps to wire Benjamin's theoretical apparatus into Heidegger's.[55] Quite apart from Benjamin's early and sustained rejections of Heidegger – Benjamin accuses Heidegger of employing the 'profoundest circumlocutions' – the merging of Heidegger and Benjamin disregards the extent to which Benjamin's inquiries into technology and re-production (elements most fundamental to both theorists) emerges precisely to repulse Heidegger's authenticity jargon. The anti-Heidegger phrase stems from the letter to Max Rychner, written in early March 1931. Benjamin attests that the 'scandalous and rough-and-ready analyses of Franz Mehring' are preferable to the 'profoundest circumlocutions of the realm of ideas currently undertaken by Heidegger's school'.[56] Unlike Heidegger, Benjamin, wielding Marxist terminology, is concerned to establish his key category of technology as a dynamic category, essentially scissioned by a tension between discrepant forces and relations of production. Technology's evaluation and dissection is part of a programmatic insistence on intellectual, theoretical analysis of the relations of production. This is conceived as a political strategy designed to foster a revolutionary activism that can take ample account of modernity's novel forms of experience and conditions of existence. As such it is far removed from Heidegger's phrasing of the question concerning technology. Heidegger imagines modern technology as a 'challenge' to nature. Modern technology is said to advance the unreasonable demand that nature supply energy. This energy is then stored and used to power other industrial forms – means to ends. In contradistinction to the 'challenge' of industry, Heidegger eulogizes peasant technologies – the tilling of the soil, of course – technologies that are barely technologies, but love-saturated instances of a cherishing, a non-invasive coaxing. The ultimate horror, in Heidegger's bucolic-romantic gobbledygook, is the river Rhine conceived not as Hölderlin's artwork but as a power source, a producer of electricity.[57]

Commentators in the 1990s have seen Benjamin's intention to be that of someone who 'sought to render experience philosophical'.[58] But more apt might be the converse: that Benjamin seeks to undermine the hypotheses of philosophy by conceptualizing specific experience and, vitally, the socio-historical conditions of transformation of experience. Philosophy is truly too bloodless for Benjamin. Despite his self-definition as cultural critic and his insulting description of philosophers in 1924 – the first year of his concentrated engagement with Marxism – as 'subaltern', 'shabby', 'the worst paid, because the most superfluous lackeys of the international bourgeoisie', academics persist in labelling Benjamin a philosopher.[59] In propelling Benjamin back into philosophy the very (institutional, disciplinary) confines that he burst (intellectually and through practice) are rigidly reinstated, thus cancelling Benjamin's redefinition of the division of intellectual labour, and his redrafting of the intellectual as activist interceding in history.

The sealed universe of the poststructuralist contribution to Benjaminology offers a temporality without history. This ahistorical temporality scrambles texts, chronologies and authors in order to dish up the key trope of deconstructionist strategy – infection. Read close enough and inside out, Walter Benjamin is contaminated, discernible in strange secret returns of the repressed in his works. Rodolphe Gasché, for example, suggests that Benjamin's only seemingly profane and mythless world 'points to what it cannot name'.[60] Though Benjamin is determined in his obliteration of Heidegger, the Black Forest *savant* is often folded back into his theory. If not Heidegger, Kant.[61] And if not Kant, perhaps Hitler, as Jacques Derrida shows, teasingly.

In his discussion of Benjamin's 'Zur Kritik der Gewalt' (1921), Derrida correctly identifies a post-First World War intensification of debate amongst European theorists about the nature of the state, justice and violence.[62] But, in allocating Benjamin's 'at once Marxist and messianic' essay to a generalized wave of anti-parliamentarian and 'counter-enlightenment' criticism 'on which Nazism so to speak surfaced and even surfed in the 1920s and the beginning of the 1930s', Derrida forces an equivalence between right and left discourse, after the war and on into the Nazi regime.[63] Both left and right contaminate each other's categories, Derrida contends, each one aiming at a primary and state-grounding political strategy dependent on violence. Derrida deconstructs Benjamin's radicalization of violence to show its return as the same (in the guise of other) in the Nazi 'Final Solution'. Benjamin's recommended violence of a general strike against the state's monopoly of violence and law – 'nihilating, expiatory and bloodless' – is shown, by Derrida, to be carried out in practice in the gas chambers.[64] Derrida cancels out Benjamin's political critical task in 'Zur Kritik der Gewalt'. Having set it up as such, he, somewhat disingenuously, dismisses the text as 'still too Heideggerian, too messianico-marxist or archeo-eschatological for me'.[65] But looked at rather in the context of debates on Marxism, and Benjamin's own developing interest in political critique in the wake of the failed German revolution, 'Zur Kritik der Gewalt' might better be seen to mark the beginning of a critical methodology, sensitive to the ideological differentiation and historicization of the class categories of justice, legality, opposition, myth and enlightenment. It is Derrida who wants now, even as he professes a twisted indebtedness to Marxism, to rescue the notion of justice, but without paying critical attention to its class inflections. Even early 'messianic' Benjamin has a more rooted, class-conscious and historical sense of the political than Derrida, who sifts out the skewing effects of economic power on Grand Bourgeois Categories. In *Spectres of Marxism: The State of the Debt, The Work of Mourning, The New International*, a book that advertises its rationale as 'a radicalization of Marxism' and provides the long-awaited encounter of deconstruction's master and Marx, Derrida thrice summons the ghost of Benjamin to vent his own haunting of European thought. Benjamin is applauded as someone who, along with Nietzsche and Derrida, believes that the weak may one day inherit the earth.[66] And somehow Derrida is able to draw Benjamin into his class-free rhetoric of domination and rebellion. Derrida's circumlocutory deconstructive efforts – all strained through metaphors of phantoms and archaic phantasms – conjure up only 'a certain spirit' of Marxism, and, from Marx, Derrida wants only his shadow, his afterglow and his powers still to provoke controversy by association.[67] He wants spirit without substance. Politically the bottom line remains a bourgeois faith in the regulated bestowal of human rights (and hovering behind them, guiltily, animal rights), and the watchwords are still reform, justice and law – albeit on an international scale. One phrase is repeated several times – curious in that it seems to propound a re-homogenization of the Marxism that has been transformed, as condition of its continued validity, into many Marxisms – without necessarily subscribing to the whole Marxist discourse on the state, on class, on ... anything.[68]

But back to Benjamin, or at least a crowded phantasmagoria of him. Filtered through the refracting lenses of Scholem, of Heidegger, of the postmodern and of poststructuralism, Benjamin returns to us now either fractured or multiplied. One conspicuous project of the 'Benjaminiana' of the last quarter-century has been to argue that in as much as Benjamin was a Jew, he was less a Marxist. In as much as he is drawn to Marxism he can do so only by wrestling with his Jewishness. He is torn between the messianic and the material, or, more extremely, between heaven and hell.[69] Angelic Benjamin floats in theory as a half-figure – half-Marxist, half-Jew – and the partiality of his identifications makes it impossible to locate his theory, and it places him on a border that cuts through all his work, and even (deconstructively? actually?) killed him.[70]

Berlin, the Fall of the Wall and Anti-Marxism

An anti-Benjamin crackdown follows on from the fall of the Berlin Wall and the self-cleansing in parts of the academy following the slow, then sudden death of Stalinism or 'actually existing socialism'. After this point, an academic distanciation from Benjamin is set in motion. A phrase occurs in academic article after article and conference paper after conference paper: Walter Benjamin has failed, spectacularly and on many counts. Benjamin is written as the failed philosopher of failure in a time of ideological failing. An article in a German newspaper, titled 'Virtuose des Scheiterns' (Virtuoso of Failure), notes that 'the intellectual milieu has turned against him'.[71] A conference held in London to mark Benjamin's hundredth birthday in July 1992 saw intellectual after intellectual testify to Benjamin's failure, when measured against contemporary ambitions: his failure to understand the meaning of law, his failure to comprehend the compassionate stance of modern Judaism and his consequent failure to mourn properly (Gillian Rose); his failure to derive an ethics (Axel Honneth); his failure as a feminist, his failure at (academic) success, due to his outsider status, and his failure to move beyond the autobiographical and micrological (Janet Wolff); his failure to find what he should have been seeking all along but did not: a notion of experience without a subject (Martin Jay); his failure as the *modus operandi* of the intellectual (Zygmunt Bauman); his theoretical failure which goes hand in hand with the failure of Marxism, and the resultant failure of contemporary Marxian-Benjaminians to neutralize historical distance and contingency and recognize the superiority of social democracy (Irving Wohlfahrt).[72] In as much as Benjamin was a Marxist he failed. And in as much as attempts are undertaken to redeem him, it has to be done under the sign of a 'Frankfurtization', amounting to an ethical domestication of his work. Axel Honneth, for one, tries to squeeze Benjamin into Habermas, but hard, violent and uncompromising edges keep jutting out. Benjamin fails, argues the third-generation Frankfurt Schüler, because he lacks a moral theory in his philosophy of history. Another German critic recently drew breath and turned his face away from Benjamin under the influence of the 'present historical moment', that moment being 'the catastrophic collapse of Marxism as a factor which determines the course of history', signalling 'the disappearance of the last transcendent goal'.[73] Certain critics, under the heady influence of a catastrophic collapse of all for which they assume Benjamin to have stood, seem to overlook the fact,

explicit in his writings and in his recorded conversations with
Brecht and others, that what has now collapsed is related precisely
to that which Benjamin condemned as product of a mechanistic
'metaphysical materialism' and that had proved even then to be
an historical disaster.

Fredric Jameson's spurning of Benjamin is motivated by more
than just the challenge of 1989. In a review of the English edition
of Benjamin's selected correspondence and the Adorno–Benjamin
letters, Jameson mournfully turns away from critical theory and
critical commentary, as epitomized by Benjamin.[74] Jameson's
review is shockingly obsessed only with the position of the writer
– that is to say, Jameson the writer is interested in Benjamin only
in as far as he reflects Jameson back to himself. For a moment
Jameson imagines a world without Hitler and what its effect on
Benjamin would have been. The crucial difference for Benjamin
in such a world would be 'the existence of a German-language
readership', writes the intellectual bound up in a world where only
words matter.[75] Ultimately, Jameson fails to find his reflection. It
is, he rues, no longer possible to be a critical intellectual like
Benjamin in postmodern times. Nobody listens to intellectuals any
more, for they can no longer 'form and inflect public taste' in a
non-literary mediatized public sphere.[76] But Jameson's main
grievance about using Benjamin stems from a curiously fetishistic
and historicist approach to knowing the past. We can no longer
understand Benjamin, he pronounces. We are separated from the
meaning of his thought by the passage of time, in a postmodernity
that has abolished some of Benjamin's touchstones and that reflects
now the flattening out and making equivalent of the whole world.[77]
Jameson wants to be able take the whole of Benjamin and somehow
tick it or, because things are seen to have changed, put a castigating
red mark against it. He is not able to see ways of using it or to ask
what is of use now even though things may have shifted, or what
is of use now because things are still the same.

Recent readings of Benjamin as prophet of anti-progress and
anti-technologism bear little relation to what is specifically
formulated in Benjamin's theory. Benjamin argues to the end that
the working class is the emancipatory force, that there is a
permanent drive through technological reformulation towards the
possibility and necessity of revolution, and that social progress is
achievable (albeit not progress as envisaged by reformists and
capitalists alike). Indeed, Benjamin's critical involvement with
Marxism should not be in question. Adorno thought him at times
too crude a Marxist. Horkheimer found his work too radical in
Popular Frontist and cold warrior times of national class concili-
ation. Scholem despised precisely Benjamin's Marxism. Both
Adorno and Scholem blamed Brecht for encouraging Benjamin to

exceed him in materialist formulations. They voiced the charge that Brecht's 'exotic' influence was 'disastrous' or 'catastrophic' for Benjamin's theorizing.[78] In as much as he is seen to be a Marxist, then as now, Benjamin is rejected.

Debates on Marxism, discussions of materialism and evaluations of aesthetics and politics in the 1920s and 1930s were more intricate and varied than is now, at times, possible to imagine. These debates emerge in the context of wild political upheaval, overturning so much of tradition. Several of these debates have been buried under subsequent historical coatings: Stalinism, Nazism, war, the Cold War, New World Orders. It takes excavation work to begin to uncover the arguments. Benjamin interacts in this now submerged environment, carrying with him traces of romanticism, an anti-capitalist utopianism. Despite his romantic desire for something other than the status quo, Benjamin does not, however, renounce his anti-nostalgic enthusiasm for new technologies and the possibilities for social recomposition which they afford.[79] The possibilities for social recomposition are suggested not least by Benjamin's reading of Marx. Benjamin reads Marx from the 1920s onwards and what he finds contained there spurs him to devise what he declares to be materialist axioms for art theory. Benjamin finds other stimuli for his cultural political theory through exchanges with Brecht and others.

It is significant that Benjamin engages in Marxism with the express purpose of enlisting its aid in formulating a political practice – largely culturally based. Benjamin is drawn specifically to Marxism's rooting in practical experience and the sense in which left political theory emerges from the practical experience of daily life. He writes in a letter to Scholem in 1934: 'That my communism – at the price of its orthodoxy, is nothing, nothing at all other than the expression of certain experiences that I have had in my thought and in my existence.'[80] Benjamin contends that 'anthropological materialism' and 'hostility to progress' are elements that are refractory towards Marxism as it is customarily understood.[81] He incorporates precisely these factors in his schematic outline of the elementary theory of historical materialism:

> The materialist representation of history brings with it an immanent critique of the concept of progress. Historical materialism bases its procedure on experience, healthy human common sense, presence of mind and the dialectic.[82]

Historical, dialectical materialists bring their experience and common sense to bear on their breakdown of history into visualizable pictures, not chronological narratives. Benjamin's conception of Marxism as rooted in practical experience also insinuates precisely what was so interesting about his researches in and with

Marxism and materialism. Benjamin's materialist approach sets out to theorize the coincidence of experience and technology. In his theorizing of modernity, and the potential and actual impact of technology on social life, Benjamin opens up a certain way of discussing experience. This discussion is not concerned with psychologistic analyses of individuals, but with social and class experiences, an aspect all too often neglected in Marxist theory.

Benjamin and Trotsky, Old Man, Hunched Man: Some Elective Affinities

If lately it has been difficult to discuss Benjamin as a Marxist, because of the impact of Stalinism and also the death of Stalinism, a new evaluation of Benjamin may be possible in the room for manoeuvre opened up by the fall of the wall in November 1989. The fall of the wall provides a striking image of the collapse of Stalinism. It has led to much trumpeting about the death of the left, but it has also vindicated some strands of anti-Stalinist leftist critique of 'actually existing socialism'. Informed by this animus, Benjamin has occasionally been brought together with Stalin's antagonist, Leon Trotsky. Terry Eagleton's *Walter Benjamin or Towards a Revolutionary Criticism* attempted to draw some analogies between the two men's theoretical literary and historiographical method.[83] Cliff Slaughter contends that of all the major writers on literature and art who have adhered to Marxism, only Walter Benjamin and Leon Trotsky have remained true to the fundamental legacy of Marx.[84] European 'open Marxists' and leftists sympathetic to Trotsky – Daniel Bensaïd, Enzo Traverso, Michael Löwy – have published work on Benjamin, excavating an alternative Marxist tradition. This alternative disentangles Marxism from the atrocities of Stalinism.[85] Such disentangling suggests it is worth assessing the affinities of Benjamin and Trotsky in order to illuminate the rumoured political black hole at the centre of Benjamin's work under the glare of political and historical light. To tear things from their site of origin, to match this one up against that one, wrote Benjamin, was the method of the allegorist, who forms through this practice dialectical syntheses: casting light from new sources. The entwining of the biographies and theories of Benjamin and Trotsky renders an allegory of a dangerous political history of the first half of the twentieth century.

Trotsky and Benjamin are linked anecdotally in death. Almost within a month of each other these two exiled Jewish revolutionaries meet their death in Spanish-speaking lands. On 21 August 1940 Stalinist agents in Mexico murdered Trotsky. His eyes were focused on disastrous events in Europe: he was halfway through the book *Hitler Speaks*. Benjamin expired on the Franco-Spanish border on 26 September 1940. The factors mobilized in Benjamin's death are not disconnected from the motivating factors in Trotsky's death. The deaths of Benjamin and Trotsky are a sign of the lethal complicity of their murderers who enjoyed an odd affinity of interests, signed and bonded in the Ribbentrop–Molotov non-aggression pact of 1939. Victor Serge, in *Memoirs of a Revolutionary*, begun in Mexico in 1942, brings the two names into constellation, suggesting their connection to be not coincidental, but epochal: 'the poets Walter Hasenclever and Walter Benjamin commit suicide. Rudolf Hilferding and Breitscheid are carried off out of our midst and handed to the Nazis. In the newspapers: suicide or murder of Krivitsky in Washington. Trotsky murdered in Mexico. Yes this is just the moment for the Old Man to die, the blackest hour for the working classes: just as their keenest hour saw his highest ascendency.'[86]

Documented connections between the two men run, of course, down a one-way street. Trotsky may have read Benjamin's journalism – for he was an avid reader of French avant-garde literature and followed those same debates in which Benjamin sometimes meddled – but there is no reference to the critic in the Old Man's writings. As might be expected, however, Benjamin's bibliographies record several books and brochures by Trotsky. After his visit to Moscow in 1927, Benjamin wrote a series of literary-political articles on the situation in post-revolutionary Soviet Union, and his essay 'New Poetry in Russia' contains a concise depiction of Trotsky's literary pronouncements.[87] In 1933 Benjamin read *The Fourth International and the USSR*. He read Trotsky enthusiastically. He was impressed by *Where is Britain going*.[88] He 'breathlessly' consumed *The History of the Russian Revolution* and *My Life*.[89] And, in 1932, Trotsky's autobiography suggested for him a new way of imagining existence. He wrote a little piece reflecting on the proverb 'once is as good as never'. In a draft version of his thoughts on the phrase, Benjamin notes the following of the fact that with work 'once is as good as never' comes into its own:

> Only not everyone is eager to uncover the innermost nature of the practices and arrangements from which this wisdom emerges. And far less is it a privilege of those folk who are rooted in the soil. But revolutionaries have best got to grips with this matter: van Gogh in his early days when he shared the life of the Belgian miners, Adolf Loos as he tore apart the environment of the Viennese middle-classes like a frangible rag, Trotsky as he erects a monument to his father's labours in Janovka.[90]

And in the finished version he includes only the thoughts on Trotsky watching his father at work with a sickle, appearing all the while as if he were only practising, 'as if he were looking for a spot where he could really make a start':

> Here we have the work habits of the experienced man who has learned every day and with every swing of the scythe to start anew. He does not stop to see what he has achieved, indeed what he has done seems to evaporate under his hands and leave no trace. Only such hands will succeed in difficult things as if they were child's play, because they are cautious when dealing with easy ones.[91]

Benjamin's typically cryptic anecdote reruns the issue of repetition, but through another spool. Repetition need not be the cheerless ideological reflex of entrapment in bourgeois economy and bourgeois categories – it might be a basic gesture in a model life that takes nothing for granted, except the reality of experience, but always tries to start afresh, mediating the new and the old correctly, in order to respond genuinely to the demand of the now, sensitive to the specific configurations in the world. Trotsky suggests that to him through his reflections on experience.

Although regarded by many as one of the greatest Marxist critics, Lukács rarely, and only disfavourably, refers to Trotsky's literary studies. Lukács' literary-critical references are to Plekhanov and Franz Mehring. Benjamin, however, was one of the few leftists who continues to refer to Trotsky through the 1920s and 1930s, in both literary-critical contexts and in political discussions. Benjamin continues to refer to Trotsky, no doubt because his distance from the Communist Party allows him to avoid the *Diktat* declaring Trotsky to be politically suspect, petit bourgeois or even a fascist agent.

In his discussion of the historiographical relevance of fascism in Trotsky's analyses of Germany in the 1930s, Ernest Mandel uses terms that coincide with concepts central to Benjamin's work.[92] Mandel labels fascism a 'new social phenomenon'. It appeared suddenly and 'seemed sharply to reverse a long-term historical trend of progress'. He continues:

> The shock experienced by attentive observers was all the greater because this historical reversal was accompanied by the even more direct brutality of physical violence against individuals. Historical and individual fate suddenly became identical for thousands of human beings, and later, for millions. Not only were social classes defeated and not only did political parties succumb, but the existence, the physical survival, of broad human groups suddenly became problematical.[93]

Mandel's description relates to Benjamin in three ways. Benjamin was one of those who, as a Marxist, a Jew and as a critical intellectual, partook of a horrific fate which also befell thousands, then millions, of others. Mandel uses the word 'shock' to describe the arrival of fascism. One of Benjamin's central concepts was the notion of the shock-experience as a way of life in capitalism itself. Also present is a key idea in Benjamin's critical theory: the debunking of historical progress as myth under capitalism. Within capitalism, argues Benjamin, progress is illusory and ideological. For every inch of progress on a technological level under these relations of production, the oppressed suffer regression on a social level: like Marx's understanding of machinery as potential liberator that in *this* moment under *this* organization of relations of production only intensifies our exploitation and, often, our discomfort. Benjamin interprets and contextualizes the disastrous empirical record of modernity, manifest in the social betrayal of faith in technology on the battlefields of the First World War, in what he calls the 'time of hell' also known as 'the modern epoch'.[94] The ruins of the twentieth century surround him and are the exploded end-product of an 'unsuccessful reception of *Technik*' in the nineteenth century.[95] The much-trumpeted potential of technology to dispense abundance for all remains unrealized, because an economic structure tethers the development of technology to the constrictions and exigencies of the specifically capitalist organization of society.

Benjamin and Trotsky sought to explain how the Stalinists and the social democrats failed to avert Hitler's ascendancy. In his commentaries on Germany in the 1930s, Trotsky countered the official communist analyses of Hitler's victory. He accounted for the rise of national socialism by pointing to the deep social crisis of capitalism. This crisis was throwing the petit bourgeois masses into disarray. Fascism, according to Trotsky, expresses the interests of finance capital at the time of a crisis of profitability and difficulties in the realization of surplus value in monopoly capitalism. Trotsky also admitted the dismal state of the German organized working classes, shaken by the mistakes of their leadership. Benjamin made reference to the conformism of the working class at this late stage. They were corrupted by the notion that they were 'swimming with the current' of history. The evidence of such painless exertion is supposed to be manifest in the advances of technical progress. Social democracy and Stalinism in their different ways abet the incapacitation of the working class. The working class is most definitely on the defensive by the time fascism digs in, and not as the KPD, at times, would have it, on the offensive. But neither Trotsky nor Benjamin assumes that this defeat is irreversible. The possibility of a renewed offensive on the part of the working class remains the only hope.

Benjamin makes a distinction between ruling-class history and the 'tradition of the oppressed', the narrative of the dispossessed.[96] Trotsky too, in a critique of futurism in *Literature and Revolution*, insisted that 'we Marxists have always lived in tradition', and cites the party's guardianship of the memory of 1905, the Paris Commune, 1848, 1789. For Benjamin and Trotsky, emphasis is placed upon the persistence of revolutionary memory, a Proustianism of history, a recollection of the history of the oppressed. Prise the power of tradition free from the ruling-class lineage that ensnares it. Cut sidewise into time and splinter the hollow continuum of ruling-class propagandism. Shatter the oppressed's empathy with their rulers. Cleave this, constellating a moment of the crisis-rocked present with a redeemed splinter from the tradition of the oppressed. Benjamin's famous phrase 'there is not one document of culture that is not at the same time a document of barbarism' finds its sentiment echoed in Trotsky's own cautionary warning against an indiscriminate celebration of tradition. The cultural legacy must be viewed dialectically. Its contradictions are historically formed. Civilization's achievements have brought knowledge of humanity and nature, but they have also perpetuated social division. Social struggle uncovers the knobbly and textured – combined and uneven – nature of progress.

But, of course, there is a difficulty in comparing a highly politicized cultural critic to an engaged revolutionary. Though they share the same historical space, Trotsky had been centrally active in a revolution and lived in the shadow of that event, as it slowly receded into time while the Stalinist bureaucracy reversed its gains. By the time of Benjamin's considered political formation, the German workers' movement had already suffered major defeats and Nazism was increasingly occupying the political centre-stage. Benjamin is, in some ways, the embodiment of 'pessimism of the intellect, optimism of the will' or, in his own words, an adherent of the concept of 'organization of pessimism', in what Brecht calls 'darkened times'. Still, theoretical affinities are plenty, and to uncover them is to lay bare aspects of the politics and aesthetics of a 'productivist' modernism. Benjamin and Trotsky were both critically opposed as much to reformism as to Stalinism. Both fought to supply an account of historical materialism that did not see human activity as simply a passive reflection of other factors, be that the economy, the will of the party, the natural, inevitable effect of mechanistic developments. Both were anti-historicist and anti-stagist. Historical change is seen not as a progressive linear evolution, but as disparate epochs or discrepancy within epochs. In *The History of the Russian Revolution*, Trotsky provided an account of a world-historical event insistent on accenting objective as well as subjective factors. Benjamin's Korschian-influenced epistemology revolves around the make-up of consciousness in conditions of capitalism. He focuses on moments of change and potential change in consciousness, through activity. Benjamin's phrase from his final piece of work finds echoes in Trotsky, with its emphasis on the self-activity of the proletariat: 'The subject of historical knowledge is the struggling, oppressed class itself.' Both Benjamin and Trotsky exhibit, in many senses, a coincidence of ideas on Popular Frontism and on the cautioning analysis of Stalinism. Both men were extremely interested in Freud and the relationship of Marxism to psychoanalysis. Both Trotsky and Benjamin had dealings with the surrealists. Benjamin saw surrealism as a practical critique of official Marxism and the tradition of metaphysical materialism. These traditions, he argues, have consistently neglected the unconscious and libidinal side of human experience. In 1938 Trotsky welcomed the support of André Breton in issuing an anti-Stalinist call for a free, uncensored revolutionary art. In their discussions of art both salvage elements of traditional inherited culture while remaining open to avant-garde movements. Trotsky evinces a Benjamin-like futurist-productivism in the preface to *Literature and Revolution*, eclipsing art and social life, evoking an activistic appropriation of culture – in calling for a self-conscious art that is 'active, vitally collectivist, and filled with limitless creative faith in the Future'. In the final chapter, 'Revolutionary and Socialist Art', Trotsky describes how post-revolutionary culture will enable the wall to fall between art and industry and art and nature: 'Technique will become a more powerful inspiration for artistic work, and later on the contradiction itself between technique and nature will be solved in a higher synthesis', while 'nature will become more artificial' as technology allows the moving of mountains, rivers and oceans in a major programme of 'improvements'. Culture forms an essential part of political debate for these men. Both questioned the relation of intellectual culture to the development of the productive forces as a whole and the relation between art's own development and the stimulus and demands of the class struggle.

The two men's comprehension of the significance of culture in political struggle is entangled with their witnessing of dramatic changes in the early twentieth century. A rapid capitalist industrialization in Germany, culminating in imperialism and the First World War exerted a shattering effect on the relations between capitalism, literature and art. This demanded analysis and reaction and politicized a whole layer of German intellectuals. The October Revolution gave further cause to question these relationships, both for intellectuals and activists within the Soviet Union and outside it. And the attempted and yet failed German revolution had an impact on questions of culture and on intellectual formations in the

Weimar Republic, having created a fatal situation in which revolutionary and reformist politicians battled seriously against each other for hegemony, only to both lose to the Nazis.

A Final Assemblage

To argue that Benjamin has a coherent project, bound up with a testing out of Marxism and a testing out of the frames of materialism, and to retrace that project, setting it in constellation with the panorama of the left in a particular historical moment, hopes to get beyond the notion of a split Benjamin. The idea that somehow he is a schizophrenic writer, sometimes materialist, sometimes mystical, but in some ways always falling apart and showing contradictory interests, displaces history into the personal(ity), instead of placing the person in history. It also denies the 'few massive heavy weights', to use Benjamin's own phraseology, that occur again and again in his writings:

> Every historical perception can be visualized in the image of a pair of scales, whose one pan is weighed down by the past, the other by knowledge of the present. The facts assembled in the former can never be too insignificant or too numerous. The latter may, however, contain only a few heavy, massive weights.[97]

The minute details of Benjamin's past might never be too numerous or insignificant for biographers and academics. But the few massive, heavy weights that recur in his writings and gain in intensity as historical life turns ever more morbid – critique of capitalist relations of exploitation, this critique's urgency, recognition of a potential squandered in the private mode of appropriation, desire for revolution, and espousal of class hatred – continue to weigh down the scale pan of the present.

Hanging On

The Benjamin memorial in Portbou is cut into a cliff. The narrow passageway forces the viewer down to the sea. Below are rocks and swirl. The way forward down to the sea is blocked by a glass wall. The way back is steep and dark. There might be a redemptive meaning of the memorial. It could be ripped away from an opportunity to mourn, impotently. It could be understood as an illustration of method, if it is shown to bring to mind a description by Benjamin of the *modus operandi* of Brecht's epic theatre:

> The blockage of the real flow of life, the moment when its course comes to a halt, can be felt as a crosscurrent, a reflux; astonishment is this reflux. Dialectic at a standstill is its actual object. It

is the cliff, down from which the gaze into the stream of things descends, and of which the people in the town of Jehoo, 'which is always full, and where no-one stays', know a song. It begins like this:

Do not insist on the wave/That breaks on your foot, as long as it/Stands in the water/New waves will break on it

But when the stream of things breaks on this cliff of astonishment, there is no difference between a human life and a word. Both are in epic theatre only the crest of a wave. It lets existence spring up from the bed of time and stand glittering for a moment in emptiness, in order that it might be bedded anew.[98]

Benjamin holds on to the moment of interruption, a freezing that can be derived from any object – a word, a person, language or activity. Brecht's 'Song of the River of Life' is pushed beyond its Heraclitean motif – 'Do not insist on the wave/That breaks on your foot, as long as it/Stands in the water/New waves will break on it.' Each moment is available for analysis, for the catastrophe is permanent, but more importantly than that, when the stream flows back, goes into reverse against the current, producing a scene of agitated suspension, it forces astonishment. That is to say, the scene, the tableau, is presented to an audience, who must themselves be agitated into thought, shocked out of contemplation.

It seems that the theses form, the fragment form, Benjamin's much-used form, quick thoughts scribbled on the run or elegantly honed slogans and figures always produce this cross-current. They confiscate old modes of conceptualizing. They attempt a blueprint of a reforged present produced of new exigencies, written for change. Written in isolation, written against the stream, they hope to force a flow back into action and lead back into the world.

Notes

Preface: An Accumulation of Technological Themes

1. Walter Benjamin, *Gesammelte Schriften* (hereafter G.S.), volume I, part 2, p. 695. *Illuminations*, Fontana, London 1992, p. 247. The translations given here sometimes deviate from the standard translations, though my reference always points the reader to those standard ones.
2. See G.S.I.2, p. 698. *Illuminations*, p. 250.
3. *Passagenwerk* (1937–40) G.S.V.1, p. 592. 'N', in Gary Smith (ed.), *Benjamin: Philosophy, History, Aesthetics*, University of Chicago Press, Chicago 1989, p. 64. Datings for the *Passagenwerk* entries are taken from the estimates made by Rolf Tiedemann, the editor of the Suhrkamp edition of the *Passagenwerk*. These estimates are presented in G.S.V.2, p. 1262.
4. See 'Über den Begriff der Geschichte', G.S.I.2 p. 698. *Illuminations*, p. 250.
5. *Passagenwerk* (1937–40) G.S.V.1, p. 592. 'N', in Smith (ed.), *Benjamin*, p. 64.
6. G.S.II.1, p. 241.
7. G.S.IV.1, p. 449.
8. See *Briefe* 1, ed. by G. Scholem and T.W. Adorno, Suhrkamp, Frankfurt/Main 1978, p. 459.
9. Siegfried Kracauer, *Das Ornament der Masse*, Suhrkamp, Frankfurt/Main 1977, p. 50. Siegfried Kracauer, *The Mass Ornament, Weimar Essays*, Harvard University Press, Cambridge, Mass. 1995, p. 75.
10. 'Konvolut N: erkenntnistheoretisches, Theorie des Fortschritts', in the *Passagenwerk* (1935–37) G.S.V.1, p. 588. 'N', in Smith (ed.), *Benjamin*, p. 60.
11. For further consideration of this issue, see Jerry Cohen, 'The Philosophy of Marcuse', in *New Left Review* no. 57 1969, p. 42.
12. Jeremy J. Shapiro, 'Translator's Preface' to Jürgen Habermas's *Towards a Rational Society*, Heinemann Educational Books, London 1971, p. vii. See also Rodney Livingstone's note at the close of Adorno's *Sound Figures*, Stanford University Press, Stanford, Cal. 1999.
13. See Celia Lury, *Cultural Rights: Technology, Legality and Personality*, Routledge, London, 1993, p. 14, for one example of an assessment of Benjamin which asserts that he is interested only in technology and not in relations of production. This has become something of a truism today, especially in Cultural Studies. John Tulloch muses on a quotation from David Buxton's *From the Avengers to Miami Vice*, Manchester University Press, Manchester 1990: 'Benjamin's position can easily lead to an exaggerated optimism attached to symbolic readings which evacuate the relations of production, thus replacing analysis of power, social structure and the economic, political and technological determinants of popular culture with a simplistic active audience populism.' See Henry Jenkins and John Tulloch, *Science Fiction Audiences*, Routledge, London 1995, p. 26.
14. T.W. Adorno and H. Eisler, *Composing for the Films*, The Athlone Press, London and Atlantic Highlands, NJ 1994, pp. 9–10.

15. See Adorno's letter to Benjamin, from 18 March 1936, in *Aesthetics and Politics*, a collection of contributions by Bloch, Lukács, Brecht, Benjamin and Adorno, New Left Books, London 1977, pp. 120–6.

16. See 'Eduard Fuchs, der Sammler und der Historiker' (1934–37), G.S.II.2, p. 467. *One Way Street and Other Writings*, New Left Books, London 1979, pp. 350–1.

17. See, for example, Scholem's 'Walter Benjamin' (1964) or 'Walter Benjamin und sein Engel' (1972), both in *Walter Benjamin und sein Engel*, Suhrkamp, Frankfurt/Main 1983. The disillusioned recantation line is also pursued in Richard Wolin, *Walter Benjamin; An Aesthetics of Redemption*, Columbia University Press, New York 1982, reissued by University of California Press in 1994.

1 Explosion of a Landscape

1. G.S.V.2, p. 1023.

2. The 1914–18 war proved to be a key experience for Benjamin. For (auto)biographical information on this point, see Werner Fuld, *Zwischen den Stühlen*, Momme Brodersen's *Walter Benjamin: A Biography* or *Spinne im eigenen Netz* and Benjamin's own remarks in *Berliner Chronik* (1932) G.S.VI.

3. See 'Die Waffen von morgen' (1925) G.S.IV.1, pp. 473–6, and 'Theorien des deutschen Faschismus' (1930) G.S.III, pp. 240–9.

4. See 'Nochmals: Die vielen Soldaten' (1929) G.S.IV.1, p. 462, and 'Theorien des deutschen Faschismus' (1930) G.S.III, pp. 239–40.

5. See 'Theorien des deutschen Faschismus' G.S.III, p. 240.

6. 'Die Waffen von morgen' (G.S.IV.1, pp. 473–6) was published in the *Vossische Zeitung*. A passage from this essay is quoted in 'Theorien des deutschen Faschismus' G.S.III, p. 240.

7. See G.S.III, p. 473.

8. See Richard Sasuly, *IG Farben* (Boni and Gaer, New York 1947) for a damning report on technological development in Germany in the early twentieth century.

9. See 'Pariser Passagen' 1 (1927–29) G.S.V.2, pp. 1010–11.

10. See G.S.IV.2, p. 910.

11. See a letter from Benjamin to Gerhard Scholem, written on 30 January 1928, published in *Briefe* 1, ed. G. Scholem and T.W. Adorno, Suhrkamp, Frankfurt/Main 1978, p. 455.

12. *Briefe* 1, p. 455.

13. On the idea of systematic orientation in thought, see 'Der Begriff der Kunstkritik in der deutschen Romantik' (1919) G.S.I.1, p. 47 passim.

14. *Briefe* 1, p. 426.

15. See *Briefe* 1, p. 355.

16. See *Einbahnstraße*, G.S.IV.1, p. 85. *One Way Street and Other Writings*, New Left Books, London 1979, p. 45.

17. G.S.IV.1, p. 85. *One Way Street and Other Writings*, p. 45.

18. *Einbahnstraße* G.S.IV.1, p. 85. *One Way Street and Other Writings*, p. 45.

19. See 'Feuermelder', in *Einbahnstraße* G.S.IV.1, p. 122. *One Way Street and Other Writings*, p. 80.

20. For a genealogy of the term, see Michael Löwy's 'Rosa Luxemburg's Conception of "Socialism or Barbarism"', in *On Changing the World*, Humanities Press, Englewood Cliffs, NJ, 1993, pp. 91–9. For a rejection of accusations of a productivist bias in Marx and an insistence that the origin of 'Socialism or Barbarism' is to be found in Marx's 1845–46 writings, see

István Mészáros's *The Power of Ideology*, Harvester Wheatsheaf, Brighton 1989, p. 34.

21. See 'Feuermelder', in *Einbahnstraße*, G.S.IV.1, p. 122. *One Way Street and Other Writings*, p. 80.

22. G.S.IV.1, p. 122, *One Way Street and Other Writings*, p. 80.

23. In German the word for elective affinities, *Wahlverwandtschaften*, has its origins in alchemy. Benjamin's invoking of the term is already a critique of straightforward scientism, just as it had been for the anti-Newtonian Goethe. Benjamin had made an extended study of Goethe's novel of that name between 1921 and 1922. See G.S.I.1, pp. 123–201. For more on elective affinity, including its relation to Max Weber's thought, see Michael Löwy's *On Changing the World: Essays in Political Philosophy from Karl Marx to Walter Benjamin*, Humanities Press, Englewood Cliffs, NJ 1993.

24. 'Zum Planetarium' in *Einbahnstraße*, G.S.IV.1, p. 148. *One Way Street and Other Writings*, New Left Books, London 1979, p. 104.

25. See G.S.IV.1, p. 148. *One Way Street and Other Writings*, p. 104.

26. See G.S.IV.1, p. 147. *One Way Street and Other Writings*, pp. 103–4.

27. See G.S.IV.1, p. 148. *One Way Street and Other Writings*, p. 104.

28. See G.S.I.1, p. 60. The publisher's note to the English edition of *One Way Street* states that 'Zum Planetarium' is 'perhaps the first and certainly the finest – because most temperate and rational – expression of that rejection of the notion of the mastery of nature by technology that was afterwards to become a hallmark of Frankfurt Marxism' (New Left Books, London 1979, p. 36). It is true that modern technology is shown to be alienated from nature in the piece, but Benjamin has little truck with the thrust of Adorno's and Horkheimer's line in *Dialektik der Aufklärung* (1947). This line seems to suggest that technology is inherently an instrument of domination. For these two, it appears that it is nature that will take its revenge on the social world.

29. This idea of technology's 'revolt' surfaces in each extended engagement with *Technik* in Benjamin's work from now on. See 'Theorien des deutschen Faschismus', G.S.III, p. 238. See also the various versions of the *Kunstwerk-Aufsatz* (1935–39), G.S.I.2, p. 468/p. 507/G.S.VII.1, p. 383. *Illuminations*, Fontana, London 1992 p. 235.

30. See theses IX, in *Über den Begriff der Geschichte* (1939–1940) in G.S.I.2, pp. 697–8. *Illuminations*, p. 249.

31. 'Zum Planetarium' in *Einbahnstraße*, G.S.IV.1, pp. 148–9. *One Way Street and Other Writings*, p. 104.

32. G.S.IV.1, p. 147. *One Way Street and Other Writings*, p. 104.

33. See Karl Marx, *Das Kapital*, volume III, *Marx Engels Werke*, Dietz Verlag, Berlin 1969 p. 828. Marx's immediate demand here is a reduction in the length of the working day.

34. G.S.II.2, p. 620.

35. See the section entitled 'Die Verdinglichung und das Bewußtsein des Proletariats', in Georg Lukács, *Geschichte und Klassenbewußtsein*, Luchterhand, Darmstadt und Neuwied 1986 pp.170–355. 'Reification and the Consciousness of the Proletariat', in *History and Class Consciousness*, Merlin Press, London 1971, pp. 83–222.

36. See Karl Marx, *Das Kapital*, volume I, *Marx Engels Werke*, Dietz Verlag, Berlin 1969 p. 467.

37. *Das Kapital*, p. 503.

38. 'Konvolut N: erkenntnistheoretisches, Theorie des Fortschritts', in the *Passagenwerk* (1937–40), G.S.V.1, pp. 595–6. 'N', in Gary Smith (ed.),

Benjamin; Philosophy, History, Aesthetics, University of Chicago Press, Chicago 1989, pp. 67–8.

39. *Passagenwerk* (pre-1935), G.S.V.1, p. 274.

40. See G.S.V.1, p. 276. Adorno's original observation is in *Noten zur Literatur*, Suhrkamp, Frankfurt/Main 1981, pp. 515–22.

41. Adorno, *Noten zur Literatur*, p. 522.

42. See 'Traumkitsch', G.S.II.2, p. 622.

43. See 'Pariser Passagen' 1 (1927–29), G.S.V.2, pp. 1006 and 1007.

44. Ernst Bloch was one of the first to recognize the surrealist connections in Benjamin's own philosophizing. This is evident in Bloch's review of *Einbahnstraße*, titled 'Revueform in der Philosophie' (1928) and included in *Erbschaft dieser Zeit* (1935), Suhrkamp, Frankfurt/Main 1985, pp. 368–71.

45. Benjamin's interest in surrealism's total critique finds an echo in Franklin Rosemont's definition. Rosemont writes: 'Contrary to prevalent misdefinitions, surrealism is not an aesthetic doctrine, nor a philosophical system, nor a mere literary or artistic school. It is an unrelenting revolt against a civilisation that reduces all human aspirations to market values, religious impostures, universal boredom and misery' (Franklin Rosemont, *André Breton and the First Principles of Surrealism*, Pluto Press, London 1978, p. 1).

46. 'Der Sürrealismus', G.S.II.1, pp. 309–10. *One Way Street and Other Writings*, p. 239.

47. This is quoted in Benjamin's preparatory notes for the surrealism essay G.S.II.3, p. 1039. Benjamin draws specifically on Pierre Naville's *La Révolution et les intellectuels* (1926), where the author attempts to lay 'foundation stones for a theory of the revolutionary intelligentsia' (reprinted Gallimard, Paris 1975).

48. 'Der Sürrealismus', G.S.II.1, p. 307. *One Way Street and Other Writings*, p. 237.

49. See G.S.II.1, p. 304. *One Way Street and Other Writings*, pp.233–4.

50. For documents pertaining to Bolshevik internationalism, see *In Defence of the Russian Revolution: A Selection of Bolshevik Writings 1917–1923*, ed. by Al Richardson, Porcupine Press, London 1995, especially pp. 119–82.

51. The quotation from Trotsky can be found in Tony Cliff, *Trotsky: The Darker the Night the Brighter the Star 1927–1940*, Bookmarks, London 1993, p. 62.

52. See, for example, a letter written to Scholem on 29 May 1926, in *Briefe* 1, pp. 425–30.

53. See G.S.VI, pp. 292–409. *Moscow Diary*, Harvard University Press, Cambridge, Mass. 1986.

54. For information on industrial struggle and the opposition see Issac Deutscher, *The Prophet Unarmed: Trotsky; 1921–1929*, Oxford University Press, Oxford 1959, pp. 275–8.

55. See Deutscher, *The Prophet Unarmed: Trotsky; 1921–1929*, p. 356.

56. See, for example, 'Moskau' (1927) G.S.IV.1, pp. 325 and 337–9. *One Way Street and Other Writings*, pp. 185–6 and 197–9.

57. See *Moskauer Tagebuch*, G.S.VI, p. 363. See also 'Moskau' (1927), G.S.IV.1, p. 323. *Moscow Diary*, Harvard University Press, Cambridge, Mass. 1986, pp. 76–7. *One Way Street and Other Writings*, p. 183.

58. See G.S.VI, p. 297. *Moscow Diary*, p. 15.

59. See G.S.VI, p. 294. *Moscow Diary*, pp. 11–12.

60. See Trotsky's 'The Suicide of Mayakovsky', in *On Literature and Art*, Pathfinder, New York 1970, pp. 174–8.

61. *Moskauer Tagebuch* G.S.VI, p. 338. *Moscow Diary*, Harvard University Press, Cambridge, Mass. 1986, p. 53.

62. See G.S.VI, pp. 338–9. *Moscow Diary*, p. 54.

63. See G.S.II.2, pp. 755–62.

64. See Leon Trotsky, *Literature and Revolution* (1924), University of Michigan, Ann Arbor 1960, p. 323.

65. *Literature and Revolution*, p. 19. Alan M. Wald suggests that it is not until 1937, while writing *The Revolution Betrayed*, that Trotsky is fully able to recognize the effects on culture of Stalin's bureaucratic tyranny. See Wald's essay 'Leon Trotsky's Contributions to Marxist Cultural Theory and Literary Criticism', in *Writing from the Left*, Verso, London 1994, p. 128.

66. See *Moskauer Tagebuch*, G.S.VI, p. 321. *Moscow Diary*, p. 39.

67. See G.S.VI, p. 366. *Moscow Diary*, p. 81.

68. See the letter to Scholem of 23 February 1927, in *Briefe* 1, p. 442.

69. See 'Moskau' (1927) G.S.IV.1 pp. 333–4. *One Way Street and Other Writings*, pp.193–4.

70. G.S.IV.1, p. 336. *One Way Street and Other Writings*, pp.195–6.

71. G.S.IV.1, pp. 316–48. *One Way Street and Other Writings*, pp.177–208.

72. GS.IV.1, pp. 321–2. *One Way Street and Other Writings*, p. 182.

73. G.S.IV.1, p. 336. See also *Moskauer Tagebuch*, G.S.VI, p. 350. *One Way Street and Other Writings*, p. 196. *Moscow Diary*, pp. 63–4.

74. G.S.IV.1, p. 326. See also *Moskauer Tagebuch*, G.S.VI, p. 327. *One Way Street and Other Writings*, p. 187. *Moscow Diary*, p. 44.

75. G.S.IV.1, p. 327. *One Way Street and Other Writings*, p. 187.

76. *Moskauer Tagebuch*, G.S.VI, p. 328. *Moscow Diary*, p. 44.

77. 'Moskau' (1927), G.S.IV.1, p. 339. *One Way Street and Other Writings*, p. 199.

78. G.S.IV.1, pp. 338–9. *One Way Street and Other Writings*, p. 198.

79. 'Der Surrealismus', G.S.II.1, p. 309. *One Way Street and Other Writings*, p. 238.

80. For an assessment of surrealist works as types of experience (*Erfahrung*), see 'Der Sürrealismus', G.S.II.1, p. 297. *One Way Street and Other Writings*, p. 227. Conceptualizing experience is a perennial concern for Benjamin and is first addressed in early pieces such as 'Über das Programm der kommenden Philosophie' (1918) (G.S.II.1, pp. 157–71). 'Erfahrung' from 1913 presents Benjamin's early thoughts on experience. See G.S.II.1, pp. 54–6.

81. 'Der Sürrealismus', G.S.II.1, p. 301. *One Way Street and Other Writings*, p. 231.

82. See G.S.II.1, p. 296; see also the notes for the surrealism essay G.S.II.3, p. 1023. *One Way Street and Other Writings*, p. 226.

83. See 'Zum Bilde Prousts' (1929), G.S.II.1, p. 319.

84. Notes for the surrealism essay, G.S.II.3, pp. 1023,1035 and 1040.

85. See G.S.II.1, p. 302. *One Way Street and Other Writings*, p. 231.

86. An English translation of this essay can be found in *October*, no. 69, Summer 1994, pp. 133–44.

87. 'Der Sürrealismus', G.S.II.1 pp. 307 and 308. *One Way Street and Other Writings*, pp. 236 and 237.

88. G.S.II.1, p. 297. *One Way Street and Other Writings*, p. 227.

89. See G.S.IV.1, pp. 396–8. *One Way Street and Other Writings*, pp. 157–9. The monograph draws, in part, on ideas about the emancipation of character from the shackles of fate, first formulated in 'Schicksal and Charakter' (1919). See G.S.II.1, pp. 171–9.

90. See 'Dadaland', in Lucy Lippard (ed.), *Dadas on Art*, Prentice Hall, New Jersey 1971, p. 24.

91. Tristan Tzara, 'Seven Dada Manifestos and Lampisteries', Calder, London 1992, p. 5.

92. 'Seven Dada Manifestos', p. 12.

93. 'Seven Dada Manifestos', pp. 12–13.

94. See G.S.II.3, p. 1022.

95. See 'Der Sürrealismus' G.S.II.1, p. 297. *One Way Street and Other Writings*, p. 227.

96. G.S.II.1, p. 309. *One Way Street and Other Writings*, p. 239.

97. Notes for the surrealism essay, G.S.II.3, p. 1041.

98. 'Der Sürrealismus', G.S.II.1, p. 310. *One Way Street and Other Writings*, p. 239.

99. See 'Pariser Passagen' 1 (1927–29), G.S.V.2, p. 1027.

100. Such accusations have been made by Norbert Bolz and van Reijen and Terry Eagleton. Bolz reads Benjamin as a deeply technocratic and anti-humanist thinker. Bolz and van Reijen state that Benjamin's anti-humanism places him beyond ethics, because the person is treated as a thing. See *Walter Benjamin* by Norbert Bolz and Willem van Reijen, Reihe Campus, Frankfurt/Main 1991 p. 92. Eagleton accuses Benjamin of 'an ultra-modernist technologism' and 'left-functionalism' when he imagines the human body as instrument or machine. See Eagleton's *The Ideology of the Aesthetic*, Blackwell, Oxford 1990, pp. 336–7.

101. See G.S.II.1, pp. 364–5. *One Way Street and Other Writings*, pp. 286–8.

102. 'Der Sürrealismus', G.S.II.1, p. 310. *One Way Street and Other Writings*, p. 239.

103. 'Konvolut a; soziale Bewegung', in *Passagenwerk* (pre-1935), G.S.V.2, p. 853.

104. See his *Walter Benjamin: Story of a Friendship*, Faber and Faber, London 1982, p. 146.

105. 'Der Sürrealismus', G.S.II.1, p. 308. *One Way Street and Other Writings*, p. 238.

106. See G.S.II.1, pp. 296 and 308–9. *One Way Street and Other Writings*, pp.226 and 238. For Aragon's views, see *Traité du style*, Gallimard, Paris 1928.

107. G.S.II.1, p. 308. *One Way Street and Other Writings*, p. 237.

108. G.S.II.1, pp. 309–10. *One Way Street and Other Writings*, p. 238.

109. G.S.II.1, p. 309. *One Way Street and Other Writings*, p. 238.

110. G.S.II.1, p. 309. *One Way Street and Other Writings*, p. 239.

111. G.S.II.1, p. 309. *One Way Street and Other Writings*, p. 238.

112. See *Einbahnstraße*, G.S.IV.1, p. 85. *One Way Street and Other Writings*, p. 45.

113. Benjamin draws on Sorel's ideas, in 'Zur Kritik der Gewalt' (1921). See G.S.II.1, pp. 179–203. *One Way Street and Other Writings*, pp. 132–54.

114. See Ernst Jünger's 'Über die Gefahr', in *Der gefährliche Augenblick*, ed. Ferdinand Bucholtz, Junker und Dünhaupt, Berlin 1931, p. 15.

115. This is not the only time that Benjamin has to veer his ideas away from reaction and fascism. See, for example, Adorno's precaution against Benjamin's use of the collective unconscious and its Jungian implications, as well as a Klagesian model of myth. This occurs in Adorno's letter to Benjamin of 2 August 1935 in *Briefe* 2, ed. G. Scholem and T.W. Adorno, Suhrkamp, Frankfurt/Main 1978, pp.671–83. In the opening section of 'Das Kunstwerk im Zeitalter seiner technischen Reproduzierbarkeit' Benjamin feels compelled to assert that he is seeking categories that will be 'completely unusable for the purposes of fascism'. G.S.I.2 p. 435/p. 473/G.S.VII.1 p. 350. *Illuminations*, Fontana, London 1992, p. 212. This reflects a sentiment expressed in a letter to Scholem in April 1931, in which Benjamin

insists that his priority is making his work 'unpalatable' to the enemy. See *Briefe* 2, Suhrkamp, Frankfurt/Main 1978, p. 531.

116. See 'Karl Kraus', G.S.II.1, p. 344. *One Way Street and Other Writings*, p. 267.

117. G.S.III, pp. 23–8.

118. For information on the controversy, see G.S.III, pp. 609–13.

119. *Einbahnstraße*, G.S.IV.1, p. 108. *One Way Street and Other Writings*, p. 66.

120. See 'Theorien des deutschen Faschismus', G.S.III, p. 250.

121. For example, Benjamin refers to war and especially the place of war and militarism in bourgeois and right-wing ideology in 'Nochmals: Die vielen Soldaten', published April/May 1929, in *Die literarische Welt* (G.S.IV.1, pp. 461–3), 'James Ensor wird 70 Jahre', published 11 April 1930 (G.S.IV.1, pp. 565–7), and 'Pariser Tagebuch', written late 1929 to early 1930 (G.S.IV.1, pp. 567–87).

122. See the first part of section called 'Zur Literaturkritik', in G.S.VI, pp. 161–80, which includes 'Programm der literarischen Kritik' (1929–30), in G.S.VI, pp. 165–6 and 'Falsche Kritik' (1930), in G.S.VI, pp. 175–6, and the essay 'Literaturgeschichte und Literaturwissenschaft' (1930), in G.S.III, pp. 283–90.

123. 'Programm der literarischen Kritik', G.S.VI, 'Fragmente' (1929–30), p. 165.

124. 'Theorien des deutschen Faschismus', G.S.III, pp. 238–50.

125. See, for example, *Briefe* 1, p. 217. Benjamin had actually been angered by elements of Bloch's book, but the review that he wrote at the time has not been found.

126. Bloch's discussions of war are concentrated in the section of *Geist der Utopie* entitled 'Karl Marx, der Tod und die Apokalypse'. The quotations in the text here come from pp. 398 and 399, in the *Gesamtausgabe*, volume 16, Suhrkamp, Frankfurt/Main 1977. Bloch reworked *Geist der Utopie* substantially for a second edition published in 1923 (see *Gesamtausgabe*, volume 3, Suhrkamp, Frankfurt/Main 1977).

127. See 'Theorien des deutschen Faschismus', G.S.III, p. 239.

128. G.S.III, p. 241.

129. See G.S.III, pp. 242 and 243.

130. See Benjamin's quotation from F.G. Jünger for an admission of masochistic, martyrish delights in cataclysmic (self-)destruction: 'Theorien des deutschen Faschismus', G.S.III, p. 246.

131. 'Theorien des deutschen Faschismus', G.S.III, pp. 242–3 and p. 244.

132. Something akin to aura is evoked by Rang's description of an eternal halo ('*Gloriole*'). 'Theorien des deutschen Faschismus', G.S.III, p. 244.

133. G.S.III, p. 240.

134. See G.S.III, p. 243.

135. G.S.III, p. 239.

136. G.S.III, p. 249.

137. See G.S.III, p. 247.

138. See G.S.III, p. 243.

139. G.S.III, p. 246.

140. G.S.III, pp. 246–7.

141. See G.S.III, p. 245.

142. 'Nochmals: Die vielen Soldaten' (1929), G.S.IV.1, p. 462.

143. G.S.III, p. 248.

144. See G.S.III, p. 246.

145. See G.S.III, p. 248.

146. See G.S.III, p. 249.

147. Compare the landscape described as the model of auratic experience in 'Kleine Geschichte der Photographie' (1931), G.S.II.1, p. 378. *One Way Street and Other Writings*, p. 250.

148. See 'Theorien des deutschen Faschismus' G.S.III, p. 243. Compare to Benjamin's later assertion in the 'Artwork essay' that the gas warfare of the First World War announces the death of aura. See G.S.I.2, p. 469/p. 508/G.S.VII.1 p. 383. *Illuminations*, p. 235.

149. G.S.III, p. 247. There is a definite politicization in Benjamin's idea of nature and landscape. Compare, for example, the differences between the attitude expressed here and Benjamin's 1928 review of Borchardt's *Der Deutsche in der Landschaft* (G.S.III, pp. 91–4), where he accepts a legitimate relationship between the German thinker, idealism and the landscape.

150. See G.S.IV.1, p. 462.

151. 'Theorien des deutschen Faschismus', G.S.III, p. 247. See also pp. 240–1.

152. See G.S.III, p. 239.

153. G.S.III, p. 244.

154. 'Ein Außenseiter macht sich bemerkbar' (1930), G.S.III, p. 220.

155. See G.S.II.1, p. 365. *One Way Street and Other Writings*, p. 287.

156. 'Theorien des deutschen Faschismus', G.S.III, pp. 238–9 and p. 249–50.

157. These comments are later repeated, in modified form, in the epilogue to 'Das Kunstwerk im Zeitalter seiner technischen Reproduzierbarkeit' (1935–39). *Illuminations*, pp. 234–5.

158. See 'Theorien des deutschen Faschismus', G.S.III, p. 238.

159. G.S.III, p. 238.

160. From Georg Lukács, *Geschichte und Klassenbewußtsein* (1923), Luchterhand, Darmstadt 1986, p. 429. *History and Class Consciousness*, Merlin Press, London 1971, p. 277.

161. 'Theorien des deutschen Faschismus', G.S.III, p. 238.

162. See G.S.III, p. 248.

163. See G.S.III, p. 247.

164. G.S.III, p. 238.

165. G.S.III, p. 249.

166. G.S.III, p. 250.

167. G.S.III, p. 238.

168. See G.S.VII.1, p. 449. Alfred Seidel's doctoral dissertation *Produktivkräfte und Klassenkampf*, Heidelberg 1922, is listed in Benjamin's 'Verzeichnis der gelesenen Schriften' as *Die Metaphysik der Produktivkräfte*.

169. Quoted in Alfred Seidel's doctoral dissertation *Produktivkräfte und Klassenkampf*, Heidelberg 1922. For the standard English translation of this quote, see Leon Trotsky's preface to *The War and the International*, Young Socialist Publication, Sri Lanka, 1971, p. vii. Similar analyses can be found in the theory of imperialism devised by Rosa Luxemburg, whose prison letters Benjamin read at the beginning of the 1920s. See G.S.VII.1, p. 447.

170. 'Theorien des deutschen Faschismus', G.S.III, p. 238.

171. G.S.III, pp. 242 and 243.

172. The final passage was scrapped by Adorno from the first edition of Benjamin's selected works in the 1950s.

173. See 'Theorien des deutschen Faschismus', G.S.III, p. 243.

174. See G.S.IV.1, p. 463.

175. See G.S.IV.1, p. 567.

176. 'Theorien des deutschen Faschismus', G.S.III, p. 250.

177. See G.S.III, p. 250.

178. G.S.III, p. 250.

179. See, for one example, 'Pariser Passagen' 1 (1927–29), G.S.V.2, p. 1033.
180. 'Theorien des deutschen Faschismus', G.S.III, p. 241.
181. See 'Erfahrung und Armut' (1933) G.S.II.1, p. 214.
182. 'Theorien des deutschen Faschismus' G.S.III, p. 249.
183. 'Zu Micky-Maus' (1931), G.S.VI, p. 144.
184. See G.S.VI, p. 145.
185. See, for one example of a contemporary analysis of Fordism, Antonio Gramsci, *Selections from the Prison Notebooks*, Lawrence and Wishart, London 1971, pp. 277–318.
186. Gramsci, *Selections from the Prison Notebooks*, pp. 309–10.
187. See Konvolut X: Marx in the *Passagenwerk* (1937–40), G.S.V.2, p. 804.
188. The original quotation is to be found in Fischer's *Karl Marx und sein Verhältnis zu Staat und Wirtschaft*, Verlag von Gustav Fischer, Jena 1932, p. 40.
189. See Fischer, *Karl Marx*, p. 40.
190. Gershom Scholem, *Walter Benjamin: die Geschichte einer Freundschaft*, Suhrkamp, Frankfurt/Main 1975, p. 209. The letter from Scholem to Benjamin is reprinted in English in Scholem's *Walter Benjamin: The Story of a Friendship*, Faber and Faber, London 1982.

2 Benjamin's Objectives

1. G.S.V.2, p. 1001.
2. 'Pariser Passagen' 1 (1927–29), G.S.V.2, p. 1011.
3. This is an art whose exemplars are not just '*Bilder*' (pictures), but, rather, '*Abbilder*' (a term that includes the idea of copies of an original, as well as intimations of the action of sourcing something external to the image). See 'Kleine Geschichte der Photographie', G.S.II.1, p. 379. *One Way Street and Other Writings*, New Left Books, London 1979, p. 250.
4. See Georg Lukács, *Theorie des Romans*, Sammlung Luchterhand, Darmstadt/Neuwied 1971. Adorno testifies to the book's influence in 'Erpreßte Versöhnung: Zu Georg Lukács; Wider den mißverstandenen Realismus' (1958), in *Noten zur Literatur*, Suhrkamp, Frankfurt/Main 1981, p. 251.
5. See Georg Lukács, 1962 introduction to *Die Theorie des Romans*, pp. 9–16.
6. See Benjamin's 'Krisis des Romans: Zu Döblins Berlin Alexanderplatz' (1930), in G.S.III, pp. 230–6.
7. Benjamin acknowledged his debt to Riegl on several occasions. See, for example, the prologue to the book on baroque mourning plays, written in 1925 (G.S.I.1), a curriculum vitae from 1928 (G.S.VI, p. 219), a review from 1929 titled 'Bücher die lebendig geblieben sind' (G.S.III, pp. 169–71), a review titled 'Strenge Kunstwissenschaft', written in 1932 (G.S.III, pp. 363–9/369–74), and all versions of the 'Artwork essay' (G.S.I.2, p. 439/p. 478 and G.S.VII.1, p. 354).
8. 'Erfahrung und Armut' (1933) G.S.II.1, p. 216.
9. *Briefe* 2, ed. G. Scholem and T.W. Adorno, Suhrkamp, Frankfurt/Main 1978, p. 531.
10. *Briefe* 2, p. 531.
11. See *Briefe* 2, p. 521.
12. See *Briefe* 2, p. 530.
13. *Briefe* 2, p. 524.

14. *Passagenwerk* (pre-1935) G.S.V.1, p. 571. 'N', in Gary Smith (ed.), *Benjamin: Philosophy, History, Aesthetics*, University of Chicago Press, Chicago 1989, p. 44.

15. See 'Kleine Geschichte der Photographie', G.S.II.1, p. 378. *One Way Street and Other Writings*, pp. 249–50.

16. 'Erfahrung und Armut' (1933), G.S.II.1, p. 215.

17. Seeking a motto for his 'Artwork essay', Benjamin chose the counterpart to Marx's poetical phrase, emphasizing enlightenment and secularization: 'all that is holy is profaned'. See the notes for the 'Artwork essay', G.S.VII.2, p. 679.

18. Marshall Berman's *All That is Solid Melts into Air: The Experience of Modernity* (Simon and Schuster, New York 1982) provides one instance of an enthusiastic misinterpretation of this famous phrase, accenting only its recognition of modernity's production of continual flux that generates further delusions, and cancelling acknowledgement of the tension between fetishism and demystification which capitalism sets in train.

19. 'Konvolut F: Eisenkonstruktion', in the *Passagenwerk* (pre-1935) G.S.V.1, p. 217. See also entry F3 a, 5, p. 220.

20. See 'Erwiderung an Oscar A. H. Schmitz' (1927) G.S.II.2, p. 753. See also 'Konvolut F: Eisenkonstruktion' in the *Passagenwerk* (pre-1935), G.S.V.1, p. 216. Benjamin reiterates these sentiments in an entry in the *Passagenwerk* (pre-1935): 'The attempt to instigate a systematic confrontation of art and photography had to fail at first. It was to be one moment in the confrontation between art and *Technik*, which arose historically' G.S.V.2, p. 828.

21. 'Erwiderung an Oscar A. H. Schmitz', p. 752.

22. Published in Tristan Tzara, *Seven Dada Manifestos and Lampisteries*, Calder, London 1992, p. 100. In 1924 Benjamin translated the essay for the magazine *G: A Magazine for Elementary Form*, journal of the 'G' group, which included Sascha Stone and Hans Richter

23. See 'Kleine Geschichte der Photographie', G.S.II.1, p. 370. *One Way Street and Other Writings*, p. 242.

24. G.S.II.1, p. 370. *One Way Street and Other Writings*, p. 242.

25. G.S.II.1, p. 381. *One Way Street and Other Writings*, pp. 252–3.

26. See, for example, Benjamin's 'Was ist das epische Theater?' 1 (1931), G.S.II.2, p. 524.

27. 'Konvolut Y: die Photographie', in the *Passagenwerk* (pre-1935), G.S.V.2, p. 832.

28. 'Kleine Geschichte der Photographie', G.S.II.1, p. 371. *One Way Street and Other Writings*, p. 243. Kracauer's essay is included in the collection *Das Ornament der Masse: Essays*, Suhrkamp, Frankfurt/Main 1977, pp. 21–39. English translation in Siegfried Kracauer, *The Mass Ornament, Weimar Essays*, Harvard University Press, Cambridge, Mass. 1995.

29. See 'Kleine Geschichte der Photographie', G.S.II.1, p. 371. *One Way Street and Other Writings*, p. 243.

30. G.S.II.1, p. 385. *One Way Street and Other Writings*, p. 256.

31. 'Der Sürrealismus', G.S.II.1, p. 300. *One Way Street and Other Writings*, p. 230.

32. See 'Kleine Geschichte der Photographie' (1931), G.S.II.1, p. 370. *One Way Street and Other Writings*, p. 242.

33. See 'Kleine Geschichte der Photographie', G.S.II.1, p. 368. *One Way Street and Other Writings*, p. 240.

34. 'Konvolut N: erkenntnistheoretisches, Theorie des Fortschritts', in the *Passagenwerk* (pre-1935), G.S.V.1, p. 572. 'N' in Gary Smith (ed.), *Benjamin;*

Philosophy, History, Aesthetics, University of Chicago Press, Chicago 1989, p. 45.

35. 'Kleine Geschichte der Photographie', G.S.II.1, p. 373. *One Way Street and Other Writings*, p. 245.

36. G.S.II.1, p. 376. *One Way Street and Other Writings*, p. 247.

37. See G.S.II.1, p. 377. *One Way Street and Other Writings*, p. 245.

38. See G.S.II.1, p. 376. *One Way Street and Other Writings*, p. 248.

39. The word awkwardly translated as 'conditionedness' is '*Bedingtsein*'. See G.S.II.1, p. 376. *One Way Street and Other Writings*, p. 248.

40. G.S.II.1, p. 376. *One Way Street and Other Writings*, p. 248.

41. G.S.II.1, p. 374. *One Way Street and Other Writings*, p. 245.

42. G.S.II.1, p. 378. *One Way Street and Other Writings*, p. 250. This definition of aura is repeated in modified but connected form in 1935 in the 'Artwork essay' and in writings on Baudelaire in 1938.

43. See G.S.II.1, p. 368. *One Way Street and Other Writings*, p. 240.

44. See G.S.II.1, p. 375. *One Way Street and Other Writings*, p. 246.

45. G.S.II.1, p. 378. *One Way Street and Other Writings*, p. 249–50.

46. See G.S.II.1, p. 371. *One Way Street and Other Writings*, p. 243.

47. See G.S.II.1, pp. 375–6. *One Way Street and Other Writings*, p. 247.

48. G.S.II.1, p. 377. *One Way Street and Other Writings*, p. 248.

49. Notes to the 1935 *Exposé* of the *Passagenwerk*, G.S.V.2, p. 1210.

50. 'Kleine Geschichte der Photographie', G.S.II.1, p. 369. *One Way Street and Other Writings*, p. 241.

51. Photographs matching these descriptions can be seen in Bernd Witte's biography of Benjamin (RoRoRo, Reinbek/Hamburg 1990), in the *Marbacher Magazin*, no. 55 edition on Walter Benjamin (1990), and in Werner Fuld, *Walter Benjamin: Zwischen den Stuhlen* (RoRoRo, Reinbek/Hamburg 1990). Benjamin's childhood photographs are also alluded to in the autobiographical pieces in *Berliner Kindheit um Neunzehnjahrhundert*. See a description from 1933 of boyhood self-portraits, where studio tripods, tapestries and scaffolds are deemed reminiscent of the boudoir and the torture chamber, in G.S.IV.1, p. 261.

52. See 'Kleine Geschichte der Photographie', G.S.II.1, p. 375. *One Way Street and Other Writings*, pp. 246–7.

53. 'Was ist das epische Theater?' 1 (1931), G.S.II.2, p. 524.

54. 'Kleine Geschichte der Photographie', G.S.II.1, p. 377. *One Way Street and Other Writings*, p. 248.

55. See 'Der Sürrealismus', G.S.II.1, p. 298. *One Way Street and Other Writings*, p. 228. See also 'Die Wiederkehr des Flaneurs' (1929), G.S.III, pp. 196–7.

56. 'Kleine Geschichte der Photographie', G.S.II.1, p. 376. *One Way Street and Other Writings*, p. 248.

57. See G.S.II.1, p. 377. *One Way Street and Other Writings*, p. 248.

58. See G.S.II.1, p. 370. *One Way Street and Other Writings*, p. 242.

59. Magic and science are not two discrete realms for Benjamin. He writes of how the most precise technology can give its productions a magical value that a painted picture can never possess. The process offers up to viewing 'image worlds that inhabit the smallest things, meaningful yet covert enough, to have found shelter in waking dreams, but which, enlarged and capable of formulation, make the difference between *Technik* and magic recognizable as a thoroughly historical variable'. 'Kleine Geschichte der Photographie', G.S.II.1, pp. 371–2. *One Way Street and Other Writings*, pp. 243–4.

60. See G.S.II.1, pp. 368 and 383. *One Way Street and Other Writings*, pp. 241 and 254.

61. 'Konvolut Q: Panorama', in the *Passagenwerk* (pre-1935), G.S.V.2, pp. 658–9.
62. G.S.II.2, p. 752.
63. 'Pariser Passagen' 1 (1927–29), G.S.V.2, p. 1026.
64. 'Kleine Geschichte der Photographie', G.S.II.1, p. 371. *One Way Street and Other Writings*, p. 243. Benjamin uses the word '*verwandt*', 'allied'.
65. Quoted in Dagmar Barnouw, *Critical Realism: History: Photography, and the Work of Siegfried Kracauer*, Johns Hopkins University Press, Baltimore 1994, p. 64.
66. 'Kleine Geschichte der Photographie', G.S.II.1, p. 379. *One Way Street and Other Writings*, p. 251.
67. See G.S.II.1, p. 383. *One Way Street and Other Writings*, p. 254.
68. See G.S.III, pp. 279–83.
69. 'Kleine Geschichte der Photographie', G.S.II.1, p. 381. *One Way Street and Other Writings*, p. 253.
70. G.S.II.1, p. 385. *One Way Street and Other Writings*, p. 256.
71. See G.S.II.1, pp. 383–4. *One Way Street and Other Writings*, p. 255. There is a reference to this photograph in Benjamin's autobiographical piece *Berliner Chronik* (1932), as part of a commentary on attempts to record Berlin. See *Berliner Chronik*, G.S.VI, p. 470. *One Way Street and Other Writings*, p. 298.
72. G.S.II.1, pp. 383–4. *One Way Street and Other Writings*, p. 255.
73. 'Konvolut K: Traumstadt und Traumhaus, Zukunftsträume, anthropologischer Nihilismus, Jung', in the *Passagenwerk* (pre-1935), G.S.V.1, p. 498.
74. See Dziga Vertov's 'Kinoks-Revolution' (first published in *Lef*, no. 3, 1923), reprinted in Harry M. Geduld (ed.), *Film Makers on Film Making*, Indiana University Press, Bloomington 1969, pp. 82–3.
75. See Hugo von Hofmannsthal, 'Der Ersatz für die Träume' (1921), in *Gesammelte Werke in Einzelausgaben*, *Prosa* 4, Fischer, Frankfurt/Main 1955, p. 45.

3 Berlin Chthonic, Photos and Trains and Films and Cars

1. G.S.V.2, p. 1011.
2. See *Der Begriff der Kunstkritik in der deutschen Romantik* (1919), G.S.I.1, p. 104.
3. 'Konvolut N: erkenntnistheoretisches, Theorie des Fortschritts' in the *Passagenwerk* (pre-1935), G.S.V.1, p. 571.
4. Though it must be said that his interpretations of both always assume mimetic causality and attempt materialist readings of direct impressions and residue.
5. 'Der Sürrealismus', G.S.II.1, p. 307. *One Way Street and Other Writings*, New Left Books, London 1979, p. 237.
6. Karl Marx, *Early Writings*, Penguin/NLR, London 1975, p. 206.
7. For original, earlier jottings of some of the themes on perception, see 'Dispositionen der Wahrnehmung', in G.S.IV.2, p. 938 (and editorial comments).
8. See *Einbahnstraße*, G.S.IV.1, p. 129. *One Way Street and Other Writings*, p. 86.
9. See G.S.IV.1, p. 129. *One Way Street and Other Writings*, p. 87.
10. T. W. Adorno, *Noten zur Literatur*, Suhrkamp, Frankfurt/Main 1981, pp. 576–7.
11. Moholy-Nagy's film sketch appeared in a supplement on tomorrow's films, added to the Berlin film journal *Film-Kurier* in May 1925. See Jeanpaul

Goergen, *Walter Ruttmann: Eine Dokumentation*, Freunde der Deutschen Kinemathek, Berlin 1989, p. 26.

12. See G.S.IV.1 for one version of this project, compiled by Theodor Adorno and Tillman Rexroth, and see G.S.VII.1 for another version, subtitled 'Fassung letzter Hand'.

13. G.S.V.2, p. 1022.

14. Bernd Witte wrote a detailed account of the history and varying versions of *Berliner Chronik* and *Berliner Kindheit um neunzehnhundert*. Witte's 'Bilder der Endzeit: Zu einem authentischen Text der *Berliner Kindheit* von Walter Benjamin' appears in the *Deutsche Vierteljahrschrift für Literaturwissenschaft und Geschichte*, Stuttgart 1984, pp. 570–92. Witte sees a development through the various versions of the text, whereby more and more biographical elements are purged and the catastrophic future is increasingly indicated in the visions of the critic, a curious mélange of child-author and historical materialist. After he abandoned his plan to commit suicide, Benjamin begins work on *Berliner Kindheit um neunzehnhundert*. The lack of publishing opportunities, apart from the appearance of a few of the articles in the *Frankfurter Zeitung* until 1935, means that Benjamin continues revising his childhood reminiscences until 1938.

15. See the editors' notes in G.S.VI, p. 799. For information on Benjamin's preparations for exile and his responses to Nazi terror, see Chryssoula Kambas's *Walter Benjamin im Exil: Zum Verhältnis von Literaturpolitik und Ästhetik*, Max Niemeyer, Tübingen 1983.

16. See *Berliner Kindheit um neunzehnhundert* (Fassung letzter Hand), G.S.VII.1, p. 385. See also an unpublished letter to Lion of 13 May 1938 held in the Benjamin-Teilnachlaß in the Akademie der Künste zu Ost Berlin.

17. 'Die Wiederkehr des Flaneurs', G.S.III, p. 194.

18. See 'Karl Kraus', G.S.II.1, p. 336. *One Way Street and Other Writings*, p. 260.

19. See G.S.II.1, p. 344. *One Way Street and Other Writings*, p. 267.

20. See 'Konvolut I: das Interieur, die Spur' in the *Passagenwerk* (pre-1935), G.S.V.1, p. 282.

21. See 'Kleine Geschichte der Photographie', G.S.II.1, p. 385. *One Way Street and Other Writings*, p. 256.

22. See '*Berliner Chronik*', G.S.VI, p. 488. *One Way Street and Other Writings*, p. 316.

23. See *Berliner Chronik*, G.S.VI, pp. 466–7. *One Way Street and Other Writings*, p. 295. For an extended rumination on this idea, see 'Pariser Passagen' 1 (1927–29), pp. 998–1000.

24. For this particular expression, see *Passagenwerk* (pre-1935), G.S.V.1, p. 138.

25. See *Berliner Chronik*, G.S.VI, p. 469. *One Way Street and Other Writings*, p. 298.

26. See G.S.V.2, p. 1010.

27. 'Der Sürrealismus', G.S.II.1, p. 297. *One Way Street and Other Writings*, p. 227.

28. See *Berliner Chronik*, G.S.VI, p. 488. *One Way Street and Other Writings*, p. 316.

29. 'Konvolut K: Traumstadt und Traumhaus, Zukunftsträume, anthropologischer Nihilismus und Jung' in the *Passagenwerk* (pre-1935), G.S.V.1, p. 490.

30. See 'Die Wiederkehr des Flaneurs', G.S.III, p. 198.

31. For the idea of the 'dreaming collective', see 'Pariser Passagen' 1 (1927–29) G.S.V.2, p. 1010.

32. *Berliner Chronik*, G.S.VI, p. 476. *One Way Street and Other Writings*, p. 305.

33. See G.S.VI, pp. 470–1. *One Way Street and Other Writings*, p. 300.
34. G.S.III, p. 261. This quotation is from a review of Werner Hegemann's *Das steinernde Berlin*.
35. See T. W. Adorno, *Minima Moralia* (1951), New Left Books, London 1974, pp. 151–2.
36. *Passagenwerk* (pre-1935), G.S.V.1, p. 497.
37. *Berliner Chronik*, G.S.VI, p. 499. *One Way Street and Other Writings*, p. 327.
38. G.S.II.2, pp. 621–2.
39. See *Berliner Chronik*, G.S.VI, p. 518. *One Way Street and Other Writings*, p. 344.
40. See K 1 a, 3 'Konvolut K: Traumstadt und Traumhaus, Zukunftsträume, anthropologischer Nihilismus und Jung', in the *Passagenwerk* (pre-1935), G.S.V.1, p. 493.
41. For an example of Benjamin's interest in the political-philosophical value of the 'too early', see 'Konvolut a: soziale Bewegung', in *Passagenwerk* (pre-1935), G.S.V.2, p. 852.
42. See *Berliner Kindheit um neunzehnhundert*, G.S.IV.1, p. 242.
43. See *Berliner Chronik*, G.S.VI, p. 501. *One Way Street and Other Writings*, p. 329.
44. See G.S.VI, p. 478. *One Way Street and Other Writings*, p. 307.
45. See G.S.VI, pp. 479–80. *One Way Street and Other Writings*, pp. 308–9.
46. See G.S.VI, pp. 471–2. *One Way Street and Other Writings*, p. 301. One of the scenes in *Berliner Kindheit um neunzehnhundert* pictures Benjamin's profanation of religion in the context of his awakening sexuality. See G.S.IV.1, p. 251 and G.S.VII.1, pp. 431–2.
47. *Berliner Chronik*, G.S.VI, pp. 478–9. *One Way Street and Other Writings*, p. 308.
48. *Berliner Chronik* is dedicated to Heinle. See 'Über Stefan George' (1928) for Benjamin's account of how deeply affected he was by Heinle's suicide (G.S.II.2, p. 623).
49. *Berliner Chronik*, G.S.VI, p. 480. *One Way Street and Other Writings*, p. 309.
50. 'Pariser Passagen' 1 (1927–29), V.2, p. 1010.
51. See 'Konvolut a: soziale Bewegung' in the *Passagenwerk* (pre-1935), p. 852.
52. See 'Die Eisenbahnkatastrophe vom Firth of Tay', in G.S.VII.1, pp. 232–7.
53. G.S.V1, p. 212.
54. For the theoretical setting of the phrase 'hope in the past', see Peter Szondi's 'Hoffnung im Vergangenen', in *Schriften*, vol. 2, Suhrkamp, Frankfurt 1978, p. 282. The phrase stems from Benjamin's 'Über den Begriff der Geschichte'. See thesis VI G.S.I.2, p. 695. *Illuminations*, Fontana, London 1992, p. 247.
55. 'Kleine Geschichte der Photographie', G.S.II.1, p. 379. *One Way Street and Other Writings*, p. 251.
56. *Berliner Chronik*, G.S.VI, p. 516. *One Way Street and Other Writings*, pp. 342–3.
57. See Sigmund Freud, *Selected Works*, vol. 11, Penguin, London 1984, pp. 427–34.
58. See *Berliner Chronik*, G.S.VI, p. 519. *One Way Street and Other Writings*, pp. 345–6.
59. 'Konvolut N: erkenntnistheoretisches, Theorie des Fortschritts', in the *Passagenwerk* (pre-1935), G.S.V.1, p. 574. 'N', in Gary Smith (ed.), *Benjamin; Philosophy, History, Aesthetics*, University of Chicago Press, Chicago 1989, p. 47.
60. See 'Aus einer kleinen Rede über Proust, an meinem vierzigsten Geburtstag gehalten' (1932), G.S.II.3, p. 1064.

61. See a letter to Gershom Scholem, quoted in Gershom Scholem (ed.), *Briefwechsel; 1933–1940*, Suhrkamp, Frankfurt/Main 1980, p. 17. *The Correspondence of Walter Benjamin and Gershom Scholem 1932–1940*, Schocken, New York 1989, pp. 9–10.

62. 'Aus einer kleinen Rede über Proust, an meinem vierzigsten Geburtstag gehalten' (1932), G.S.II.3, p. 1064.

63. For some instances of Bloch's notion of the 'darkness of the lived moment' and the force of the 'not-yet', see the chapter 'Zur Metaphysik unseres Dunkels, nicht-mehr bewussten, noch-nicht bewussten, unkonstruierbaren Wirproblems', in *Geist der Utopie* (second edition from 1923), Gesamtausgabe, vol. 3, Suhrkamp, Frankfurt/Main 1977, pp. 237–87.

64. (Written between 1937 and 1940), G.S.I.3, p. 1238. For the source of the quotation, see G.S.V.1, pp. 603–4.

65. G.S.IV.1, p. 304. 'Das bucklichte Männlein' was printed in the *Frankfurter Zeitung* on 12 August 1933 and appears in *Berliner Kindheit um neunzehnhundert*, G.S.IV.1, p. 302–4.

66. 'Konvolut K: Traumstadt und Traumhaus, Zukunftsträume, anthropologischer Nihilismus und Jung', in the *Passagenwerk* (pre-1935), G.S.V.1, p. 497.

67. 'Pariser Passagen' 1 (1927–29), G.S.V.2, p. 1013.

68. For Benjamin's first utterances on empathy and history, see 'Pariser Passagen' 1, p. 1014.

69. *Passagenwerk* (pre-1935), G.S.V.2, pp. 678–9.

70. 'Erwiderung an Oskar A. H. Schmitz'; written between the end of January and early March 1927, published on 11 March 1927 in *Die literarische Welt* (G.S.II.2, pp. 751–5). 'Zur Lage der russischen Filmkunst'; published 11 March 1927 in *Die literarische Welt* (G.S.II.2, pp. 747–50).

71. For a note on the direct line of development from phantasmagoria, panorama to film, see 'Konvolut Q: Panorama', in the *Passagenwerk* (pre-1935), G.S.V.2, p. 658. See also 'Pariser Passagen' 1, p. 1008.

72. 'Pariser Passagen' 1, p. 1011.

73. ''Konvolut Q: Panorama', in the *Passagenwerk* (pre-1935), G.S.V.2, p. 658.

74. See *Passagenwerk* (pre-1935), G.S.V.1, p. 498.

75. 'Erfahrung und Armut' (1933), G.S.II.1, p. 214.

76. G.S.II.1, p. 214.

77. G.S.II.1, p. 215.

78. 'Der Autor als Produzent' (1934), G.S.II.2, p. 699. *Reflections*, Schocken Books, New York 1986, p. 235.

79. 'Theater und Rundfunk', G.S.II.2, p. 775.

80. G.S.II.2, p. 775.

81. 'Franz Kafka' (1934), G.S.II.2, p. 436. *Illuminations*, p. 133.

82. 'Kleine Geschichte der Photographie', G.S.II.1, p. 379. *One Way Street and Other Writings*, p. 251.

83. *Berliner Chronik*, G.S.VI, p. 470. *One Way Street and Other Writings*, p. 298.

84. G.S.VI, p. 503. *One Way Street and Other Writings*, p. 331.

4 Dream Whirled: *Technik* and Mirroring

1. See Karl Korsch, *Marxism and Philosophy* (1923), Monthly Review Press, New York 1970.

2. Georg Lukács, *Geschichte und Klassenbewußtsein*, Sammlung Luchterhand, Darmstadt/Neuwied 1986, p. 72. *History and Class Consciousness*, Merlin Press, London 1971, p. 10.

3. Viktor Shklovsky, *Zoo or Letters not about Love* (1923), Cornell University Press, Ithaca, NY 1971, p. 116.

4. For a detailed analysis of the manifestos and work of these groupings, see Christina Lodder, *Russian Constructivism*, Yale University Press, New York/London 1983.

5. A German edition of Arvatov's work exists. See Boris Arvatov, *Kunst und Produktion; Entwurf einer proletarisch-avantgardistischen Ästhetik (1921–1930)*, Hanser, Munich 1972. Arvatov's treatises analyse social and technological mutations of the aesthetic, and his arguments are closely resembled in Benjamin's 'Der Autor als Produzent' (1934).

6. 'Zur Lage der russischen Filmkunst', published 11 March 1927, in *Die literarische Welt*, G.S.II.2, p. 750.

7. 1935 *Exposé*, G.S.V.1, p. 49. *Charles Baudelaire: a Lyric Poet in the Era of High Capitalism*, New Left Books, London 1973, p. 162. Attempts at a major plan of the *Exposé* for the *Passagenwerk* had been occupying Benjamin since March 1934. See G.S.V.2, pp. 1111 and 1206.

8. 'Konvolut K: Traumstadt und Traumhaus, Zukunftsträume, anthropologischer Nihilismus und Jung', in the *Passagenwerk* (pre-1935), G.S.V.1, p. 500. The first part of the quotation was written in slightly modified form in *'Pariser Passagen'* 1 (1927–29), G.S.V.1, p. 1030. Added in or around 1935 is a section asserting that *Technik* possesses a 'dialectical essence', whose negative side carries out goals that are alien to nature, with means that are alien or hostile to nature.

9. 1935 *Exposé*, G.S.V.1, p. 48. *Charles Baudelaire*, p. 162.

10. G.S.V.1, p. 59. *Charles Baudelaire*, p. 176.

11. See 'Konvolut Y: die Photographie', in the *Passagenwerk* (pre-1935), G.S.V.2, p. 825, and the notes for the 1935 *Exposé*, G.S.V.2, p. 1209.

12. G.S.V.1, p. 56. *Charles Baudelaire*, pp. 173–4.

13. Adolf Loos, 'Ladies' Fashion', in *Spoken into the Void: Collected Essays 1897–1900*, MIT Press, Cambridge, Mass. 1982, p. 102.

14. Supplementary notes to 'Der Autor als Produzent', G.S.VII.2, p. 812.

15. Supplementary notes to 'Der Autor als Produzent', G.S.VII.2, p. 812.

16. 'Der Autor als Produzent', G.S.II.2, p. 687. *Reflections*, Schocken Books, New York 1986, p. 224.

17. G.S.II.2, p. 687. *Reflections*, p. 224.

18. G.S.II.2, p. 693. *Reflections*, p. 230.

19. See G.S.II.2, p. 688. *Reflections*, p. 225. Benjamin makes alterations to this self-quotation. It was published in March 1934 in a Swiss magazine, *Der öffentliche Dienst*, but in this original version there is no specification of the Soviet Union, and simply the identification of a tendency that alters modes of communication within capitalism. See 'Die Zeitung', G.S.II.2, pp. 628–9.

20. See supplementary notes to 'Der Autor als Produzent', in G.S.VII.2, p. 812. For Brecht's usage of the term 'culinary', see his 'Über kulinarische Kritik', in *Gesammelte Werke: Schriften zur Literatur und Kunst* 1, vol. 18, Suhrkamp, Frankfurt/Main 1967, p. 97.

21. Supplementary notes to 'Der Autor als Produzent', in G.S.VII.2, p. 812.

22. See 'Der Autor als Produzent', G.S.II.2, p. 695. *Reflections*, pp. 231–2.

23. The motif of class betrayal occurs in a number of Benjamin's writings, including reviews of Siegfried Kracauer's *Die Angestellten* (G.S.III, pp. 219–28) and in writings on Baudelaire, whom he calls a secret agent for the other side.

24. For the critique of Döblin's stance, see G.S.II.2, pp. 690–1. *Reflections*, pp. 227–8.

25. G.S.II.3, p. 1464. Benjamin also quotes this passage in 'Der Irrtum des Aktivismus: Zu Kurt Hillers Essaybuch *Der Sprung ins Helle*' (1932), G.S.III, p. 351.

26. See 'Der Autor als Produzent', G.S.II.2, pp. 690–1 and 701. *Reflections*, pp. 226–7 and 237–8.

27. G.S.II.2, p. 696. *Reflections*, p. 233.

28. See *Der Begriff der Kunstkritik in der deutschen Romantik* (1919), G.S.I.1, p. 78.

29. 'Der Autor als Produzent', G.S.II.2, p. 701. *Reflections*, p. 237.

30. G.S.II.2, p. 701. *Reflections*, p. 238.

31. G.S.II.2, p. 696. *Reflections*, p. 233.

32. See G.S.VII.1, p. 463.

33. See G.S.VI, p. 620.

34. 'Der Autor als Produzent', G.S.II.2, p. 689. *Reflections*, p. 225.

35. G.S.II.2, p. 686. *Reflections*, p. 222.

36. See G.S.II.2, p. 698. *Reflections*, pp. 234–5.

37. The value of counteracting the illusionistic moment is also stressed in a comment on Ottwald in some supplementary notes to 'Der Autor als Produzent'. See G.S.VII.2, p. 812.

38. See G.S.III, pp. 364–5/370. For the two versions of 'Strenge Kunstwissenschaft', see G.S.III, pp. 363–74.

39. 'Der Autor als Produzent', G.S.II.2, p. 685. *Reflections*, p. 222.

40. See G.S.II.2, p. 685. *Reflections*, p. 222.

41. G.S.II.2, p. 684. *Reflections*, p. 221.

42. See Tretyakov, 'Woher und Wohin: Perspektiven des Futurismus', reprinted in *Ästhetik und Kommunikation* No.4, 1971. Or, in English, 'From Where to Where?', in *Russian Futurism Through its Manifestoes, 1912–1928*, ed. Anna Lawton and Herbert Eagle, Cornell University Press, Ithaca, NY 1988. This essay appeared in *Lef*, no. 1, 1923.

43. 'Der Autor als Produzent', G.S.II.2, p. 686. *Reflections*, p. 223.

44. G.S.II.2, p. 691. *Reflections*, p. 228.

45. G.S.V.2, p. 1217.

46. For a reference by Zhdanov to Stalin's designation, see Igor Golomstock, *Totalitarian Art*, IconEditions, HarperCollins, New York 1990, p. 85.

47. Meyer Schapiro, *Abstract Art in Modern Art; 19th and 20th Centuries*, George Braziller, New York 1978, p. 211.

48. 'Unsere Wendung' is printed in *Die Linkskurve* 3, Jahrgang no. 10, from October 1931, pp. 1–8. (*Die Linkskurve* is available as an unaltered reprint of the Berlin edition, ed. Johannes Becher, Kurt Kläber, Hans Marchwitza, Erich Weinert and Ludwig Renn, and published by Verlag Detlev Auvermann K.G., Glashütten im Taunus 1970.)

49. See Maxim Gorky et al., *Soviet Writers' Congress 1934: The Debate on Socialist Realism and Modernism in the Soviet Union*, Lawrence and Wishart, 1977. Radek's condemnation of Joyce is on p. 153.

50. Aragon's theoretical backing of socialist realism can be found in his *Pour un réalisme socialiste*, Denoël, Paris 1934.

51. See G.S.II.2, pp. 695–6. *Reflections*, pp. 232–3.

52. See 'Konvolut Y: die Photographie', in the *Passagenwerk* (pre-1935) G.S.V.2, pp. 826, 828 and 832.

53. See 'Konvolut Q: Panorama', in the *Passagenwerk* (pre-1935), G.S.V.2, pp. 658–9 and the reference to progress in the 'Photography file' of the *Passagenwerk* (pre-1935), G.S.V.2, p. 828.

54. See 1935 *Exposé*, G.S.V.1, p. 48 and 'Konvolut Q: die Photographie' in the *Passagenwerk* (pre-1935), G.S.V.1, p. 658.

55. See 1935 *Exposé*, G.S.V.1, p. 48.

56. Examine this quotation: 'The mirrors that hang dully and uncared for in bars are the symbol of Zola's naturalism; how they reflect one another in an interminable row, a counterpart to the endless memory of memory into which, through the quill of Marcel Proust, his own life was transformed.' 'Paris, die Stadt im Spiegel' (1929), G.S.IV.1, p. 359.

57. See a letter from Adorno to Benjamin in response to the 'Artwork essay' of 18 March 1936, G.S.I.3, p. 1004.

58. Georg Lukács, *The Historical Novel* (1936–37), Penguin, London 1976, pp. 235–6.

59. *Passagenwerk*, G.S.V.2, pp. 666–73. This file was largely completed by 1935.

60. See 'Konvolut Q: Panorama', in the *Passagenwerk* (pre-1935), G.S.V.2, p. 655.

61. See, for example, R1, 3, G.S.V.2, pp. 666–7.

62. See R 1, 6, G.S.V.2, p. 667. See also R 2, a 3, G.S.V.2, p. 672.

63. See 'Konvolut R: Spiegel', in the *Passagenwerk* (pre-1935), G.S.V.2, pp. 666–7. See also 'Paris, die Stadt im Spiegel' (1929), G.S.IV.1, p. 358.

64. See *Passagenwerk*, G.S.V.1, pp. 537–8.

65. See G.S.V.1, pp. 559–60.

66. See 1935 *Exposé*, G.S.V.1, p. 54. *Charles Baudelaire*, pp. 170–1.

67. 'Konvolut K: Traumstadt und Traumhaus, Zukunftsträume, anthropologischer Nihilismus, Jung', in the *Passagenwerk* (pre-1935), G.S.V.1, p. 495. See also M°, 14 G.S.V.2, p. 1023.

68. See *Die deutsche Ideologie*, *Marx Engels Werke*, vol. 3, Dietz Verlag, Berlin 1983, pp. 25–26.

69. See 'Ein Außenseiter macht sich bemerkbar' (1930), G.S.III, p. 220.

70. Marx mentions phantasmagoria in *Das Kapital*, vol. I, *Marx Engels Werke*, Dietz Verlag, Berlin 1969, p. 86.

71. See Marx, *Capital*, The Modern Library, New York 1906, p. 84; in this translation, as in the more recent Penguin *Capital*, vol. 1, the German word *sachlich* is translated as 'material': 'the relations connecting the labour of one individual with that of the rest appear, not as direct social relations between individuals at work but as what they really are, material relations between persons and social relations between things.' 'Sachlich' is an interesting word, for it means 'material', 'objective', 'businesslike', 'functional'. In one word Marx combines the idea of people treating each other as objects, while also getting across the extent to which such a relationship is functional, apt, the necessary mode of intercourse in capitalism. This concrete state of relations is, at the same time, however, abstract for it misses out, or makes into an add-on the real core of human relations, the sensuousness of substantial, human interaction.

72. G.S.V.1, p. 118.

73. For an extremely detailed account, see *Hairstyles and Fashion: A Hairdresser's History of Paris, 1910–1920*, edited by Steven Zdatny, Berg, Oxford 1999.

74. G.S.V.1, p. 123.

75. G.S.V.1, p. 459.

76. G.S.V.1, p. 120.

77. See *Passagenwerk* (pre-1935), G.S.V.1, p. 118.

78. G.S.V.2, p. 674.

79. G.S.II.1, pp. 371–2. *One Way Street and Other Writings*, New Left Books, London 1979, pp. 243–4.

80. An idea worked out by Ernst Bloch most thoroughly.
81. G.S.V.2, p. 694. The first appearance in English of the 'autonomic nervous system', according to the OED, is 1898.
82. G.S.V.2, p. 694.
83. G.S.V.2, p. 696.
84. G.S.V.2, p. 694
85. G.S.V.2, p. 692.
86. G.S.V.2, p. 686.
87. G.S.V.2, pp. 675, and 686.
88. G.S.I.2, p. 664.
89. G.S.V.2, p. 674. Du Camp's Paris study is published in instalments from 1869 to 1875. See G.S.V.2, p. 1292.
90. Les Fleurs du Mal, Picador, London 1982 pp. 329–35.
91. G.S.V.2, p. 695.
92. G.S.V.2, p. 1062.
93. G.S.V.2, p. 692, and G.S.I.2, p. 660.
94. G.S.V.2, pp. 692, and 694.
95. G.S.V.2, p. 684.
96. G.S.V.2, p. 693.
97. G.S.V.2, p. 692.
98. G.S.V.2, p. 693.
99. G.S.V.2, pp. 677, 680, and 1011.
100. G.S.V.1, pp. 459–60.
101. G.S.V.1, p. 127.
102. G.S.V.1, p. 123.
103. G.S.V.2, pp. 695–6.
104. See 'Konvolut O: Prostitution, Spiel', in the Passagenwerk (pre-1935), G.S.V.1, pp. 616–17.
105. See G.S.V.1, p. 615.
106. See 'Konvolut J: Baudelaire', in the Passagenwerk, G.S.V.1, pp. 435–6.
107. Karl Marx, Early Writings, Penguin/NLR, London 1975, p. 350.
108. Passagenwerk, G.S.V.1, p. 436.
109. See, for example, Passagenwerk, G.S.V.1, p. 455.
110. See G.S.V.1, p. 464.
111. See 'Konvolut G: Ausstellungswesen, Reklame, Grandville, in the Passagenwerk (pre-1935), G.S.V.1, p. 245.
112. Marx, Das Kapital, vol. I, p. 86.
113. Ibid., p. 83.
114. See G.S.V.1, p. 51. The original phrase from Marx can be found in Das Kapital, vol. 1, p. 85.
115. See 1935 Exposé, G.S.V.1, p. 50.
116. See G.S.V.2, p. 1117.
117. See Gershom Scholem, Walter Benjamin und sein Engel, Suhrkamp, Frankfurt/Main 1983, p. 26.
118. See G.S.V.2, p. 1118.
119. Quoted in Leon Trotsky, Literature and Revolution, University of Michigan Press, Ann Arbor 1960, p. 137.
120. See Kants gesammelte Schriften; akademische Ausgabe, vol. 5, Berlin 1913, p. 283.
121. 'Der Autor als Produzent', G.S.II.2, p. 692. Reflections, p. 229.
122. G.S.II.1, p. 385. One Way Street and Other Writings, New Left Books, London 1979, p. 256.

123. See, for example, 'Der Autor als Produzent' (1934), G.S.II.2, p. 692. *Reflections*, p. 229.

124. See G.S.II.2, p. 693. *Reflections*, p. 230.

125. 'Nichts gegen die Illustrierte', G.S.IV.1, p. 449. The article to which Benjamin is responding is in G.S.IV.2, pp. 1019–22.

126. 'Der Autor als Produzent', G.S.II.2, p. 698. *Reflections*, p. 234.

127. See notes to 'Das Kunstwerk im Zeitalter seiner technischen Reproduzierbarkeit', written in Autumn 1935, G.S.I.3, p. 1040.

128. G.S.V.1, p. 194.

129. Letter from T. W. Adorno to Benjamin, 2 August 1935, in *Briefe* 2, Suhrkamp, Frankfurt/Main 1978, p. 678.

130. See G.S.V.2, p. 1211.

131. See 1935 *Exposé*, G.S.V.1, p. 50.

132. G.S.V.1, p. 59.

133. See G.S.V.1, p. 59.

134. For a reference to this title and its rejection, see a letter to Gretel Adorno, 16 August 1935, in *Briefe* 2, p. 687. See also G.S.V.2, p. 1117.

135. 'Konvolut K: Traumstadt und Traumhaus, Zukunftsträume, anthropologischer Nihilismus, Jung', in the *Passagenwerk* (pre-1935), G.S.V.1, p. 499.

136. Notes for the 1935 *Exposé*, G.S.V.2, p. 1225.

137. See 1935 *Exposé*, G.S.V.1, p. 47. See also notes for the 1935 *Exposé*, G.S.V.2, pp. 1224–5. *Charles Baudelaire*, pp. 159–60.

138. G.S.V.1, pp. 46–7. *Charles Baudelaire*, pp. 159–60.

139. 'Konvolut K: Traumstadt und Traumhaus, Zukunftsträume, anthropologischer Nihilismus, Jung', in *Passagenwerk* (pre-1935), G.S.V.1, p. 497.

140. See R 2, 2 (pre-1935), G.S.V.2, p. 669.

141. 'Konvolut N: erkenntnistheoretisches, Theorie des Fortschritts', in the *Passagenwerk* (pre-1935), G.S.V.1, p. 570.

142. See 'Pariser Passagen' 1, G.S.V.2, p. 1033.

143. From Adorno's letter written in June 1935, G.S.VII.2, p. 858. See also the letter written on 2 August 1935 in *Briefe* 2, pp. 671ff.

5 Murmurs from Darkest Europe

1. See Tony Cliff, *Trotsky: The Darker the Night the Brighter the Star 1927–1940*, Bookmarks, London 1993, p. 187.

2. Reference to this quotation from Stalin can be found in Cliff, *Trotsky*, p. 111.

3. See, for example, Trotsky's article 'The Turn in the Communist International and the Situation in Germany', written on 26 September 1930 and reprinted in his *The Struggle against Fascism in Germany*, Pathfinder, New York 1971, p. 55–74.

4. See J. Danos and M. Gibelin, *June '36. Class Struggle and the People's Front in France*, Bookmarks, London 1986, pp. 33–4.

5. *Briefe* 2, ed. G. Scholem and T.W. Adorno, Suhrkamp, Frankfurt/Main 1978, pp. 604–5. *The Correspondence of Walter Benjamin and Gershom Scholem 1932–1940*, Schocken, New York 1989, p. 109.

6. *Briefe* 2, pp. 604–5. *The Correspondence of Walter Benjamin and Gershom Scholem 1932–1940*, p. 109.

7. See *Briefe* 2, p. 605. *The Correspondence of Walter Benjamin and Gershom Scholem 1932–1940*, p. 110.

8. See Danos and Gibelin, *June '36*, pp. 35–6.

9. See Cliff, *Trotsky*, p. 192.

10. For his critique of popular frontism, see *Trotsky on France*, Pathfinder, New York 1979.
11. See Cliff, *Trotsky*, p. 204.
12. *Briefe* 2, p. 732.
13. See Chryssoula Kambas, 'Politische Aktualität: Walter Benjamin's Concept of History and the Failure of the French Popular Front', in *New German Critique* no. 39, Fall 1986, pp. 93–4.
14. See Dawn Ades et al., *Art and Power; Europe under the Dictators 1930–1945*, Catalogue to the Hayward Gallery Exhibition, South Bank Centre 1995, pp. 108–9.
15. For Trotsky's account of events in Spain, see his *The Spanish Revolution 1931–1939*, Pathfinder, New York 1973. See also the collected articles in *The Spanish Civil War: A View from the Left*, *Revolutionary History*, vol. 4, nos. 1/2 1991–92.
16. See Victor Serge, *Memoirs of a Revolutionary 1901–1941*, Oxford University Press, Oxford 1980, pp. 345–6.
17. See James Joll, *Europe since 1870; An International History*, Penguin, London 1990, pp. 369–70.
18. *Briefe* 2, p. 747.
19. See 'Tagebuchnotizen 1938', in G.S.VI, p. 534. 'Conversations with Brecht', in *Reflections*, Schocken Books, New York 1986, p. 213.
20. G.S.VI, pp. 536–7. *Reflections*, pp. 215–16.
21. G.S.VI, pp. 535–6. *Reflections*, pp. 214–15.
22. G.S.VI, p. 537. *Reflections*, p. 216.
23. G.S.VI, p. 534. 'Conversations with Brecht', in *Reflections*, p. 213.
24. G.S.VI, p. 539. 'Conversations with Brecht', in *Reflections*, pp. 218–19.
25. G.S.VI, p. 539. 'Conversations with Brecht', in *Reflections*, 1986, p. 219.
26. See *Briefe* 2, p. 771.
27. See *Briefe* 2, p. 772.
28. 'Tagebuchnotizen 1938', in G.S.VI, p. 538. 'Conversations with Brecht' in *Reflections*, p. 217.

6 The Work of Art in the Age of Unbearable Capitulation

1. This is called 'erste Fassung' in the *Gesammelte Schriften* and appears on pp. 431–69 in G.S.I.2.
2. This is called' zweite Fassung' in the *Gesammelte Schriften*, and appears on pp. 350–84 in G.S.VII.1. This chapter refers primarily to this second version of the 'Artwork essay', the version in which Benjamin first hoped the essay would appear. All quotations in the chapter are taken from this version, unless otherwise stated and it functions here as the normative text; hence footnote indications, such as 'slightly different wording'. This is not the version that appears in *Illuminations* (Fontana, London 1992) and so page references to Harry Zohn's English translation direct the reader only to the third version, in *Illuminations*, when an identical or similar passage occurs.
3. See G.S.I.3, pp. 1001–6. This version had been assumed lost for decades until its discovery in the Max-Horkheimer-Archive, but it was not published, in volume VII.1 of Benjamin's *Gesammelte Schriften*, until 1991. Adorno's letter is translated in *Aesthetics and Politics*, a collection of contributions by Bloch, Lukács, Brecht, Benjamin and Adorno, New Left Books, London 1977, pp. 120–6.
4. See G.S.I.2, pp. 709–39.
5. See G.S.I.3, p. 1029.

6. See G.S.I.3, pp. 999–1000.

7. See G.S.I.3, p. 992/pp. 996–7.

8. See Chryssoula Kambas, *Walter Benjamin im Exil: Zum Verhältnis von Literaturpolitik und Ästhetik*, Max Niemeyer, Tübingen 1983, p. 154. István Mészáros discusses the 'post-Marxian ideological opportunism' of the Institute once in the United States, an orientation that is exported back to post-war West Germany and its influence here is branded by Mészáros 'Americanizing'. See István Mészáros, *The Power of Ideology*, Harvester Wheatsheaf, Brighton 1989, pp. 48–9.

9. G.S.I.3, pp. 997–8.

10. See a letter from Benjamin to Scholem, written on 29 June 1933 and reprinted in *Briefwechsel; 1933–1940*, ed. Gershom Scholem, Suhrkamp, Frankfurt/Main 1980, p. 82. *The Correspondence of Walter Benjamin and Gershom Scholem 1932–1940*, Schocken, New York 1989, p. 62.

11. Notwithstanding, the editors of Benjamin's posthumous collected works are always keen to underplay the battles around Benjamin's work, displaying little sympathy for any perspective that shows Benjamin as bound to his publishers for money like a worker to an employer, and therefore compromised. For information about Benjamin's dire financial situation in Parisian exile in the 1930s see the biographical details reported in Werner Fuld's *Walter Benjamin: Eine Biographie*, RoRoRo, Reinbek/Hamburg 1990, pp. 223–72. The editors of the *Gesammelte Schriften* accuse commentators of an over-exposure of events during the production of the 'Artwork essay'. They assert that focusing on documents relating to the organization of the work and editorial matters mediate unfavourable impressions of Benjamin's 'relation to Horkheimer' and his 'relation to the Institute'. See G.S.I.3, p. 1020.

12. This is called 'dritte Fassung' in the collected works, but previous work editions refer to it as the 'zweite Fassung'. G.S.I.2, pp. 471–508.

13. See the letter from Adorno to Benjamin, 18 March 1936, in G.S.I.3, p. 1006.

14. See *Briefe* 2, ed. G. Scholem and T.W. Adorno, Suhrkamp, Frankfurt/Main 1978, p. 699. Benjamin is alluding to the 'Artwork essay'. See G.S.I.3, p. 984 for the editorial comments to this effect from Tiedemann and Schweppenhäuser.

15. See G.S.I.2, p. 435/p. 473/G.S.VII.1, p. 350. *Illuminations*, Fontana, London 1992, p. 212. Or at least, the English reference should relay the same message, but this particular edition in my possession does not. 'The concepts which are introduced into the theory of art in what follows differ from the more familiar terms in that they are completely useless [*omitted*: for the purposes of Fascism. They are on the other hand, useful] for the formulation of revolutionary demands in the politics of art.' Fontana sold around 7,000 copies of the corrupted text, before the mistake was pointed out and a new page prepared. For a footnote on this blunder, see Ben Watson, *Art, Class and Cleavage: Quantulumcunque Concerning Materialist Esthetix* Quartet, London 1998, p. 49, note 120.

16. 'Der Autor als Produzent', G.S.II.2, p. 689. *Reflections*, Schocken Books, New York 1986, p. 226.

17. See *Briefe* 2, p. 690. See also Benjamin's letter to Gretel Adorno from 9 October 1935, in G.S.V.2, p. 1148.

18. G.S.I.3, p. 983.

19. G.S.I.2, p. 435/p. 473/G.S.VII.1, p. 350. *Illuminations*, p. 211.

20. See 'Kleine Geschichte der Photographie' (1931), G.S.II.1, p. 370. *One Way Street and Other Writings*, New Left Books, London 1979, p. 242.

21. See *Briefe* 2, pp. 698–9.

22. See 'Eduard Fuchs, der Sammler und der Historiker', G.S.II.2, p. 474. *One Way Street and Other Writings*, pp. 357–8.

23. 'Eduard Fuchs, der Sammler und der Historiker', G.S.II.2, p. 475. *One Way Street and Other Writings*, p. 358.

24. G.S.I.2, pp. 468–9 (slight modification)/ pp. 507–8 (slight modification)/G.S.VII.1, p. 383. *Illuminations*, p. 235.

25. See G.S.I.2, pp. 467–8/p. 506/G.S.VII.1, p. 382. *Illuminations*, p. 234.

26. A section devoted to these ideas is in Fischer's *Karl Marx und sein Verhältnis zu Staat und Wirtschaft*, Verlag von Gustav Fischer, Jena 1932, pp. 35–6. Benjamin drew on this study while researching the *Passagenwerk*.

27. 'Paralipomena, Varianten und Varia' to the first version of 'Das Kunstwerk im Zeitalter seiner technischen Reproduzierbarkeit', G.S.I.3, p. 1039.

28. Benjamin notes Raphael's reading of Marx and Greek art in 'file N' in the *Passagenwerk* (1935–37), G.S.V.1, pp. 580–1.

29. G.S.I.2, p. 435/p.473/G.S.VII.1, p. 350. *Illuminations*, p. 212.

30. G.S.I.2, p. 456 (with slightly different syntax)/G.S.VII.1, p. 372.

31. See G.S.I.2, pp. 451–2 (different version)/G.S.VII.1, p. 370. Compare the different passage in the later version (G.S.I.2, p. 492/*Illuminations*, Fontana, London 1992, p. 224).

32. This analysis is closely matched in the analysis of the 'culture industry' undertaken by Adorno and Horkheimer. However, the critical role of the proletariat is missing there.

33. G.S.I.2, p. 462/p. 500/G.S.VII.1, p. 378. *Illuminations*, p. 242.

34. See G.S.I.2, p. 457 (slightly different wording)/pp. 500–1 (slightly different wording)/G.S.VII.1, p. 378. *Illuminations*, p. 230.

35. See G.S.I.2, p. 436/p. 475/G.S.VII.1, p. 351. *Illuminations*, p. 213.

36. See G.S.I.2, p. 436/pp. 474–5/G.S.VII.1, p. 351. *Illuminations*, p. 213.

37. Notes for the second version of 'Das Kunstwerk im Zeitalter seiner technischen Reproduzierbarkeit', G.S.VII.2, p. 677.

38. See G.S.III, p. 499.

39. G.S.I.2, p. 441/p. 481/G.S VII.1, p. 356. *Illuminations*, p. 218.

40. G.S.I.2, p. 447 (slight change in syntax)/p. 486/G.S.VII.1, p. 362. *Illuminations*, p. 220.

41. For a reprint of Zhdanov's 1934 speech to the first Congress of Soviet Writers, see *Art in Theory 1900–1990: An Anthology of Changing Ideas*, ed. Charles Harrison and Paul Wood, Blackwell, Oxford 1992, pp. 409–12. Amongst other pronouncements on the aesthetics of socialist realism, Benjamin must have been particularly interested to read former surrealist Louis Aragon's 'Pour un réalisme socialiste' in 1936. See G.S.VII.1, p. 471.

42. Benjamin continues this line of inquiry in the discussion of realism, photography and painting in 'Pariser Brief' II (1936), G.S.III, pp. 495–507.

43. G.S.I.2, p. 459 (slight change in syntax)/p. 496/G.S.VII.1, p. 374. *Illuminations*, p. 227, emphasis in original.

44. G.S.I.2, p. 458/p. 495/G.S.VII.1, p. 373. *Illuminations*, p. 226.

45. G.S.I.2, p. 458 (with modifications)/p. 495/G.S.VII.1, p. 373. *Illuminations*, p. 226, emphasis in original.

46. 'Konvolut Y: die Photographie' in the *Passagenwerk* (1935–37), G.S.V.2, p. 833.

47. Notes for the second version of 'Das Kunstwerk im Zeitalter seiner technischen Reproduzierbarkeit', G.S.VII.2, p. 677.

48. See G.S.I.2, pp. 449–50/p. 488/G.S.VII.1, p. 365. *Illuminations*, p. 222.

49. G.S.I.2, pp. 461–2/G.S.VII.1, pp. 376–7.

50. G.S.I.2, p. 459/p. 496/G.S.VII.1, p. 374. *Illuminations*, p. 227.

51. Hans Richter, *The Struggle for the Film* (late 1930s/1976), Scolar Press, Aldershot, 1986.

52. Hans Richter, *Filmgegner von Heute – Filmfreunde von Morgen* (1929) Facsimile, Verlag Hans Rohr, Zurich 1968. Richter's ideas in both books are strikingly similar to Benjamin's, though neither credits the other.

53. For Benjamin's misgivings about abstract, avant-garde film practice and its 'arrogant' attitude to audiences, see entry K 3 a, 1, in the *Passagenwerk* (pre-1935), G.S.V.1, p. 500.

54. 'Krisis der Kunst', in 'Fragmente, Autobiographische Schriften', G.S.VI, p. 183.

55. G.S.I.2, p. 461/p. 499/G.S.VII.1, pp. 375–6. *Illuminations*, p. 229.

56. See G.S.I.2, p. 461/pp. 499–500/G.S.VII.1, p. 376. *Illuminations*, pp. 229–30.

57. See G.S.I.2, p. 500/G.S.VII.1, p. 376. *Illuminations*, p. 230.

58. Notes for the second version of 'Das Kunstwerk im Zeitalter seiner technischen Reproduzierbarkeit', G.S.VII.2, p. 678/p. 679.

59. See G.S.I.2, p. 443/p. 483/G.S.VII.1, p. 358. *Illuminations*, p. 218.

60. G.S.I.2, p. 443/G.S.VII.1, p. 357. 'Schein' can also be translated as appearance or illusion.

61. G.S.VII.1, p. 368.

62. G.S.VII.2, p. 667.

63. Benjamin's discussions of play include the 1928 review 'Spielzeug und Spielen', in G.S.III, pp. 127–32 and the illustrated essays in G.S.IV.2, pp. 609–26.

64. G.S.VII.1, pp. 368–9.

65. G.S.VII.1, p. 369.

66. See G.S.I.2, pp. 446–7/G.S.VII.1, p. 362.

67. See G.S.I.2, p. 441/p. 480/G.S.VII.1, p. 355. *Illuminations*, p. 217.

68. See G.S.I.2, p. 440/p. 479 (with slight modifications)/G.S.VII.1, p. 355. *Illuminations*, pp. 216–17.

69. See G.S.I.2, p. 445/p. 485/G.S.VII.1, p. 360. *Illuminations*, p. 219.

70. See G.S.VII.1, pp. 368–9.

71. See G.S.I.2, p. 440/p. 479 (the entrenched rule of Nazism presumably encourages Benjamin to drop the reference to self-organized mass movements in this later version)/G.S.VII.1, p. 355. *Illuminations*, pp. 216–17.

72. G.S.I.2, p. 469/p. 508/G.S.VII.1, p. 383. *Illuminations*, p. 235.

73. G.S.I.2, p. 439/p.478/G.S.VII.1, pp. 353–4. *Illuminations*, p. 216.

74. G.S.I.2, p. 440/p. 480/G.S.VII.1, p. 355. *Illuminations*, p. 217.

75. G.S.I.2, p. 439/p. 478/G.S.VII.1, p. 353. *Illuminations*, p. 215.

76. See *Briefe* 2, pp. 669–70.

77. See Serge Guilbaut, *How New York Stole the Idea of Modern Art*, University of Chicago Press, Chicago 1983, p. 22.

78. See *Briefe* 2, pp. 715–16.

79. Cited in Guilbaut, *How New York Stole the Idea of Modern Art*, p. 26.

80. See G.S.I.2, p. 442/p. 481/G.S.VII.1, p. 356. *Illuminations*, p. 218.

81. See G.S.I.2, p. 438/p. 477/G.S.VII.1, p. 353. *Illuminations*, p. 215.

82. G.S.I.2, pp. 437–8/pp. 476–7/G.S.VII.1, p. 352. *Illuminations*, pp. 214–15.

83. G.S.I.2, pp. 448–9/G.S.VII.1, p. 362/p. 364.

84. G.S.I.2, p. 445/p. 485/G.S.VII.1, p. 361. *Illuminations*, pp. 219–20.

85. G.S.V.1, pp. 499–500.

86. See G.S.I.2, pp. 464–5/p. 503/G.S.VII.1, p. 380. *Illuminations*, p. 232.

87. See Adorno's letter to Benjamin of 6 September 1936, in G.S.VII.2, p. 864.

88. G.S.I.2, p. 466/G.S.VII.1, p. 381.

89. See Karl Marx, *Early Writings*, Penguin/NLR, London 1975, pp. 353–4.

90. See the conclusion of paragraph 10, G.S.I.2, p. 450 and paragraph X, G.S.VII.1, p. 365. These aspects of Benjamin's work on technology and alienation are frequently overlooked in the secondary literature, due, in part, to a concentration on the third version of the 'Artwork essay'.

91. G.S.I.2, p. 451/p. 489/G.S.VII.1, p. 366. *Illuminations*, pp. 222–3. Although Pirandello's observations apply specifically to silent film, the trashing of categories of presence are generally transferable to sound film also.

92. See G.S.I.2, p. 490/G.S.VII.1, p. 367. This thought can be aligned with Marx's thesis on commodity fetishism. Commodity fetishism has been interpreted by some as some sort of a recasting of Marx's ideas on alienation from the 1844 manuscripts.

93. G.S.I.3, p. 1045.

94. See G.S.I.2, p. 452/p. 490/G.S.VII.1, p. 367. *Illuminations*, p. 223.

95. In the final version of the essay Benjamin reverses the argument, emphasizing the audience's placement on the side of the camera. Its placement here amounts to identification with the objectifying, penetrating eye. Identification with the actor is allowed only in so far as the actor tests critically, impersonally, in the same way as the camera, empathizing with the camera. '*The public only identifies with the actor by identifying with the apparatus. It adopts its viewpoint: it tests.* That is not a viewpoint to which cult values may be exposed.' G.S.I.2, p. 488. *Illuminations*, p. 222.

96. See Kleine Geschichte der Photographie, G.S.II.1, p. 379. *One Way Street and Other Writings*, p. 251.

97. G.S.I.2, p. 451/G.S.VII.1, p. 369.

98. See Karl Marx *Das Kapital*, vol. 1, *Marx Engels Werke*, Dietz Verlag, Berlin 1969, p. 442. See also p. 402.

99. See additional notes to the 'Artwork essay', G.S.I.3, p. 1051.

100. See G.S.I.2, p. 464/p. 503 (the need to accommodate the self to shocks is stressed)/G.S.VII.1, p. 380. *Illuminations*, pp. 231–2.

101. G.S.V.1 (1935–37), pp. 226–7.

102. See 'Paralipomena, Varianten und Varia' to the first version of 'Das Kunstwerk im Zeitalter seiner technischen Reproduzierbarkeit', G.S.I.3, p. 1040.

103. G.S.I.3, p. 1040.

104. Incidentally it is at this point that Habermas's objections set in. He questions whether the techniques and technologies used in cultural production can be seen to be at all analogous to those of all technology. See 'Technology and Science as Ideology', in *Towards a Rational Society*, Heinemann Educational Books, London 1971.

105. See the chapter on the culture industry in *Dialektik der Aufklärung* (1944), by Theodor W. Adorno and Max Horkheimer, Fischer, Frankfurt/Main 1969. Adorno's rejection of mimesis as a representation of apparently realistic contents has been located in his adherence to a '*Bilderverbot*' that necessitates the promotion of enigmatic images. See Joseph Früchtl *Mimesis: Konstellation eines Zentralbegriffs bei Adorno*, Königshausen und Neumann, Würzburg 1986.

106. See G.S.VII.1, p. 368. See also notes for the second version of 'Das Kunstwerk im Zeitalter seiner technischen Reproduzierbarkeit', G.S.VII.2, p. 666.

107. G.S.VII.1, p. 368. See also G.S.VII.2, p. 666.

108. Such mimesis intersects with Benjamin's category of 'non-sensuous similarity' ('*unsinnliche Ähnlichkeit*'), as explicated in two essays, written in 1933, 'Lehre vom Ähnlichen' and 'Über das mimetische Vermögen', G.S.II.1, pp. 204–10 and pp. 210–13.

109. Sorel's *Réfléxions sur la Violence*, whose influence can be traced in Benjamin's 'Zur Kritik der Gewalt' (1921), develops a connected argument. 'Art is an anticipation of the way all work will feel in the society of the future'. Quoted in Fredric Jameson, *Marxism and Form*, Princeton University Press, Princeton 1971, p. 155.

110. See G.S.I.2, p. 462/G.S.VII.1, pp. 376–7. He does, however, also note in a footnote present in the second version of the essay, that Disney's tendency to locate bestiality and violence as normal accompaniments of existence allows the cartoons' revolutionary innovations to be appropriated by fascists. This makes the response to filmic americana somewhat more ambivalent.

111. G.S.V.2, p. 802.

112. G.S.I.2, p. 461/G.S.VII.1, p. 375.

113. See G.S.I.2, p. 461/p. 500/G.S.VII.1, p. 376. *Illuminations*, p. 230.

114. G.S.I.2, p. 461 (difference in syntax)/p. 500/G.S.VII.1, p. 376. *Illuminations*, pp. 229–30. Benjamin is drawing on Arnheim here.

115. G.S.I.2, p. 464 (with a short addition)/p. 502(with an additional paragraph)/G.S.VII.1, p. 379. *Illuminations*, pp. 231–2.

116. See G.S.I.2, pp. 445–6/p. 485/G.S.VII.2, p. 361. *Illuminations*, p. 220. In 'Kleine Geschichte der Photographie' the slogan had been rather a counterbalance to the image, disjointing the intensification of the analogue.

117. See, for example, 'Paralipomena, Varianten und Varia' for the second version of 'Das Kunstwerk im Zeitalter seiner technischen Reproduzierbarkeit', G.S.I.3, p. 1045.

118. See G.S.I.2, p. 444.

119. 'Paralipomena, Varianten und Varia' for the second version of 'Das Kunstwerk im Zeitalter seiner technischen Reproduzierbarkeit', G.S.I.3, p. 1045.

120. This approach contrasts with that of Adorno and Horkheimer, who similarly ask when technological scientific progress becomes catastrophic regression, but then locate the 'dialectic of enlightenment' in the flipover from humanity's domination over nature into nature's domination over humanity.

121. See notes for the second version of 'Das Kunstwerk im Zeitalter seiner technischen Reproduzierbarkeit', G.S.VII.2, p. 666.

122. See G.S.I.2, p. 469/G.S.VII.1, p. 383. A similar formulation uses different examples in G.S.I.2, p. 508. *Illuminations*, p. 235.

123. 'Paralipomena, Varianten und Varia' for the second version of 'Das Kunstwerk im Zeitalter seiner technischen Reproduzierbarkeit', G.S.I.3, p. 1045.

124. See G.S.VII.2, pp. 665–6.

125. See G.S.VII.1, p. 359.

126. G.S.VII.1, p. 359.

127. See G.S.VII.1, p. 359.

128. G.S.VII.1, p. 359. 'Once is as good as never' is a German proverb, but it is also attributed to Nietzsche, and understood there to be a melancholic reflection on the uselessness of a life that can be lived only once. In a short piece which includes a reflection on Trotsky, in 1932, called 'Einmal ist Keinmal', Benjamin regards the repetitive gesture demanded by 'once is as good as never' not as a dismal ensnarement in bourgeois economy and bourgeois categories, but rather as a essential gesture in a model life that

always attempts to start afresh – with presence of mind – and aims to respond sincerely to the specific requirements of the current moment. See G.S.IV.2, p. 1009 and G.S.IV.1, p. 434.

129. G.S.VII.1, p. 368.
130. See notes for the second version of the 'Artwork essay' in G.S.VII.2, p. 667.
131. See G.S.VII.1, pp. 359–60.
132. See G.S.VII.1, p. 360.
133. See 'From Where to Where?' (1923), in *Russian Futurism through its Manifestoes, 1912–1928*, ed. Anna Lawton and Herbert Eagle, Cornell University Press, Ithaca, NY 1988, p. 212.
134. G.S.VII.1, p. 360.
135. G.S.VII.1, p. 360.
136. 'Konvolut W: Fourier' in the *Passagenwerk* (1935–37), V.2, p. 777.
137. The accusation of technological determinism or fetishism has often been levelled at Benjamin's essay. Celia Lury, in *Cultural Rights: Technology, Legality and Personality*, voices a familiar charge: 'at times, he fails to distinguish between the technical possibilities of reproducibility allowed by particular cultural means, and the inevitably selective realization of those possibilities as they occur in particular social contexts' (Routledge, London and New York 1993, p. 14). This chapter has attempted to argue that the differentiation of *Technik*, and the concern with consequent relations of artistic production and reception, reveal precisely Benjamin's sensitivity to social context. Such sensitivity counters any simple charge of technological determinism because of its supposition of possibilities.
138. See G.S.VII.1, p. 359.
139. See 'Paralipomena, Varianten und Varia' for the second version of 'Das Kunstwerk im Zeitalter seiner technischen Reproduzierbarkeit', G.S.I.3, p. 1045.
140. *Das Ornament der Masse: Essays*, Suhrkamp, Frankfurt/Main 1977, p. 52. Siegfried Kracauer, *The Mass Ornament, Weimar Essays*, Harvard University Press, Cambridge, Mass. 1995, p. 77.
141. G.S.I.2, p. 469/p. 507/G.S.VII.1, p. 383. *Illuminations*, p. 235.
142. See Benjamin's discussion of the fascist art of propaganda in 'Pariser Brief I': 'André Gide und sein neuer Gegner' (1936), G.S.III, pp. 488–90.
143. G.S.I.2, p. 467 (slightly different wording)/p. 506/G.S.VII.1, p. 382. *Illuminations*, pp. 243–4.
144. See 'Pariser Brief I': 'André Gide und sein neuer Gegner' (1936), G.S.III, p. 489.
145. See G.S.III, p. 488.
146. G.S.I.2, p. 469/p. 508/G.S.VII.1, p. 384. *Illuminations*, p. 235.
147. *Passagenwerk* (1935–37), G.S.V.1, p. 152.
148. 'Eduard Fuchs, der Sammler und der Historiker' (1934–37), G.S.II.2, p. 475. *One Way Street and Other Writings*, p. 358.
149. See G.S.I.3, p. 1045.
150. See 'Pariser Brief I': 'André Gide und sein neuer Gegner' (1936) G.S.III, p. 488. See also an entry in 'Konvolut N: erkenntnistheoretisches, Theorie des Fortschritts', in the *Passagenwerk* (1937–40) for Benjamin's valorization of 'healthy human common sense' (G.S.V.1, p. 596/N, in Gary Smith (ed.), *Benjamin: Philosophy, History, Aesthetics*, University of Chicago Press, Chicago 1989, pp. 67–8).
151. See Kracauer's *From Caligari to Hitler* (1947), Princeton University Press, Princeton 1974, p. 269.

152. 'Das Ornament der Masse' is in Siegfried Kracauer's *Das Ornament der Masse: Essays*, pp. 50–63. In English, in Siegfried Kracauer, *The Mass Ornament, Weimar Essays*, pp. 75–86. From the early 1920s onwards, Benjamin and Kracauer were acquainted with each other personally and showed an interest in each other's projects. They occasionally corresponded with each other.

153. See G.S.I.2, p. 451/G.S.VII.1, p. 369.

154. G.S.I.2, p. 506. *Illuminations*, p. 234.

155. G.S.VII.1, pp. 370–1.

156. See the letter from Adorno to Benjamin of 18 March 1936, reprinted in G.S.I.3, p. 1006.

157. See G.S.VII.1, p. 370.

158. G.S.VII.1, p. 370.

159. G.S.VII.1, p. 371.

7 Time for an Unnatural Death

1. 'Konvolut X: Marx', G.S.V.2, p. 819.

2. G.S.I.2, p. 695. *Illuminations*, Fontana, London 1992, p. 247.

3. See 'Theorien des deutschen Faschismus', G.S.III, p. 238 and the 'Artwork essay', G.S.I.2, p. 469/p. 507/G.S.VII.1, p. 383. See *Illuminations*, p. 235.

4. *Passagenwerk* (1937–40), G.S.V.1, p. 592. 'N', in Gary Smith (ed.), *Benjamin: Philosophy, History, Aesthetics*, University of Chicago Press, Chicago 1989, p. 64.

5. Editorial notes on 'Über den Begriff der Geschichte', G.S.I.3, pp. 1223 and 1226.

6. G.S.I.3, p. 1226.

7. See G.S.I.3, pp. 1223 and 1226.

8. G.S.II.2, p. 540.

9. See G.S.I.3, p. 1228.

10. Editorial notes on 'Über den Begriff der Geschichte', G.S.I.3, p. 1226.

11. G.S.I.2, p. 699. *Illuminations*, p. 251.

12. G.S.I.3, p. 1244. See also G.S.I.2, p. 697. *Illuminations*, p. 249.

13. G.S.I.2, p. 698. *Illuminations*, pp. 249–50.

14. See G.S.I.2, p. 698. *Illuminations*, p. 250.

15. See especially Gershom Scholem's 'Walter Benjamin und sein Engel', in Scholem's collection titled *Walter Benjamin und sein Engel*, Suhrkamp, Frankfurt/Main 1983. The essay 'Walter Benjamin und sein Engel' also appears in Siegfried Unseld (ed.), *Zur Aktualität Walter Benjamins*, Suhrkamp, Frankfurt/Main 1972.

16. See Brecht's *Arbeitsjournal: 1938–1942*, Suhrkamp, Frankfurt/Main 1973, p. 294. For Adorno's critique of Benjamin's procedure with images, specifically in the Baudelaire work, see his letter of 10 November 1938 in *Briefe 2*, Suhrkamp, Frankfurt 1978, p. 785. In 'Virtuose des Scheiterns' Ralf Konersmann exacerbates the debate and argues that Benjamin was never a Marxist and was permanently distanced from historical materialism. Historical materialism for him is 'only a metaphor' (in *Freitag*, no. 36, 28 August 1992, p. 13).

17. See notes for 'Über den Begriff der Geschichte', G.S.I.3, p. 1231.

18. See G.S.I.3, p. 1232.

19. 'Konvolut N: erkenntnistheoretisches, Theorie des Fortschritts', in the *Passagenwerk* (1937–40), G.S.V.1, p. 596. 'N', in Smith (ed.), *Benjamin*, p. 67.

20. G.S.V.1, p. 575. 'N', in Smith (ed.), *Benjamin*, p. 48.

21. See entry N 3, 3, where Benjamin uses the expression '*bildhaft*' (pictorial or vivid) to describe the needs of materialist historiography. G.S.V.1, p. 578. 'N' in Smith (ed.), *Benjamin*, p. 51.

22. G.S.I.2, p. 693. *Illuminations*, p. 245.

23. G.S.I.2, p. 693. *Illuminations*, p. 245.

24. The cryptic correspondence has been interpreted variously. While some commentators identify here, and in the theses in general, a secularization of theology, others perceive a theologization of Marxism. Mention has also been made of an elective affinity between theological messianism and Marxism. Such an affinity is seen to transfigure both. Alternatively, analyses, such as that offered by Phillipe Ivernel, in his article 'Paris, Capital of the Popular Front', who 'identifies the theological dimension purely and simply with the political dimension', make the term theology completely redundant. Ivernel's article is in *New German Critique*, no. 39, Fall 1986, pp. 61–84.

25. There are many interpretations that insist on the formative influence of Judaism in Benjamin's thought. For a consideration of Benjamin's intellectual relationship to Judaism (especially its motif of redemption), in comparison with the orthodox Judaism of Samson Raphaël Hirsch, Hermann Cohen's reform Judaism, the Zionism of Buber and Herzl, and Kafka's idealization of *Ostjudentum*, see Enzo Traverso's *Les Marxistes et la question juive; histoire d'un débat (1843–1943)*, La Breche-Pec, Montreuil 1990. Translated into English, it is available as *The Marxists and the Jewish Question: The History of a Debate 1843–1943*, Humanities Press, New Jersey 1994.

26. Notes for 'Über den Begriff der Geschichte', G.S.I.3, p. 1232.

27. See 'Der Sürrealismus', G.S.II.1, pp. 296 and 308–9. *One Way Street and Other Writings*, New Left Books, London 1979, pp. 226 and 238.

28. Notes for 'Über den Begriff der Geschichte', G.S.I.3, p. 1231.

29. The quotation is taken from *Socialism and the Political Struggle* (1883), quoted at the start of Adam Westoby's *The Evolution of Communism*, Polity, Cambridge 1989.

30. See *Marx Engels Werke*, vol. 20, Dietz Verlag, Berlin 1962, p. 146.

31. G.S.II.2, p. 475. *One Way Street and Other Writings*, p. 358.

32. 'Konvolut N: erkenntnistheoretisches, Theorie des Fortschritts', in the *Passagenwerk* (1937–40), G.S.V.1, p. 607. 'N' in Smith (ed.), *Benjamin*, p. 78.

33. 'It is impossible that things should not turn out all right.' Quoted in James Joll's *Europe since 1870: An International History*, Penguin, London 1990, p. 188.

34. See 'Konvolut X: Marx' in the *Passagenwerk* (1937–40), G.S.V.2, p. 808.

35. G.S.I.2, p. 699. *Illuminations*, p. 250.

36. See notes for 'Über den Begriff der Geschichte', G.S.I.3, p. 1232.

37. G.S.I.2, p. 698. *Illuminations*, p. 250.

38. Reference to Marx's 'Randglossen zum Program der deutschen Arbeiterpartei' is made in 'Über den Begriff der Geschichte', G.S.I.2, p. 699. *Illuminations*, pp. 250–1. It is also cited in the 'Marx file' of the *Passagenwerk*, G.S.V.2, pp. 808 and 809.

39. See the entry X 12 a, 1 in 'Konvolut X: Marx', in the *Passagenwerk* (1937–40), G.S.V.2, p. 820.

40. 'Konvolut X: Marx', in the *Passagenwerk* (1937–40), G.S.V.2, pp. 820–1.

41. 'Konvolut J: Baudelaire', in the *Passagenwerk*, G.S.V.1, p. 456.

42. It has been noted that Benjamin's assault on Dietzgen is neither strictly fair nor accurate. For more on this, see Ben Watson, *Art, Class and Cleavage: Quantulumcunque Concerning Materialist Esthetix*, Quartet, London 1998, pp. 98–108.

43. G.S.I.2, p. 699. *Illuminations*, p. 251. (*Vormärz* is roughly the period 1815–48).

44. See 'Konvolut N: erkenntnistheoretisches, Theorie des Fortschritts', in the *Passagenwerk* (1937–40), G.S.V.1, p. 605. 'N' in Smith (ed.), *Benjamin*, p. 76.

45. See 'Sur Scheerbart' G.S.II.2, pp. 630–1.

46. See 'Konvolut J: Baudelaire', in the *Passagenwerk*, G.S.V.1, pp. 455–6.

47. 'Konvolut N: erkenntnistheoretisches, Theorie des Fortschritts', in the *Passagenwerk* (1937–40), G.S.V.1, p. 598. 'N' in Smith (ed.), *Benjamin*, p. 70.

48. G.S.V.1, p. 596. 'N', in Smith (ed.), *Benjamin*, p. 68. See also 'Eduard Fuchs, der Sammler und der Historiker' (1934–1937), G.S.II.2, p. 487. *One Way Street and Other Writings*, pp. 368–9.

49. See 'Eduard Fuchs', G.S.II.2, p. 488. *One Way Street and Other Writings*, p. 370.

50. See G.S.I.2, p. 700. *Illuminations*, p. 252.

51. See Karl Marx's 'Die Methode der politischen Ökonomie' in the 'Einleitung zur Kritik der politischen Ökonomie' in *Marx Engels Werke*, vol. 13, Dietz Verlag, Berlin 1961, pp. 631–3.

52. 'Konvolut N: erkenntnistheoretisches, Theorie des Fortschritts', in the *Passagenwerk* (1937–40), G.S.V.1, pp. 598–9. 'N', in Smith (ed.), *Benjamin*, p. 70.

53. See 'Konvolut J: Baudelaire', in the *Passagenwerk* (1937–40), G.S.V.1, p. 432.

54. For further discussion of this point, see T.W. Adorno, 'Fortschritt', in Peter Bulthaup (ed.), *Materialien zu Benjamins Thesen 'Über den Begriff der Geschichte'*, Suhrkamp, Frankfurt/Main 1975.

55. G.S.V.1, p. 596. 'N', in Smith (ed.), *Benjamin*, p. 68.

56. See G.S.I.3, p. 1160. *Charles Baudelaire: A Lyric Poet in the Era of High Capitalism*, New Left Books, London 1973, p. 103.

57. G.S.V.1, p. 593. 'N', in Smith (ed.), *Benjamin*, p. 66.

58. 'Konvolut J: Baudelaire', in the *Passagenwerk*, G.S.V.1, p. 451. Benjamin read Marx's tract at Brecht's house in Skovsbostrand in 1938. See G.S.VII.1, p. 474.

59. G.S.I.2, p. 632. *Charles Baudelaire*, p. 133.

60. See the 'Mode file', in the *Passagenwerk*, G.S.V.1, pp. 110–32.

61. The first reference to eternal return is in the 1937–40 section of the *Passagenwerk* file titled 'die Langeweile, ewige Wiederkehr'. Benjamin quotes from Nietzsche's *Nachlaß* in the *Passagenwerk*, G.S.V.1, pp. 173ff. At the same time Adorno was using the idea of 'eternal return' in his critique of Wagner's static dynamism.

62. See G.S.V.1, pp. 171, 457–8.

63. See especially Benjamin's discussion of the book in the introduction and conclusion to the 1939 *Exposé* of the *Passagenwerk*, G.S.V.2, pp. 1255–8.

64. See a letter from Benjamin to Horkheimer on 6 January 1938, in G.S.I.3, pp. 1071–2.

65. 'Konvolut J: Baudelaire', in the *Passagenwerk*, G.S.V.1, p. 429.

66. 'Zentralpark' (1938), G.S.I.2, p. 680.

67. 'Konvolut D: die Langeweile, ewige Wiederkehr', in the *Passagenwerk* (1937–40), G.S.V.1, p. 177.

68. *Passagenwerk* (1937–40), G.S.V.1, p. 178.

69. See 'Teilung der Arbeit und Manufaktur', in *Das Kapital*, *Marx Engels Werke*, Dietz Verlag, Berlin 1969, pp. 356–90.

70. See 'Über einige Motive bei Baudelaire' (1939), G.S.I.2, p. 636. *Charles Baudelaire*, p. 137.
71. G.S.I.2, p. 631. *Charles Baudelaire*, pp. 132–3.
72. G.S.I.2, p. 645. *Charles Baudelaire*, p. 147.
73. See G.S.I.2, p. 630. *Charles Baudelaire*, p. 132. See also Benjamin's 1939 review of the Encyclopédie Française, G.S.III, p. 583n.
74. See 'Zentralpark' (1938), G.S.I.2, p. 614.
75. 'Über einige Motive bei Baudelaire' (1939), G.S.I.2, p. 631. *Charles Baudelaire*, pp. 132–3.
76. See G.S.I.2, p. 632. *Charles Baudelaire*, p. 133.
77. G.S.I.2, p. 630. *Charles Baudelaire*, p. 132.
78. See G.S.I.2, p. 632. *Charles Baudelaire*, p. 133. See also 'Konvolut m: Müßigang', in the *Passagenwerk* (1937–40), G.S.V.2, p. 966.
79. See 'Konvolut m: Müßigang', p. 962.
80. *Passagenwerk*, (1937–40) G.S.V.2, p. 963.
81. G.S.I.2, p. 684.
82. *Passagenwerk*, G.S.V.2, pp. 961–70.
83. See 'Teilung der Arbeit und Manufaktur', in *Das Kapital*; Vol. 1, *Marx Engels Werke*, Dietz Verlag, Berlin 1969 p. 390.
84. See 'Konvolut J: Baudelaire' in the *Passagenwerk*, G.S.V.1, pp. 425–6; also 'Zentralpark' (1938–39), G.S.I.2, p. 679.
85. See Karl Marx, *Der 18te Brumaire des Louis Napoleon* in *Marx Engels Werke*, volume 8, Dietz Verlag, Berlin 1960.
86. This quotation appears in G.S.I.3, p. 1169. *Charles Baudelaire*, p. 106.
87. See G.S.I.3, p. 1168.
88. See 'Das Paris des Second Empire bei Baudelaire', G.S.I.2, p. 561.
89. See *Passagenwerk* (1935–37), G.S.V.1, p. 547.
90. See G.S.V.1, p. 426/p. 538.
91. See *Passagenwerk* (1937–40), G.S.V.1, p. 562.
92. See *Passagenwerk* (pre-1935), G.S.V.1, pp. 121–2.
93. The letter is reprinted in *Frankfurter Adorno Blätter IV*, ed. Theodor W. Adorno Archiv, edition text + kritik 1995, pp. 26–40.
94. The book shows this, but it cannot account for it; hence its success in the bourgeois press (winning the Prix Interallie), and Benjamin's fundamental suspicion of it.
95. The lecture is called 'The Bastille, Old French State Prison', delivered in 1931, and is in G.S.VII.1, pp. 165–73.
96. See Paul Wood and Charles Harrison (eds.), *Art in Theory; An Anthology of Changing Ideas*, Blackwell, Oxford 1992.
97. The review appeared in the *Neue Rhenische Zeitung*, and was reprinted in *Die Neue Zeit* in 1886, which is where Walter Benjamin found it when researching the social-democratic journal.
98. Quotations from the review are cited in Benjamin's *Passagenwerk*, G.S.V.2, pp. 747–9.
99. *Das Kapital*, Volume III, *Marx Engels Werke*, Dietz Verlag, Berlin 1969 p. 838.
100. See G.S.III, pp. 174–5.
101. G.S.V.1, p. 478.
102. See G.S.V.1, p. 353.
103. G.S.I.2, p. 515. See *Charles Baudelaire*, p. 14.
104. See G.S.I.3, p. 1161. See *Charles Baudelaire*, p. 104. Benjamin uses this argument to contest the simple 'class passportism' of vulgar-Marxism.
105. See G.S.V.2, p. 747.

106. See *Twenty Prose Poems of Baudelaire*, translated with an introduction by Michael Hamburger, Editions Poetry London, 1946, pp. 45–7.
107. G.S.I.2, p. 514. See *Charles Baudelaire*, p. 12. This is repeated in slightly different form in 'Zentralpark', G.S.I.2, pp. 658–9.
108. Paul Nizan, *The Conspiracy*, Verso, London, p. 235.
109. G.S.V.1, p. 562.
110. G.S.I.2, p. 515. *Charles Baudelaire*, p. 14.
111. G.S.V.1, p. 537.
112. See, for example, G.S.V.1, p. 424.
113. G.S.V.1, p. 423
114. See G.S.V.1, p. 374.
115. See G.S.VII.2, p. 819.
116. G.S.V.1, p. 233.
117. G.S.V.1, p. 235.
118. Paul Nizan, *The Conspiracy*, Verso, London 1988, p. 235.
119. *Frankfurter Adorno Blätter* IV, edition text und kritik, 1995, p. 34.
120. *Frankfurter Adorno Blätter* IV, p. 35.
121. See the letter to Horkheimer of 3 August 1938, in G.S.I.3, pp. 1082–4.
122. G.S.I.3, p. 1083.
123. See Konvolut X: Marx, in the *Passagenwerk* (1937–40), G.S.V.2, pp. 822–3.
124. See G.S.V.2, pp. 1255–8.
125. See G.S.I.3, p. 1095.
126. See the letter from Benjamin to Adorno of 23 February 1939, in *Briefe* 2, pp. 806–7.
127. 1939 exposé of the *Passagenwerk*, G.S.V.2, pp. 1257–8.
128. See 'Konvolut A: Passagen, magasins de nouveautés, calicots', in the *Passagenwerk* (1937–40), G.S.V.1, p. 108.
129. See 'Konvolut J: Baudelaire', in the *Passagenwerk*, G.S.V.1, p. 469.
130. See 'Konvolut J: Baudelaire', in the *Passagenwerk*, G.S.V.1, p. 469.
131. 'Konvolut J: Baudelaire', in the *Passagenwerk*, G.S.V.1, p. 436.
132. See G.S.V.1, p. 469.
133. G.S.V.1, p. 469.
134. 'Konvolut G: Ausstellungswesen, Reklame, Grandville', in the *Passagenwerk* (1935–37), G.S.V.1, p. 260.
135. 'Konvolut D: die Langeweile, ewige Wiederkehr', in the *Passagenwerk* (1937–40), G.S.V.1, p. 178.
136. See 'Konvolut J: Baudelaire', in the *Passagenwerk*, G.S.V.1, p. 475.
137. 'Konvolut G: Ausstellungswesen, Reklame, Grandville', in the *Passagenwerk* (1937–40), G.S.V.1, p. 267. See also G.S.I.3, p. 1179.
138. See 'Über den Begriff der Geschichte', G.S.I.2, p. 704. *Illuminations*, p. 255.
139. G.S.I.3, p. 1241.
140. G.S.I.3, p. 1241. The first and the last sentence here feature, scratched in several languages, on the glass of Dani Karavan's memorial to Walter Benjamin, erected at Portbou in 1994.
141. G.S.I.3, pp. 1237, 1245.
142. See I. Bibikova, C. Cooke and V. Tolstoy, *Street Art of the Revolution: Festivals and Celebrations in Russia 1918–1933*, Thames and Hudson, London 1990, p. 54 and figs. 21 and 22.
143. See Bibikova, Cooke and Tolstoy, *Street Art of the Revolution*, p. 13.
144. G.S.I.3, pp. 1240 and 1252.
145. G.S.I.3, p. 1252. Splinters is *Splitter* in Benjamin's German.
146. G.S.I.3, pp. 1240–1.

147. Marx, *Grundrisse*, The Pelican Marx Library, London: Penguin/New Left Review 1973, p. 105.

148. *Grundrisse*, p. 107.

149. It could be argued that this structure is echoed in Trotsky's notion of 'combined and uneven development', developed through his struggle against Stalinist stagism and historicism.

150. See Marx, *Grundrisse*, pp. 173, 711–12.

151. G.S.I.3, p. 1243.

152. See G.S.I.3, pp. 1223 and 1226.

153. See 'Über den Begriff der Geschichte', G.S.I.2, pp. 702–3. *Illuminations*, p. 254.

154. G.S.I.2, p. 701. *Illuminations*, pp. 252–3. Benjamin's philosophy of history references this figure termed '*Jetztzeit*', the visioning of a moment laden with energies. '*Jetztzeit*' implies such a rejection of empty time and progress as is already muted in the philosophy of history underpinning 'Das Leben der Studenten' (1915). See G.S.II.1, p. 75/G.S.II.3, p. 915. The critique of homogeneous, mechanical time is first formulated, in *Urform*, in Benjamin's 1916 essay 'Trauerspiel und Tragödie', G.S.II.1, p. 134.

155. See G.S.I.2, p. 703. *Illuminations*, p. 254.

156. See notes for 'Über den Begriff der Geschichte' G.S.I.3, p. 1235/p. 1238/ p. 1329.

157. See entry J 55, 13 in 'Konvolut J: Baudelaire' for a comment on allegory and modern experience in respect of Baudelaire. *Passagenwerk*, G.S.V.1, p. 413.

158. See 'Zentralpark', G.S.I.2, p. 671.

159. The terms deployed to discuss allegory – fragmentation, ruin, discontinuity – are similar to the terms Benjamin uses to discuss film. For example, in writings on Baudelaire, he writes: 'Everything affected by the allegorical intention is cut off from the continuities of life: it is smashed and conserved simultaneously. Allegory holds on tight to the ruins.' 'Konvolut J: Baudelaire', in the *Passagenwerk*, G.S.V.1, pp. 414–15. In his study of baroque tragedy allegory had been identified in Schopenhauer's terms, as a form that works directly on the recipient, spurring them to deed. See G.S.I.1, p. 338. *The Origin of German Tragic Drama*, New Left Books, London 1977, p. 162.

160. G.S.I.2, pp. 669–70.

161. 'Konvolut J: Baudelaire', in the *Passagenwerk*, G.S.V.1, p. 417.

162. 'Zentralpark', G.S.I.2, p. 671.

163. See G.S.I.2, p. 700. *Illuminations*, p. 252. See also G.S.I.3, pp. 1237 and 1241. For a connection drawn between film and hate, see entry K 3 a,1, in G.S.V.1, p. 500.

164. See Fischer's *Karl Marx und sein Verhältnis zu Staat und Wirtschaft*, Verlag von Gustav Fischer, Jena 1932, p. 33.

165. 'Konvolut J: Baudelaire', in the *Passagenwerk*, G.S.V.1, p. 414.

166. See G.S.I.2, p. 700. *Illuminations*, p. 252.

167. G.S.I.3, p. 1240.

168. G.S.I.3, pp. 1237 and 1245.

169. G.S.I.3, p. 1256.

170. G.S.I.3, p. 1254.

171. See G.S.I.3, pp. 1258–9.

172. From *Partisan Review* 8, no. 1, cited in Alan M. Wald, *The Responsibility of Intellectuals: Selected Essays on Marxist Traditions in Cultural Commitment*, Humanities Press, Atlantic Heights, NJ 1992, pp. 46–7.

173. See 'Zentralpark', G.S.I.2, p. 660 and also in the *Passagenwerk*, G.S.V.1, p. 428. See also G.S.I.3, p. 1139.
174. See 'thesis V', 'thesis IV' and 'thesis VIII', G.S.I.2, pp. 695 and 696. *Illuminations*, 1992, pp. 247 and 248–9.
175. 'Über den Begriff der Geschichte', G.S.I.2, p. 703. *Illuminations*, p. 254.
176. See G.S.I.2, p. 634. *Charles Baudelaire*, p. 135.
177. G.S.I.2, p. 702. *Illuminations*, p. 254. See also entry D 10a, 5 in the *Passagenwerk* (1937–40), G.S.V.1, p. 178.
178. 'Konvolut N: erkenntnistheoretisches, Theorie des Fortschritts', in the *Passagenwerk* (1937–40), G.S.V.1, p. 589. 'N', Smith (ed.), *Benjamin*, p. 61.
179. See 'Über den Begriff der Geschichte', G.S.I.2, p. 697. *Illuminations*, pp. 248–9.
180. G.S.I.2, p. 695. *Illuminations*, p. 247.
181. G.S.I.2, pp. 697–8. *Illuminations*, p. 249.
182. See 'Engagement', in *Noten zur Literatur*, Suhrkamp, Frankfurt/Main 1981, p. 430.
183. G.S.I.2, p. 701. *Illuminations*, p. 253.
184. C.L.R. James, *Notes on Dialectics: Hegel, Marx, Lenin* (1948), Allison and Busby, London 1980, p. 99.
185. James, *Notes on Dialectics*, pp. 100–1.
186. 'Über den Begriff der Geschichte', G.S.I.2, p. 702. *Illuminations*, p. 254.
187. G.S.I.2, p. 700. *Illuminations*, p. 251.
188. See 'Pariser Passagen' 1 (1927–29), G.S.V.2, p. 1026.
189. G.S.I.2, p. 698. *Illuminations*, p. 250.
190. G.S.I.2, p. 700. *Illuminations*, p. 251.
191. *Marx Engels Werke*, vol. 3, Berlin: Dietz Verlag, Berlin 1983 p. 547.
192. See Leon Trotsky, *The History of the Russian Revolution*, Pluto Press, London 1985, p. 326. Incidentally, this was a book that Benjamin 'breathlessly' devoured. See Benjamin, *Briefe* 2, Suhrkamp, Frankfurt 1978, p. 785.
193. V.I. Lenin, *Collected Works*, vol. 38, Progress Publishers, Moscow 1972, pp. 259–60.
194. See G.S.I.2, p. 703. *Illuminations*, p. 254.
195. Editorial notes on 'Über den Begriff der Geschichte', G.S.I.3, pp. 1223 and 1227.
196. See Bertolt Brecht's *Arbeitsjournal: 1938–1942*, Suhrkamp, Frankfurt/Main 1973, p. 294.

8 Benjamin's Finale: Excavating and Remembering

1. See, for some examples, Terry Eagleton, *Walter Benjamin or Towards a Revolutionary Criticism*, Verso, London 1981; Norbert Bolz and Willem van Reijen, *Walter Benjamin*, Reihe Campus, Frankfurt/Main 1991; Bernd Witte, *Walter Benjamin mit Selbstzeugnissen und Bilddokumenten*, RoRoRo, Reinbek/Hamburg 1990; *Text + Kritik* nos. 31/32 1979, ed. Heinz Ludwig Arnold' special issue on Walter Benjamin.
2. See, for example, *Illuminations*, Fontana, London 1992; P. Gebhardt, M. Grzimek, D. Harth, M. Rumpf, U. Schödlbauer and B. Witte (eds), *Walter Benjamin – Zeitgenosse der Moderne*, Scriptor, Kronberg/Ts. 1976.
3. See, for example, Werner Fuld, *Walter Benjamin: Eine Biographie*, RoRoRo, Reinbek/Hamburg 1990.
4. By Gary Smith (with designer Hans Puttnies), Anabas Verlag, Gießen 1991.
5. See, for example, Gary Smith (ed.), *Benjamin: Philosophy, History, Aesthetics*, University of Chicago Press, Chicago 1989.

6. See, for example, Helmut Salzinger, *Swinging Benjamin* (1973), Kellner, Hamburg 1990.

7. See the introduction by Susan Sontag to Walter Benjamin's *One Way Street and Other Writings*, New Left Books, London 1979, p. 7.

8. G.S.I.2, p. 445/p. 485/G.S.VII.1, p. 360. *Illuminations*, Fontana, London 1992, p. 219.

9. See 'Kleine Geschichte der Photographie' (1931), G.S.II.1, p. 371. *One Way Street and Other Writings*, p. 243.

10. G.S.II.1, p. 372. *One Way Street and Other Writings*, p. 244.

11. Quoted in Christopher Phillips (ed.), *Photography in the Modern Era*, Aperture, New York 1989, pp. 239–40.

12. The quotation stems from Zygmunt Bauman. It was uttered at a conference on Walter Benjamin held at Birkbeck College, London in July 1992, largely reprinted in *New Formations* no. 20, Summer 1993. This quotation from Bauman is on p. 48. The collection of papers was republished by Lawrence and Wishart in 1998, though Iain Chambers substituted for Susan Buck-Morss.

13. Notes for 'Über den Begriff der Geschichte', G.S.I.3, p. 1224.

14. G.S.I.2, p. 695. *Illuminations*, p. 247.

15. The phrase 'celebrated opacity' stems from Gary Smith and appears on the book jacket of Jeffrey Mehlman's *Walter Benjamin for Children: An Essay on his Radio Years*, University of Chicago Press, Chicago 1993.

16. For an interpretation of Benjamin as an anti-fascist intellectual and not a Marxist or historical materialist, see Gerhard Wagner, *Walter Benjamin; Die Medien der Moderne*, ed. the Hochschule für Film und Fernsehen Konrad Wolf, Potsdam-Babelsberg 1992. Notably, the standard reception of Benjamin in the Eastern bloc praised his anti-fascism, while rejecting what was construed as a neo-Marxist New Left radicalism. See, for example, the abstract of V. G. Arslanov's 1983 book in *Literatur über Walter Benjamin: kommentierte Bibliographie 1983–1992*, ed. Reinhard Markner and Thomas Weber, Argument-Verlag, Berlin 1993, p. 26.

17. The phrase 'mimetic delirium' stems from Rainer Nägele's *Theater, Theory, Speculation: Walter Benjamin and the Scenes of Modernity*, Johns Hopkins University Press, Baltimore 1991, p. xiv.

18. The idea of posthumous fame is discussed in Hannah Arendt's introduction to her selection of writings by Walter Benjamin. See *Illuminations*, pp. 7ff.

19. See Ralf Konersmann's 'Virtuose des Scheiterns: Warum man vielleicht aufhören sollte, Benjamin zu zitieren', in *Freitag* no. 36, 28 August 1992, p. 13.

20. See Benjamin's radio lecture 'Bert Brecht' (1930), G.S.II.2, pp. 660–7.

21. 'Konvolut k: Die Kommune', G.S.V.2, p. 949.

22. For a deeply melancholic reading of Benjamin, see Gillian Rose, 'Walter Benjamin – Out of the Sources of Modern Judaism', in *New Formations* no. 20, Summer 1993, pp. 59–81. The essay is also published in Rose's *Judaism and Modernity; Philosophical Essays*, Blackwell, Oxford 1993, pp. 175–210. The melancholic or Saturnine approach is also executed in exemplary form in Susan Sontag's widely available introduction to Benjamin's *One Way Street*, New Left Books, London 1979, pp. 7–28.

23. Zygmunt Bauman, 'Walter Benjamin, the Intellectual', in *New Formations* no. 20, summer 1993, p. 47. The reorganized reprint of the collection places the quotation on p. 72.

24. See Bertolt Brecht's poem 'An Walter Benjamin, der sich auf der Flucht vor Hitler entleibte' (1941), in *Marbacher Magazin* no. 55/1990, ed. Rolf Tiedemann, C. Gödde and H. Lonitz, p. 319.

25. *Berliner Kindheit um Neunzehnhundert*, G.S.VII.1, p. 385.

26. See, for example, a letter from Walter Benjamin to Gerhard Scholem of 20 March 1933, published in *Briefe* 2, ed. G. Scholem and T.W. Adorno, Suhrkamp, Frankfurt/Main 1978, pp. 565–7. *The Correspondence of Walter Benjamin and Gershom Scholem 1932–1940*, Schocken, New York 1989, p. 34.

27. See Bertolt Brecht's poem 'Zum Freitod des Flüchtlings W.B.' (1941), in *Marbacher Magazin* no. 55/1990, eds Rolf Tiedemann, C. Gödde and H. Lonitz, p. 318.

28. For further information which, drawing on a batch of documents found in Spain, casts doubts on the factuality of Benjamin's death as suicide, see Ingrid and Konrad Scheurmann eds, *For Walter Benjamin: Documentation, Essays and a Sketch*, Inter Nationes, Bonn 1993, pp. 265–97. They suggest his death may not have been self-willed but brought on by illness, and surmise that the myth of self-termination was perpetrated via mistranslation and misunderstanding.

29. It is worth noting that while the monument seems to be Benjamin's monument, it might be viewed differently. The monument, states the Portbou tourist leaflet available from the stand at the harbour, is not just in memory of Benjamin, but also commemorates all European exiles, fleeing in both directions, in the years 1933 to 1945. This heightened sensitivity to exile and refugee status as a mass experience might be born of Catalonia's specific experience of fascism.

30. *Briefe* 2, p. 767.

31. See Walter Benjamin's 'Linke Melancholie' (1930), G.S.III.

32. G.S.II.2, p. 456. *Illuminations*, p. 99.

33. Scholem quoted in Zygmunt Bauman, 'Walter Benjamin, the Intellectual', p. 48. Scholem addresses Benjamin's relationship to loneliness in *Walter Benjamin und sein Engel*, Suhrkamp, Frankfurt/Main 1983, p. 34.

34. For a dispersal of history in a recounting of Benjamin's aesthetics, see Inez Müller, *Walter Benjamin und Bertolt Brecht: Ansätze zu einer dialektischen Ästhetik in den dreißiger Jahren*, Röhrig, St. Ingbert 1993. Müller's doctoral thesis blames Benjamin and the avant-garde for the failure of history to provide a revolution, rather than considering the dialectical relationship between these factors, quite apart from missing the crucial role of the Nazis and Stalinists in firmly closing down the possibilities.

35. See 'Bibliographie der zu Lebzeiten gedruckten Arbeiten' with its 442 entries in order to debunk this myth. G.S.VII.1, pp. 477–519.

36. See 'Memorandum zu der Zeitschrift *Krisis und Kritik*', G.S.VI, pp. 619–21 and 825–8. See also Bertolt Brecht, *Gesammelte Werke: Schriften zur Literatur und Kunst* 1, vol. 18, Suhrkamp, Frankfurt/Main 1967, p. 86–7.

37. This may be further illuminated by reference to one of Benjamin's notes on the practice of criticism from 1931. It discusses the necessary interdependence of theory and praxis in political criticism, best exemplified in Lenin's writing. See G.S.VI, p. 180.

38. *Briefe* 1 ed. G. Scholem and T.W. Adorno, Suhrkamp, Frankfurt/Main 1978, p. 418.

39. See 'Literaturgeschichte und Literaturwissenschaft' (1931), in G.S.III, pp. 283–90 and also the two versions of 'Strenge Kunstwissenschaft' (1932), in G.S.III, pp. 363–9/pp. 369–74.

40. Editor's note by Hannah Arendt, in *Illuminations*, p. 256.

41. See Hannah Arendt's Introduction to *Illuminations*, pp. 32–3.

42. See Arendt, Introduction, p. 50.

43. See *Literatur über Walter Benjamin*, ed. Reinhard Markner and Thomas Weber, Das Argument Verlag, Berlin 1993, p. 8.

44. See Angela McRobbie, 'The *Passagenwerk* and the Place of Walter Benjamin in Cultural Studies: Benjamin, Cultural Studies, Marxist Theories of Art', in *Cultural Studies* vol. 6, no. 2, May 1992, pp. 147–69.

45. Gerhard-Gershom Scholem, *On Jews and Judaism in Crisis*, Schocken Books, New York 1976, p. 187.

46. 'Selbstbetrug' and 'Selbsttäuschung' are the terms Scholem uses to describe Benjamin's sympathies for dialectical materialism in a letter written on 30 March 1931. See *Briefe* 2, p. 525/p. 528. Suicide is raised in the letter of 6 May 1931 (*Briefe* 2, p. 533). See also Mark Lilla, 'The Riddle of Walter Benjamin', in *The New York Review*, 25 May 1995, p. 39.

47. See a letter from Scholem written on 30 March 1931, in *Briefe* 2, p. 526.

48. See a letter from Scholem written on 6 May 1931, in *Briefe* 2, pp. 532–3.

49. See the letter from Scholem to Benjamin sent on 30 March 1931, in *Briefe* 2, pp. 525–9.

50. See 'Über das Programm der kommenden Philosophie', G.S.II.1, pp. 157–68.

51. *Briefe* 2, p. 523.

52. *Briefe* 2, p. 523.

53. See Arendt's Introduction to *Illuminations*, p. 50.

54. See Paul de Man, 'The Task of the Translator', in *Yale French Studies* no. 69, 1985, pp. 25–46.

55. See various contributions to *Walter Benjamin's Philosophy: Destruction and Experience*, ed. Andrew Benjamin and Peter Osborne, Routledge, London 1994. Disregarding Benjamin's confessed antagonism towards Heidegger, the contributions from Caygill, Düttmann, Hamacher, Andrew Benjamin and Comay all spend their time Heidegger-spotting in Benjamin. Adherence predominantly to themes thrown up by Heidegger means that critical figures and constellations in Benjamin's historico-political aesthetics remain largely unexamined in this collection. Unobserved, though key, Benjaminian figures include phantasmagoria, the critique of progress, evaluations of cultural production and reception, the optical unconscious, the *flâneur*, historicist empathy, montage, commodity fetishism. These figures all emerge out of Benjamin's productive and critical dialogues with Marxist historiography, politics and aesthetics. Their absences mark a void.

56. *Briefe* 2, p. 524.

57. See Martin Heidegger, *The Question Concerning Technology and Other Essays*, Harper and Row, New York 1977, pp. 14–16.

58. See, for example, *Walter Benjamin's Philosophy: Destruction and Experience*, pp. x–xiii. The book announces, in possessive and defensive terms, on its back cover and in its introduction, that Benjamin must be viewed as a philosopher. The editors maintain that 'it is Benjamin the Philosopher, who stands behind' every other sort of Benjamin who might be named.

59. See the letter to Scholem, written 10 May 1924, in *Briefe* 1, p. 344.

60. See Rodolphe Gasché's essay 'Objective Diversions: On Some Kantian Themes in Benjamin's *The Work of Art in the Age of Mechanical Reproduction*', in *Walter Benjamin's Philosophy*, p. 201.

61. See, for example, Gasché's essay in *Walter Benjamin's Philosophy*. Despite Benjamin's shaping of major themes in candid rejection of Kant, Kant

persists, insists Gasché, in undergirding Benjamin's theory. This undergirding is present most crucially in 'Das Kunstwerk im Zeitalter seiner technischen Reproduzierbarkeit'. This, Gasché reveals, is decidedly non-profane. Gasché interprets Benjamin's usage of space-time categories as recourse to Kantianism, and, binding the perceived elimination of space and time to the dematerialization of the art object, claims that Benjamin's theory has 'all the allure of the Kantian aesthetics with its subjective bent'. Gasché connects the (disappearance of the) object and the (emergence of the) subject. But he needs to recognize the decisiveness of Benjamin's formulations about modern collective subjectivity – not old bourgeois subjectivity – in the context of mass experience, as well as the novel quality of critical, appropriative perception. Gasché concludes that Benjamin's reversal of evaluation of Kant's aesthetic categories – such as distraction or contemplation – indicates that he is trapped and stranded within the Kantian schema, and his 'temporary affiliations with historical materialism' can force no exit. Surely it is Gasché's analysis that is trapped and stranded within binaries, unable to recognize Benjamin's reliance on the conceptual power of dialectics.

62. See Jacques Derrida, 'Force of Law: The Mystical Foundation of Authority', in *Deconstruction and the Possibility of Justice*, ed. Drucilla Cornell et al., Routledge, New York 1992, pp. 29–67. Or see Jacques Derrida, *Gesetzeskraft. Der mystische Grund der Authorität*, Suhrkamp, Frankfurt 1991 (French and English versions also in *Cardozo Law Review* vol. 11, 1990).

63. Derrida, 'Force of Law', p. 64.

64. Derrida, 'Force of Law', pp. 52 and 62.

65. Derrida, 'Force of Law', p. 62.

66. See Jacques Derrida, *Spectres of Marxism: The State of the Debt, The Work of Mourning, The New International*, Routledge, London 1994, p. 55.

67. For references to 'a certain spirit' of Marxism, see Derrida, *Spectres of Marxism*, pp. 75, 86, 90, 92 and elsewhere.

68. See Derrida, *Spectres of Marxism*, p. 84.

69. See the concluding sentiments of Graeme Gilloch, *Myth and Metropolis: Walter Benjamin and the City*, Polity Press, Oxford 1996.

70. See Jacques Derrida, 'Ein Porträt Benjamins', Burkhardt Lindner (ed.), in *Links hatte noch alles sich zu enträtseln: Walter Benjamin im Kontext*, Syndikat, Frankfurt/Main 1978.

71. See Ralf Konersmann, 'Virtuose des Scheiterns; Warum man vielleicht aufhören sollte, Benjamin zu zitieren', in *Freitag* no. 36, 28 August 1992, p. 13.

72. These arguments appear in the conference papers reprinted in *New Formations* no. 20, Summer 1993, and in the Lawrence and Wishart reprint from 1998.

73. See Bernd Witte, 'Allegorien des Schreibens: Eine Lektüre von Walter Benjamins Trauerspielbuch', in *Merkur*, Heft 2, February 1992, pp. 125–36.

74. Jameson's review is titled 'An Unfinished Project', and is in *London Review of Books*, 3 August 1995, pp. 8–9. It is a review of *The Correspondence of Walter Benjamin 1910–1940*, ed. G. Scholem and T.W. Adorno, Chicago 1994 and T.W. Adorno and Walter Benjamin: *Briefwechsel 1928–1940*, ed. Henri Lonitz, Suhrkamp, Frankfurt/Main 1994.

75. Jameson, 'An Unfinished Project', 3 August 1995, p. 8.

76. Jameson, p. 8.

77. Jameson, p. 9.

78. See, for examples, Adorno's letter to Benjamin, dated 18 March 1936 and translated in *Aesthetics and Politics*, ed. F. Jameson, Verso, London 1980; also Scholem, *Walter Benjamin und sein Engel*, p. 26. Mark Lilla in his review article 'The Riddle of Walter Benjamin' echoes this in passing. He describes Benjamin's encounter with Brecht as 'a deferential relationship that had an unfortunate effect on his writing', in *The New York Review*, 25 May 1995, p. 40.

79. Benjamin's fascination with technology and his excitement at its potentials emerge in various places. His frequent engagement with the meaning of the technological opens up a number of concerns insufficiently charted by Michael Löwy whose description of Benjamin foregrounds his commitment to ecological and anti-war concerns and so restricts Benjamin's positive evaluation of technological potential to a brief phase from 1933 to 1935, labelled by Löwy 'a short-lived experiment in progressivism' and correlated to his friendship with Brecht. See Löwy's 'Revolution against "Progress"', in *On Changing the World*, Humanities Press, Atlantic Heights, NJ 1993 p. 155.

80. Letter from Walter Benjamin to Gerhard Scholem, 6 May 1934, published in *Briefe* 2, p. 604. *The Correspondence of Walter Benjamin and Gershom Scholem 1932–1940*, p. 110.

81. 'Konvolut a: soziale Bewegung', in the *Passagenwerk* (pre-1935), G.S.V.2, p. 852.

82. 'Konvolut N: erkenntnistheoretisches, Theorie des Fortschritts', in the *Passagenwerk* (1937–40), G.S.V.1, p. 596. 'N', in Gary Smith (ed.), *Benjamin; Philosophy, History, Aesthetics*, University of Chicago Press, Chicago 1989, p. 67–8.

83. See Terry Eagleton, *Walter Benjamin or Towards a Revolutionary Criticism*, Verso, London 1981.

84. See Cliff Slaughter, *Marxism, Ideology and Literature*, Macmillan, London 1980.

85. See, for example, Daniel Bensaïd, *Walter Benjamin: sentinelle messianique. A la gauche du possible*, Plon, Paris 1990, Enzo Traverso, *Les Marxistes et la question juive; histoire d'un débat (1843–1943)*, La Breche-Pec, Montreuil 1990, or Michael Löwy, *On Changing the World: Essays in Political Philosophy from Karl Marx to Walter Benjamin*, Humanities Press, Atlantic Heights, NJ 1993.

86. Victor Serge, *Memoirs of a Revolutionary 1901–1941*, Oxford University Press, London 1980, pp. 364–5.

87. See G.S.II.2, p. 758.

88. See *Briefe* 1, p. 409.

89. *Briefe* 2, p. 553.

90. G.S.IV.2, p. 1009.

91. G.S.IV.1, p. 434.

92. See Mandel's introduction to Leon Trotsky's *The Struggle against Fascism in Germany*, Pathfinder, New York 1971, pp. 9–46.

93. Mandel, p. 9.

94. 'Pariser Passagen' 1 (1927–29) V.2, p. 1010.

95. 'Eduard Fuchs, der Sammler und der Historiker' (1934–1937), G.S.II.2, p. 475. *One Way Street and Other Writings*, p. 358.

96. 'Über den Begriff der Geschichte' (1939–40), G.S.I.2, p. 697. *Illuminations*, p. 248.

97. 'Konvolut N: erkenntnistheoretisches, Theorie des Fortschritts', in the *Passagenwerk* (1935–37), G.S.V.1, p. 585. 'N' in Smith (ed.), *Benjamin*, p. 57.
98. G.S.II.2, p. 531. Jehoo is a town in Brecht's first epic drama *Mann ist Mann.*

Bibliography

Below is a select bibliography of books that have been consulted in the preparation of this work. Gary Smith provides a bibliography of secondary literature on Walter Benjamin, mainly articles, from 1921 to 1979 in *New German Critique* no. 17, Spring 1979, pp. 189–208. For an extensive bibliographical inventory of writings on Walter Benjamin written up to 1982, see Momme Brodersen, *Walter Benjamin: Bibliografia critica generale* (1913–83), Centro Internazionale Studi di Estetica, Palermo 1984. For an international bibliographical listing, which extends Brodersen's catalogue, see *Literatur über Walter Benjamin; kommentierte Bibliographie 1983–1992*, ed. Reinhard Markner and Thomas Weber, Argument-Verlag, Berlin 1993.

Occasionally the original dates of publication appear inside square brackets, when there exists a sizable gap between time of first publication or writing and the publication date of the edition listed.

Books by Walter Benjamin

Benjamin, Walter, *Gesammelte Schriften*, volumes I–VII, ed. Rolf Tiedemann and Hermann Schweppenhäuser, Suhrkamp, Frankfurt/Main 1972–91
Walter Benjamin, *Briefe*, two volumes, ed. Gershom Scholem and T.W. Adorno, Suhrkamp, Frankfurt/Main 1978
Benjamin, Walter and Scholem, Gershom, *Briefwechsel: 1933–1940*, ed. Gershom Scholem, Suhrkamp, Frankfurt/Main 1980
Benjamin, Walter, *Allegorien kultureller Erfahrung; Ausgewählte Schriften 1920–1940*, Reclam, Berlin 1984

A Selection of English Translations of Walter Benjamin's Writings

Benjamin, Walter, *Charles Baudelaire: A Lyric Poet in the Era of High Capitalism*, New Left Books, London 1973
Benjamin, Walter, *The Origin of German Tragic Drama*, with an introduction by George Steiner, New Left Books, London 1977
Benjamin, Walter, *One Way Street and Other Writings*, with an introduction by Susan Sontag, New Left Books, London 1979
Benjamin, Walter, *Understanding Brecht*, with an introduction by Stanley Mitchell, New Left Books, London 1983
Benjamin, Walter, *Reflections*, with an introduction by Peter Demetz, Schocken Books, New York 1986
Benjamin, Walter, *Moscow Diary*, with an afterword by Gary Smith [originally an edition of the journal *October*], Harvard University Press, Cambridge, Mass. 1986
Benjamin, Walter and Scholem, Gershom, *The Correspondence of Walter Benjamin and Gershom Scholem 1932–1940*, ed. Gershom Scholem, Schocken, New York 1989

Benjamin, Walter, *Illuminations*, ed. and with an introduction by Hannah Arendt, Fontana, London 1992

Benjamin, Walter, *The Correspondence of Walter Benjamin 1910–1940*, ed. G. Scholem and T.W. Adorno, Chicago 1994

Benjamin, Walter, *Selected Writings, Volume 1, 1913–1926*, The Belknap Press of Harvard University Press, Cambridge, Mass. 1996.

Benjamin, Walter, *Selected Writings, Volume 2, 1927–1934*, The Belknap Press of Harvard University Press, Cambridge, Mass. 1999

Books and Articles about or Substantially about Walter Benjamin

Abbas, Ackbar, 'On Fascination; Walter Benjamin's Images', in *New German Critique* no. 48, Fall 1989, pp. 43–62

Adorno, T.W., *Über Walter Benjamin*, Suhrkamp, Frankfurt/Main 1970

Alter, Robert, *Necessary Angels: Tradition and Modernity in Kafka, Benjamin and Scholem*, Harvard University Press, Cambridge, Mass. 1991

Arendt, Hannah, *Benjamin, Brecht: Zwei Essays*, Piper, Munich 1971

Ash, Beth Sharon, 'Walter Benjamin: Ethnic Fears, Oedipal Anxieties, Political Consequences', in *New German Critique* no. 48, Fall 1989, pp. 2–42

Benjamin, Andrew and Osborne, Peter (eds.), *Walter Benjamin's Philosophy: Destruction and Experience*, Routledge, London 1994

Bensaïd, Daniel, *Walter Benjamin: sentinelle messianique. A la gauche du possible*, Plon, Paris 1990

Bolz, Norbert and Faber, Richard (eds.), *Walter Benjamin: Profane Erleuchtung und rettende Kritik*, Königshausen und Neumann, Würzburg 1982

Bolz, Norbert and Witte, Bernd (eds.), *Passagen; Walter Benjamins Urgeschichte des 19. Jahrhunderts*, Wilhelm Fink, Munich 1984

Bolz, Norbert and Faber, Richard (eds.), *Antike und Moderne: Zu Walter Benjamins 'Passagen'*, Königshausen und Neumann, Würzburg 1986

Bolz, Norbert and van Reijen, Willem, *Walter Benjamin*, Reihe Campus, Frankfurt/Main 1991

Brecht, Bertolt, 'An WB, der sich auf der Flucht vor Hitler entleibte', in *Brecht's Gedichte*, vol. 6, Suhrkamp, Frankfurt/Main 1964, p. 49

Brodersen, Momme, *Walter Benjamin: Bibliografia critica generale (1913–1983)*, Centro Internazionale Studi di Estetica, Palermo 1984

Brodersen, Momme, *Spinne im eigenen Netz; Walter Benjamin, Leben und Werk*, Elster Verlag, Bühl-Moos 1990

Brodersen, Momme, *Walter Benjamin: A Biography*, Verso, London 1996

Buci-Glucksmann, Christine, *Walter Benjamin und die Utopie des Weiblichen*, Hamburg 1984

Buci-Glucksmann, Christine, 'Catastrophic Utopia: The Feminine as Allegory of the Modern', in *Representations* no. 12, Spring 1986, pp. 220–9

Buck-Morss, Susan, *The Origin of Negative Dialectics: Theodor W. Adorno, Walter Benjamin and the Frankfurt Institute*, Harvester Press, Brighton 1977

Buck-Morss, Susan, *The Dialectics of Seeing: Walter Benjamin and the Arcades Project*, MIT Press, Cambridge, Mass. 1989

Buck-Morss, Susan, 'Aesthetics and Anaesthetics: Walter Benjamin's Artwork Essay Reconsidered', in *October* no. 62, Fall 1992, pp. 3–41

Bullock, Marcus, *Marxism and Romanticism: The Philosophical Development of Literary Theory and Literary History in Walter Benjamin and Friedrich Schlegel*, Peter Lang, New York 1987

Bulthaup, Peter (ed.), *Materialien zu Benjamins 'Über den Begriff der Geschichte'*, Suhrkamp, Frankfurt/Main 1975

Cadava, Eduardo, *Words of Light: Theses on the Philosophy of History*, Princeton University Press, Princeton 1997

Caygill, Howard, *Walter Benjamin: The Colour of Experience*, Routledge, London 1998

Caygill, Howard, Coles, Alex and Klimowski, Andrzej, *Walter Benjamin for Beginners*, Icon Books, Cambridge 1998

César, Jasiel, *Walter Benjamin on Experience and History*, Mellen Research University Press, San Francisco 1992

Chow, Rey, 'Walter Benjamin's Love Affair with Death', in *New German Critique* no. 48, Fall 1989, pp. 63–86

Cohen, Margaret, 'Walter Benjamin's Phantasmagoria', in *New German Critique* no. 48, Fall 1989, pp. 87–107

Cohen, Margaret, *Profane Illumination: Walter Benjamin and the Paris of Surrealist Revolution*, University of California Press, Berkeley 1993

Derrida, Jacques, *The Truth in Painting* [1978], University of Chicago Press, Chicago 1987

Derrida, Jacques, *Gesetzeskraft: Der mystische Grund der Authorität*, Suhrkamp, Frankfurt/Main 1991

Derrida, Jacques, 'Force of Law: The Mystical Foundation of Authority', in *Deconstruction and the Possibility of Justice*, ed. Drucilla Cornell et al., Routledge, New York 1992 pp. 29–67

Derrida, Jacques, *Spectres of Marxism: The State of the Debt, The Work of Mourning, The New International*, Routledge, London 1994

Dieckhoff, Reiner, *Mythos und Moderne*, Janus Verlag, Cologne 1987

Doderer, Klaus (ed.), *Walter Benjamin und die Kinderliteratur: Aspekte der Kinderkultur in den zwanziger Jahren*, Juventa Verlag, Weinheim, Munich 1988

Eagleton, Terry, *Walter Benjamin or Towards a Revolutionary Criticism*, Verso, London 1981

Frisby, David, *Fragments of Modernity*, Polity Press, Cambridge 1985

Fuld, Werner, *Walter Benjamin; Eine Biographie*, RoRoRo, Reinbek/Hamburg 1990

Fürnkäs, Josef, *Sürrealismus als Erkenntnis; Walter Benjamin, Weimarer Einbahnstraße und Pariser Passagen*, Metzler, Stuttgart 1988

Jameson, Fredric, 'An Unfinished Project', *London Review of Books*, 3 August 1995, pp. 8–9

Garber, Klaus, *Rezeption und Rettung*, Max Niemeyer, Tübingen 1987

Garber, Klaus, *Zum Bilde Walter Benjamins: Studien, Porträts, Kritiken*, Wilhelm Fink, Munich 1992

Gebhardt, Peter, Grzimek, Martin, Harth, Dietrich, Rumpf, Michael, Schödlbauer, Ulrich and Witte, Bernd (eds.), *Walter Benjamin – Zeitgenosse der Moderne*, Scriptor, Kronberg/Ts. 1976

Gilloch, Graeme, *Myth and Metropolis: Walter Benjamin and the City*, Polity Press, Oxford 1996

Greffrath, Krista, *Metaphorischer Materialismus; Untersuchungen zum Geschichtsbegriff Walter Benjamins*, Wilhelm Fink, Munich 1981

Günther, Henning, *Walter Benjamin: Zwischen Marxismus und Theologie*, Walter Verlag, Olten-Freiburg im Breisgau 1974

Hart-Nibbrig, C.L., 'Das Déjà-vu des ersten Blicks: Zu Walter Benjamins Berliner Kindheit um Neunzehnhundert', in *Deutsche Vierteljahresschrift für Literaturwissenschaft und Geistesgeschichte* 47, Heft 4, 1973, pp. 711–29

Hering, Christoph, *Der Intellektuelle als Revolutionär; Walter Benjamins Analyse intellektueller Praxis*, Wilhelm Fink, Munich 1979

Hering, Christoph, *Die Rekonstruktion der Revolution*, Lang Verlag, Frankfurt/Main 1983

Jennings, Michael, *Dialectical Images: Walter Benjamin's Theory of Literary Criticism*, Cornell University Press, Ithaca, NY 1987

Jerzewski, Roland, *Zwischen anarchistischer Fronde und revolutionärer Disziplin; Zum Engagement-Begriff bei Walter Benjamin und Paul Nizan*, Metzler, Stuttgart 1991

Kaiser, Gerhard, *Benjamin, Adorno; Zwei Studien*, Athenäum, Frankfurt/Main 1974

Kambas, Chryssoula, *Walter Benjamin im Exil: Zum Verhältnis von Literaturpolitik und Ästhetik*, Max Niemeyer, Tübingen 1983

Kambas, Chryssoula, 'Politische Aktualität: Walter Benjamin's Concept of History and the Failure of the French Popular Front', in *New German Critique* no. 39, Fall 1986

Konersmann, Ralf, 'Virtuose des Scheiterns: Warum man vielleicht aufhören sollte, Benjamin zu zitieren', in *Freitag* no. 36, 28 August 1992, p. 13

Leslie, Esther, 'Wrapping the Reichstag; Re-visioning German History', in *Radical Philosophy* 77, May/June 1996

Leslie, Esther, 'Exotic of the Everyday: Critical Theory in the Parlour', in *Things* 4, summer 1996

Leslie, Esther, 'Walter Penetrates Deeply into the Web', in *Mute* 7, winter 1997

Leslie, Esther, 'On Making-up and Breaking-up: "Woman" and "Ware", "Craving" and "Corpse" in Walter Benjamin's *Arcades Project*', in *Historical Materialism* 1, winter 1997

Leslie, Esther, 'The Multiple Identities of Walter Benjamin', *New Left Review* 226, November/December 1997

Leslie, Esther, 'Professional Faces: Explaining the Shadows; On August Sander', in *Things* 7, winter 1997–78

Leslie, Esther, 'Walter Benjamin: Traces of Craft', in *Journal of Design History* vol. 11 no. 1, spring 1998, special issue on Modernism and Modernity in Design

Leslie, Esther, 'Drawing the Line: Painting History and History Painting', in *Art, Technology, Technique; Art, Criticism, Theory* 4, 1998

Leslie, Esther, 'Telescoping the Microscopic Object: Walter Benjamin, the Collector' in *De-, Dis-, Ex-* no. 3, March 1999

Leslie, Esther, 'Elective Affinities: the Hunched Man, the Old Man and B.B.', *Revolutionary History* vol. 7, no. 2, summer 1999

Leslie, Esther, 'Space and West-end Girls; Walter Benjamin versus Cultural Studies', in 'Hating Tradition Properly', *New Formations* 38, 1999

Leslie, Esther, 'Souvenirs and Forgetting; Walter Benjamin's Memory-work', in *Material Memories; Design and Evocation*, ed. Marius Kwint, Christopher Breward and Jeremy Aynsley, Berg, Oxford/New York 1999

Liessmann, Konrad Paul, 'Der verführerische Charme des Ungefähren; Eine Polemik zum 100. Geburtstag von Walter Benjamin', in *Freitag* no. 29, 10 July 1992, p. 11

Lilla, Mark, 'The Riddle of Walter Benjamin', in *The New York Review*, 25 May 1995, pp. 37–42

Lindner, Burkhardt (ed.), *'Links hatte noch alles sich zu enträtseln'; Walter Benjamin im Kontext*, Syndikat, Frankfurt/Main 1978

Lonitz, Henri (ed.), *T.W. Adorno & Walter Benjamin: Briefwechsel 1928–1940*, Suhrkamp, Frankfurt/Main 1994.

Löwy, Michael, *On Changing the World: Essays in Political Philosophy from Karl Marx to Walter Benjamin*, Humanities Press, New Jersey 1993

Lunn, Eugene, *Marxism and Modernism: A Historical Study of Lukács, Brecht, Benjamin and Adorno*, University of California Press, Berkeley 1982

Marcus, Laura and Nead, Lynda (eds.), *The Actuality of Walter Benjamin*, Lawrence and Wishart, London 1998

Markner, Reinhard and Weber, Thomas (eds.), *Literatur über Walter Benjamin: kommentierte Bibliographie 1983–1992*, Argument-Verlag, Berlin 1993

McCole, John, *Walter Benjamin and the Antinomies of Tradition*, Cornell University Press, Ithaca, NY 1993

McRobbie, Angela, 'The *Passagenwerk* and the Place of Walter Benjamin in Cultural Studies; Benjamin, Cultural Studies, Marxist Theories of Art', in *Cultural Studies* vol. 6 no. 2, May 1992, pp. 147–69

Mehlman, Jeffrey, *Walter Benjamin for Children: An Essay on his Radio Years*, University of Chicago Press, Chicago 1993

Menke, Bettine, *Sprachfiguren: Name, Allegorie, Bild nach Benjamin*, Wilhelm Fink, Munich 1991

Menninghaus, Winfried, *Walter Benjamins Theorie der Sprachmagie*, Suhrkamp, Frankfurt/Main 1980

Menninghaus, Winfried, *Schwellenkunde: Walter Benjamins Passage des Mythos*, Suhrkamp, Frankfurt/Main 1986

Missac, Pierre, *Walter Benjamin's Passages*, MIT Press, Cambridge, Mass. 1995

Müller, Inez, *Walter Benjamin und Bertolt Brecht: Ansätze zu einer dialektischen Ästhetik in den dreißiger Jahren*, Röhrig, St. Ingbert 1993

Nägele, Rainer (ed.), *Benjamin's Ground: New Readings of Walter Benjamin*, Wayne State University Press, Detroit 1988

Nägele, Rainer, *Theater, Theory, Speculation. Walter Benjamin and the Scenes of Modernity*, Johns Hopkins University Press, Baltimore 1991

Opitz, Michael and Wizisla, Erdmut (eds.), *'Aber ein Sturm weht vom Paradiese her'; Texte zu Walter Benjamin*, Reclam, Leipzig 1992

Parini, Jay, *Benjamin's Crossing*, Henry Holt and Company, New York 1997

Pensky, Max, *Melancholy Dialectics: Walter Benjamin and the Play of Mourning*, University of Massachusetts Press, Amherst 1993

Reisch, Heiko, *Das Archiv und die Erfahrung*, Königshausen und Neumann, Würzburg 1992

Roberts, Julian, *Walter Benjamin*, Macmillan, London 1982

Salzinger, Helmut, *Swinging Benjamin* [1973], Kellner, Hamburg 1990

Scheurmann, Ingrid and Scheurmann, Konrad (eds.), *For Walter Benjamin: Documentation, Essays and a Sketch*, Inter Nationes, Bonn 1993

Schiller-Lerg, Sabine, *Walter Benjamin und der Rundfunk: Programmarbeit zwischen Theorie und Praxis*, K.G. Saur, Munich 1984

Scholem, Gershom, *Walter Benjamin: die Geschichte einer Freundschaft*, Suhrkamp, Frankfurt/Main 1975

Scholem, Gershom, *Walter Benjamin: The Story of a Friendship*, Faber and Faber, London 1982

Scholem, Gershom, *Walter Benjamin und sein Engel*, Suhrkamp, Frankfurt/Main 1983

Smith, Gary (ed.), *On Walter Benjamin: Critical Essays and Recollections*, MIT Press, Cambridge, Mass. 1988

Smith, Gary (ed.), *Benjamin: Philosophy, History, Aesthetics*, University of Chicago Press, Chicago 1989

Smith, Gary (with designer Hans Puttnies), *Benjaminiana*, Anabas Verlag, Gießen 1991

Steiner, Uwe, *Die Geburt der Kritik aus dem Geiste der Kunst: Untersuchungen zum Begriff der Kritik in den frühen Schriften*, Königshausen und Neumann, Würzburg 1989

Stoessel, Marleen, *Aura: Das vergessene Menschliche; Zu Sprache und Erfahrung bei Walter Benjamin*, Edition Akzente, Hanser, Munich 1983

Stüssi, Anna, *Erinnerung an die Zukunft: Walter Benjamins Berliner Kindheit um Neunzehnjahrhundert*, Vandenhoeck und Ruprecht, Göttingen 1977

Unseld, Siegfried (ed.), *Zur Aktualität Walter Benjamins*, Suhrkamp, Frankfurt/Main 1972

Vietta, Silvio, 'Großstadtwahrnehmungen und ihre literarische Darstellung: Expressionistischer Reihungsstil und Collage', in *Deutsche Vierteljahresschrift für Literaturwissenschaft und Geistesgeschichte* Heft 2, 1974, pp. 354–73

Wagner, Gerhard, *Walter Benjamin: Die Medien der Moderne*, ed. the Hochschule für Film und Fernsehen Konrad Wolf, Potsdam-Babelsberg 1992

Wawrzyn, Lienhard, *Walter Benjamins Kunsttheorie: Kritik einer Rezeption*, Luchterhand Typoskript, Darmstadt/Neuwied 1973

Wiesenthal, Liselotte, *Zur Wissenschaftstheorie Walter Benjamin*, Athenäum, Frankfurt/Main 1973

Wilson, Elizabeth, 'The Invisible Flâneur', in *New Left Review* no. 191, January–February 1992, pp. 90–110

Witte, Bernd, 'Bilder der Endzeit: Zu einem authentischen Text der Berliner Kindheit von Walter Benjamin' in *Deutsche Vierteljahrschrift für Literaturwissenschaft und Geistesgeschichte*, Stuttgart 1984, pp. 570–92

Witte, Bernd, *Walter Benjamin mit Selbstzeugnissen und Bilddokumenten*, RoRoRo, Reinbek/Hamburg 1990

Witte, Bernd, 'Allegorien des Schreibens: Eine Lektüre von Walter Benjamins Trauerspielbuch', in *Merkur* Heft 2, February 1992, pp. 125–36

Wolin, Richard, *Walter Benjamin: An Aesthetics of Redemption*, Columbia University Press, New York 1982 [reissue with a new introduction from University of California Press 1994]

Special Journal Issues and Exhibition Catalogues on Walter Benjamin

Text + Kritik nos. 31/32, 1979 ed. Heinz Ludwig Arnold; special issue on Walter Benjamin

New German Critique no. 17, Spring 1979; special issue on Walter Benjamin

Philosophical Forum no. 15, 1983/84; special issue on Walter Benjamin

New German Critique no. 34, Winter 1985; special section on Walter Benjamin

New German Critique no. 39, Fall 1986; special issue on Walter Benjamin

New German Critique no. 48, Fall 1989; special section on Walter Benjamin

Marbacher Magazin no. 55/1990, ed. Rolf Tiedemann, C. Gödde and H. Lonitz; Sondernummer Walter Benjamin to accompany an exhibition at the Deutsches Literaturarchiv and the Literaturhaus Berlin in 1990

Perspektiven Sonderheft 2, 1990; special issue on Walter Benjamin

Bucklicht Männlein und Engel der Geschichte: Walter Benjamin, Theoretiker der Moderne, Werkbund Archiv Berlin 1991 to accompany the exhibition at the Martin Gropius-Bau, Berlin in 1990

Modern Language Notes 107 no. 3 1992; special issue on Walter Benjamin

Diacritics nos 3–4, 1993; 'Commemorating Walter Benjamin'

Internationale Zeitschrift für Philosophie Jahrgang 2, no. 1 1993; Themenheft Walter Benjamin

New Formations no. 20, summer 1993; 'The Actuality of Walter Benjamin'

Frankfurter Adorno Blätter IV, ed. Theodor W. Adorno Archiv, edition text + kritik 1995, includes 'Neue Baudelairiana' by Walter Benjamin

De-, Dis-, Ex-, no. 3, March 1999; 'The Optic of Walter Benjamin'

Other Books and Articles Consulted

Ades, Dawn et al. *Art and Power: Europe under the Dictators 1930–1945*, Catalogue to the Hayward Gallery Exhibition, South Bank Centre 1995

Adorno, Theodor W. and Horkheimer, Max, *Dialektik der Aufklärung* [1944], Fischer, Frankfurt/Main 1969

Adorno, Theodor W., *Ästhetische Theorie*, Suhrkamp, Frankfurt/Main 1971

Adorno, Theodor W., *Minima Moralia* [1951], New Left Books, London 1974

Adorno, Theodor W., *Noten zur Literatur*, Suhrkamp, Frankfurt/Main 1981

Adorno, T.W. and Eisler, Hanns: *Composing for the Films* [1947], The Athlone Press, London and Atlantic Highlands, NJ 1994

Althusser, Louis, *Lenin and Philosophy and Other Essays*, New Left Books, London 1971

Althusser, Louis and Balibar, Etienne, *Reading Capital*, New Left Books, London, 1975

Amberger, Waltraud, *Männer, Krieger, Abenteuer*, Fischer, Frankfurt/Main 1987

Anderson, Perry, *Considerations on Western Marxism*, New Left Books, London 1976

Anderson, Perry, *Arguments within English Marxism*, New Left Books and Verso, London 1980

Angress, W.T., 'Pegasus and Insurrection; Die Linkskurve and its Heritage', in *Central European History* no. 1 1968, pp. 35–55

Appiganesi, Lisa (ed.), *Postmodernism*, ICA Documents, Free Association Books 1989

Aragon, Louis, *Traité du style*, Gallimard, Paris 1928

Aragon, Louis, *Pour un réalisme socialiste*, Denoël, Paris 1934

Aragon, Louis, *Le Paysan de Paris*, Gallimard, Paris 1953

Aragon, Louis, 'John Heartfield and Revolutionary Beauty' [1935], in *Praxis: A Journal of Radical Perspectives on the Arts* no. 4, 1978, pp. 3–7

Arato, Andrew and Gebhardt, Eike, *The Essential Frankfurt School Reader*, Urizen Books, New York 1977

Arvatov, Boris, *Kunst und Produktion; Entwurf einer proletarisch-avantgardistischen Ästhetik* [1921–30], Hanser, Munich 1972

Bahne, S., *Die KPD und das Ende von Weimar*, Campus, Frankfurt/Main 1976

Barnouw, Dagmar, *Weimar Intellectuals and the Threat of Modernity*, Indiana University Press, Bloomington and Indianapolis 1988

Bartetzko, Dieter, *Illusionen in Stein: Stimmungsarchitektur im deutschen Faschismus, ihre Vorgeschulte in Theater- und Film-Bauten*, RoRoRo, Reinbek/Hamburg 1985

Barthes, Roland, *Camera Lucida*, Jonathan Cape, London 1982

Bathrick, David and Huyssen, Andreas (eds.), *Modernity and the Text: Revisions of German Modernism*, Columbia University Press, New York 1989

Baudelaire, Charles, *Les Fleurs du Mal*, Picador, London 1982

Baudelaire, Charles, *Der Künstler und das moderne Leben*, Reclam, Leipzig 1990

Baxandall, Lee and Morawski, Stefan (eds.), *Marx and Engels on Literature and Art*, Telos Press, St. Louis 1973

Becher, Johannes, Kläber, Kurt, Marchwitza, Hans, Weinert, Erich and Renn, Ludwig (eds.), *Die Linkskurve* [unaltered reprint of the Berlin edition], Verlag Detlev Auvermann K.G., Glashütten im Taunus 1970

Beetham, David, *Marxists in Face of Fascism*, Manchester University Press, Manchester 1983

Benjamin, Andrew (ed.), *Problems of Modernity*, Routledge, London 1989

Benjamin, Andrew, *Art, Mimesis and the Avant-Garde*, Routledge, London 1991

Berg-Ganschow, U. and Jacobsen, W. (eds.), *Film ... Stadt ... Kino ... Berlin*, Argon, Berlin 1987

Berger, John, *The Moment of Cubism and Other Essays*, Pantheon, New York 1969

Berger, John, *About Looking*, Writers and Readers, London 1980

Berman, Marshall, *All That is Solid Melts into Air: The Experience of Modernity*, Simon and Schuster, New York 1982

Berman, Russell, 'Lukács' Critique of Bredel and Ottwalt', in *New German Critique* no. 10, 1972, pp. 155–78

Bibikova, I. and Cooke C. and Tolstoy, V., *Street Art of the Revolution: Festivals and Celebrations in Russia 1918–1933*, Thames and Hudson, London 1990

Birchall, Ian, 'Des marteaux matériels', in *French Studies; a Quarterly Review* vol. XLIV, no. 3, July 1990, pp. 300–18

Blackburn, Richard J., *The Vampire of Reason*, Verso, London 1990

Bloch, Ernst, *Vom Hasard zur Katastrophe: Politische Aufsätze aus den Jahren 1934–1939*, Suhrkamp, Frankfurt/Main 1972

Bloch, Ernst, *Geist der Utopie* [first edition 1918], *Gesamtausgabe*, vol. 16, Suhrkamp, Frankfurt/Main 1977

Bloch, Ernst, *Geist der Utopie* [second edition 1923], *Gesamtausgabe*, vol. 3, Suhrkamp, Frankfurt/Main 1977

Bloch, Ernst, Lukács, Georg, Brecht, Bertolt, Benjamin, Walter and Adorno, Theodor, W., *Aesthetics and Politics*, New Left Books, London 1977

Bloch, Ernst, *Erbschaft dieser Zeit* [1935], Suhrkamp, Frankfurt/Main 1985

Bloch, Ernst, *The Utopian Function of Art and Literature*, MIT Press, Cambridge, Mass. 1988

Bloom, Harold (ed.), *Gershom Scholem*, Chelsea House Publishers, New York/New Haven/Edgemont 1987

Bohrer, Karl Heinz, *Die Ästhetik des Schreckens: Die pessimistische Romantik und Ernst Jüngers Frühwerk*, Ullstein, Frankfurt/Main 1983

Bohrer, Karl Heinz (ed.), *Das Erhabene*, Sonderheft Merkur, Hefte 9/10 1989

Bolz, Norbert, *Auszüge aus der entzauberten Welt*, Wilhelm Fink, Munich 1989

Brauneck, Manfred (ed.), *Die Rote Fahne: Kritik, Theorie, Feuilleton 1918–1933*, Wilhelm Fink, Munich 1973

Bravermann, Harry, *Labor and Monopoly Capital*, Monthly Review Press, New York/London 1974

Brecht, Bertolt, *Gesammelte Werke: Schriften zur Literatur und Kunst 1*, vol. 18, Suhrkamp, Frankfurt/Main 1967

Brecht, Bertolt, *Arbeitsjournal*, two volumes, Suhrkamp, Frankfurt/Main 1973

Breines, Paul, 'Praxis and its Theorists: The Impact of Lukács and Korsch in the 1920s', in *Telos* no. 11, Spring 1972, pp. 67–103

Breton, André, *Manifestoes of Surrealism*, University of Michigan Press, Ann Arbor, Mich. 1972

Breton, André, 'Introduction to the Discourse on the Paucity of Reality', in *October* no. 69, Summer 1994, pp. 133–44.

Brüggemann, Heinz, *Literarische Technik und soziale Revolution; Versuche über das Verhältnis von Kunstproduktion, Marxismus und literarischer Tradition in den theoretischen Schriften Bertolt Brechts*, Rowohlt, Reinbek/Hamburg 1973

Buchloh, Benjamin, 'From Faktura to Factography', in *October: The First Decade; 1976–1986*, MIT Press, Cambridge, Mass. 1987

Buckmiller, Michael (ed.), *Zur Aktualität von Karl Korsch*, Europäische Verlagsanstalt, Frankfurt/Main 1981

Bürger, Peter, *Theorie der Avant-Garde*, Suhrkamp, Frankfurt/Main 1972

Burgin, Victor, *Thinking Photography*, Macmillan, London 1982

Butler, Christopher, *Early Modernism; Literature, Music and Painting in Europe 1900–1916*, Oxford University Press, Oxford 1994

Buxton, David, *From the Avengers to Miami Vice*, Manchester University Press, Manchester 1990

Cadars, Pierre and Courtade, Francis, *Geschichte des Films im Dritten Reich*, Büchergilde Gutenberg, Frankurt/Main 1976

Caputi, Jane, *The Age of Sex Crime*, Women's Press, London 1988

Callinicos, Alex, *Althusser's Marxism*, Pluto Press, London 1976

Callinicos, Alex, *Marxism and Philosophy*, Oxford University Press, Oxford 1983

Callinicos, Alex, *Making History: Agency, Structure, Change in Social Theory*, Polity Press and Blackwell, Oxford 1987

Callinicos, Alex, *Against Postmodernism*, Polity Press, Oxford 1989

Céline, Louis-Ferdinand, *Journey to the End of the Night*, Calder, London 1988

Chatwin, Bruce, 'Ernst Jünger, An Aesthete at War', in *What am I Doing Here?: Selected Essays by Bruce Chatwin*, Picador, London 1992

Cliff, Tony, *Trotsky: The Darker the Night the Brighter the Star 1927–1940*, Bookmarks, London 1993

Cohen, G.A., *Karl Marx's Theory of History: A Defence* [1978], Clarendon Press, Oxford 1991

Cohen, Jerry, 'The Philosophy of Marcuse', in *New Left Review* no. 57, 1969, pp. 35–51

Cullerne Bown, Matthew and Elliott, David (eds.), *Soviet Socialist Realist Painting 1930s–1960s*; Catalogue to an exhibition at the Museum of Modern Art in Oxford, 12 January–15 March 1992

Danos, J. and Gibelin, M., *June '36. Class Struggle and the People's Front in France*, Bookmarks, London 1986

Deak, Istvan, *Weimar Germany's Left-Wing Intellectuals: A Political History of the Weltbühne and its Circle*, University of California Press, Berkeley 1968

Debord, Guy, *Society of the Spectacle*, Black & Red, Detroit 1983

Deutscher, Issac, *The Prophet Unarmed: Trotsky; 1921–1929*, Oxford University Press, Oxford, 1959

Dews, Peter, *Logics of Disintegration: Post-Structuralist Thought and the Claims of Critical Theory*, Verso, London 1987

Donald, James (ed.), *Fantasy and the Cinema*, British Film Institute, London 1989

Eagleton, Terry, *Marxism and Literary Criticism*, University of California Press, Berkeley 1976

Eagleton, Terry, *The Ideology of the Aesthetic*, Blackwell, Oxford 1990

Eagleton, Terry, *Ideology: An Introduction*, Verso, London 1991

Eberle, Matthias, *World War One and the Weimar Artists*, Yale University Press, New York/London 1985

Eisenstein, Sergei, 'Methods of Montage', in *Film Form*, ed. Jay Leyda, Harcourt Brace Jovanovitch, New York and London 1949, pp. 72–83

Eisenstein, Sergei, *The Film Sense*, Faber and Faber, London 1986

Elliott, David, *New Worlds; Russian Art and Society 1900–1937*, Thames and Hudson, London 1986

Elliott, David (ed.), *Photography in Russia 1840–1940*, Thames and Hudson, London 1992

Emmerich, W., 'The Red One-Mark Novel and the Heritage of Our Time; Notes on Michael Rohrwasser's Saubere Mädel – Starke Genossen; Proletarishe Massenliteratur?', in *New German Critique* no. 10, Winter 1977, pp. 179–89

Engels, Friedrich, *Anti-Dühring* [1876–78], in *Marx Engels Werke*, vol. 20, Dietz Verlag, Berlin 1962

Evans, David, *John Heartfield: Photomontages 1930–1938*, Kent Fine Art, New York 1992

Fähnders, W. and Rector, M., *Linksradikalismus und Literatur*, Rowohlt, Reinbek/Hamburg 1974

Fähnders, W., *Proletarische-revolutionäre Literatur*, Metzler, Stuttgart 1977

Fichte, J. G., *The Science of Knowledge* [1794], Cambridge University Press, Cambridge 1982

Fischer, Ernst, *The Necessity of Art: A Marxist Approach* [1959], Penguin Books, London 1963

Fischer, Hugo, *Karl Marx und sein Verhältnis zu Staat und Wirtschaft*, Verlag von Gustav Fischer, Jena 1932

Fleron, Frederic and Fleron, Lou Jean, 'Administration Theory as Repressive Political Theory; The Communist Experience', in *Telos* no. 12, Summer 1972, pp. 63–92

Foucault, Michel, *Vom Licht des Krieges zur Geburt der Geschichte*, Merve, Berlin 1986

Freud, Sigmund, *Selected Works* vol. 11, Penguin, London 1984

Freund, Gisèle, *Photographie et société*, Editions du Seuil, Paris 1974

Friedel, H., *Kunst und Technik in den 20er Jahren*, Stadtische Galerie im Lenbachhaus, Munich 1980

Früchtl, Joseph, *Mimesis: Konstellation eines Zentralbegriffs bei Adorno*, Königshausen und Neumann, Würzburg 1986

Fuller, Peter, *Seeing Berger*, Writers and Readers, London 1981

Fussell, Paul, *The Great War and Modern Memory*, Open University Press, London 1975

Gadamer, Hans Georg, *The Relevance of the Beautiful and Other Essays*, Cambridge University Press, Cambridge 1987

Gallas, Helga, *Marxistische Literaturtheorie*, Sammlung Luchterhand, Darmstadt/Neuwied 1971

Gay, Peter, *Weimar Culture: The Outsider as Insider*, Penguin Books, London 1974

Geduld, Harry M. (ed.), *Film Makers on Film Making*, Indiana University Press, Bloomington and Indianapolis 1969

Geras, Norman, *Marx and Human Nature: Refutation of a Legend*, Verso, London 1983

Goergen, Jeanpaul, *Walter Ruttmann: Eine Dokumentation*, Freunde der Deutschen Kinemathek, Berlin 1989

Golomstock, Igor, *Totalitarian Art*, IconEditions, HarperCollins, New York 1990

Gorky, Maxim et al., *Soviet Writers' Congress 1934: The Debate on Socialist Realism and Modernism in the Soviet Union*, Lawrence and Wishart, London 1977

Gramsci, Antonio, *Selections from the Prison Notebooks*, Lawrence and Wishart, London 1971

Guilbaut, Serge, *How New York Stole the Idea of Modern Art*, University of Chicago Press, Chicago 1983

Habermas, Jürgen, *Towards a Rational Society: Student Protest, Science and Politics*, Heinemann Educational Books, London 1971

Hadjinicolaou, Nicos, *Art History and Class Struggle*, Pluto Press, London 1978

Haraway, Donna, *Simians, Cyborgs, and Women: The Reinvention of Nature*, Free Association Books, London 1991

Harrison, Charles and Wood, Paul (eds.), *Art in Theory 1900–1990: An Anthology of Changing Ideas*, Blackwell, Oxford 1992

Hayter, Alethea, *Opium and the Romantic Imagination*, Crucible, Northamptonshire 1988

Hegel, Georg Wilhelm Friedrich, *Wissenschaft der Logik* [1832–45], vol. 1, Suhrkamp, Frankfurt/Main 1986

Heidegger, Martin, *The Question Concerning Technology and Other Essays*, Harper and Row, New York 1977

Herf, Jeffrey, 'Technology, Reification, Romanticism', in *New German Critique* no. 12, Fall 1977, pp. 175–91

Herf, Jeffrey, *Reactionary Modernism: Technology, Culture, and Politics in Weimar and the Third Reich*, Cambridge University Press, Cambridge 1984

Hessel, Franz, *Ein Flaneur in Berlin* (originally *Spazieren in Berlin*) [1929], Arsenal, Berlin 1984

Hewitt, Andrew, *Fascist Modernism: Aesthetics, Politics and the Avant-Garde*, Stanford University Press, Stanford 1993

Hinz, Berthold (ed.), *Die Dekoration der Gewalt: Kunst und Medien im Faschismus*, Anabas Verlag, Gießen 1979

Hinz, Berthold, *Art in the Third Reich*, Blackwell, Oxford 1980

Hobsbawn, Eric and Ranger, Terence (eds.), *The Invention of Tradition*, Cambridge University Press, Cambridge 1984

von Hofmannsthal, Hugo, 'Der Ersatz für die Träume' [1921], in *Prosa* 4: *Gesammelte Werke in Einzelausgaben*, Fischer, Frankfurt/Main 1955

Huyssen, Andreas, *After the Great Divide: Modernism, Mass Culture, Postmodernism*, Indiana University Press, Bloomington and Indianapolis 1986

Hyman, John, *The Imitation of Nature*, Blackwell, Oxford 1989

Jacobs, Carol, *The Dissimulating Harmony: The Image of Interpretation in Nietzsche, Rilke, Artaud and Benjamin*, Johns Hopkins University Press, Baltimore 1978

James, C.L.R., *Notes on Dialectics: Hegel, Marx, Lenin* [1948], Allison and Busby, London 1980

Jameson, Fredric, *Marxism and Form*, Princeton University Press, Princeton, NJ 1971

Jameson, Fredric, *Late Marxism: Adorno, or the Persistence of the Dialectic*, Verso, London 1990

Jameson, Fredric, *Postmodernism or the Cultural Logic of Late Capitalism*, Verso, London 1991

Jauss, Hans Robert, *Toward an Aesthetic of Reception*, Harvester Press, Brighton, 1982

Jay, Martin, *The Dialectical Imagination: A History of the Frankfurt School and the Institute of Social Research 1923–1950*, Little, Brown and Co., Boston 1973

Jay, Martin, *Permanent Exiles: Essays on the Intellectual Migration from Germany to America*, Columbia University Press, New York 1986

Jenkins, Henry and Tulloch, John, *Science Fiction Audiences*, Routledge, London 1995

Jennings, Humphrey, *Pandaemonium – 1616–1886: The Coming of the Machine as Seen by Contemporary Observers*, Picador, London 1987

Joll, James, *Europe since 1870; An International History*, Penguin, London 1990

Joyce, James, *Ulysses* [1922], Bodley Head, London 1969

Jünger, Ernst (ed.), *Das Antlitz des Weltkrieges: Fronterlebnisse deutscher Soldaten*, Neufeld und Henius Verlag, Berlin 1930

Jünger, Ernst, 'Über die Gefahr', in *Der gefährliche Augenblick*, ed. Ferdinand Bucholtz, Junker und Dünhaupt, Berlin 1931

Jünger, Ernst, *In Stahlgewittern* [1920], Ernst Klett, Stuttgart 1961

Jünger, Ernst, *Das abendteuerliche Herz*, Ernst Klett, Stuttgart 1961

Jünger, Ernst, *Sämtliche Werke*, Klett-Cotta, Stuttgart 1980

Kaes, Anton (ed.), *Weimarer Republik; Manifeste und Dokumente zur deutschen Literatur 1918–1933*, Metzler, Stuttgart 1983

Kahn, Douglas, *John Heartfield; Art and Mass Media*, Tanam, New York 1985

Kant, Immanuel, *Kants gesammelte Schriften*; akademische Ausgabe, vol. 5, Reimer, Berlin 1913

Kellner, Douglas, *Karl Korsch; Revolutionary Theory*, Texas Press, Texas 1974

Kellner, Douglas, *Critical Theory, Marxism and Modernity*, Polity Press, Cambridge 1989

Kleinspeh, Thomas, *Der flüchtige Blick; Sehen und Identität in der Kultur der Neuzeit*, Rowohlt, Reinbek/Hamburg 1989

Koch, Gertrud, 'Mimesis and *Bilderverbot*' in *Screen* no. 34/34, Autumn 1993, pp. 211–22

Korsch, Karl, *Karl Marx*, Russell and Russell, New York 1963

Korsch, Karl, *Marxism and Philosophy* [1923], Monthly Review Press, New York 1970

Koslowski, Peter, *Der Mythos der Moderne: Die dichterische Philosophie Ernst Jünger*, Wilhelm Fink, Munich 1991

Kracauer, Siegfried, *Die Angestellten*, Suhrkamp, Frankfurt/Main 1971

Kracauer, Siegfried, *From Caligari to Hitler* [1947], Princeton University Press, Princeton 1974

Kracauer, Siegfried, *Das Ornament der Masse: Essays*, Suhrkamp, Frankfurt/Main 1977

Kracauer, Siegfried, *Kino*, Suhrkamp, Frankfurt/Main 1979

Kracauer, Siegfried, *Straßen in Berlin und Anderswo*, Arsenal, Berlin 1987

Kracauer, Siegfried, *The Mass Ornament, Weimar Essays*, Harvard University Press, Cambridge, Mass. 1995

Krauss, Rosalind and Livingston, Jane (eds.), *L'Amour fou: Photography and Surrealism*, Abbeville Press, New York 1985

Kuenzli, Rudolf E. (ed.), *Dada and Surrealist Film*, Willis Locker and Owens, New York 1987

Lacis, Asja, *Revolutionär im Beruf: Berichte über proletarisches Theater – über Meyerhold, Brecht, Benjamin und Piscator*, Rogner und Bernhard, Munich 1971

Lacoue-Labarthe, Pierre, *Heidegger, Art and Politics*, Blackwell, Oxford 1988

Larsson, L.O., *Die Neugestaltung der Reichshauptstadt: Albert Speers Generalbebauungsplan für Berlin*, Hatje, Stuttgart 1978

Lawton, Anna and Eagle, Herbert (eds.), *Russian Futurism through its Manifestoes, 1912–1928*, Cornell University Press, Ithaca, NY 1988

Lees, Andrew, *Cities Perceived: Urban Society in European and American Thought 1820–1940*, Manchester University Press, Manchester 1985

Lefebvre, Lucien and Martin, Henri-Jean, *The Coming of the Book: The Impact of Printing 1450–1800*, Verso, London 1990

Lenin, V.I., *Collected Works*, vol. 27, Lawrence and Wishart, London 1965

Lenin, V.I., *Collected Works* vol. 38, Progress Publishers, Moscow 1972

Lethen, Helmut, *Neue Sachlichkeit 1924–1932: Zur Literatur des weissen Sozialismus*, Metzler, Stuttgart 1975

Lewis, Helena, *Dada Turns Red*, Edinburgh University Press, Edinburgh 1990

Lippard, Lucy (ed.), *Dadas on Art*, Prentice Hall, New Jersey 1971

Lodder, Christina, *Russian Constructivism*, Yale University Press, New York/London 1983

Loos, Adolf, *Spoken into the Void: Collected Essays 1897–1900*, MIT Press, Cambridge, Mass. 1982

Lüddecke, W., *Der Film im Agitation und Propaganda der revolutionären Arbeiterbewegung 1919–1933*, Oberbaumverlag, Berlin 1973

Lukács, Georg, 'Technology and Social Relations', in *New Left Review* no. 39, 1966, pp. 27–34

Lukács, Georg, *Die Theorie des Romans* [1916], Sammlung Luchterhand, Darmstadt/Neuwied 1971

Lukács, Georg, *History and Class Consciousness* [1923], Merlin, London 1971

Lukács, Georg, *Studies in European Realism*, Merlin, London 1972

Lukács, Georg, *The Historical Novel* [1936–37], Penguin, London 1976

Lukács, Georg, *Geschichte und Klassenbewußtsein* [1923], Sammlung Luchterhand, Darmstadt/Neuwied 1986

Lukács, Georg, *Chrostismus und Dialektik* [1925], Áran Verlag, Budapest 1996.

Lury, Celia, *Cultural Rights: Technology, Legality and Personality*, Routledge, London 1993

Luxemburg, Rosa, *Gesammelte Werke* vol. 1.2, Dietz Verlag, Berlin 1972

Maier, Charles, 'Between Taylorism and Technology: European Ideologies and the Vision of Productivity in the 1920s', in *Journal of Contemporary History*, 1970, pp. 27–61

de Man, Paul, *Blindness and Insight: Essays in the Rhetoric of Contemporary Criticism*, 2nd edition, University of Minnesota Press, Minneapolis 1983

de Man, Paul, 'The Task of the Translator', in *Yale French Studies* no. 69, 1985, pp. 25–46

Marinetti, Filippo Tommaso, *Selected Writings*, ed. R.W. Flint, Farrar, Straus and Giroux, New York 1971

Marx, Karl, *Der 18te Brumaire des Louis Napoleon* in *Marx Engels Werke*, vol. 8, Dietz Verlag, Berlin 1960

Marx, Karl, 'Einleitung zur Kritik der politischen Ökonomie', in *Marx Engels Werke*, vol. 13, Dietz Verlag, Berlin 1961

Marx, Karl, *Das Kapital*, three volumes, *Marx Engels Werke*, Dietz Verlag, Berlin 1969

Marx, Karl, *Grundrisse*, The Pelican Marx Library, London: Penguin/New Left Review 1973

Marx, Karl, *Early Writings*, Penguin/NLR, London 1975

Marx, Karl and Engels, Friedrich, *Marx Engels Werke*, vol. 20, Dietz Verlag, Berlin 1962

Marx, Karl and Engels, Friedrich: *Marx Engels Werke*, vol. 3, Berlin: Dietz Verlag, Berlin, 1983

Marx, Karl and Engels, Friedrich, *Über Geschichte der Philosophie*, Reclam, Leipzig 1985

Mattenklott, Gert and Scherpe, K.R. (eds.), *Positionen der literarischen Intelligenz zwischen bürgerlicher Reaktion und Imperialismus*, Scriptor, Kronberg/Ts. 1973

Mészáros, István, *Marx's Theory of Alienation*, Merlin, London 1970

Mészáros, István, *The Power of Ideology*, Harvester Wheatsheaf, Brighton 1989

Müller, Reinhard (ed.), *Die Säuberung, Moskau 1936: Stenogramm einer geschlossenen Parteiversammlung*, RoRoRo, Reinbek/Hamburg 1991

Nadeau, Maurice, *The History of Surrealism* [1944], Plantin Publishers, London 1987

Naremore, J. and Brantlinger, P. (eds.), *Modernity and Mass Culture*, Indiana University Press, Bloomington and Indianapolis 1991

Naville, Pierre, *La Révolution et les intellectuels* [1926], Gallimard, Paris 1975

Neue Gesellschaft für Bildende Kunst, *Inszenierung der Macht: Ästhetische Fazination im Faschismus*, Nishen, Berlin 1987

New German Critique no. 40; Special Issue on Weimar Film Theory, Winter 1987

New German Critique no. 56; special issue on T.W. Adorno, Summer 1992

New Left Review Board (eds.), *Western Marxism: A Critical Reader*, Verso, London 1983

Nizan, Paul, *The Conspiracy*, Verso, London 1988

Nochlin, Linda, *Realism*, Penguin Books, London 1971

Pfotenhauer, Helmut, *Ästhetische Erfahrung und gesellschaftliches System*, Metzler, Stuttgart 1975

Pike, David, *Lukács and Brecht*, University of North Carolina Press, Chapel Hill/London 1985

Rabinbach, Anson, 'Toward a Marxist Theory of Fascism and National Socialism: A Report on Developments in West Germany', in *New German Critique* no. 3, Fall 1974, pp. 127–53

Rabinbach, Anson, 'Ernst Bloch's Heritage of Our Times and Fascism', in *New German Critique* no. 11, Spring 1977, pp. 5–21

de Ras, M.E.P., *Körper, Eros und weibliche Kultur: Mädchen in Wandervogel und in der bündischen Jugend 1900–1933*, Centaurus Verlagsgesellschaft, Pfaffenweiler 1988

Revolutionary History vol. 4, nos. 1/2, 1991–92: *The Spanish Civil War: A View from the Left*

Richards, Thomas, *The Commodity Culture of Victorian England*, Verso, London 1990

Richardson, Al (ed.), *In Defence of the Russian Revolution: A Selection of Bolshevik Writings 1917–1923*, Porcupine Press, London 1995

Richter, Hans, *Filmgegner von Heute – Filmfreunde von Morgen* [1929] Facsimile, Verlag Hans Rohr, Zurich 1968

Richter, Hans, *The Struggle for the Film* [late 1930s/1976], Scolar Press, Aldershot, 1986.

Ridless, Robin, *Ideology and Art: Theories of Mass Culture from Walter Benjamin to Umberto Eco*, Peter Lang, New York 1984

Roberts, John, *Postmodernism, Politics and Art*, Manchester University Press, Manchester 1990

Roberts, John, *Selected Errors 1981–1990*, Pluto Press, London 1993

Roberts, John (ed.), *Art Has No History!*, Verso, London 1994

Rose, Gillian, *Judaism and Modernity: Philosophical Essays*, Blackwell, Oxford 1993

Rosemont, Franklin, *André Breton and the First Principles of Surrealism*, Pluto Press, London 1978

Ross, Kristin, *The Emergence of Social Space: Rimbaud and the Paris Commune*, University of Minnesota Press, Minneapolis 1988

Roters, Eberhard, 'Die Opferung und Verklärung der Braut', in Ursula Prinz (ed.), *Androgyn; Sehnsucht und Vollkommenheit*, Dietrich Reimer Verlag, Berlin 1987

Sasuly, Richard, *I.G. Farben*, Boni & Gaer, New York 1947

Schäfer, Hans-Dieter, *Das gespaltene Bewußtsein: deutsche Kultur und Lebenswirklichkeit 1933–1945*, Carl Hanser Verlag, Munich 1982

Schapiro, Meyer, *Modern Art: 19th and 20th Centuries*, George Braziller, New York 1978

Scheerbart, Paul, *Lesabéndio* [1913], Suhrkamp, Frankfurt/Main 1986

Scherpe, K. (ed.), *Die Unwirklichkeit der Städte*, Rowohlt, Reinbek/Hamburg 1988

Schiller, Friedrich, *On the Aesthetic Education of Man: In a Series of Letters* (bilingual edition), Clarendon Press, Oxford 1989

Schivelbusch, Wolfgang, *The Railway Journey: The Industrialization of Space and Time in the 19th Century*, Berg, Leamington Spa/Hamburg/New York 1986

Schmidt, A., *The Concept of Nature in Marx*, New Left Books, London 1970

Schmitt, H.J. and Schramm, G. (eds.), *Sozialistische Realismuskonzeptionen; Dokumente zum 1. Allunionskongress der Sowjetschriftsteller*, Suhrkamp, Frankfurt/Main 1974

Schneider, Manfred, *Die erkaltete Herzensschrift: Der autobiographische Text im 20. Jahrhundert*, Hanser, Munich 1986

Scholem, Gershom, *On Jews and Judaism in Crisis*, Schocken Books, New York 1976

Schuster, P.K. (ed.), *Nationalsozialismus und entartete Kunst*, Prestel, Munich 1988

Seidel, Alfred, *Produktivkräfte und Klassenkampf* (Doctoral Dissertation, submitted to the University of Heidelberg) 1922 [available from the University of Heidelberg]

Serge, Victor, *Memoirs of a Revolutionary 1901–1941*, Oxford University Press, Oxford 1980

Shklovsky, Viktor, *Zoo or Letters not about Love* [1923], Cornell University Press, Ithaca, NY 1971

Slater, Phil, *Origin and Significance of the Frankfurt School: A Marxist Perspective*, Routledge and Kegan Paul, London 1977

Slaughter, Cliff, *Marxism, Ideology and Literature*, Macmillan, London 1980

Sloterdijk, Peter, *Critique of Cynical Reason*, Verso, London 1988

Sohn-Rethel, Alfred, *Ökonomie und Klassenstruktur des deutschen Faschismus* [written between 1937 and 1941], Suhrkamp, Frankfurt/Main 1973

Sontag, Susan, *On Photography*, Penguin Books, London, 1979

Speer, Albert, *Inside the Third Reich*, Macmillan, New York 1970

Stein, Gerd, *Dandy – Snob – Flaneur; Exzentrik und Dekadenz*, Fischer, Frankfurt/Main 1985

Stollmann, Rainer, 'Fascist Politics as a Total Work of Art', in *New German Critique* no. 14, Spring 1978, pp. 41–60

Szondi, Peter, *Schriften*, vol. 2, Suhrkamp, Frankfurt/Main 1978

Taylor, Brandon and van der Will, Wilfried (eds.), *The Nazification of Art*, Winchester Press, Hampshire 1990

Taylor, Robert K., *The Word in Stone: The Role of Architecture in the National Socialist Ideology*, University of California Press, Berkeley 1974

Text + Kritik no. 68 1980, ed. Heinz Ludwig Arnold; special issue on Siegfried Kracauer

Toeplitz, Jerzy, *Geschichte des Films* vol. 2, 1928–33, Henschel, Berlin 1979

Traverso, Enzo, *Les Marxistes et la question juive: histoire d'un débat (1843–1943)*, La Breche-Pec, Montreuil 1990

Traverso, Enzo, *The Marxists and the Jewish Question: The History of a Debate 1843–1943*, Humanities Press, New Jersey 1994

Tretyakov, Sergei, 'Woher und Wohin; Perspektiven des Futurismus', in *Ästhetik und Kommunikation* no. 4, 1971

Trotsky, Leon, *Terrorism and Communism*, Labour Publications Company, London 1921

Trotsky, Leon, *Literature and Revolution* [1923], University of Michigan Press, Ann Arbor 1960

Trotsky, Leon, *Germany 1931–1932*, New Park Publications, London 1970

Trotsky, Leon, *On Literature and Art*, Pathfinder, New York 1970

Trotsky, Leon, *The Struggle against Fascism in Germany*, Pathfinder, New York 1971

Trotsky, Leon, *The War and the International*, Young Socialist Publication, Sri Lanka, 1971

Trotsky, Leon, *The Spanish Revolution 1931–1939*, Pathfinder, New York 1973

Trotsky, Leon, *Trotsky on France*, Pathfinder, New York 1979

Trotsky, Leon, *The History of the Russian Revolution*, Pluto Press, London 1985

Tzara, Tristan, *Seven Dada Manifestos and Lampisteries*, Calder, London 1992

Vespignani, Renzo, *Faschismus*, Elefanten Press, Berlin 1989

Virilio, Paul, *Fahren, Fahren, Fahren ...*, Merve, Berlin 1978

Virilio, Paul and Lotringer, Silvère: *Der reine Krieg*, Merve, Berlin 1984

Virilio, Paul, *Speed and Politics*, Foreign Agents Series, Semiotext[e], New York 1986

Virilio, Paul, *Die Sehmaschine*, Merve, Berlin 1989

Virilio, Paul, *War and Cinema: The Logistics of Perception*, Verso, London 1989

Voloshinov, Valentin, *Marxism and the Philosophy of Language*, Harvard University Press, Cambridge, Mass. 1973

Wald, Alan M., *The Responsibility of Intellectuals: Selected Essays on Marxist Traditions in Cultural Commitment*, Humanities Press, New Jersey 1992

Wald, Alan M., *Writing from the Left*, Verso, London 1994

Watson, Ben, *Art, Class and Cleavage*: *Quantulumcunque Concerning Materialist Esthetix*, Quartet, London 1998

Weigel, Sigrid, *Topographien der Geschlechter*, RoRoRo, Reinbek/Hamburg 1991

Werneburg, Brigitte, 'Ernst Jünger and the Transformed World', in *October* no. 62, Fall 1992, pp. 43–64

Westoby, Adam, *The Evolution of Communism*, Polity Press, Cambridge 1989

Willett, John, *The New Sobriety: Art and Politics in the Weimar Period 1917–1933*, Thames and Hudson, London 1978

Williams, Raymond, *Marxism and Literature*, Oxford University Press, Oxford 1978

Williams, Raymond, *The Politics of Modernism; Against the New Conformists*, Verso, London 1989

Williams, Rosalind, *Dream Worlds: Mass Consumption in Late 19th Century France*, University of California Press, Berkeley 1982

Wilson, Elizabeth, *Adorned in Dreams: Fashion and Modernity*, Virago, London 1989

Wilson, Elizabeth, *The Sphinx in the City: Urban Life, the Control of Disorder, and Women*, Virago, London 1991

Winckler, Lutz (ed.), *Antifaschistische Literatur*, vol. 1, Scriptor, Kronberg/Ts. 1977

Wolff, Janet, 'The Invisible Flâneuse; Women and the Literature of Modernity', in *Theory, Culture and Society* no. 3, 1984–85, pp. 37–46

Wolff, Janet, *Feminist Sentences: Essays on Women and Culture*, University of California Press, Berkeley 1990

Wollen, Peter, *Signs and Meanings in the Cinema*, Secker and Warburg/BFI, London 1982

Wulf, J., *Theater und Film im dritten Reich*, Ullstein, Frankfurt/Main 1983

Zdatny, Steven (ed.), *Hairstyles and Fashion: A Hairdresser's History of Paris, 1910–1920*, Berg, Oxford 1999

Index